ERIC N. COMPTON

PRINCIPLES
OF *Banking*

Third edition

EDUCATION POLICY & DEVELOPMENT

AMERICAN
BANKERS
ASSOCIATION

1120 Connecticut Avenue, N.W.
Washington, D.C. 20036

Library of Congress Cataloging-in-Publication Data

Compton, Eric N., 1925–
   Principles of banking.

   Includes bibliographies and index.
   1. Banks and banking—United States. I. Title.
   HG2491.C647 1988 332.1'2'068 88–6307
   ISBN 0-89982-353-X

To my wife, Maire Cathleen,
whose encouragement, patience, and support have been constant,
and
To Maureen, Eric, Margaret Mary, and Anne Marie,
for their love and understanding.

CONTENTS

EXHIBITS

TABLES

ABOUT THE AUTHOR

Eric N. Compton, the author of seven textbooks on banking, is a vice president in Chase Manhattan Bank's Metropolitan Community Bank. He is responsible for the marketing of cash management services to customers of that department.

Mr. Compton's banking career began in New York City in 1950 and includes experience in installment loans, marketing training, credit training, and management development. He has also served as a relationship manager in the bank's branch system and as a team leader in its government banking division.

In 1961 he joined the faculty of the American Institute of Banking in New York and served in that capacity until 1986. He is also a past president and trustee of that chapter.

PREFACE

Journalism instructors traditionally tell their students that writing a good news story requires asking and answering five basic questions: Who? What? When? Where? Why? Without the answers to these questions, there is no real story. The same five questions apply to the writing of a good textbook on banking.

Who are the people involved in commercial banking? There are about one million of them, in every part of the country. The teller at a bank in Arizona, the loan clerk in Washington, the administrative assistant in Florida, the auditor in Maine, and the securities clerk in Michigan are all part of an industry that is essential to the American economy, and the principles that guide their daily work are common to all of them.

What do these people do? In their individual ways, they render services: a wide range of financial services to a wide variety of customers, and the end result is the growth and profitability of the banks they represent.

When does their industry operate? Every day of the year, around the clock, the banks are functioning, and their operations directly affect every member of the population and every segment of the economy.

Where does all this happen? Banks operate in every corner of the United States, in the nation's largest cities and its smallest local communities. Some banks hold billions of dollars in deposits and others hold only a fraction of that amount. The basic activities are the same in the giant money-center banks and in the smallest community banks.

Why do banks function as they do? The answer is that they fill a basic need. Banks function the way they do in order to provide services that satisfy the financial needs of their customers.

Some fundamental *principles* guide all banks in their daily operations. Those principles flow from experience, from regulation and bank policy, and from training.

Commercial banking has sometimes been considered an industry in which change takes place slowly and infrequently. Banks are sometimes thought of as institutions that operate today as they did years ago, and bankers themselves have been characterized as resistant—or even hostile—to change. But banking—and bankers—are changing.

It has been said that more changes have occurred in U.S. banking since 1961 than in the previous 200 years of American history. Recent changes also have been far more dramatic. The introduction of the large-denomination CD (certificate of deposit), the expansion of EFTS (electronic funds transfer systems), the proliferation of bank cards, and the trend toward diversified operations through bank holding companies have forever changed the face of banking in our country. More recently, however, additional developments have had a massive impact on the industry. The only safe prediction is that many more changes will continue to occur. Banking today truly is in a state of flux.

In 1979 the first edition of *Principles of Banking* attempted to present an overview of what commercial banks were doing, why they were doing it, and when and where significant changes were occurring. Within 4 years a second edition was made necessary by all the developments that were shaping the industry. In the relatively short time that has elapsed since that publication, history has repeated itself. Change has become the one constant factor in commercial banking; understanding this is of primary importance for all those who aspire to leadership roles in the future.

In the 4 years since publication of the second edition of *Principles of Banking* we have witnessed

- a widespread move toward full-scale interstate banking, with removal of the barriers that have prevented it in the past
- a continuing decrease in the commercial banks' share of the total financial marketplace, as new competitors appear and existing competitors aggressively seek to expand their range of services
- an increase in expressions of serious concern by members of Congress, by regulatory authorities, and by the public itself over the soundness of the entire banking system and the protection that depositors receive
- an increase in customer dissatisfaction, reflecting the fact that many individuals are now required to pay new or increased service charges
- a trend among many large banks toward reducing the number of brick-and-mortar branches, with a corresponding increase in alternate systems for delivery of services, such as electronic funds transfer systems
- a continuation of the shift of deposits from interest-free to interest-bearing accounts

At year-end 1985, commercial banks held only 33 percent of the total assets of all financial institutions, compared with 57 percent in 1946.[1] Sears Roebuck, Ford Motor Company, General Electric Credit Company, brokerage firms, and insurance companies have become increasingly important suppliers of financial services. The president of the nation's second largest commercial bank has stated flatly that "I can't do anything in consumer lending that GMAC (General Motors Acceptance Corporations) can't do."[2] The number of bank failures grew from 48 in 1983 to 79 in 1984, 120 in 1985, and 138 in 1986,[3] and the chairman of the Federal Deposit Insurance Corporation predicted a further increase in 1987.[4] In

1985 every one of the nation's 10 largest banks showed 70 percent or more of its total deposits in interest-bearing relationships.[5] This change in the banks' basic deposit structure has affected every aspect of funds management and bank profitability.

Peter Drucker, nationally recognized as an authority on management topics, has said, "In turbulent times, the first task of management is to make sure of an institution's capacity for survival . . . and its capacity to adapt to sudden change and avail itself of opportunities."[6]

For banking, the times are indeed turbulent; but management cannot face the challenges and seize the opportunities alone. Management must have the support of competent, dedicated staff members who possess knowledge of the principles that govern banking. That knowledge includes an understanding of the changes that are taking place in the entire financial services industry, of which commercial banking remains a critical part.

Banking formerly was evolutionary; it has now become revolutionary. Much of what we now take for granted—from space exploration to microwaves and videocassette recorders—was science fiction a few short years ago. Similarly, in banking we find new approaches, new techniques, and new services that previous generations of bankers would have considered unthinkable. Knowledge of principles must be timely; just as lawyers, physicians, and accountants must try to keep up with all the developments that affect their professions, bank staff members must seek an understanding of the environment that affects them now and will affect them in the future.

This third edition of *Principles of Banking* is intended to provide both basic principles and timeliness. It presents, in modular form, a sequential overview of commercial banking, from colonial times to the present day, and leads the reader from the fundamentals of negotiable instruments to the contemporary issues and developments in the industry. The banks of tomorrow may differ greatly from the institutions of today, yet their survival in a difficult financial environment and the profits they are able to generate will be the result of their ability to understand and adapt to change. This text is designed to help you develop those abilities.

NOTES

1. Robert E. Litan, "Taking the Dangers Out of Deregulation in Turbulent Times," *American Banker*, January 20, 1987, p. 10.

2. In Robert M. Garsson, "'86 in Washington: Banking Industry Has Had Better Years in the Capital," *American Banker*, February 4, 1987, p. 1.

3. "Bank Failures 1982–86," *American Banker*, January 6, 1987, p. 12.

4. Nathaniel C. Nash, "F.D.I.C. Chief Sees Bank Failure Rise," *The New York Times*, January 22, 1987, p. D17.

5. "Bank Scoreboard," *Business Week*, April 8, 1985, p. 107.

6. In Paul A. Willax, "Belated New Year's Resolutions for Bankers," *American Banker*, February 11, 1987, p. 4.

ACKNOWLEDGMENTS

The individual who is selected by the American Bankers Association to compile a textbook incurs a serious obligation along with the honor and privilege of authorship. In attempting to fulfill that obligation, I have had the assistance of many bankers throughout the country, whose efforts have played an important part in the completion of this Third Edition of *Principles of Banking*.

Special thanks must go to the members of the ABA Task Force, assembled for the project, who so willingly gave of their time and expertise and contributed so many valuable suggestions. The members include T. Eugene Allred, Senior Vice President, Sovran Bank, N.A., Fairfax, Virginia; Moses Bond, Group Vice President, Trust Company Bank, Atlanta, Georgia; Bethany Brown, Assistant Vice President, Bank of Boston, Boston, Massachusetts; Loyd Hoskins, Vice President, Colorado State Bank, Denver, Colorado; M.A. Muirhead, Vice President, First Republic Bank, Dallas, Texas; Duane C. Ostlund, Vice President, First Bank, N.A., Robbinsdale office, Robbinsdale, Minnesota; and Joseph C. Piscitello, Vice President, Melrose Park Bank & Trust, Melrose Park, Illinois.

Throughout the preparation of this text, I have had the consistent encouragement of the Education Policy and Development Group of the American Bankers Association. In particular, I must extend my gratitude to George T. Martin, project manager. His unfailing patience and guidance have been invaluable, and this text would have been impossible without his wholehearted support.

Finally, to my wife, Maire Cathleen, and to our children, Maureen, Eric, Margaret, and Anne, and their spouses, my appreciation for their loving participation.

1.

THE
EVOLUTION
OF
U.S. BANKING

LEARNING OBJECTIVES

After completing this chapter, you will be able to

•

identify the basic differences between
American banking and the systems in other major countries

•

trace the development of banking from colonial times

•

discuss the importance of the National Bank Act

•

cite the reasons for the Glass-Steagall, Monetary Control, and
Garn-St Germain Acts and describe their impact on banking

•

define such banking terms as wildcat banking, national bank,
transaction account, money market deposit account, and NOW and
Super-NOW accounts

•

explain the role of the Comptroller of the Currency as a
regulator of banking

American banking has been described in recent years as the most overregulated, overrestricted, and overexamined of all our industries; yet today's banking system evolved from one with virtually no examination, regulations, or restrictions. The history of American banking indicates that many successive crises led to a series of acts of Congress that created the system we now have. Not only is it entirely different from the system that existed in colonial times, it also differs from the banking systems found in other major countries throughout the world. The differences between American banking and banking in countries such as Great Britain, Germany, Japan, or France consist primarily in the *number* of banks and their *geography*.

In many countries, a handful of giant banks have the largest share of the financial marketplace. In the United States, however, some 14,000 commercial banks compete with other types of financial institutions, such as savings and loan associations (S&Ls), credit unions, savings banks, and nonbank entities (brokerage firms, retailers, insurance companies, and other organizations providing financial services). While multibillion-dollar banks exist in New York, Chicago, Atlanta, Dallas, Los Angeles, and other U.S. money centers, thousands of smaller banks also serve local communities and meet the financial needs of their customers. Thus, in the United States, the financial marketplace is fragmented, and even the largest banks have only a small part of it.

The second major difference is closely tied to the first and consists in the geographical dispersion of our banks. There is no true counterpart in the United States to the banks in other countries, which operate networks of branches on a nationwide basis. A customer of a major bank in England, Germany, France, or Italy can deal with thousands of branches of the same bank in every part of the country. In Canada, a customer of a major bank may use one branch in Vancouver, on the Pacific Ocean, and another in one of the Maritime provinces bordering the Atlantic Ocean. Developments in the United States in the mid-1980s have, to some extent, changed the basic framework, but essentially, nationwide full-scale branch banking does not exist.

The uniqueness of the U.S. banking system derives from events in our country's financial history. The system that exists today is the product of a most interesting evolution, in which the developments relate directly to the philosophy and mood of the population in each generation.

EARLY BANKING SYSTEMS

The earliest settlers on our shores differed from one another in many ways. They came from a variety of religious, national, and ethnic backgrounds, yet they shared one basic desire—a hunger for freedom. Their willingness to risk everything in leaving their familiar homelands and making the arduous journey to a primitive, largely unexplored New World reflected their wish to escape from every form of persecution, tyranny, and government control over freedom of speech and worship and other aspects of everyday life. The early colonists sought as much independence as possible, with a minimum amount of government intervention.

In some cases the colonists left countries where a strong central bank was the dominant force on the financial scene. Institutions such as the Bank of England, the Reichsbank, the Banque de France, and the Bank of Sweden were established long before America was colonized. It might have seemed logical for the colonists to establish some comparable institution; however, the spirit of free enterprise prevailed, and the early settlers moved to the opposite extreme.

In the colonies, an individual who wished to open a general store or tavern was free to do so. Similarly, a group of individuals could establish a new bank with a minimum of difficulty and with an almost complete absence of government regulation or supervision. Following the American Revolution, each of the 13 original states stoutly defended its right to regulate banking within its borders. No central bank comparable to those in other countries was established. Banks opened their doors—and, unfortunately, closed them—with great regularity.

Of course, not all the banks of the colonial and early federal eras failed. The Bank of New York, and some commercial banks organized in Massachusetts and Philadelphia during the 1780s, have survived to the present. However, these are the rare exceptions to the general rule.

The system of "currency" used in colonial times led to many bank failures. *Specie*, or hard currency, consisted of gold and silver; but only an extremely limited amount of this was available to meet the needs of the economy. Specie flowed out of the colonies in payment for goods purchased from European suppliers. As a result, many types of paper "money" began to appear.

The concept of depositing the proceeds of loans to depositors' accounts had not yet been introduced. Therefore, when a loan was approved the bank would give its customer a supply of its own notes to use as a payment medium. Each bank issued its own notes, presumably backed by specie; however, in many cases the notes proved to be either counterfeit or worthless. The public came to distrust this system. Creditors often refused to accept bank notes, doubting whether the issuing bank was still in business. Even if the bank was still functioning, creditors could not be sure whether it would agree to exchange its notes for the far more desirable specie. The problem was compounded by the lack of a standard paper currency. The Continental Congress in 1777 issued 42 separate forms of currency, and the individual states also issued their own notes (exhibit 1.1).

EXHIBIT 1.1
BANK NOTE ISSUED BY THE BANK OF MORGAN, GEORGIA, 1857

Congress finally became persuaded of the need for strengthening the faith of the public and improving the monetary system. Alexander Hamilton had been responsible for the founding of the Bank of New York in 1784; when he became secretary of the Treasury he proposed the formation of a new bank that would have the direct involvement and backing of the federal government. His plan was approved by Congress, and the First Bank of the United States opened in Philadelphia in 1791.

THE BANKS OF THE UNITED STATES

The First Bank of the United States was granted a 20-year charter by Congress. It opened eight branches to disburse and collect notes that were exchangeable for gold or silver. The federal government used the First Bank for deposits and payments.

However, the First Bank was the object of strong opposition from several sides. Critics pointed out that the Constitution contained no provision for government involvement in banking, and the independent, private bankers whose institutions operated under the liberal laws of their individual states saw the First Bank as a forerunner of a centralized bank supervisory system that would limit their freedoms. In addition, the First Bank operated as a type of policeman by accepting the notes of other banks from customers and presenting those notes for redemption in specie. This benefited the public, but was resented by banks that did not want their outstanding notes redeemed at the cost of their precious supply of specie. The First Bank was properly capitalized and well managed, which generated widespread public confidence; however, the opposition to its continued existence was so strong that Congress refused to renew the charter, and it closed in 1811.

The period from 1811 to 1816 witnessed the same weaknesses that had existed prior to the formation of the First Bank, but on a much larger scale. The population and the economy had grown, and the War of 1812 had created a need for credit. The number of undercapitalized, poorly run state banks grew steadily: in 1815, more than 200 private banks were issuing their own notes.

As bank failures increased, public confidence deteriorated. Congress reacted in 1816 by granting a charter to the Second Bank of the United States, again for a 20-year period. The Second Bank, like the First, was well capitalized and properly managed. It operated 29 branches, acted as a lender to other banks, and issued its respected and accepted notes when the money supply had to be increased. It acted as a depository for the federal government and collected the notes issued by other banks. It also had the backing of the U.S. Supreme Court, which issued a decision in 1819 (*McCulloch v. Maryland*) holding that the Second Bank was a necessary and proper instrument of the federal government.

However, President Andrew Jackson and other banks bitterly opposed the Second Bank. Congress refused to renew its charter, and the Second Bank went out of existence in 1836.

1836–63: A PERIOD OF CHAOS

The period from 1836 to 1863 has been described as the darkest in our banking history. Certainly, many events occurred that had a profound impact on banks (see exhibit 1.2). The need for a sound and trustworthy banking system had never been greater, yet there was no response to that need. The geographic expansion, population growth, and economic prosperity of the years preceding the Civil War created an ideal climate for the growth of commercial banking, but many of the banks that opened were poorly capitalized and lacked prudent management. They failed to meet the economic needs of a growing nation. Of the 2,500 state banks created between 1836 and 1860, more than 1,000 closed within 10 years of their formation; by 1862 over $100 million had been lost through bank failures.[1] Forged, depreciated, and counterfeit notes were so prevalent that various publications listed as many as 5,500 types of worthless paper. Public resentment of banks became so strong that by 1852 nine states had enacted laws prohibiting banking.[2] Despite those laws, by 1860 the total number of state banks had increased to 1,562, with outstanding loans of $692 million against deposits of $254 million and capital of $422 million.[3]

Merchants, naturally suspicious about the viability of an issuing bank or the genuineness of notes, often refused to accept notes in payment. Public trust in the banking system was at its lowest point, particu-

---

EXHIBIT 1.2
IMPORTANT DATES, 1791–1863

1791—First Bank of the United States, Philadelphia, is chartered for 20 years.

1812—War with Britain brings need for credit; state-chartered banks proliferate.

1816—Second Bank of the United States, Philadelphia, is chartered for 20 years.

1823—Nicholas Biddle heads Second Bank of the United States.

1836—Second Bank of the United States' charter expires; state chartering surges.

1837—Panic from collapse of cotton prices brings mass bank, trading company failures.

1841—President John Tyler vetoes new national bank chartering. Cabinet resigns in protest.

1842—Louisiana is first state to require reserves to back deposits.

1848—Gold is found in California, attracting miners and deposit takers. Karl Marx publishes "The Communist Manifesto."

1853—New York City banks start first U.S. clearing house.

1862—Legal Tender Act approves nationally issued paper money.

1863—National Currency Act (amended significantly June 3) creates federally chartered banks.

---

larly in the South and West, where new banks opened and operated with even less control.

Some banks instituted an abusive practice that became known as *wildcat banking*. To discourage noteholders from presenting their notes and demanding specie in exchange, these banks established locations at remote points in the wilderness, where only wildcats were said to roam. This practice further eroded public confidence, made it even more difficult for business transactions to take place, and increased the need for overall reform.

1863–64: THE NATIONAL BANK ACT

In 1863, for the third time in less than a century, America was engaged in a war, this time one that divided the nation against itself. Two years of bitter conflict had created a financial crisis in the federal government and forced President Abraham Lincoln to seek new methods of obtaining the funds he desperately required. In 1862 the Treasury Department spent $475 million but received only $52 million, and the rate of inflation stood at 13 percent.[4] Lincoln's secretary of the Treasury, Salmon P. Chase, was given the task of finding new sources of revenue while at the same time overhauling and reforming the banking system.

Chase introduced drastic legislation, passed by Congress in 1863 as the National Currency Act and later amended to form what has become known as the National Bank Act. This act created the foundation for the banking system of today. It also provided a solution to the government's financial woes by generating new revenues through the sale of Treasury bonds. The National Bank Act had four basic provisions.

First, the act created a new type of financial institution, called a *national bank*. Each such bank was privately owned, but received its charter—its authority to conduct banking business—directly from the federal government. Strict qualifying standards for charters were imposed. The stockholders, whose contributions formed the bank's capital, were personally liable if the bank failed, and Congress set limits on each bank's lending operations. All state-chartered banks were invited to apply for national bank charters, which were granted if the bank met the standards.

Second, a new office was created within the Department of the Treasury: The *Office of the Comptroller of the Currency* (OCC). The title may be misleading. The Comptroller does *not* regulate the nation's money supply, but rather has the responsibility for chartering, examining, and regulating all national banks. The Comptroller requires periodic reports of financial condition from each national bank and reports to Congress on the findings and functions of the office.

Third, the National Bank Act introduced a new type of uniform currency, the *national bank note*. Except for the issuing bank's name, these notes were standard in design (exhibit 1.3). Before it could issue its notes, each national bank was required to buy a quantity of government bonds from the Treasury Department and to pledge the bonds as security against the notes. This requirement gave the public confidence in the notes, raised money for the federal government, and kept the amount of each bank's outstanding notes proportionate to its capital.

Finally, the act established a system of *required reserves*. Every national bank was required to keep reserves against its deposits and notes as an additional protection for its depositors. Reserves could consist of vault cash plus a balance maintained with a national bank in a money-center city. Since New York City had become the nation's financial center, reserve balances were often kept with the New York banks, which paid interest on them.

Salmon Chase intended that all state banks voluntarily convert to national charters. In actual practice, few chose to do so. They preferred to stay with a system that did not call for the chartering procedures and other restrictions imposed on national banks. Therefore, Congress passed additional legislation in 1865 that placed a 10 percent tax on all notes issued by state banks. This law, together with the increasing acceptance of checks throughout the country, led the state banks to discontinue issuing notes. The practice of depositing loan proceeds directly to customers' accounts was established.

The fact that every commercial bank must be chartered either by the federal government (through the OCC) or by the banking authorities in its own state has created the *dual banking system*. Under this system, which has existed since 1864, the state-chartered and national banks exist side by side, competing with one another and generally offering the same services and operating in the same fundamental way. The Comptroller of

EXHIBIT 1.3
NATIONAL BANK NOTE, 1900

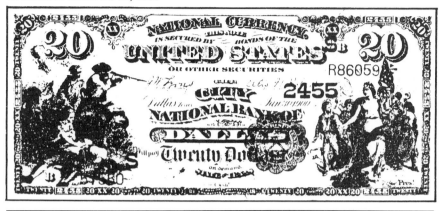

the Currency supervises the national banks, which presently number about 4,800. These banks can be recognized by the word "national," which must appear somewhere in their legal names. Examples include First National Bank (of Boston, Chicago, and so forth), Bank of America N.T. & S.A. (National Trust and Savings Association), and Citibank or Chase Manhattan Bank, N.A. (National Association). A bank may convert from one type of charter to the other at any time if it gains the necessary approvals.

WEAKNESSES AFTER 1864

The National Bank Act was a landmark in U.S. banking history. In terms of addressing the abuses and problems that had existed before its passage, in terms of helping the federal government raise funds, and in terms of forming the basis for a sound system in which the public could place its trust, the act served its purposes very well. Today it is difficult to imagine how the banking system could have survived without the reforms the act introduced. However, with the passage of time the nation was faced with new problems that required new legislation. A list of important events that followed the National Bank Act appears as exhibit 1.4.

Check Collection Problems

One problem in the system developed with the increased use of checks. By 1913 America was a nation of 48 states, and the daily flow of checks from coast to coast created a major problem. No system existed for the rapid presentation and collection of these checks. It might take weeks for a merchant in Texas who had accepted a check drawn on a bank in North Carolina to learn that the check was good—or that it had not been honored.

EXHIBIT 1.4
IMPORTANT DATES, 1865–1913

1865—Tax on state bank notes is authorized. Allotment system is established for aggregate circulation of national bank notes.

1870—Legislation raises ceiling of national bank notes in circulation.

1873—National financial crisis begins in September. Stock market closes for 10 days.

1874—U.S. Treasury is made the redeeming agency for national banks.

1875—Resumption Act authorizes resumption of specie payments for paper bills.

1875—American Bankers Association, the industry trade organization, is founded.

1879—Resumption of specie payments begins Jan. 1.

1884—Fiscal crisis begins in New York in May. More than 110 banks fail.

1890—Financial crisis, concentrated in the East, begins in the fall, peaking in November. Pooled loan certificates are used to stem runs.

1893—Panic of 1893, brought on by shrinkage in deposits, strikes hard in West and South.

1896—Populist Party's presidential bid, based on call for minting of silver, fails. Silver agitation starts to fade.

1900—Capital requirements are eased for small-town national banks. Gold Standard Act permits banks to issue notes for 100 percent of capital instead of 90 percent.

1900—Boston Clearing House begins uniform clearing procedure in New England that becomes basis for modern check-clearing operations.

1901—American Institute of Banking is formed.

1907—Panic almost brings down Wall Street. J.P. Morgan personally leads efforts to save brokerages, major banks.

1908—Reserve requirement for federal deposits is eliminated.

1913—Federal Reserve Act creates Federal Reserve System.

Most commercial banks had established account relationships with other banks, where they maintained balances in exchange for certain services. (A bank that maintains an account for another bank is called a *correspondent bank*.) As the volume of checks increased, banks used their correspondents to collect checks for them, but this process took an excessive amount of time.

An Inflexible Currency

A second weakness identified after 1864 involved the nation's money supply. The dollar amount of outstanding national bank notes at any one time legally was tied to the amount of government bonds in circulation. When business was booming, it would have been desirable to increase the supply of notes in order to finance transactions; however, the opposite actually took place. When the economy prospered, the government found that its revenues, chiefly derived from taxes, increased. The government responded to this by trying to reduce its outstanding debt and interest payments and calling in some of the bonds for redemption. In turn, this caused the amount of national bank notes in circulation to decrease. The National Bank Act thus created a uniform type of trustworthy national currency, but did so in a way that hurt, rather than helped, the rapidly growing economy.

Pyramiding Reserves

The third post-1864 weakness resulted from the system of required reserves established by the act. Each national bank had to maintain reserves with another, and the smaller, rural banks used the larger, city banks for this purpose. The city banks, in turn, left their reserves with even larger, stronger banks. The end result was a concentration of reserves held by the banks in New York City. The structure of reserves resembled a pyramid with New York City banks at the apex. To meet the interest payments on these reserves, the New York City banks used the deposited funds to make short-term loans, usually to brokerage firms.

When banks outside New York City needed large amounts of currency, they were forced to draw down their reserves. This caused an eventual drain on the New York banks, which were then compelled to call in loans in order to raise immediate funds. In some cases actual money panics resulted; for example, in 1873 a number of bank failures and a crisis in the New York stock market resulted when the brokers whose loans had been called in by the banks were forced to liquidate their own holdings to make required repayments. The stock market closed for 10 days, and thousands of companies went into bankruptcy because they could no longer obtain credit.[5]

THE FEDERAL RESERVE SYSTEM

By 1908 it had become clear that the weaknesses in the banking system were having increasingly adverse effects on the entire economy, and a National Monetary Commission was created to determine what changes needed to be made. In 1912 President Woodrow Wilson publicly stated that reforms had become absolutely necessary. After lengthy Congressional discussion and analysis of the ideas presented by banking associations, economists, and regulatory authorities, Congress passed the Federal Reserve Act in 1913.

The Federal Reserve Act is a fascinating example of compromise legislation; it responded to the wishes of many different groups while correcting many of the defects in the banking system. For those who feared an excessive concentration of federal power in Washington, it provided a measure of local control. For those who opposed the idea of a strong central bank, it provided for private ownership. For those whose chief concern was the money supply, it offered a new type of currency, the Federal Reserve note, which did not have to be backed by bonds but would be accepted as legal tender (exhibit 1.5). In every way, the Federal Reserve Act served to remedy the previous drawbacks to sound and efficient banking, and thus gave the economy a far more responsive system.

The Federal Reserve Act divided the country into 12 geographic districts, established a Federal Reserve bank in each one, and provided

EXHIBIT 1.5
FEDERAL RESERVE BANK NOTE, 1914

that member banks could send checks directly to them for collection; thereafter, the district Fed would take care of presenting the checks to the individual banks on which they were drawn (see exhibit 1.6). The new check collection system contained mechanisms to ensure that the presenting and collection process would require far less time than the previous methods.

To solve the problem of the money supply, the Federal Reserve Act gave the Fed authority to issue notes and removed the requirement that these be backed by government bonds. Today, these notes constitute our

EXHIBIT 1.6
FUNCTIONS OF THE FEDERAL RESERVE SYSTEM

Bank For Banks

| Loans | Check Collection | | Currency | Safekeeping |

Supervision | Automated Transfer

Bank For The Federal Government

| U.S. Government Checking Account | Sale, Redemption Interest Payments on Government Securities |

Monetary Policy

| Reserve Requirement | Discount Rate | Open Market Operations |

basic currency. After passage of the act, national banks stopped issuing their own notes. The act also made it possible for banks to obtain ready supplies of coin and currency when needed since the Fed can, on very short notice, deliver cash to its member banks.

The problem of pyramiding reserves also was solved through the 12 geographic districts. Member banks in the Federal Reserve System kept their reserves with the Federal Reserve bank in their own district. Thus, pools of reserve funds were maintained in every part of the country rather than concentrated in one area. The act also gave the Fed authority to change the percentage of required reserves whenever necessary, and to extend credit under certain conditions. The original act provided that only member banks in the Federal Reserve System could borrow from it. Subsequently, the act was amended so that all financial institutions offering transaction accounts can apply to the Fed for short-term credit.

The importance of the Fed as the nation's primary force for controlling the flow of money and credit and the organization and tools of the Federal Reserve System are discussed in more detail in chapter 2.

The Federal Reserve Act overcame these three major obstacles to sound and efficient banking and gave the U.S. economy a far more responsive system. However, just as Salmon Chase and his associates could not have foreseen the economic changes that made that act necessary, so the lawmakers and bankers who drew up the Federal Reserve Act could not have predicted the collapse of the stock market in 1929, the Great Depression, and the banking crisis that followed.

THE GLASS-STEAGALL ACT

Following the end of World War I, America embarked on an era of unrestrained growth and wild optimism. The commercial banks financed much of this growth and participated in the optimism, making investments and extending credit on the apparent assumption that the economy would continue to expand indefinitely.

During the "Roaring Twenties," the banking environment still reflected the unrestrictive laws of the preceding century. Some states allowed new banks in small communities to open with as little as $6,000 in initial capital. By 1929, 72 percent of the 24,912 commercial banks had capital of less than $100,000 each.[6] Depositors who wished to speculate in the stock market found it easy to obtain credit from the banks. Margin credit—borrowed money used to buy stocks—increased by $800 million in a single year (1927) to a total of $3.6 billion; 90 percent of a purchase of stock could be financed through bank loans or directly by brokers.[7]

The prevailing philosophy that the business boom would continue forever, and that stock prices would only continue to rise, was put to rest when the stock market crash of October 28, 1929, decreased paper values by $14 billion in a single day.

During 1930 more than 1,300 commercial banks closed their doors, and by 1933 an additional 7,000 had failed. About $7 billion in deposits disappeared as a result of these bank failures. Other countries also felt the impact of the collapse. In 1931 Austria's largest bank, Credit Anstalt, collapsed, as did Danat Bank in Germany; this was followed by a run on all German banks, and in the same year Britain abandoned the gold standard.

Many of the U.S. banks that were forced out of business were small banks in agricultural areas; however, a single failure in New York City caused the loss of $200 million in deposits. The banks became the hub of a vicious circle. The stock market investments in which they had speculated had lost much of their value; the investors and brokerage firms to which the banks had loaned billions of dollars were unable to repay; and businesses in growing numbers went into bankruptcy, fired their workers, and defaulted on their bank loans. The nation's unemployment rate reached 25 percent. Large numbers of depositors lost their lifetime savings, unable to withdraw funds from the banks to meet their everyday living expenses simply because there was no cash to distribute.

A further problem arose because, prior to 1933, commercial banks had paid interest on demand deposits (checking accounts) and competed aggressively with one another, offering higher rates in order to attract new deposits. The interest expense created by this policy could be offset only by increasing interest income on loans and investments; therefore, credit had become extremely easy to obtain. When the loans and investments proved worthless, many banks had no alternative other than to liquidate.

By the time Franklin D. Roosevelt was sworn in as president in March 1933, 22 states had declared "bank holidays" and the nation's banking system had lost its most valuable asset—the confidence of the public. Roosevelt immediately declared a 7-day national bank holiday and stated that literally thousands of institutions were "unfit to reopen." The desperate condition of the entire system led Congress to pass the Glass-Steagall Act in 1933.

The Glass-Steagall Act significantly altered the operations of commercial banks and helped to restore public confidence. It contained four major provisions, as follows:

- Interest payments on demand deposits were prohibited.
- Commercial banks were ordered to divest themselves of all underwriting of revenue bonds and corporate stock issues, and were prohibited from investing in common stock except when acting on behalf of customers.
- The Federal Reserve was authorized to control bank loans made in connection with securities transactions.
- A new agency, the Federal Deposit Insurance Corporation (FDIC), was created to provide protection for bank depositors.

Over the years, the section of Glass-Steagall separating commercial from investment banking repeatedly has been challenged. In the late 1980s, for example, many banks have sought permission to engage in securities activities in order to compete more effectively with other providers of financial services. In some cases, this permission was granted and the banks were given certain securities-related powers, subject to judicial review.

FEDERAL DEPOSIT INSURANCE CORPORATION

The Glass-Steagall Act authorized the start of FDIC operations on January 1, 1934, guaranteeing insurance coverage on all deposits up to $2,500. This maximum limit on coverage periodically has increased and as of 1987 stood at $100,000. The Federal Deposit Insurance Act of 1935 amended Glass-Steagall and established the current format for FDIC operation. FDIC is authorized to

- set standards for its member banks' operations
- examine them to ensure their compliance with the standards
- take action to prevent troubled banks from failing
- pay depositors if an insured bank fails

National banks, already required to be Fed members, *must* belong to FDIC; other commercial banks may join if they wish. Mutual savings banks also may be FDIC members. Savings and loan associations, which do not fall under the legal definition of banks, are not eligible for FDIC membership. S&Ls use a similar federal agency, the Federal Savings and Loan Insurance Corporation (FSLIC), for the protection of their customers.

Today about 98 percent of all commercial and savings banks are FDIC members. They are legally required to identify their membership through displays in their branches and in their advertising. Each member pays an annual insurance premium of one-twelfth of one percent of its average total deposits. If the insurance fund built up through these assessments should ever prove insufficient to meet its needs, FDIC is authorized to borrow up to $3 billion directly from the Treasury Department at any time. This borrowing privilege has never been used. The FDIC fund currently amounts to over $10 billion.

FDIC operations are directed in Washington, D.C., by a three-member board of governors, of which the Comptroller of the Currency is an *ex officio* member. Regional FDIC offices also exist. FDIC was also given the authority to establish maximum interest rates on savings and time deposits at banks whose rates were not otherwise regulated.

As a result of the implementing of FDIC, the number of bank failures and forced mergers dropped sharply from 4,326 in 1933 to 275 in 1934; from 1934 through 1942, 393 insured banks failed; and from 1943 through 1978 there were 162 insured-bank failures.[8]

Irvine Sprague, former FDIC chairman, has said that of the 50 largest failures in U.S. banking history, 46 were handled in such a way that no depositor or creditor of a failed bank lost one penny. In 1984 FDIC, by providing $4.5 billion in various forms of assistance, prevented the collapse of the nation's eighth largest bank, Continental Illinois, which had assets of over $40 billion. This "bailout" reflected the philosophy that the banking system simply cannot tolerate the failure of a major bank, and that therefore an institution above a certain size should never be allowed to fail.[9]

There were 138 bank failures in 1986. FDIC and FSLIC have assumed an active role in trying to *prevent* failures, and during the 1980s both agencies frequently intervened when troubled banks were identified. The FDIC maintains a "problem list" of those banks that perform poorly, based on its CAMEL (capital, assets, management, earnings, and liquidity) ratings. In 1986 there were over 1,400 institutions on this list.

During the 1980s, U.S. thrift institutions—savings banks and S&Ls— encountered severe difficulties because of the basic nature of their business. As the nation's largest home-mortgage lenders, thrifts carried portfolios of long-term loans on which interest rates could not be changed. Changes in the money markets forced these thrifts to pay out far more in interest on deposits than they could earn on their loans. Consequently, savings banks and S&Ls showed large operating losses. FDIC and FSLIC repeatedly stepped in to prevent them from failing. Typically, a takeover of a troubled thrift would be arranged with FDIC or FSLIC assistance. The acquiring institution might be either a stronger thrift or a commercial bank. Although these interventions were expensive for the insurers, it would have been even more costly if the institutions had been allowed to fail and FDIC and FSLIC had been required to pay the depositors.

THE MONETARY CONTROL ACT

Congress passed the Depository Institutions Deregulation and Monetary Control Act (commonly known by the last three words of the title) in 1980. It has been called the most important single piece of banking legislation since 1933. Designed to improve the Fed's ability to control monetary policy and to provide greater competitive equality among financial institutions, the major provisions of the Monetary Control Act were as follows:

- Maximum FDIC and FSLIC coverage was increased to $100,000 per account.
- The term *transaction accounts* was coined to describe all accounts that permit any type of payments to third parties. *All* institutions offering transaction accounts were required to maintain reserves against their deposits, either directly with the Fed or through Fed member banks.

- Regulation Q, implemented in 1934 to set maximum interest rates on all forms of savings and time deposits, was to be gradually phased out so that financial institutions could compete freely for these deposits. By 1987 the phase-out had been completed.
- A Depository Institutions Deregulation Committee (DIDC) was formed and was made responsible for the timing and amount of changes in interest-rate ceilings during the phase-out period.
- The Fed's "discount window," through which loans are made, was expanded so that all financial institutions could apply for short-term credit.
- The Fed was ordered to implement a system of explicit pricing for all its services, including check collection, securities safekeeping, wire transfers of funds, and suppying coin and currency. These services and functions will be described in chapter 2.
- Thrift institutions and credit unions were given additional powers to make them more competitive with commercial banks. For example, federally chartered savings banks were given the right to offer consumer and commercial loans and trust services.
- *Negotiable order of withdrawal* (NOW) accounts, which give customers the ability to earn interest on balances against which checks can be issued, were authorized for all financial institutions.[10]

Effects of the Monetary Control Act

The act drastically affected every type of financial institution in the United States. By making all of them subject to reserve requirements, it prevented attrition from the Federal Reserve System and thereby gave the Fed added control over the flow of money and credit. By increasing maximum insurance coverage, the act gave depositors at insured banks further assurance that their funds were safe. This was extremely important at a time when questions were being raised as to whether the banks were "safe." By eliminating rate ceilings on savings and time deposits, it provided for free competition. Thrift institutions were allowed to expand into new areas of financial services. Finally, by requiring the Fed to levy specific prices on its services, the act forced banks to begin passing along per-item charges for many services directly to their customers.

Traditionally, the three major categories of bank customers—businesses, agencies of government, and individuals—were accustomed to leave demand deposits, earning no interest, with their banks. The basis of the deposit structure at commercial banks was the checking account, or demand deposit, relationship.

In 1961 in New York, through the introduction of the large-denomination (issued for $100,000 or more) negotiable *certificate of deposit* (CD), that deposit structure began to change. The size of these CDs meant that they were exempt from the interest-rate restrictions of Federal

Reserve Regulation Q. Banks could complete freely in offering them, and the fact that CDs were issued in negotiable form meant that they could easily be sold in the secondary market if the holder wished to convert them into cash before maturity. CDs of this type soon became the favored interest-earning vehicle for the banks' affluent customers, and by 1983 they accounted for over 15 percent of the total assets of all insured commercial banks.[11]

In 1971 brokerage firms introduced a new type of mutual fund, the *money market fund*, to accommodate customers with less than $100,000 to invest. When banks, restricted by federal regulation, could pay only 5 or 5¼ percent interest on savings accounts, money market funds were paying 8 percent or more. By 1982 these funds had peaked at $230 billion, with Merrill Lynch alone holding $50 billion.[12]

Disintermediation is the term used to describe an outflow of money from one type of financial institution to another, or from one type of relationship to another, as customers seek higher yields on their excess funds. In the early 1980s, both commercial banks and thrifts sought congressional help because huge sums of money were being withdrawn from the banks' deposit accounts to be placed in the mutual funds.

To help maintain competition among financial institutions, Congress passed the Garn-St Germain Act in 1982. Its major provision directed the DIDC to authorize a new type of account, the *money market deposit account* (MMDA), at commercial banks and thrifts. The first such accounts were authorized in December 1982. MMDAs had the following characteristics:

- There was no minimum maturity, but depository institutions were required to reserve the right to demand at least 7 days' notice before withdrawal.
- The accounts were available to all depositors and were insured by FDIC or FSLIC.
- A minimum balance of $2,500 was required, and accounts which met this requirement were exempt from interest rate ceilings.
- No restrictions were placed on the size or frequency of withdrawals by mail, by messenger, or in person, but check transactions were limited to three per month.
- Banks and thrifts could establish their own minimum denominations for each transaction.

Within 2 years, the amount held in MMDAs at all financial institutions was estimated at $394 billion, and money market funds had experienced a corresponding decline in popularity.

A second provision of the Garn-St Germain Act expanded FDIC authority to provide assistance in order to keep insured commercial and savings banks from failing. As mentioned earlier, FDIC has used this expanded power extensively in recent years.[13]

Late in 1982 the DIDC took further action, as authorized under the Garn-St Germain Act, and created another type of deposit relationship called the *Super-NOW account*. This account had no interest rate ceiling and was made available to individuals, government agencies, and certain nonprofit organizations. The Super-NOW account had no limits on monthly transaction volume.

In 1985 the DIDC eliminated minimum deposit requirements on Super-NOW and MMDA accounts, and as of March 31, 1986, all rate ceilings were eliminated. Banks *may* set minimum balance figures if they wish.

The introduction to this text mentioned the drastic change that has occurred in the deposit structure at the largest U.S. commercial banks. As increasing numbers of banks, for competitive reasons, have offered new types of interest-bearing accounts, that structure has continued to change throughout the country. During the 1980s the percentage of interest-bearing time and savings deposits in the entire banking system has consistently been in the 70 percent to 75 percent range; in other words, only 25 percent to 30 percent of total bank deposits have remained in non-interest-bearing demand deposits.

The introduction of these various types of interest-bearing relationships, which maintain the customer's check-writing privileges, has provided bank depositors with a new freedom of choice. It is no longer necessary for an individual to keep funds in a non-interest-bearing demand deposit in order to issue checks. Money easily is moved from one type of account to another, and consumers are quick to take advantage of yield opportunities.

SUMMARY

Banking in colonial times reflected a belief that the highest possible degree of freedom, with a minimum of government intervention, should be allowed and that banks should be permitted to operate as freely as other forms of business ventures. However, experience proved that banking cannot be granted the same latitude that other businesses enjoy under our free-enterprise system. Bank operations have far too great an impact on the national economy for them to function without any government regulation. However, the extent and type of that regulation has caused serious concern among bankers in recent years.

Since colonial times the diversity of laws in different areas, combined with the absence of a centralized banking authority, contributed to the evolution of a unique banking system in the United States. In 1987 full-scale interstate banking still was not possible for commercial banks. The number of U.S. banks—and the concentration of assets—also contrasts with the systems in other countries. In Canada, for example, five banks hold some 90 percent of the total bank assets; six clearing banks in

England control about 70 percent; the three largest French banks hold approximately 55 percent; and in West Germany three banks hold 45 percent. The 100 largest U.S. commercial banks control only 53.9 percent of total bank assets.[14]

In 1863 and 1864, 1913, and 1933, Congress enacted legislation that imposed certain controls and standards on banks while leaving them with some freedom to compete. Generally, banking laws have been passed to stabilize the financial system in times of crisis and to remove weaknesses in the system.

In 1980 and 1982, adapting to current economic conditions, a measure of *deregulation* was granted to allow commercial banks and thrifts to compete more effectively with other financial institutions.

The evolution of American banking is marked by a series of crises, each of which weakened public confidence in the soundness of the system. Those crises, however, have been met with solutions that strengthened the system and rebuilt public confidence. Although concerns still exist, and although bankers and lawmakers often have disagreed about the extent and type of controls that should be placed on banking, their joint efforts have helped to build an industry of which its one million employees can be justly proud. No doubt crises will continue to occur, but solutions to them can be found so that the system remains sound.

QUESTIONS FOR DISCUSSION

1. What problems existed in the colonial banking system before 1791?

2. How did the two Banks of the United States represent improvements over their predecessors?

3. What caused both Banks of the United States to go out of business?

4. What problems did wildcat banking create?

5. Why was counterfeiting so prevalent during the nineteenth century?

6. List the four major provisions of the National Currency (National Bank) Act.

7. Does the United States have a dual banking system? Why?

8. Identify three basic weaknesses in the banking system that existed after 1864.

9. How did the Federal Reserve Act address those three weaknesses?

10. What banking crisis led to establishment of the FDIC?

11. List four major provisions of the Monetary Control Act of 1980.

12. Why did large numbers of thrift institutions experience severe financial problems in the 1970s and 1980s?

13. What factors led to the establishing of Money Market Deposit Accounts?

14. How do Super-NOW accounts differ from MMDAs?

NOTES

1. Bartlett Naylor, "Bankers Spilled Blood in Nation's Early Years," *American Banker*, 150th anniversary issue (January 1987), p. 24.

2. Elvira Clain-Stefanelli and Vladimir Clain-Stefanelli, *Chartered For Progress: Two Centuries of American Banking* (Washington, D.C.: Acropolis Books, Ltd., 1975), pp. 68–69.

3. Paul Studenski and Herman E. Krooss, *Financial History of the United States*, 2d ed. (New York: McGraw-Hill Book Company, Inc., 1963), p. 121.

4. Naylor, "Bankers Spilled Blood," p. 24.

5. Jeffrey Marshall, "'Twixt Booms and Panics: Banking in the Gilded Age," *American Banker*, 150th anniversary issue (January 1987), p. 26.

6. Robert M. Garsson, "'The Ballyhoo Years' End in a Crash and a Hangover," *American Banker*, 150th anniversary issue (January 1987), p. 36.

7. Tom Ferris, "From the Doghouse to the Country Club," *American Banker*, 150th anniversary issue (January 1987), p. 50.

8. Richard C. Keller, "Glass-Steagall: Fact vs. Folklore," *The Bankers Magazine* (September-October 1984), p. 84; and Joseph F. Sinkey, Jr., *Problem and Failed Institutions in the Commercial Banking Industry* (Greenwich, Conn.: JAI Press, Inc., 1979), p. 15.

9. "FDIC's Search for a Lasting Solution to the Continental Crisis," *American Banker*, September 12, 1986, pp. 4–10.

10. The full text of the Monetary Control Act may be found in *Federal Reserve Bulletin* (June 1980), pp. 444–53. See also Board of Governors of the Federal Reserve System, *The Monetary Control Act of 1980* (Washington, D.C.: U.S. Government Printing Office, 1981).

11. Deborah J. Danker and Mary M. McLaughlin, "Profitability of Insured Commercial Banks in 1983," *Federal Reserve Bulletin* (November 1984), p. 804.

12. Harvey Rosenblum, "Banks and Nonbanks: Who's In Control?," *The Bankers Magazine* (September-October 1984), p. 16.

13. "FDIC Policy and Criteria on Aid to Operating Insured Banks," *American Banker*, December 5, 1986, p. 10.

14. Martha R. Seger, "Given Effective Legislative Controls, Interstate Access Will Help Banking," *American Banker*, January 4, 1985, p. 1.

For More Information

Board of Governors of the Federal Reserve System. *The Monetary Control Act of 1980*. Washington, D.C.: Government Printing Office, 1981.

Clain-Stefanelli, Elvira and Vladimir. *Chartered for Progress: Two Centuries of American Banking*. Washington, D.C.: Acropolis Books, 1975.

Klebaner, Benjamin J. *Commercial Banking in the United States: A History*. Hinsdale, Ill.: 1974.

Reed, Edward W., Richard V. Cotter, Edward K. Gill, and Richard K. Smith. *Commercial Banking*, 3d ed. Englewood Cliffs, N.J.: Prentice-Hall, Inc., 1984.

Studenski, Paul, and Herman E. Krooss. *Financial History of the United States*, 2d ed. New York: McGraw-Hill Book Co., Inc., 1963.

Trescott, Paul B. *Financing American Enterprise: The Story of Commercial Banking*. New York: Harper & Row, 1963.

2.

BANK ORGANIZATION
AND
THE FEDERAL
RESERVE

LEARNING OBJECTIVES

After completing this chapter, you will be able to

•

explain the concept of full-service banking

•

describe the operations of thrift institutions and credit unions

•

list the contributions of commercial banks to the economy

•

distinguish between demand deposits and other deposit types

•

identify the basic objectives of the Federal Reserve

•

list the basic tools the Fed uses to control the flow of money and credit

•

describe the basic services provided by the Fed to banks and the
government

•

define the terms credit union, share draft, savings bank,
savings and loan association, commercial paper, monetary and fiscal
policy, open-market operations, discount rate,
and bank holding company

Financial needs—and services—are as individual as the customers who come to a bank, thrift, credit union, or other financial institution. Consider the following six situations:

- Ellen Smith receives Social Security payments each month, but in the past year she has had three checks lost through mailbox theft. In each case she had to wait for the government agency to issue replacement checks. Each lost check created a hardship for Ellen Smith and an expense for the Social Security Agency; both parties would like to find a better way.
- Matthew and Verna Robinson came to the United States several years ago from the Caribbean. They have both worked and have always wanted a home of their own. They have now found the exact house they want, but in order to buy it they will need a mortgage loan.
- Joe Terry has won a substantial amount from the state lottery. After all taxes are paid, he would like to establish a trust fund to pay for his grandchildren's education. He is not sure about the best way to do this.
- Gary Williams operates a general merchandise store and has learned that a firm in Italy can supply a product he needs at a very attractive price. Unfortunately, the Italian firm requires prepayment to ship the goods, and Gary does not have the cash on hand to pay the supplier. He needs a method of satisfying the Italian company while protecting his own interests.
- Lynn DePalma has been successful in her own business as an interior decorator. She has never worked for a company that offered a pension plan. She is unsure whether new tax legislation allows her to set aside a portion of her income for retirement security and wonders how to do this.
- Charlie McGowan is treasurer of the local school board. Because of changes in its billing and collection system, the board now finds itself with a large sum of money that will not be needed for several months. For the local taxpayers' benefit, Charlie would like to invest the excess funds at a good yield while making sure that they are fully protected.

What do these everyday situations have in common? In each case, the individuals could go to one or more types of financial institutions for the services they need. However, only at their local commercial bank can all of these people obtain all their required services.

TYPES OF FINANCIAL INSTITUTIONS

One characteristic of the U.S. financial scene is the diversity of the financial institutions that compete for funds. Savings banks, savings and loan associations, credit unions, and commercial banks are distinct entities that offer overlapping services. Like the U.S. system of banking, these differing institutions have evolved over time to meet specific needs.

In Europe, *savings banks* were organized in the nineteenth century to promote thrift among individuals of modest income and to provide them with interest on their savings. During the same period, individuals in America found that the commercial banks—which were organized to serve the needs of businesses and government—often did not welcome them as depositors. The first savings banks in the United States began operating in 1817 and 1819. At year-end 1985 there were 659 U.S. savings banks, with total assets of $326 billion.[1] Most of these banks are located in the northeastern part of the country and in New York. Indeed, savings banks legally cannot exist in many states.

Savings banks may be mutual (owned by the depositors) or corporate in nature, and may be chartered federally or by the state. As a result of the Monetary Control and Garn-St Germain Acts, savings banks now are free to conduct an increased amount of business with corporations. They offer a wide range of financial services, although their emphasis is still on using the savings of individuals to extend home mortgage loans and make other investments.

Savings and loan associations (S&Ls) originally were called building societies because their purpose was to serve as a source of home mortgage credit for individuals at a time when commercial banks usually were unwilling to extend such loans. Today, some 3,200 S&Ls in the United States have total assets in excess of $1.1 trillion.[2] The S&Ls hold almost 50 percent of the total mortgage debt on one- to four-family homes; however, under the expanded powers granted by the Monetary Control and Garn-St Germain Acts, they have diversified into other forms of lending, including loans to businesses. Like the savings banks, S&Ls may be either state-chartered or federally chartered. Their operations are supervised by the Federal Home Loan Bank Board (FHLBB), and their insurance coverage is provided by the Federal Savings and Loan Insurance Corporation (FSLIC). Many S&Ls in recent years have converted their charters in order to become "banks" and offer a wider range of financial services.

Credit unions are cooperative, non-profit, voluntary organizations composed of groups of individuals that have some common bond. In most cases the individuals work for the same employer or are members of the same branch of the armed forces; in other cases the common bond may be social, fraternal, or geographic. There are some 17,000 credit unions in the United States, with total assets of over $157 billion.[3] Originally, they specialized in small loans to individuals—again, because commercial banks generally did not make those loans—but, like the savings banks and S&Ls, credit unions now offer other types of credit. Members of credit unions can use *share drafts* (negotiable, check-like instruments) as a means of making payments.

Although savings banks, S&Ls, and credit unions are important components of the overall financial services industry in the United States, and although all three have grown substantially in recent years, the dominant type of financial institution remains the commercial bank. Unfortunately, the various types of financial institutions are sometimes confused with one another, and the meaning of the word ''bank'' may sometimes be unclear.

COMMERCIAL BANKS

Under the Bank Holding Company Act of 1956, a *bank* has two essential characteristics:

- It accepts demand deposits.
- It makes commercial loans.

Commercial banks obviously have these characteristics. Today, however, other financial institutions often compete directly with commercial banks in offering financial services, and terms such as ''nonbank banks'' have become part of our language. The one characteristic that distinguishes commercial banks from all other competitors is this: Commercial banks are *full-service* institutions.

In the situations mentioned at the beginning of this chapter, other types of financial institutions might have offered each customer the necessary services. Yet only a commercial bank could have offered all of the services to all of the customers.

The Robinsons could have found a thrift institution, or possibly a credit union, that would extend the necessary home mortgage loan. Ellen Smith could have established an account with a thrift or credit union and arranged for automatic monthly crediting of her account with her Social Security payments through a form of electronic funds transfer. As a result of legislation in the 1980s, many thrift institutions now offer various investment programs—thus, Joe Terry could go through a thrift to set aside funds for future needs. Gary Williams might be able to arrange for credit with a commercial finance company or other organization willing to advance the funds he needed. Lynn DePalma's funds for her eventual retirement could be placed with a savings bank, S&L, brokerage firm, or other financial intermediary; similarly, Charlie McGowan could place the school board funds with one of these financial institutions for investment purposes.

The point is that a commercial bank would have been able to accommodate all of these needs, in addition to providing other services to all its other customers: businesses, government units, correspondent banks, and consumers. It is a full-service institution. By serving the financial needs of all types of customers, the 14,000 commercial banks remain the dominant entities in the competitive U.S. financial marketplace.

THE IMPORTANCE OF BANKS

If one wished to measure the importance of banks to the economy, several yardsticks could be used. The 14,000 banks, the 40,000 offices they operate, the 1 million workers they employ, and their total assets— $2.8 trillion as of year-end 1986—could be used for that purpose. More important, however, is the contribution that banks make to every aspect of the national economy. Banking is the one industry that is related to every other. Without the services the banks provide, other industries would find it difficult or impossible to continue operating.

For example, the U.S. automobile industry employs hundreds of thousands of workers, creates sales worth many billions of dollars each year, has thousands of stockholders in its corporations, and provides a market for many other industries, such as steel, aluminum, glass, plastic, and textiles. The services of commercial banks are critical to the functioning of the entire automobile industry.

Assume that John Smith buys a car from his local dealer (possibly using the proceeds of a bank loan) and gives the dealer a check. The dealer deposits that check with his own bank and, in turn, issues his own check or makes a money transfer to pay the manufacturer. The manufacturer uses a bank for loans to finance further growth and development. It makes deposits in its banks and uses checks on those deposit accounts to pay its employees, taxes, and vendors. If necessary the auto manufacturer can easily move funds to and from banks in every corner of the world, can obtain daily computerized information on the status of all its bank accounts, can establish pension and profit-sharing plans with banks for the benefit of its employees, can have a bank perform various securities services for stockholders, and can invest excess funds with it. No other single agency or institution can meet all the manufacturer's needs.

COMMERCIAL BANK ORGANIZATION

The typical commercial bank in the United States is *corporate* in structure: it is a legally chartered business venture that has directors, officers, and stockholders and is organized for profit. The charter is granted either by the state in which the bank is organized or by the federal government through the Comptroller of the Currency. (The chartering process and the regulatory procedures that banks must follow are detailed in chapter 13.) The bank's board of directors constitutes the active, governing body of the corporation. They are responsible for its operations and performance, and can be held legally liable for their actions. Directors are elected by the bank's stockholders and generally operate through various committees such as credit, auditing, and trust. Directors also appoint the bank's officers.

The chairman of the bank (or bank holding company) usually is the chief executive officer and is the person responsible for the basic policies of the institution. The president is typically the chief administrative officer, responsible for supervising operations and implementing policies. Depending on the size and scope of the institution, various officer levels may be designed so that individuals have specific responsibility for units under their jurisdiction.

With the passage of time and the changes that have taken place in the overall financial services industry, new needs have arisen in the organization, policies, and structure of commercial banks. Alfred P. Sloan, the genius who helped make General Motors one of the world's largest and most profitable corporations, stated many years ago that "the circumstances of the ever-changing market and ever-changing product are capable of breaking any business organization if that organization is unprepared for change." His words apply directly to banking today. To prepare for inevitable changes, banks are emphasizing professional training and development of personnel.

Through training and development, employees learn the functions of banks, the competitive factors that affect banks, and the need for new or enhanced skills to meet the challenges of the future. The industry-sponsored American Institute of Banking leads banking education with formal courses and certificate programs. In addition, many banks offer internal courses and seminars to help employees realize their potential and master important knowledge areas.

Every bank employee must be guided by a code of ethics that reflects the position of trust he or she occupies. Beyond the basic requirement of unquestioned honesty, bank employees must be sensitive to the need for absolute confidentiality. The banker must remain above suspicion. Every report of insider trading, illegal loans, or breaches of confidence casts a cloud over the entire industry, and any question or doubt regarding a specific action must be resolved in favor of straightforward propriety.

BANK FUNCTIONS

Large industries and corporations, individual consumers, small businesses, and agencies of federal, state, and local government all rely on commercial banks to meet every type of financial need.

The largest commercial banks today may offer over 200 separate financial services and products, but not all of these are essential to continued profitable operations. For example, every bank does not have an international department or a trust department. If some of the 200 services were to be eliminated, the large bank still could serve most of its customers. The key question, then, is this: What are the essentials of banking? What are the most basic functions of banks, without which they could not exist and without which the U.S. economy could not remain productive and strong?

If all the activities of a commercial bank are studied, three functions stand out as major contributions to the economy. They are the building blocks upon which banking and the economy rest. In addition, they satisfy the legal requirement that defines a bank. The three functions are

- the deposit function
- the payments function
- the credit function

Unlike those in many other countries, American banks are not owned and operated by the government. They are owned by their stockholders. There is no central bank in the United States fully comparable to the Banks of England, Sweden, Italy, or Japan. The objective of U.S. banks is to render services while generating profits. The deposit, payment, and credit functions make it possible for that objective to be achieved.

THE DEPOSIT FUNCTION

Hundreds of billions of dollars are deposited with, and drawn against, commercial banks each year. Why? What actually is deposited? Who are the depositors? The answers to these questions require an understanding of the U.S. *money supply*. This term is used to describe the total amount of funds available to the general public for spending; that is, funds in nongovernment hands. The money supply includes

- M_1: coin and currency in circulation, demand deposits (with some exceptions) at banks, traveler's checks, and funds withdrawable on demand at other financial institutions
- M_2: M_1 plus savings and small-denomination time deposits
- M_3: M_2 plus large-denomination time deposits
- M_4: M_3 plus certain other liquid assets

Of these, M_1 is the most widely quoted, because it reflects funds that are immediately available for spending. Coin and currency makes up only about 25 percent of M_1. By far, the largest component of M_1 is *demand deposits*—funds that can be withdrawn at any time without advance notice to the bank.

The most common type of demand deposit is the checking account. The total amount on deposit, or any part of it, is payable on demand and can be converted into coin and currency if the funds are collected and available. If an individual with an available balance of $100 in a checking account issues a check for that amount, he or she can present it to a teller and immediately receive $100 in cash.

But is a check *money*? Using the true definition of that word, it is not. Money is the legal tender issued and backed by a government. A check may be acceptable as a form of payment; indeed, over one hundred million checks flow through the banking system every day, and well over 90 percent of all payments are made by check. However, a check can be refused, since there may be doubt as to whether it is "good." With actual money, this problem does not exist. The currency in circulation in the United States today consists of Federal Reserve notes, each of which bears the printed legend, "This note is legal tender for all debts, public and private." A check is accepted on faith and trust, whereas legal tender—money—is issued and backed by a government.

Because the largest single element in the money supply is the demand deposit, against which checks are issued, it follows that the bulk of a bank's daily deposit activity involves checks rather than coin and currency. The dollar value of all the checks deposited with banks each day is far greater than the amount of coin and currency, simply because checks are so widely used as a form of payment.

Checking account customers have bills to pay and expenses to meet. The deposit function necessarily precedes the payment function; the latter could not exist without the former. When we are given a check, we accept it because we believe that it is "good" and that funds have been deposited to cover it.

Converting Checks into Money

When a check is used to make a payment, what can the recipient do to convert it into money? He or she could physically take it to the bank on which it was drawn and ask for legal tender in exchange. However, with over 14,000 commercial banks, against any of which the check could have been drawn, this is impossible for every recipient to do. The check might have been drawn on a bank across the street or on one located thousands of miles away. To resolve this problem, the commercial banking system has provided a mechanism for converting checks into money.

Consider a cross section of the depositors at a commercial bank. A farmer receives checks in payment for produce. A state or local government receives checks in payment of taxes. A worker receives salary checks. A retired person receives pension checks from former employers and a Social Security check from the government. Stockholders receive dividend checks from corporations. By depositing their checks with banks, all these customers can convert what would otherwise be mere pieces of paper into spendable funds quickly, cheaply, and efficiently.

Safety and Convenience

Two additional reasons for depositing money with banks are safety and convenience. Every depositor believes that deposits left with a bank will be protected at all times and that the bank is responsible for safeguarding them and making them available at some future date. If a bank robbery or some type of embezzlement should occur, the depositor is protected against loss. Banks must always be conscious of the need to protect depositors' funds and use them prudently for loans and investments. A bank should never be unable to honor a legitimate request for payment against an account.

Banks try to make their offices and facilities available to customers at convenient times and locations. Extra banking hours, drive-in facilities, and automated teller machines (ATMs) have become commonplace. Banks try to maintain facilities near where their customers live, work, or shop, and try to simplify transactions for them.

The more than 59,000 ATMs now operating in the United States provide added convenience for customers. Of all commercial banks with deposits of $1 billion or more, 91 percent have ATMs, as do 93 percent of banks in the $500 million to $1 billion range.[4] Average usage per ATM per month is approximately 6,000 transactions. These machines have become familiar sights in every part of the country.

Demand Deposits Vs. Savings and Time Deposits

At a bank, the deposit may be made either into a checking or savings account, or used to establish some form of time deposit. The depositor's intent is not the same in each case. Deposits into checking accounts are made because the customer intends to withdraw the funds in the very near future to meet current expenses. In today's economy, customers tend to leave the smallest amount possible in excess checking-account balances, which by law cannot earn interest. Instead, they deposit all funds that are not immediately needed into some form of savings account or time deposit. Such funds are set aside for future goals or emergencies while earning interest.

Savings accounts are different from *time deposits*. The customer who opens a savings account does not establish a maturity date when it will be closed; deposits and withdrawals affecting the account may be made over a period of many years. On the other hand, a time deposit has a specific maturity—7 days or more from the date of deposit. Whenever a time deposit is withdrawn before maturity, there is a penalty for the early ("premature") withdrawal.

All savings accounts and time deposits can earn interest. The NOW account, which can be offered by every type of financial institution, combines the features of a savings account with a time deposit: it allows the user to earn interest on a type of savings account against which checks can be issued. Super-NOW accounts provide the same benefits, generally while paying higher rates of interest. Common types of time deposits include certificates of deposit and Christmas, Hanukkah, and Vacation Club accounts.

Traditionally, checking accounts existed only at commercial banks. Today, thrift institutions compete aggressively for these accounts, and members of credit unions have an equivalent type of customer relationship, since they can issue share drafts instead of checks.

Federal laws also allow banks to offer automatic transfer services (ATS). If a depositor issues checks against insufficient or nonexistent funds in a checking account, the bank can automatically transfer funds from the customer's savings account to cover them. If the bank offers banking-at-home plans, the user can issue payment instructions and conduct other banking business by telephone.

In its simplest form, banking consists of obtaining funds through deposits and putting those funds to profitable use in loans and investments. Thus, it is logical to expect banks to be aware at all times of the actual amounts available as deposits and the types of deposits these amounts represent. The ratio between demand deposits on one hand, and time and savings deposits on the other, is extremely important for two reasons. The bank must pay an interest expense on the latter, and there is an essential difference in the rate of turnover. The turnover rate for demand deposits is extremely high. They can be used for short-term loans and investments. Time deposits, however, remain for longer periods and are used in longer-term loans and investments.

When they are accepted from customers, all forms of deposits simultaneously become both assets and liabilities for a bank. They are liabilities because the amount of every deposit is owed to the customer and will have to be repaid at some future date. On the balance sheet, all deposits are shown as actual liabilities (as debts of the bank). On the other hand, they can be considered assets for the bank in the sense that they can be put to profitable use.

THE PAYMENTS FUNCTION

As mentioned earlier, checks are safe and convenient vehicles for payment, and are accepted on faith and trust. Indeed, unless prior arrangements (such as ATS agreements or overdraft privileges) have been made with the bank, the issuing of a check by someone who knows that there are insufficient funds to cover it is an act of fraud.

Before checks gained such wide acceptance, the payments function often involved methods that left a great deal to be desired. Money, for example, is easily lost or stolen. If a payment is made in cash, any receipt that is given also can be lost; and if no receipt is issued, it may be impossible to prove that the payment actually was made.

By contrast, every customer who uses checks as a payment vehicle receives certain forms of protection. The risk of losing cash disappears; the paid check remains the best evidence of payment; and the bank's bookkeeping system is designed to assure that the customer's exact instructions, as contained in the check, are followed in every detail.

Electronic Funds Transfer Systems

By continually improving the payments mechanism and by supplying the personnel, equipment, and technology to handle 100 million checks every day, banks have made a great contribution to the economy. However, this huge volume automatically creates expenses and problems. Even with automation, the cost to banks for processing and exchanging checks grows each year. That cost recently was estimated at over $20 billion per year. There is a constant search for a better way to serve the interests of customers and banks, and this has led to the development of various *electronic funds transfer systems* (EFTS).

Whenever automated, paperless bookkeeping entries can be used to debit one account and credit another, tremendous benefits can be gained. Electronic transfers are far less costly, more accurate, and faster than paper-based payment systems.

Social Security Administration officials have had great success in persuading recipients to accept direct deposit of their monthly payments, which avoids the use of checks and guarantees payment on the due date. Many employers also use direct deposit for their payroll activity so that an employee's account, wherever it is located, can be credited with his or her net pay. In growing numbers, customers are using ATMs to obtain cash without issuing checks. A depositor can authorize in advance direct payments from his or her bank to cover insurance premiums, mortgage and loan payments, and other fixed charges. Point-of-sale (POS) terminals have become a common sight in supermarkets and other types of stores; they accept a customer's plastic card to initiate a transfer of funds as a means of paying for merchandise.

When electronic transfers of funds were introduced, it was thought that a "checkless society" eventually would develop and that every type of payment would be made without the use of checks. This no longer appears realistic. Every new application of an EFTS reduces check usage, but it now seems that there will always be situations in which checks will continue to be used.

THE CREDIT FUNCTION

The borrowing and lending of money have been accepted parts of financial affairs since the earliest days of civilization. In the ruins of ancient Babylon, written evidence was found of a loan made to a farmer who agreed to make repayment with interest when his crops were harvested and sold. In farm areas of the United States today, an equivalent transaction takes place; the farmer who borrows from a bank executes a written promise of repayment just as his predecessor did in Babylon thousands of years ago.

In the Middle Ages, goldsmiths—who held their clients' precious metals and other assets in safekeeping—often made loans against the value of those assets. Such lenders often are mentioned in literature and in history. The American Revolution was financed in large part through loan certificates issued by the Continental Congresses, and every subsequent war in which the United States was involved created heavy government borrowing.

Today, many sources of credit are available to customers. Individual consumers can approach personal finance or auto finance companies for credit and can borrow from insurance companies against the cash surrender value of their policies or from brokerage firms against the value of their securities. Individuals also can buy merchandise on credit through a retailer, obtain mortgage or home equity loans from thrift institutions, borrow from a credit union to which they belong, or as savings depositors, use their passbooks as security for loans.

Businesses of every type and size likewise have many sources of credit open to them. Thrift institutions, given expanded powers under the Monetary Control and Garn-St Germain Acts, may extend commercial loans, as do many commercial financing firms. One business may extend credit to another—for example, by supplying materials in advance of payment. Insurance companies often make the large, long-term loans needed for the construction of office buildings, shopping centers, and factories. Large corporations, such as General Electric Credit and General Motors Acceptance Corporation, also make large commercial loans.

Instead of borrowing from banks, many large corporations with excellent credit ratings borrow directly from one another by issuing unsecured, short-term promissory notes. These are known as *commercial paper*. Billions of dollars in commercial paper are actively traded in the securities markets every day.[5] Federal, state, and local governments use a wide variety of long- and short-term borrowing techniques to raise funds. Banks often borrow directly from one another or approach the Federal Reserve for credit.

Despite the diversity of available lenders, banks remain the dominant force in the credit market. More money is borrowed each year from banks than from any other source. Banks have not become the largest lenders simply because they are required to make commercial loans under the legal definition of banks; they do so because the loans constitute their largest source of income. Typically, two-thirds of a bank's yearly earnings result from interest on loans. Moreover, lending fulfills the bank's traditional role of serving their customers and communities.

In keeping with their full-service philosophy, banks extend credit under virtually every conceivable set of conditions to every segment of the market. No other lender can match them in either the size or diversity of the credit extended. There are bank loans to meet the needs of the small or large business, the government, and the consumer. The terms of bank loans may be as short as 30 days or as long as 30 years. Some are made with a form of security, known as collateral; most are made on an unsecured basis, with the bank relying entirely on the borrower's written promise to repay. On a given day, a bank may extend a $250 personal loan to an individual, a large loan to a government agency, and an even larger loan to a business.

Businesses, governments, and consumers are the three main categories of borrowers. Banks provide about $70 out of every $100 borrowed by businesses and about $50 out of every $100 borrowed by governments. Despite the many other sources of credit open to them, many consumers continue to borrow from commercial banks; in 1986 bank loans to individuals amounted to more than $240 billion, not including mortgage debt or outstanding credit card debt. This represented 45.7 percent of total consumer debt.[6]

The ability of banks to serve the credit needs of these three groups is vital to the prosperity of the American economy. In addition, by granting loans and crediting the proceeds to customers' accounts, banks are directly responsible for *creating* money, thereby directly affecting the nation's money supply.

How do banks create money? Essentially, by generating a cycle of funds (exhibit 2.1). Assume that reserve requirements are 20 percent, that all loan proceeds are deposited into checking accounts, and that all payments are deposits to a checking account in the same bank. A $1,000 cash deposit is made in the bank by *A*. After the 20 percent reserve is deducted, the bank can lend $800 to *B*. Following the reserve deduction, $640 is available to lend to *C*. Continuing the same process, the bank theoretically could lend $512 to *D* and $409 to *E*. From the original cash deposit of $1,000, a total of $2,361 in new funds has been created through this succession of bank loans.

Banks can build up their deposits by increasing loans, as long as they provide for reserve requirements and depositors' withdrawals.

FEDERAL RESERVE FUNCTIONS AND SERVICES

The essential functions of banks are closely related to those of the Federal Reserve. The deposit, payment, and credit functions of the former are linked to those of the latter, and the operations of both have an immediate and direct effect on the national economy.

Under the Federal Reserve Act, the Fed is the primary agent of *monetary policy*. This means the Fed may take specific actions to influence the flow of money and credit and, therefore, the entire economic environment. However, the Fed must take into consideration *fiscal policy*: the

EXHIBIT 2.1
HOW BANKS CREATE MONEY

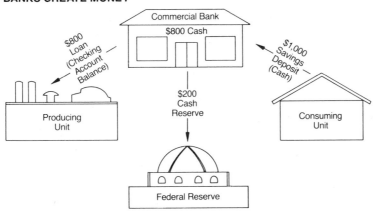

	Assets		**Liabilities**	**Cash reserves**	
Stage	**Reserve**	**Loan**			
1. A deposits $1,000 cash.	$1,000		$1,000	$1,000	total reserves
				− 200	20 percent required Fed reserve
The bank makes an $800 loan to B.		$800	800	800	available to loan
				− 160	required 20 percent Fed reserve
Total	$1,800		$1,800		
2. The bank makes a $640 loan to C.		640	640	$640	available to loan
				− 128	20 percent Fed reserve
Total 1–2	$2,440		$2,440		
3. The bank makes a $512 loan to D.		512	512	$512	available to loan
				− 103	20 percent Fed reserve
Total (1–3)	$2,952		$2,952		
4. The bank makes a $409 loan to E.		409	409	$409	available to loan
				82	20 percent Fed reserve
Total (1–4)	$3,361		$3,361	$327	still available to loan

Total assets: $3,361.
Total liabilities: $3,361.
Total new funds created: $2,361.

Source: American Bankers Association, *The Business is Banking* (Washington, D.C., 1980).

activities of the Congress and president in the areas of taxation and government spending. In effect, fiscal policy determines how much revenues the government will collect and how much it will spend; monetary policy provides the economic tools or mechanisms that are intended to work in tandem with fiscal policy. However, fiscal policy always carries political implications, whereas the Fed's monetary policy is intended to be divorced from political concerns.

Central banks, which have functions and objectives similar to those of the Fed, have existed in other countries for many years. The Bank of England was established in the seventeenth century, and the Bank of France was created under Napoleon I in 1800. However, the Fed differs from the central banks of other countries in the degree of independence granted to it by the 1913 act. The Fed is owned by its member banks—not by the government. This, and the fact that its actions do not have to be ratified by the president or by Congress, make the Federal Reserve unique.

In order to promote economic growth and stability, the Fed endeavors to

- provide stability in the overall price level and the purchasing power of the dollar
- contribute to a high national level of employment
- maintain a sound and reasonable system for international balance-of-payments transactions
- combat inflationary and recessionary trends as they develop

Many other economic factors influence whether the goals of the Fed will be achieved. The system consistently focuses on these four targets, shifting emphasis from one to another as conditions dictate.

The four basic objectives are interdependent. An economy can neither grow nor remain prosperous with high levels of unemployment. Large and persistent deficits in our balance of payments, such as those caused by excess American imports over exports, affect the international value of the dollar and America's reserve position. During an inflationary cycle, the real value of earned income and accumulated savings is reduced.

Although the Federal Reserve possesses a high degree of independence, it does interact with the other policy-making entities of the federal government. The chairman of the Fed's Board of Governors reports regularly to Congress and meets frequently with the president and the government's chief financial officers. By virtue of his office, the chairman is also a member of the Depository Institutions Deregulation Committee (DIDC). Other members of the Board of Governors maintain constant liaison with those agencies that are chiefly concerned with economic developments and policies.

In the original Federal Reserve Act, the secretary of the Treasury and the Comptroller of the Currency were *ex officio* members of the Board of Governors; however, a 1935 amendment to the act eliminated their membership. The Board of Governors consists of seven individuals, named by the president and approved by the Senate. They have overall responsibility for supervising the Federal Reserve System and are headquartered in Washington. Each of the 12 Federal Reserve banks (one in each geographic district) has a 9-member board; 6 of its directors are elected by the member banks in that district, while the other 3 are appointed by the Fed's Board of Governors.

FEDERAL RESERVE ORGANIZATION

Because the ownership and control of any central banking system in the United States has always been controversial, the Federal Reserve Act ingeniously combined the interests of the government and the private sector. As mentioned earlier, ownership of the system rests with member banks, who are stockholders. Like the stockholders in any corporation, they receive dividends as a result of the profitable operations performed by the Fed in any given year. A member bank may withdraw from the Fed by selling its Federal Reserve stock back to the Fed.

All national banks *must* belong to the Fed; state-chartered banks may join if they wish and if they meet the Fed's requirements. Although fewer than half of all commercial banks are members, the member banks control over 70 percent of all deposits in the banking system.

The ability of the Fed to control the flow of money and credit obviously depends on the extent of bank membership in the system, since the Fed cannot regulate or supervise nonmember banks. Therefore, any reduction in Fed membership has an adverse effect on that basic ability. In response to the withdrawal of many banks from Fed membership in the late 1970s, the Monetary Control Act addressed this important issue.

Since 1913, member banks have been required to keep reserves with the Fed on a non-interest-bearing basis. In exchange, they were given access to Federal Reserve services and enjoyed certain privileges. When interest rates in the money markets rose during the late 1970s, many banks determined that they would benefit by giving up their Fed membership and thereby gaining the use of reserve funds that could be put to profitable use in loans and investments. Withdrawal from the Federal Reserve System meant that these banks would have to obtain equivalent services from their correspondent banks instead.

As mentioned earlier, the Monetary Control Act significantly changed the original Federal Reserve Act by defining transaction accounts and requiring *all* financial institutions that offered these accounts to keep reserves, either directly with the Fed or through a Fed member. In this way, the Monetary Control Act eliminated the basic reason that banks had given for withdrawing from Fed membership.

TOOLS OF MONETARY AND CREDIT POLICY

Increasing the money supply is expected to increase the rate of inflation; causing the money supply to grow less rapidly is expected to reduce that rate. The Fed studies the periodic figures on M_1, and in order to regulate the flow of money and credit, it employs three fundamental tools or techniques: its *open-market operations*, its *discount rate*, and its *reserve requirements*. As a result of the Monetary Control Act, a timetable for phasing in thrift institutions and nonmember banks under the new system of reserves was established, and the ability of the Fed to use reserve requirements as a tool of monetary policy was increased accordingly. The other two instruments, open-market operations and discount-rate changes, should be thought of as being coordinated and employed with a single purpose rather than as independent mechanisms used separately.

Open-Market Operations

The open-market operations of the Federal Reserve Open Market Committee (FOMC) constitute the most important, yet at the same time most flexible, instrument for Fed implementation of monetary policy. The FOMC comprises the seven members of the Board of Governors, plus the president of the New York Fed and four other Federal Reserve bank presidents. By law, all open-market operations must be directed and regulated by the FOMC, whose basic function involves determining the amount of government obligations to be sold and redeemed each week. After each meeting of the FOMC, a directive is issued to the New York Fed, which has been designated as the agent to buy and sell (issue) Treasury bills, notes, and bonds for the accounts of all the Reserve banks. The volume of transactions handled through the open-market account is in excess of $10 billion per day, most of which consists of trading in Treasury bills.

As an example of how FOMC decisions affect monetary policy, assume that a directive instructs the New York Fed to *buy* Treasury bills. As each sale is made to the Fed, the reserve accounts of the member banks, through which the sales flow, will be credited. Thus, the members will gain the use of funds, formerly held as reserves, that can now be put to profitable use. Credit will become easier to obtain. This may satisfy a short-term FOMC objective, based on a seasonal or regional shift in the money supply, or it may be intended to have a long-term effect on the overall economy.

The Discount Rate

As a result of the Monetary Control Act, all financial institutions that offer transaction accounts now have the privilege of applying to the Fed for short-term credit. Whenever such a request is approved, the Fed charges the borrowing institution interest at the *discount rate*. The discount rate is set by each of the 12 district banks, and they can change the discount rate whenever appropriate, subject to review by the Board of Governors. Generally, the discount rate is uniform throughout the system. Table 2.1 shows changes in the discount rate in recent years.

If the Fed raises the discount rate, borrowing by any financial institution becomes more costly, and the increased cost is passed along through the banking system so that credit becomes more difficult to obtain. On the other hand, a lowering of the discount rate immediately makes credit less expensive and easier to obtain. Either change affects the national economy.

Borrowing from the Fed is a privilege, not an automatic right. Each request is reviewed according to purpose, frequency of requests, and amount of existing indebtedness to the Fed. If the loan request is approved, the borrowing institution executes a promissory note and secures it with acceptable collateral. Loans granted by the Fed are usually made for very short periods of time, such as overnight or for 2 days.

TABLE 2.1
DISCOUNT RATES CHARGED BY FEDERAL RESERVE BANKS, 1973–87

Year	Rate at Year-end (percent)	Number of Rate Changes During Year
1973	7.50	
1974	7.75	4
1975	6.00	9
1976	5.25	4
1977	6.00	4
1978	9.50	12
1979	12.00	7
1980	14.00	12
1981	12.00	4
1982	8.50	14
1983	8.50	0
1984	8.00	5
1985	7.50	2
1986	5.50	4

Note: As of September 1, 1987, the rate remained unchanged at 5.5 percent from the year-end 1986 figure.
Source: *Federal Reserve Bulletin* (July 1987), p. A7.

Reserve Requirements

Until the Monetary Control Act was passed in 1980, *only* member banks were affected by the Fed's system of reserve requirements. Reducing those requirements freed funds to meet the needs of the economy and made bank credit easier to obtain; increasing the requirements had the opposite effect. Prior to 1980, a member bank with deposits of over $400 million was required to keep reserves of 3.0 percent against its savings and time deposits and 16.25 percent against demand deposits. No interest was paid on reserves at the Fed.

The Monetary Control Act requires *all* financial institutions that offer transaction accounts to maintain reserves. However, the size of the required reserve has been reduced; a bank with deposits of over $400 million now must keep only 12 percent against demand deposits. The reserves remain with the Fed on a non-interest-bearing basis.

Banks that find that their reserves at the Fed are temporarily larger than the required figure may lend these *Fed funds* to another institution whose reserves are temporarily short. The transaction takes place through adjustments of the reserves of the two institutions on the account books of the Fed itself. No money changes hands between the two institutions. The Fed sets the interest rate at which these temporary loans of Fed funds are made.[7]

When a customer of one bank asks that a transaction—for example, a money transfer—be made in Fed funds, the transaction takes place through the reserve accounts at the Fed. Any such transfer or transaction constitutes immediately available value.

FEDERAL RESERVE SERVICES

Under the terms of the Federal Reserve Act, the services provided by the Fed include check collection, supplying coin and currency, making wire transfers of funds, providing safekeeping, and extending credit. With the exception of credit, these services were provided from 1913 to 1980 without charge as an offset to the reserves that member banks were required to maintain. Since 1980, the Fed has imposed a system of *explicit pricing* for all its services. Banks are charged for each check collected by the Fed, each shipment of coin and currency, and each wire transfer. The banks, in turn, pass these charges along to their customers.

Additional services provided by the Fed include economic surveys, tables of statistical data, and financial reports.

Fed services are extremely important to the government as well as to the banks. The Fed operates the checking account for the U.S. government; every individual who receives an income tax refund or other disbursement of funds from the government by check is actually receiving an instrument drawn on the Fed, and all inflows of funds to the federal government go through the Fed. The Federal Reserve is also the fiscal agent for the Department of the Treasury. It is responsible for issuing and redeeming all government obligations and for the safekeeping of unissued Treasury bills, notes, and bonds. Supplies of unissued currency are kept in the Fed's vaults, as are assets and securities of other countries that have been entrusted to the Fed for safekeeping.

The Federal Reserve has an important examining function. Its examiners regularly visit the banks under Fed jurisdiction to ensure that they are obeying all laws and regulations and are accurately showing their financial condition. Through this examining process, the Fed helps the federal government maintain a sound national banking system.

THE FED AND BANK HOLDING COMPANIES

A holding company is a legal entity that holds a controlling interest through ownership of the stock of various subsidiaries. It need not sell, manufacture, distribute, or otherwise engage in any operations of its own; it simply serves as a vehicle for stock ownership. By law, a *bank holding company* (BHC) is an organization that holds a controlling interest in the stock of one or more banks. During the 1960s and 1970s, virtually every major commercial bank in the United States converted to a holding company format, with the bank the major subsidiary in each case. Through this form of organization, the holding company could engage in certain types of profitable business outside the precise realm of banking.

Under the terms of the Bank Holding Company Acts (1956 and 1970), the Fed was given authority to supervise and regulate all bank holding companies, regardless of the component bank's membership status in the Fed. The legislation allows the Fed to publish lists of the activities that are permitted or denied for all bank holding companies and to make decisions on all requests they may make for acquisitions or for the right to engage in various types of business.

FEDERAL RESERVE REGULATIONS

The broad powers of the Fed are applied through the various regulations that control all member banks and BHCs (table 2.2). To see how they apply, it is helpful to group the regulations by subject matter (table 2.3). The various Federal Reserve regulations provide the means by which the Fed carries out congressional policies and controls the flow of money and credit. They deal with relationships between the Fed and its members, the protection of consumers, extensions of consumer credit and home mortgages, and the activities of banks, bank holding companies, brokerage firms, and other securities dealers.

The new Federal Reserve Regulation CC, created as a result of the Competitive Equality Banking Act of 1987, was not yet in final form at the time *Principles of Banking* went to press. Students should obtain current information on Regulation CC and corresponding amendments to Reg-

TABLE 2.2
FEDERAL RESERVE REGULATIONS

Letter Identification	Subject
A	Loans to Depository Institutions
B	Equal Credit Opportunity
C	Home Mortgage Disclosure
D	Reserve Requirements
E	Electronic Funds Transfers
F	Securities of Member Banks
G	Margin Credit
H	Fed Membership Requirements
I	Member Stock in Federal Reserve
J	Check Collection and Funds Transfer
K	International Banking Operations
L	Interlocking Bank Relationships
M	Consumer Leasing
N	Relationships With Foreign Banks
O	Loans by Members to Officers
P	Member Bank Protection Standards
Q	Interest on Deposits
R	Interlocking Relationships With Securities Dealers
S	Reimbursement for Providing Financial Records
T	Margin Credit
U	Margin Credit
V	Loan Guarantees for National Defense Work
W	Extensions of Consumer Credit[a]
X	Borrowers Who Obtain Margin Credit
Y	Bank Holding Companies
Z	Truth in Lending
AA	Consumer Complaint Procedures
BB	Community Reinvestment
CC	Expedited Funds Availability

Source: Board of Governors of the Federal Reserve System, *A Guide to Federal Reserve Regulations* (September 1981).
a. Regulation W was abolished after the conclusion of the Korean War.

ulation J either from their instructors or from the Federal Reserve.

Federal Reserve supervision of member banks begins when an institution applies for admission to the system. As members, these banks are subject to periodic examination by the Fed and to all its regulations, as well as to the banking laws of other agencies. For example, annual examinations of all national banks are made by the Office of the Comptroller of the Currency. Since all such banks must be Fed members, the Comptroller's examiners furnish the Fed with copies of all examination reports. The Fed may then conduct its own examinations if it feels these are necessary.

The Fed is also responsible for approving changes in a member bank's capital structure and for approving new branches of member banks, assuming such approval is consistent with that of the Comptroller of the Currency (in the case of national banks) and with state laws on

TABLE 2.3
FEDERAL RESERVE REGULATIONS BY SUBJECT MATTER

Area of Coverage	Letter Identification
Bank holding companies	Regulation Y
Federal reserve banks: Organization and operations	Regulations A, BB, I, J, N, V
Foreign banking business	Regulations K, M, N
Interlocking directorates	Regulations L and R
Consumer protection	Regulations B, C, E, M, Z, AA, CC
Monetary policy	Regulations A, D, Q
Electronic funds transfers	Regulation E
Securities credit	Regulations G, T, U, X
Financial privacy	Regulation S
Fed membership requirements	Regulation H
Member bank loans to executive officers	Regulation O
Community reinvestment	Regulation BB

Source: Board of Governors of the Federal Reserve System, *A Guide to Federal Reserve Regulations* (September 1981).

branching. The Fed also regulates and supervises the overseas lending and investing functions of U.S. banks.

SUMMARY

Financial services in the United States today can be obtained from a wide variety of financial institutions: savings banks, S&Ls, credit unions, commercial and consumer finance companies, and retailers. Commercial banks, however, remain the only full-service institutions providing the entire spectrum of services for businesses, governments, and consumers under a single roof. The three basic functions of banks—the deposit function, the payments function, and the credit function—affect every segment of the U.S. economy. Because a bank is legally defined as an institution that accepts demand deposits and makes commercial loans, these functions are the cornerstones of the banking business. Banks accept various types of deposits, process both checks and electronic funds transfers as payment vehicles, and extend credit in the form of secured and unsecured short- and long-term loans.

The Federal Reserve System was created as a means of addressing the basic weaknesses that were perceived to exist in banking after 1864. The Fed differs in organization from the central banks in other countries, but parallels them in its objectives to control the flow of money and credit and otherwise provide for economic growth and stability in the nation. The Fed devotes its attention to the rate of growth in the money supply, the domestic rate of inflation, the global changes in the value of the dollar, the balance of payments in our international trade, and the federal deficit itself among other problem areas. Through its ability to change the discount rate and reserve requirements, through its open-market operations, and through its regulatory and examining powers, the Fed strives to maintain a sound national banking system and to promote economic well-being.

QUESTIONS FOR DISCUSSION

1. What is the legal definition of a bank?

2. What is the principal function of a savings and loan association?

3. What is the largest component of the U.S. money supply?

4. What is the legal difference between a savings deposit and a time deposit?

5. How do commercial banks create money?

6. What are the three basic functions of commercial banks?

7. What are the three major classes of borrowers from banks?

8. How do electronic funds transfer systems substitute for checks?

9. What are the four objectives of the Fed in regulating the flow of money and credit?

10. Which financial institutions are required to keep reserves with the Fed?

11. How are the members of the Board of Governors elected or appointed?

12. What three tools or techniques does the Fed use to control the flow of money and credit?

13. What is meant by the term *discount rate*?

14. What is meant by the term *explicit pricing*?

NOTES

1. Mark Basch, "The Growth of Savings Banks," *American Banker*, 150th anniversary issue (January 1987), p. 75.

2. "The Thrift Industry at a Glance," *American Banker*, September 9, 1986, p. 31.

3. L. Michael Cacace, "Credit Unions' Deposits Keep Soaring," *American Banker*, September 9, 1986, p. 1.

4. Richard R. Dart, "ATM Services—1985," *American Banker*, December 4, 1985, p. 15.

5. At year-end 1985, commercial paper outstanding amounted to $303 billion. See *Federal Reserve Bulletin* (April 1986), p. A23.

6. *Federal Reserve Bulletin* (February 1986), p. A40.

7. American Bankers Association, *Bank Fact Book* (Washington, D.C., 1983), p. 5.

For More Information

Burke, William. *The Fed: The Nation's Central Bank*. San Francisco: Federal Reserve Bank of San Francisco, 1978.

Friedman, David H. *Money and Banking*. Washington, D.C.: American Bankers Association, 1985.

Golembe, Carter H., and David S. Holland. *Federal Regulation of Banking*. Washington, D.C.: Golembe Associates, 1986.

Hutchinson, Harry D. *Money, Banking, and the United States Economy*. 5th ed. Englewood Cliffs, N.J.: Prentice-Hall, Inc., 1984.

Johnson, Roger T. *Historical Beginnings: The Federal Reserve*. Boston, Mass.: Federal Reserve Bank of Boston, 1977.

Meek, Paul. *Open Market Operations*. New York: Federal Reserve Bank of New York, 1978.

3.

THE LANGUAGE AND DOCUMENTS OF BANKING

LEARNING OBJECTIVES

After completing this chapter, you will be able to

●

describe the operation of the barter system

●

discuss the advantages of the credit balances system

●

name the requirements for negotiable instruments

●

identify the parties to drafts and their roles

●

define what constitutes a check

●

define the terms certified check and cashier's check

●

explain the basic types of endorsements

●

describe the liabilities of endorsers and the
concept of holder in due course

E very industry and profession has its own jargon to describe whatever is unique to that particular line of work. Lawyers, doctors, engineers, and accountants all learn specialized terminologies and become familiar with the forms and documents used in their daily tasks. To work efficiently, bank employees must understand the language of banking and the meaning and importance of the documents that are used in it. Trading, buying, selling, and borrowing are as old as civilization itself, and the manner in which these transactions are handled and the terms used to describe them have evolved into the language and docu- · ments that are so important in banking today.

EARLY METHODS OF EXCHANGE

When people can not produce what they need or want, they find others who possess those articles and establish methods of obtaining them. The oldest and simplest of these methods still is used in some societies; it involves the direct physical exchange of goods, and is known as *barter*. An example of barter is exchanging animal skins for foodstuffs. Mutual wants or needs are met through the transfer of merchandise—a system with some basic weaknesses. For barter to take place, it is necessary for the articles of value to be portable and for the parties to agree on their value. An individual who wants a particular item must find someone willing to trade and arrange a meeting so that the exchange can take place.

The inconveniences of the barter system gradually led to the introduction of some form of money as an accepted medium of exchange. However, long before money as we know it came into existence, various commodities (such as salt, grain, fish or meat, and gunpowder) were used as units of payment. Jewelry and decorative objects could also be used for trade. In time, precious metals such as gold and silver came to be accepted as the medium of exchange. These required safekeeping, usually in the hands of a goldsmith, who issued a written receipt to the owner. These receipts were used as a medium of payment and are an early example of paper currency.

CREDIT BALANCES

Although money offers advantages over the barter system, it nevertheless possesses disadvantages of its own. It still must be moved from one place to another, with the risk of loss or theft. The farther the distance between buyer and seller, the greater the risk. For example, a British merchant wishing to import lace from France had to find a method of transporting money to the supplier, and could then only hope that it would arrive safely. As commerce grew and as merchants began to expand their operations and to put their faith and trust in other merchants with whom they dealt, a more satisfactory system of payment was developed using *credit balances*. This new system eliminated the risks involved in carrying and transporting money, and created the basis for much of the language and many of the documents used today in commercial banking.

Under the system of credit balances, merchants agreed that a specific payment would not be required for every transaction. Instead of delivering money to the seller, the buyer of goods was told to establish some form of book entry for the sale, thus recording the fact that a certain amount was owed to the seller. It was through the system of credit balances that the word *bookkeeping* came into existence. The seller maintained documents providing evidence of the transaction, with the understanding that the credit balance shown on the books could be applied to future dealings between the two parties. In this way, the French supplier had a record to substantiate the fact that the buyer in England was indebted for a given amount.

The same French merchant, however, might at some point owe money to another party in England. Could the same system be adapted to provide a means of payment to a third party? The answer was yes: The merchant in England had a record of the amount he owed to the French merchant. If given instructions by the latter, in a secure form so that there could be no dispute, the English merchant could pay out part or all of the French merchant's credit balance to the specified third party. For security reasons, the French merchant would have to issue instructions in writing, would have to specify the amount to be paid, and would have to name the beneficiary of the payment. No payment would be made without specific instructions from the French merchant.

Today's banking system is a modern version of the credit balance system. Substitute your bank for the English merchant holding a credit balance (your funds deposited with the bank) and substitute yourself for the French merchant, to whom that balance is owed. If you wish to pay a bill by issuing a check against the balance held by your bank, as the *drawer* of the check, you will issue a properly dated and signed "letter" instructing the bank to pay a specified amount to the *payee*, who is the beneficiary. The bank on which the check is drawn is the *drawee*. The bank accepts your instructions and makes the requested payment, much as the English merchant who held the credit balance would have done.

NEGOTIABLE INSTRUMENTS

The system of credit balances offered major improvements over both the barter system and actual payments in money. Merchants who knew and trusted their customers were willing to accept written instructions from them to make payments by reducing their credit balances. In turn, they could use the same system to pay their own expenses and debts. All that was needed was agreement on the language and form of the letter of instructions.

Inevitably, disputes arose among merchants as to whether payments had been made in exact accordance with instructions, whether the proper party had received payment, whether the instructions had been carried out on time, and so forth. To provide a uniform means of settling these disputes and to establish a standard system for making payments, lawmakers and courts in various countries gradually agreed on a format and the procedures to be followed. Safeguards were written into the laws to protect all the parties to commercial transactions.

In the United States a single statute, the *Uniform Commercial Code* (UCC), was drafted in 1953 to facilitate the handling of banking and business transactions. This code revised and consolidated many of the laws that had preceded it. In whole or in part, it has been adopted throughout the country.

The UCC contains nine articles, of which article 3 is the most important for purposes of this discussion. It defines the term *negotiable instrument* and sets forth the liabilities and rights of all the parties who deal with checks, drafts, notes, and other banking documents such as certificates of deposit.

The *negotiable* feature of an instrument allows it to circulate freely and to be accepted in lieu of legal tender in certain payment transactions. In this context, negotiation means that an instrument is transferred from one party to another so that the latter becomes the holder (beneficiary). This can be done by delivery alone—as when one individual hands a check to another in payment of a debt—or by delivery and endorsement. *Delivery* means the voluntary physical transfer of possession with the intention of transferring title and rights to the instrument; *endorsement* is a further transfer of title and rights by the holder.

Article 3 of the UCC sets forth six requirements for negotiable instruments, as follows:

- They must be in writing. No verbal order to pay or promise to pay qualifies.
- They must contain an unconditional order or promise to pay a specific amount of money. The legal term is "a sum certain in money." This term is used so that there can be no dispute as to the amount of the instrument. A promissory note bearing interest at 10 percent is negotiable; one bearing interest at "the prevailing rate" is not.
- They must be unconditional. Negotiable instruments are not governed by or subject to any other agreement involving the parties.
- They must be signed by the drawer or maker. Here, the word *signed* also includes marks, thumbprints, and printed, typed, or stamped signatures.

- They must be payable on demand or at a definite future time (for example, "90 days from date" or "on June 28, 19XX"). A demand instrument is payable at sight or on presentation.
- They must be made payable either to *bearer* or to *order*. An instrument payable to "cash" is a bearer instrument; "to order" means the instrument is payable to a named party or to another to whom that party has transferred the rights to the instrument. The phrase "Pay to the order of . . ." on checks is an example of the application of this requirement.

An instrument must meet all the above criteria to qualify as a negotiable instrument under the terms of the UCC. The parties to it may be willing to use and accept it, but the provisions of the UCC do not apply.

Drafts and Checks

The standard, simplified letter of instructions by which one party instructed the holder of a credit balance to make payment to a third party became known as a *bill of exchange* or, more commonly, a *draft*. The term bill of exchange is still used in international transactions. A draft is a written order directing that payment be made.

As mentioned earlier, there are three parties to drafts. The *drawer* issues the draft; the *drawee* (the holder of the credit balance owed to the drawer) is instructed to make the payment; and the *payee* is the party named to receive the payment. At the outset, banks were not involved in negotiating drafts. Drafts were entirely within the province of merchants and goldsmiths.

Drafts still are widely used in certain types of transactions. A merchant may draw a draft on another; an insurance company may draw drafts on a bank; or one bank may draw a draft on another. Drafts may be either *time* (payable at some future date) or *demand* instruments.

As banks gradually replaced the goldsmiths and merchants as the holders of credit balances, the items drawn on them were simplified and made more uniform. A demand draft drawn on a bank typically is a *check* (exhibits 3.1 and 3.2). The drawer of a check issues specific written instructions for a payment of funds against an account.

Of course, it is possible for one party to play more than one role in a transaction. If Mary Smith issues a check payable to cash, endorses it, presents it to a bank, and converts part or all of her demand deposit balance into coin and currency, Mary is both the drawer and the payee.

Every check is a demand draft drawn on a bank; therefore, every check is a type of draft, but not every draft is a check. Checks must be demand instruments; drafts may be either time or demand. Checks must be drawn on a bank; drafts need not be. When all necessary conditions are met, checks must be charged to the issuer's account; drafts need not be, since the drawer of a draft can reserve the right to examine and approve it

EXHIBIT 3.1
A STANDARD CHECK

Payee   Drawer

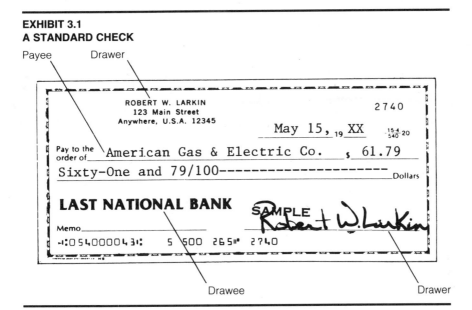

Drawee   Drawer

EXHIBIT 3.2
ELEMENTS OF A CHECK

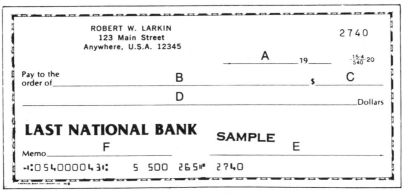

A. Date
B. Pay To The Order Of . . .
C. Amount in Numerals

D. Written Amount
E. Signature
F. Memo . . . (purpose of check)

before any charge to an account takes place. It is for this reason that insurance companies frequently use drafts rather than checks. They wish to examine each draft and assure its validity before actually allowing a bank account to be reduced.

Promissory Notes

Another payment medium often used in business transactions is the promissory note. Notes differ from drafts and checks in a very important way: Notes are *promises* to pay and involve only two parties, while drafts and checks are *orders* to pay and involve three parties. Checks are always demand instruments; notes may be time or demand. Checks must be drawn on banks; notes may be executed without the involvement of a bank.

The promissory note is one of the essential documents in banking. Every loan made by a bank is supported by some form of note that spells out the terms of repayment and which is signed by the borrower. The note provides legal evidence of a debt.

Certified Checks

Many everyday situations occur in which the party to whom a typical check is offered will not accept it. An individual closing title on a new home or buying an expensive automobile or item of jewelry may be told that he or she must provide an instrument that gives the payee a greater assurance of actual payment. A check is *not* legal tender; it is only a claim to money, and doubt can exist regarding the strength or validity of the claim. By giving the payee a *certified check* (exhibit 3.3), the problem is resolved and the transaction can be completed.

To certify a check, the drawer presents it to the drawee bank, which must immediately verify that there are sufficient available funds in the drawer's account to cover it. The amount of the check is usually charged to the drawer's account at once and placed in a special account, "certified checks outstanding." When a drawee certifies a check, it transforms the

EXHIBIT 3.3
CERTIFIED CHECK

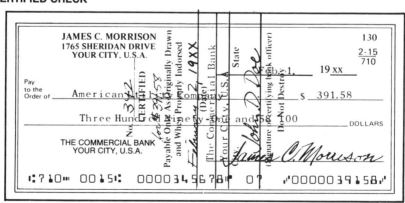

drawer's order to pay into the bank's promise to pay. Certified checks are a legal liability of the bank.

Certification takes place by having an official bank stamp and signature placed on the item. Banks legally are not required to certify checks, but regularly do so (usually for a fee) as a customer service. The certified check is marked or mutilated in some way so that it will not be charged to the drawer's account again. The drawee may also use some form of perforation as part of the certification stamp to prevent any tampering with the amount.

While the payee of a certified check assumes that the drawee guarantees payment, under special circumstances the drawer may ask that payment be stopped on the item. If, for example, the check has been stolen or lost, the interests of both the drawee and drawer should be protected. The UCC states that a bank is not obliged to accept a stop-payment order on a check that has been certified; however, if the drawer signs an affidavit explaining the problem and indemnifying the bank against claims or losses, the request can be honored.

Cashier's Checks

Another negotiable instrument frequently seen in banking is the *cashier's check*, also known as an *official check* or *treasurer's check* (exhibit 3.4). The certified check is issued by a customer and certified by the drawee bank; the cashier's check is issued by and drawn on the bank itself. The bank is both the drawer and drawee. Banks often use cashier's checks to pay their own obligations or to pay out loan proceeds. These checks also may be sold to customers who require an official instrument of the bank.

EXHIBIT 3.4
CASHIER'S CHECK

Back Beach First National Bank	$\frac{63-000}{000}$
	88597
BACK BEACH, U.S.A. ____ May 2 ____ 19 XX	
PAY TO THE ORDER OF ____ ABC Developers, Inc.	$ 178.00
THE SUM 1 7 8 DOLS 0 0 CT. ____ DOLLARS	
Cashier's Check	
REMITTER ____ Kit Walker	*Margaret A. King*
	AUTHORIZED SIGNATURE
⑈088597⑈ ⑆0000⑈ 0000⑇ ⑈000 0004⑈	

NEGOTIATION OF FINANCIAL INSTRUMENTS

The holder of a negotiable instrument often finds it necessary or desirable to transfer his or her title and rights to it to another party. For example, the holder of a stock certificate may want to sell or pledge it. A merchant who holds a note payable at a future date may need funds immediately and therefore may seek to transfer the note to another in exchange for cash. A person who has received a check may wish to deposit it into an account, convert it into coin and currency, or give it to someone else. Each of these transfers of legal right and title is an example of *negotiation*.

As mentioned earlier, transfers of rights to negotiable instruments may be accomplished simply by delivery to another party. More frequently, however, endorsement is part of the process. There are four principal types of endorsements (see exhibit 3.5), each of which serves a particular purpose.

A *blank endorsement* consists simply of the signature of the instrument's previous holder. With a *special endorsement* the previous holder, in addition to signing the instrument, names the party to whom rights are being transferred. For example, the individual might add the line: "Pay to AIB National Bank." With a *restrictive endorsement*, in addition to signing

EXHIBIT 3.5
FOUR TYPES OF ENDORSEMENTS

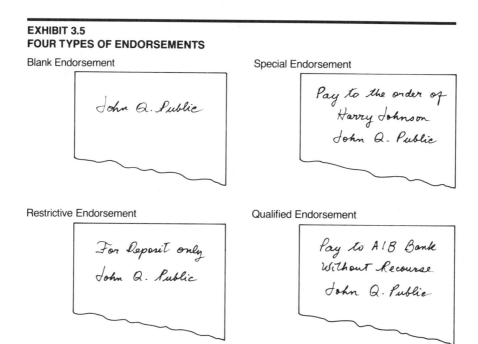

Blank Endorsement

John Q. Public

Special Endorsement

Pay to the order of
Harry Johnson
John Q. Public

Restrictive Endorsement

For Deposit only
John Q. Public

Qualified Endorsement

Pay to AIB Bank
Without Recourse
John Q. Public

the instrument, the previous holder identifies the purpose of the transfer and restricts the use to which the instrument can be put. The most common example of a restrictive endorsement occurs when checks are endorsed with the words "For deposit only."

Restrictive and special endorsements are often used in combination on a single instrument. John Smith, for example, may endorse a check payable to him with the words "Pay to AIB Bank; For Deposit Only" and his signature. The UCC affirms that when AIB Bank accepts this endorsed check, it is legally required to increase the endorser's account balance and to hold the funds until withdrawal instructions are received.

The fourth kind of endorsement is the *qualified endorsement*. When the endorser of an instrument wishes to limit or escape what would otherwise be his or her legal liability, he or she may use the words "Without Recourse," or other words with a similar meaning, as part of the endorsement. In this way the endorser is attempting to claim that he or she will *not* make good if called on to do so. A qualified endorsement must be accepted and acknowledged by the receiving (depositing) bank or else the cancellation of the general contract of the endorser is not binding.

Because the volume of checks in circulation has reached such huge proportions and the use of endorsements has become so common, the UCC allows certain endorsements that are not handwritten. Rubber-stamped, typed, or printed endorsements are valid under the code and are widely accepted by banks.

The Expedited Funds Availability Act, passed in 1987 as part of the Competitive Equality Banking Act, also affects endorsement standards—particularly in regard to placement of endorsements on the backs of checks. Specific information on the new standards was unavailable, however, at the time this text was published. You may wish to contact the Federal Reserve for current information.

The endorsement on an instrument need not be applied by the previous holder. Banks frequently act on a customer's behalf by placing a rubber-stamp endorsement on deposited checks (for example, "Credited to account of within-named payee") and guaranteeing the absence of the previous holder's personal signature and endorsement.

Liabilities of Endorsers

On any given day, millions of checks are endorsed and transferred to other parties, including banks that give cash for them or accept them on deposit. In addition, stock certificates, promissory notes, and other negotiable instruments are endorsed and change hands every day. Every endorser may not be fully aware of the legal liabilities that his or her action creates. Obviously, good faith and trust are of paramount importance. An endorser who knowingly transfers rights to a fraudulent check is not acting in good faith, but an endorser who has no knowledge of any defect in, or problem with, a check must still be held liable. All endorsers should understand this concept of liability.

Every endorser of a negotiable instrument assumes four specific liabilities and responsibilities. Under the terms of article 3 of the UCC, the endorser warrants

- that he or she has good title to the instrument or is authorized to obtain payment on behalf of one who has good title, and that the transfer is otherwise rightful
- that all signatures are genuine and authorized (although it is recognized that the endorser may not know or be in a position to know that this is true)
- that the instrument has not been materially altered and that no defense to payment of any party is good against him or her
- that he or she has no knowledge of any bankruptcy proceedings affecting the instrument

There is an additional, most important *general liability*. The endorser promises to make good on the item if it is dishonored and if he or she is promptly and properly notified of that dishonor. This liability is the one that the user of a qualified endorsement seeks to escape.

By endorsing a negotiable instrument, the endorser promises—even though this promise is not specifically stated in every transaction—that he or she will pay the value of that instrument to the next, or any subsequent, party if the instrument is dishonored for any reason. The qualified endorsement is the only instance in which this guarantee of reimbursement does not apply.

The endorser's liability is vital to the efforts of banks to minimize risk and loss. When Jane Doe presents her endorsed payroll check to a teller and either deposits it or receives cash in exchange for it, she is promising the bank that she will make good if the check is returned for any reason. The UCC stipulates that by her endorsement Jane Doe is stating that the check is genuine and that she has legal rights to it and can do with it as she wishes. The bank can accept the endorsed check from her, secure in the knowledge that it has a valid claim against her if the check is not honored when it is presented to the drawee bank.

Holder in Due Course

The legal protection given to any party accepting an endorsed negotiable instrument is outlined in the UCC under the heading "Holder in Due Course." A bank, individual, or other party accepting such an item is entitled to this protection and should not be penalized in any way for defects in, or subsequent problems with, the instrument.

To qualify legally as a *holder in due course* and thus to obtain the superior rights conveyed by that title, one must receive the instrument

- for value
- in good faith
- under proper conditions of delivery and negotiation
- without notice that it is overdue or has been dishonored
- without any notice of claim against the instrument or defense against it

If an instrument payable to order is transferred with no endorsement, the concept of a holder in due course does not apply, and the party to whom the instrument was transferred does not have the corresponding protection under the UCC.

When the bank accepts Jane Doe's endorsed payroll check for deposit, or gives her coin and currency for it, the principle of holder in due course applies. The bank has acted in good faith, for it surely would not have accepted the check had it known that the instrument was stolen, forged, or otherwise invalid. By crediting Jane Doe's account or giving her cash, the bank has accepted the check in exchange for value. As an endorser, Jane Doe is liable; as a holder in due course, the bank legally is protected.

Consider what would happen if the teller handling this transaction neglects to obtain Jane Doe's endorsement on the check. Under that set of circumstances, the bank would not be considered a holder in due course and would not have the protection that a holder enjoys.

A holder in due course may recover on an instrument regardless of any disputes or defenses that may exist between the prior parties. He or she takes the instrument free from all claims to it on the part of any party with whom he or she has not dealt. A holder in due course normally seeks recovery from the previous or last-named endorser, although the UCC also gives that holder the right of recovery from the original drawer or maker. If a teller accepts an endorsed check on deposit or gives cash for it and the item is dishonored for any reason, the bank turns to the endorser for recovery. If the check, for example, was endorsed and deposited, upon finding that it had been returned unpaid by the drawee, the bank would simply charge its amount back to the depositor's account.

To illustrate the principle, assume that Hazel Adams has purchased a used car from Margaret Jones and has given her a personal check in payment. To pay a debt to William Crosby, Margaret, in turn, endorses Hazel's check and gives it to him. Hazel later feels that the car is defective and is not what she agreed to buy; therefore, she places a stop-payment order on the check at her bank. Crosby, an innocent party to their dispute, is a holder in due course. He acted in good faith by accepting the endorsed check, and he gave something of value for it by canceling or reducing Margaret's debt. His first legal protection under the UCC consists of a valid claim against the endorser—Margaret. If that claim is not satisfied, he may then try to recover from Hazel, the drawer of the check.

If the law did not contain this protective feature, it would be difficult or impossible to persuade a bank or any other party to accept an endorsed negotiable instrument. All forms of commerce and exchanges of property, including transfers of stock certificates and notes, would suffer greatly as a result. The doctrine of holder in due course was intended to provide legal protection and recourse for the transferees.

SUMMARY

From the dawn of civilization, various systems have been developed to manage the transactions that take place whenever goods or services are bought or sold. From the earliest and simplest barter system, the system of credit balances gradually evolved. Credit balances created the need for bookkeeping and for a secure written instrument that could direct that a payment be made from one party to another through a third. The concept of negotiable instruments, and the need for a specific body of law governing the use and standards of these instruments, arose from this same system. Drafts, checks, notes, cashier's checks, and certified checks are handled every day in commercial banking. The parties to these instruments, and the banks that handle them, should be aware of their rights and obligations. This is especially true in the case of endorsed instruments, to which the concept of a holder in due course applies.

QUESTIONS FOR DISCUSSION

1. What weaknesses exist in the barter system and in the use of money as a payment medium?

2. In what ways did the system of credit balances represent an improvement over other forms of payment?

3. Define the following terms: draft, check, certified check, cashier's check, holder in due course, endorsement.

4. What are the differences between checks and promissory notes?

5. Why is the principle of holder in due course important to tellers?

6. Identify four characteristics an instrument must have if it is legally to qualify as negotiable.

7. If an endorsed check is accepted and deposited to an account, what action will the bank take if the item is dishonored?

For More Information

American Bankers Association. *Banking Terminology*. Washington, D.C., 1985.

Brauns, Robert A.W., Jr., and Sarah Slater. *Bankers Desk Reference*. Boston, Mass.: Warren Gorham & Lamont, Inc., 1978.

Conboy, James C., Jr. *Law and Banking: Principles*. Washington, D.C.: American Bankers Association, 1986.

Smith, Craig. *Law and Banking: Applications*. Washington, D.C.: American Bankers Association, 1986.

4.

THE
DEPOSIT
FUNCTION

LEARNING OBJECTIVES

After completing this chapter, you will be able to
●
explain the importance of the deposit function in banks
●
define the terms cash item,
provisional credit, float, house check, split deposit, kiting, and batch proof
●
distinguish among a customer's book, collected, and available balances
●
list the characteristics of cash and noncash items
●
identify the ways in which deposits to accounts can be made
●
describe the processing of deposit items by tellers
●
discuss the problem of counterfeit currency

A mong the diverse and important services performed by banks every day, it is difficult to single out any particular activity as being the one on which all the others rest. If such a choice had to be made, however, the *deposit function* would stand out as the essential service without which banks could not operate. Deposits are the raw material that makes it possible for banks to provide the other services. Just as a manufacturer requires a steady inflow from suppliers in order to prepare and market a product, the bank cannot function without daily deposit activity.

Banks could not perform their two other fundamental functions—payment and credit—without the deposit function. Some 100 million checks flow through banks each day. Bank customers can issue checks because they have already deposited the funds to cover them, and payees can accept the checks because they believe that the checks are covered. The payees are confident that the banking system will accept those checks as deposits and, by presenting them to the drawees, be able to convert them into available funds. Without the deposit function, the payment function could not exist.

The same principle applies to the credit function. Contrary to a popular misconception, most of the funds loaned or invested by banks *do not* come from the banks' own resources; about 90 percent of bank loans and investments are made through the use of depositors' money. If the inflow of deposits ceased, the banks would no longer have the funds to extend credit; their lending activities would at first be restricted, and eventually eliminated. The U.S. economy, which depends heavily on bank borrowings to finance its expansion and meet its needs, would suffer a serious setback. Businesses, governments, and consumers all would find that a major source of credit was no longer available to them.

The deposit function allows the payees of checks to convert those pieces of paper, which essentially are claims to money, into usable funds. Consider the case of a large insurance company, located in Milwaukee. Each month it receives many thousands of checks from its policyholders in payment of their premiums. Theoretically, the company could present each check directly to its drawee. In practice, the drawee might be across the street—or thousands of miles away. Physically presenting each check is obviously impossible for the insurance company. Instead, the company deposits the checks with its bank or banks. Banks are willing to perform all the work of receiving and processing deposited checks because those deposits provide them with the funds they need to make loans and investments.

The payee of a check assumes that it is "good" unless and until it hears otherwise. However, every check is a written set of instructions to a drawee, directing that a payment be made. The drawee, wherever it is located, must make the final decision regarding honoring the check and charging it to the drawer's account.

WHAT ARE DEPOSITS?

On any given day, a bank teller may serve a rapid succession of customers, each of whom wishes to make a deposit into an account. The teller must never assume that accepting deposits is a simple, routine job, consisting chiefly of examining and counting coin and currency, receiving checks, and issuing receipts. Tellers must be thoroughly familiar with the nature of the items they are handling and know which properly can be accepted at once and which should be questioned further or given special processing. A teller must always be aware that the bank, by the mere act of accepting a deposit, exposes itself to serious liability and risk.

Assume that a teller must deal with five customers in sequence who present for deposit

- coin and currency only
- an endorsed payroll check drawn on the teller's own bank; that is, the bank of deposit is also the drawee
- an endorsed check payable to the depositor, drawn on another bank in the same community
- an endorsed check the customer has received from a relative in a distant city
- a promissory note, payable to the customer

The teller has been confronted with five unique situations. The teller must decide whether each item can be accepted for deposit, and know the processing each will receive. Each deposit must be examined and processed quickly and accurately.

The five situations in this scenario are common ones, but do not represent all the various possibilities a teller may encounter in receiving deposits. Individuals may present checks drawn in a foreign currency, or "payable through" drafts they have received in settlement of insurance claims. Other customers may wish to deposit traveler's checks to an account, or may give the teller coupons representing periodic interest payments on bonds they own.

Cash Items

In the language of banking, the term *cash items* often creates confusion. The importance of this term cannot be overemphasized. The general public may think it refers only to currency and coin; in banking it has an entirely different significance, referring to a position taken by banks because of their belief in the "goodness" of the typical, everyday check.

As mentioned earlier, checks are *not* money; they are *claims* to money. The drawee bank must in each case decide whether the amount claimed can and should be charged to the drawer's account. Despite the huge volume of checks that changes hands every day, only 1 out of every 200 will be dishonored; the remaining 199 justify the basic assumption that a check is "good" until proved otherwise and therefore can be accepted with confidence.

The entire system operates on an exception basis. When customers deposit checks, no notification takes place unless those checks are returned for any reason.

Banks are willing to assume that the vast majority of checks deposited each day will be honored by the drawees; therefore, they call these *cash items* and give the customers *immediate, provisional* credit at the time of deposit.

The words "immediate" and "provisional" have great significance for the bank and for the depositor. The word "immediate" means that the bank increases the depositor's account balance by crediting the amount of the check on the day it is received. The word "provisional" means that the bank reserves the right to reverse that credit if necessary.

Assume that the ABC Company receives 200 checks today and deposits them in its local bank. Assuming that all the checks are "good," the bank posts the total amount as a credit to the ABC Company's account, thereby creating a liability for itself. Since it is money that is owed to the customer, every deposit represents a liability for the bank.

The granting of immediate and provisional credit on these 200 checks has an immediate effect on the ABC Company's *book* (or ledger) balance. However, the possibility always exists that one or more of the deposited checks will not be honored by a drawee. Therefore, both the bank and its customer must be aware that there can be significant differences between a *book* balance and the customer's *collected* or *available* balance. These terms reflect the importance of *float* in our banking system.

In the situation mentioned, the dollar total of the 200 checks deposited by the ABC Company consists of *uncollected funds* while the items are in the process of being routed to the drawees, examined by the drawees, and either honored or rejected. The term *float* describes items that have been taken on deposit but are in the process of collection. At any time, a customer's book balance may include a certain amount of float, adjusted each day as deposited items are presented to drawees and either accepted or returned.

The ABC Company's book balance, less the float, is its *collected* balance. The collected balance represents only funds that have completed the processing cycle and are known to be good.

One peculiarity of our banking system is that "money" can be in two places at the same time. The drawers of the 200 checks deposited by the

ABC Company have bank balances against which the checks are drawn; those balances will not be reduced by their banks until the checks are honored and posting takes place. Until that happens, the checks merely are letters of instruction that are somewhere in the collection cycle. Meanwhile, however, the ABC Company has been credited for the checks in its book balance. Although checks are not money, their payees consider them to be equivalent to money. In other words, the ABC Company is given immediate, provisional credit for the 200 checks as deposit items before the balances of the drawers of the 200 checks are reduced.

Because there is always the possibility that one or more deposited checks may be returned, banks generally do not allow customers to draw against uncollected funds. They may do so, however, when the customer is well known and of good credit standing; in these cases the banks assume the risk.

A further difference may exist between a deposit account's *collected* balance and its *available* balance. Within a certain time frame, the bank that accepted the 200 checks deposited by the ABC Company may consider the checks to have been honored by the drawees; at that point, the bank will eliminate the float and consider the book balance to have become a collected balance. Nevertheless, the bank may not be willing to allow the ABC Company to withdraw that entire amount. The available balance can be described as the balance that the bank would allow the customer to withdraw were the account to be closed on that day. Banks generally prepare schedules of availability showing how soon various types of deposited checks will be made available for the customers' use. Bank availability schedules and their effects on customers will be discussed further in chapter 7. Because they are uniform in nature and do not require individual, special handling, cash items can be processed quickly, cheaply, and in large volume. By treating the typical check as a cash item (assuming that it is "good" until otherwise notified), banks have been able to develop quick and efficient handling methods that cost the customer relatively little.

In the deposit examples described earlier, the first customer deposited coin and currency with the teller. The teller is dealing with legal tender; there are no uncollected funds and no reason for delay in increasing the customer's balance.

The second, third, and fourth customers presented checks that must be approved for payment by their respective drawees; nevertheless, they are treated as cash items and will increase the account balance on an immediate, provisional basis. The check presented by the second customer will remain within the same bank at which it is deposited; it is known as a check *on-us* (sometimes referred to as a *house* check). The third item involves a drawee bank in the same geographic area as the bank of deposit; it generally is called a *local*, or *clearing*, check. The fourth customer presented a check drawn on a bank in a distant city. Checks of this type are called *transit* items. Every bank has internal policies for classifying checks as local or transit, depending on the geography of the area, the number of banks that serve that area, and the facilities for exchanging and settling for checks drawn on other banks.

Each of the three checks is payable on demand, is not accompanied by any documents or special instructions that would make customized handling necessary, can be handled quickly and inexpensively in bulk, and is payable in an immediately determinable amount of U.S. currency; therefore, all are treated as cash items.

Every bank uses a variety of techniques to reduce float, since deposited checks that remain as uncollected funds for a period of time have a severe impact on both the bank and its customers. Those techniques are discussed in chapter 7.

Noncash Items

The fifth customer presented the teller with a completely different situation. The promissory note is not a cash item; it will require individual, specialized handling. Several characteristics distinguish cash from noncash items, and they are processed differently (see table 4.1). When customers present noncash items, the teller accepting them should make it clear that immediate account credit cannot be given and that an advice of credit will be sent to the customer only when the specialized collection process has been completed. Because there is no immediate credit, no float is created. For the same reason, the credit that is finally posted is not provisional; the item is known to have been presented and honored.

When a deposited cash item is dishonored by the drawee, the amount of the deposit is charged back to the customer's account. When a

TABLE 4.1
CHARACTERISTICS OF DEPOSITED ITEMS

Cash Items	Noncash Items
• Give customer immediate, provisional account credit	• Give customer delayed (deferred) credit
• Create float (time lag between account crediting and collection)	• Do not create float (account not credited until collection is completed)
• May be payable on demand	• May or may not be payable on demand
• Must not have documents attached	• May have documents attached
• Must not carry special instructions or require special handling	• Individual, special handling required; may carry customer's or other instructions
• Inexpensive; processed in bulk	• More expensive to handle
• Payable in U.S. funds	• May or may not be payable in U.S. funds
Examples	**Examples**
• Checks	• Promissory notes
	• Drafts with attached documents
	• Coupons
	• Foreign checks

noncash item is dishonored, however, no charge-back to the depositor occurs, simply because no credit was posted at the time of receipt.

Noncash items usually are handled by a special department within the bank. There they can be given the customized processing required in each case. If the volume warrants it, that department may be subdivided into "city" collections (for noncash items payable locally) and "country" items. Foreign collections are another specialized category because they present different problems, such as currency conversion.

Every bank retains the right to establish policies regarding the cash and noncash classification of deposited items. For example, a bank may accept coupons from U.S. government bonds for immediate credit in the case of a well-known customer, despite the fact that the coupons normally would be treated as noncash items.

Holds

The question of availability of funds influences the bank's decision regarding the amount of time that should elapse before a customer is permitted to use deposited funds. To protect itself, a bank may place a *hold* on an account for a certain number of days, thereby preventing withdrawals by the customer. In effect, this delays the availability of funds to the customer. During the late 1980s, many consumers protested the substantial holds that some banks were imposing. As a result, some states passed legislation that has limited the number of days that deposited funds can be held before they are made available to the customer. In 1987, Congress passed a nationwide law on this topic.

A temporary schedule of availability applies from August 31, 1988 to September 1, 1990; it establishes 6 business days as the maximum delay in availability. Effective September 1, 1988, cash, wire transfers, government checks, and cashier's, teller's, and certified checks, deposited into new accounts, must be given *1-day* availability when the initial deposit consisting of such items is $5,000 or less. On the excess above $5,000 there is a maximum delay of 8 business days in availability.

As of September 1990, a permanent schedule of availability will become effective, requiring banks to make the following deposited items available for withdrawal on the next business day: cash deposits, wire transfers, government checks, cashier's, teller's, and certified checks, and the first $100 of all deposits. Other local checks must become available to the depositor in 2 business days, and transit checks must be made available in 4 business days following the deposit.

HOW ARE DEPOSITS MADE?

Historically, most deposits have been made at tellers' windows, in the brick-and-mortar facilities of banks. However, to increase and expedite the inflow of deposits and for the greater convenience of customers, banks today have developed many additional ways in which deposits can be made. These alternatives both reduce congestion on the banking floor and shorten waiting time at tellers' stations.

Convenience Services

Retail stores, restaurants, theaters, and other businesses that receive checks and currency in payment for goods and services often need to make deposits after banking hours and on weekends. The *night depository* makes this possible. The customer is given a bag or pouch with a safety lock and a key to a compartment in the bank wall. The locked bag is placed in the compartment whenever the customer finds a convenient time. The deposit will be opened and examined under special conditions by bank personnel on the next business day.

Counting and verifying each night deposit generally is done under a system called *dual control*, involving two bank personnel. Dual control is also used in many other phases of the bank's daily operations. Access to vaults and the handling of debit and credit entries are among the types of transactions that usually require the participation of two staff members, so that one may verify what another has done. Use of dual control in the night deposit operation helps protect the bank if a dispute arises over the existence or amount of a deposit.

Many banks provide facilities known as *lobby depositories* or *quick-deposit boxes* for the convenience of customers. The depositor places a deposit in an envelope, seals the envelope, and drops it into a secure receptacle on the banking floor. In this way the customer avoids waiting for a teller, and the deposits can be examined and proved—again, using dual control—during nonpeak periods. After each deposit has been examined and verified, receipts are sent to the customers.

Banks encourage the use of *mail deposits* as another way to speed up the handling of deposits, reduce traffic in the bank, and make banking more convenient for customers. Bank personnel can process the deposits without the pressures created by long lines of impatient customers; thus, errors are reduced. Receipts for mail deposits are sent out after examination and verification.

The *drive-in* or *drive-through window* has become a familiar sight in banks throughout the country, and some institutions reportedly handle as much as two-thirds of their daily deposit activity through these facilities. Transactions are processed as they would be at any other teller station, but customers appreciate the convenience of doing their banking while remaining in their cars.

Electronic Funds Transfer Systems

The development of electronic funds transfer systems (EFTS) has opened up additional ways in which deposits to accounts can be made without the need for a customer to visit the bank or spend much time there. Many applications of EFTS also represent an effort to substitute paperless entries (involving debits and credits to accounts) for checks, thereby reducing the daily volume of 100 million checks that now flow through the banking system.

For example, programs for *direct deposit* of incoming funds increase in popularity each year. The deposit may be made to an account at any type of financial institution. The direct deposit of Social Security checks to beneficiaries' accounts allows for greater efficiency and reduced handling costs. The government agency avoids the cost of actual checks, the expense of issuing them, and the costs of processing claims for lost, stolen, or forged checks. At the same time, the beneficiaries benefit because their monthly Social Security payments are virtually guaranteed to be in their accounts and available for use on the specified date.

Direct deposit also is used with payrolls. Many corporate employees agree to direct deposit of their salaries and wages each pay period. Some companies have combined the use of payroll direct deposit with the installation of an ATM on the company's premises. This convenience allows the employee to use the machine to withdraw cash from an account that has been credited (through direct deposit) with his or her net pay.

In direct deposit programs, information regarding each payment is entered on magnetic tape by the payer (usually a government agency or employer). The tapes are processed through *automated clearing houses* (ACHs), which are regional facilities affiliated with the National Automated Clearing House Association. Over 10,000 financial institutions of all types now participate in regional ACHs. Without the processing of a single check, funds are transferred electronically from the account of the payer to the account of the beneficiary, wherever it may be. Thirty-one of the 32 regional ACHs process transactions through the Fed; the New York ACH processes payments within its region independent of the Fed. Each of the 32 ACHs routes all payment information to the payee's designated bank or other financial institution.

As another manifestation of EFTS, *automated teller machines* (ATMs) are becoming both more familiar and more widely accepted by customers. ATMs allow for deposits, cash withdrawals or advances against accounts, transfers of funds between accounts, and balance inquiries. They offer the bank customer 24-hour service every day of the year. The start-up costs of an ATM are high, but the result is a substantial cost saving for the bank.

When EFTS applications first were introduced, a prediction was made that the use of checks eventually would be abandoned in favor of simple debit and credit entries to accounts—paperless entries, created electronically. This prediction has proved to be completely false. As of 1987, check usage continues to grow at the rate of 4 percent to 5 percent each year.

At the same time, the annual volume of ACH transactions has grown at a much faster rate. People and organizations made 586 million payments through ACH facilities in 1985, with government-originated payments accounting for 51 percent of the volume. During 1986 the ACH volume increased by about 27 percent, to 743 million transactions, and payments originated by government entities dropped to 46 percent, indicating greater acceptance of the program by businesses and consumers.[1]

Many banks that receive large deposits from customers originate ACH transactions for those customers. In Springfield, Illinois, for example, three insurance companies use the Marine Bank in that city to collect premium payments for them and credit their accounts. In cases such as this, the originating bank prepares a tape containing all the necessary information regarding each account that is to be debited, forwards the tape to an ACH for routing, and posts a single credit for the total as a direct deposit to its customer's account.[2]

Corporations increasingly are using electronic transfers of funds to pay suppliers. For example, in 1986 General Motors Corporation announced that it would begin making 400,000 monthly bill payments to its suppliers by electronically crediting their accounts. By itself, this activity represents $4 billion in monthly payment volume.[3]

Applications of electronic funds transfers can tie the deposit function directly to the payment function. Many customers have adopted a system that automatically transfers funds out of their accounts. These customers authorize their banks to debit their accounts and to move funds automatically to designated payees. The payees receive the benefits of direct deposit activity and avoid the delays and costs associated with the use of checks. These transfer programs are most effective when a fixed amount of money must be paid at the same time each month.

In growing numbers, consumers have shown a willingness to accept systems that use *point-of-sale* (POS) terminals as a means of electronically transferring funds to payee accounts, where direct depositing takes place. These POS systems are used when the buyer of goods or services uses a plastic card at a supermarket, gas station, or other facility to initiate a direct transfer of funds. In mid-1986 over 17,000 POS installations were in operation; however, it was predicted at that time that the number would increase to 178,000 within 5 years.[4]

There is no float involved in EFTS applications involving a direct deposit of funds. The account credit is electronic. This removes any question as to whether a payment is "good," and EFTS transaction costs are far lower than those of checks.

Transfers Between Banks

Wire transfers represent yet another way in which deposits are made to accounts without the involvement of tellers. Billions of dollars move from bank to bank in this manner every day. The Federal Reserve operates a network that links the 12 Fed districts and enables banks to transfer to and from the reserve accounts of member institutions. Fed funds transfers often are requested by banks when corporate customers wish to move large dollar amounts. Because the reserve account of one bank is debited while that of another bank is credited, immediate availability of the transferred funds is guaranteed.

Assume, for example, that a company headquartered in Alabama must move funds from its local bank to an institution in Detroit that maintains a payroll account for the firm's employees in that area. On receipt of properly authorized instructions, the Alabama bank charges the company's account and instructs the Detroit bank, by wire, to credit the payroll account. The system is rapid and efficient, since it reduces the movement of funds to mere bookkeeping entries.

Under the provisions of the Monetary Control Act, the Fed is compelled to levy a specific charge for each wire transfer instruction that it handles. Banks, in turn, pass these charges along to their customers, either by increasing the minimum balance required to support the wire transfer service or by charging direct activity fees.

Transfers Within a Bank

A final example of deposits that do not originate with bank tellers can be seen in the multitude of credit tickets prepared each day by departments within a bank. The most common method of paying out loan proceeds is to post a credit to the borrower's account. Proceeds of securities sales and the collection of noncash items likewise result in this form of deposit activity.

EXAMINING DEPOSITS

Before a deposit is accepted from a customer and a receipt issued, it is essential that the deposit be examined so that the bank knows what it is accepting. The first step in this process is to remove any noncash items from the rest of the deposit and route them to the proper department for specialized handling. All cash items are then carefully examined.

Counterfeit Currency

The handling of currency poses a special problem for tellers. In recent years counterfeiting of currency has reached record proportions, as new and more sophisticated photographic, printing, and copying equipment has enabled counterfeiters to print large quantities of bogus currency. Counterfeit bills may be of such high quality that they are extremely hard to detect. Government agencies have expressed great concern over this increasing problem, and an alert teller can be extremely valuable in the effort to reduce counterfeiting.

When a bogus bill is identified in a deposit, the teller should immediately subtract its amount from that deposit and arrange for the bill to be forwarded to the Federal Reserve. The Fed will, in turn, send the bill to the Secret Service unit of the U.S. Treasury Department. This unit is responsible for trying to identify the source of the counterfeit money so that arrest and eventual prosecution can take place. Under *no* circumstances should a counterfeit bill be returned to the depositor. To do this would serve only to keep the phony money in circulation. Depositors, in effect, lose the amount of any such bills that are found in their deposits of currency.

Endorsements

Checks presented for cashing or depositing should be examined for proper endorsement. By insisting on proper endorsements, tellers serve the best interests of both the bank and its customers. Under the principle of holder in due course, the customer who endorses a check and receives cash or deposit credit for it has agreed to make good if need be. Further, the endorsement provides an audit trail if proof of payment to a specific party ever is needed. For example, checks issued by a unit of the federal government and those issued by many insurance companies require specific endorsements as a means of proving that the funds were paid to the proper beneficiary.

Business Deposits

As a general rule, currency and checks are counted and examined at the teller's window; however, many business customers make large deposits of coin and currency, making the normal process impossible. Supermarkets, amusement parks, and transportation companies are among those customers who often make large deposits of already-rolled or already-bagged coins and bundles of bills. Standard bank practice permits the accepting of these deposits without actual counting and verifying by a teller at the time the deposit is made. In these cases, the bank and depositor agree that the amount of the deposit is subject to later verification, which may involve dual control.

EXCESS CASH

The coin and currency received by a bank in the course of a day are stored in its vaults after proof procedures have been completed. If a bank has an excess of coin and currency on hand—that is, an amount over and above its projected near-term needs—the bank may do one of two things. It may turn the surplus over to the Fed to be added to its reserve account. Or, the bank may deposit the surplus with a correspondent bank, which performs services in exchange for compensating balances. When a bank requires additional coin and currency—for example, to prepare for a busy payroll day or during the hectic Christmas season—it may obtain a supply from either of these two sources.

Banks should take every reasonable precaution against keeping excess cash at tellers' stations. Typically, the supply of coin and currency is counted and controlled each day. Cash, in and of itself, generates no profit for the bank; indeed, the sight of an overabundance of cash spilling over the drawers at a teller's window can tempt a would-be robber, and if a holdup should occur the bank's loss will be greater. Delivering excess cash to the Fed or to a correspondent releases other funds for loan and investment purposes, thereby helping the bank's earnings.

PROBLEM SITUATIONS

Banks always will be targets for individuals who seek to rob or defraud them in one way or another, and one of the challenges every teller faces in the course of a day's work requires dealing with persons who may try to take advantage of a momentary lapse in concentration or the pressures of an especially hectic hour, when lines are at their longest and the teller inevitably becomes fatigued. Even when what appears to be nothing more than a routine cash item is involved, banks are often defrauded.

The *split deposit* is a common technique that illustrates individual fraud. A person opens a bank account and later presents a check payable to him or her, asking that part of it be deposited and the remainder paid out in cash. A teller who grants this request assumes a very real risk. Establishing a bank account *does not* give a customer the right to use the bank as an automatic medium for cashing checks. The check presented by the customer may have been stolen, or may be dishonored by the drawee for some valid reason. If the bank that gives cash for it is unable to recover the funds, as is often the case, the bank suffers a direct loss. The problem can be avoided by having the customer deposit the entire check and issue a check of his or her own for the amount requested in cash, provided there are sufficient *available* funds in the account to cover that amount.

Another common fraud involving the deposit function uses a technique called *kiting*. A customer establishes accounts with two or more banks and uses a check drawn on one—against insufficient or uncollected funds—as a means of obtaining cash from another. A deposit consisting of checks drawn on other banks never justifies paying out money unless the bank is completely sure of the creditworthiness and integrity of the depositor. Even in instances where banks felt entirely comfortable in allowing a customer to draw against uncollected funds, frauds have taken place.

Other problems in the accepting of cash items often involve the exact designation of the named payee. For example, if an error has been made in the spelling of a payee name the check must be endorsed twice—once with the incorrect spelling and again with the proper spelling. The bank must accept instructions only from that payee or from another party to whom the named payee has transferred rights to the instrument. A check payable to a corporation, estate, business name, or other form of legal entity should not be accepted for deposit to an individual account unless there are strong reasons for doing so as an exception. This again illustrates the importance of careful examination of endorsements.

SORTING AND PROVING DEPOSITS

Depending on their size, the volume of deposited items they handle each day, and the extent to which they have automated their systems, banks have developed various methods of sorting and proving deposited checks after the customer has left a teller's window. The most widely used method is known as the *batch proof* method. It is based on the theory that if the necessary sorting work on all deposited items is done correctly, and if accurate totals have been created for each sorting category, the sum of the totals for each category must equal the total amount processed for the day. Even though *counter errors* (errors that offset one another) may occur, the batch proof system more than compensates by making it unnecessary for every individual deposit to be proved separately.

Whether the batch proof system or another system is used, and regardless of the bank's size or volume of activity, the following two steps must be completed after all deposits have been received at tellers' windows:

- The total deposited amount must be proved.
- Separate, accurate control totals must be developed to show the destinations to which deposited checks have been sent and the amount that has been sent to each.

Deposited and cashed checks are sorted into three groups: on-us, local, and transit. The totals for these three groups must equal the tellers' daily activity after all cash substitution tickets, accounting for currency and coin, are included.

Exhibit 4.1 shows the check processing flow in those banks with a daily deposit volume large enough to warrant a centralized department. In smaller banks, the sorting and routing work may be done directly by the tellers. Chapter 7 covers the details of check processing through the routing of checks to their drawee banks.

SUMMARY

Accepting deposits simultaneously serves the best interests of banks and their customers. Were it not for the check-handling capability that banks have developed, the economy would suffer tremendously because each payee would have to assume the tasks of sorting, routing, and presenting every check. By rendering this service, banks also provide for themselves the daily inflow of raw material that they need in order to generate profits.

Although the technology that has made electronic funds transfers possible has reduced check volume, and although banks have implemented many systems of accepting deposits that do not require the customer's presence at a teller's window, the bulk of daily deposit activity continues to take place through tellers. They must be able to recognize the nature of the items that are presented for deposit, screen out the noncash

EXHIBIT 4.1
THE CHECK PROCESSING WORKFLOW

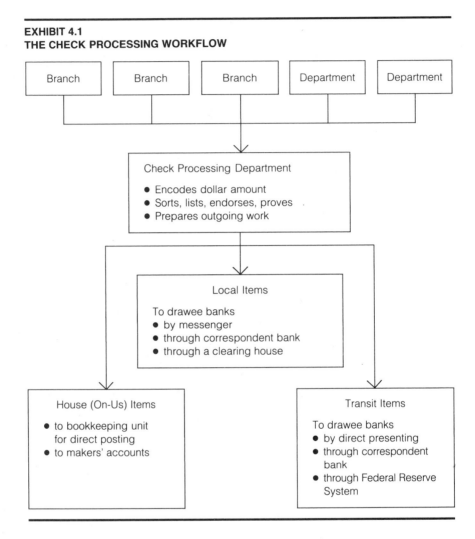

items, understand how deposited cash items affect the customer's balance, and process the work with speed and accuracy. Speed is important not only from the standpoint of reducing customers' waiting time; it is important that deposited items be processed quickly so that float can be reduced. Deposited items in the process of collection have no real value to either the bank or the customer. Likewise, accuracy is essential because both bank and customer depend on and expect it.

No teller should ever feel that receiving deposits is a simple process that creates no risk or liability for the bank. On the contrary, each teller must understand and apply the criteria for immediate credit and the principle of holder in due course, and recognize the potential for loss that may result from his or her actions. Tellers constantly must be on guard to protect the bank against fraud.

QUESTIONS FOR DISCUSSION

1. What is the relationship between a bank's deposit function and its credit function?

2. What is the importance of the words "immediate" and "provisional" as they are applied to deposited cash items?

3. Define the term *float*. How is float created? What is its importance to the bank?

4. What risk is created if a customer is allowed to draw against deposits that are in the process of collection?

5. What is an on-us check? A clearing item? A transit check?

6. What benefits or advantages do ATMs offer to customers? What are the benefits they offer to banks?

7. What is the difference between a customer's book balance and the customer's available balance?

8. Identify five characteristics of cash items taken on deposit.

9. What actions should a teller take when a counterfeit bill is found in a deposit?

10. Mention two reasons why the amount of tellers' cash should be kept to a minimum.

11. What advantages does the system of direct deposit offer to the payee of funds? What benefits does a bank gain by offering this service? What is the advantage to the corporation using direct deposit to pay its employees?

12. How does the batch proof system operate? Is this system used in your bank?

NOTES

1. See Tom Ferris, "Chase is No. 1 at Automated Clearing House," *American Banker*, May 13, 1986, p. 1; and Jeffrey Kutler, "Automated Clearing House System Still Struggling," *American Banker*, March 16, 1987, p. 24.

2. Ferris, "Chase is No. 1," p. 1.

3. Tom Ferris, "GM Readies Electronic Bill Paying," *American Banker*, October 1, 1986, p. 1.

4. Jeffrey Kutler, "Number of POS Terminals to Grow Tenfold by 1990," *American Banker*, February 25, 1987, p. 11.

For More Information

Friedman, David H. *Deposit Operations*. Washington, D.C.: American Bankers Association, 1987.

5.

BANK-DEPOSITOR RELATIONSHIPS

LEARNING OBJECTIVES

After completing this chapter, you will be able to

●

explain the importance of identity, capacity, and authority in account relationships

●

list the types of accounts commercial banks offer today

●

identify the competition that commercial banks face

●

describe the effects of interest expense on commercial banks

●

define such banking terms as attorney-in-fact, rights of survivorship, taxpayer identification number, Form 1099, money market account, and corporate resolution

●

name the legal distinctions between proprietorships, partnerships, and corporations

Although its traditions stretch back for over 200 years, banking in the United States has changed more since World War II than in its entire previous history. Changes in the deposit structure, changes in technology, changes in the competitive financial services industry, and changes in the services offered by banks have been numerous and continuous.

The banking environment also has changed. As international and domestic economies have grown, as new industries have been formed, and as bank customers of every type have become more knowledgeable regarding interest-earning opportunities, many time-honored attitudes of banks have been revised. For example, many banks have become aggressive marketers. A bank account no longer is the symbol of the well-to-do individual, and the use of bank services no longer is restricted to a select group of customers. Banks have come to resemble supermarkets of finance, offering many services that did not exist 30 years ago. Large-denomination CDs, home equity loans, NOW and money market accounts, loans to finance boats, condominiums, or cooperative apartments, checking accounts tied to personal lines of credit, overdraft privileges, and investment opportunities or bank card usage are among these new services.

Of course, every bank does not offer every type of service to every customer. The philosophy that an institution should be "all things to all people" no longer applies in banking. Through its knowledge of the marketplace and of its customers' wants and needs, each bank must determine which services it can best offer on a profitable basis, taking into consideration its own resources and capabilities.

COMPETITION

Competition from thrift institutions and credit unions for customer deposits and the entry of the money market fund into the financial services marketplace were topics introduced in chapters 1 and 2. Customers who in the past were forced to go to commercial banks for many services now have far more freedom of choice. Areas that were once the exclusive province of the banks have been opened up to competitors, so that the share of the total assets in the marketplace held by commercial banks has shrunk at an alarming pace. At the same time, banks have been prohibited by various laws and regulations from competing freely by offering all the services that others can offer. Sophisticated customers today show no hesitation in moving funds from one financial intermediary to another, whenever and wherever advantages and benefits can be found.

Nevertheless, commercial banks as a group continue to hold the bulk of the nation's deposits. Banks held $2.29 trillion in deposits as of year-end 1986, as opposed to $1.09 trillion at all thrift institutions and $152 billion at credit unions.[1]

Aside from those two categories of competitors, no discussion of the current financial marketplace would be complete without mentioning such organizations as Sears, Roebuck and Company, Merrill Lynch, American Express, General Motors Acceptance Corporation, and Ford Motor Company. Some of these competitors have made no secret of their objective of becoming the true financial supermarkets of the future. To do so, they can expand by offering a range of services that no bank legally can match and by moving across state lines to any location they choose.

Sears, Roebuck and Company, for example, is a fully integrated provider of financial services. It owns a bank in Delaware, a major insurance company (Allstate), one of the nation's largest brokerage firms (Dean Witter), and one of the leading companies in home mortgage financing and servicing (Coldwell Banker). Sears has over 26 million active credit cardholders, whose amounts outstanding are over $14 billion. Sears operates more than 300 "financial centers" in its 800 store locations. These offer consumers a complete package of insurance, investment, CDs, money market accounts, and real estate financing. The Discover card, introduced by Sears, will create even more competition for banks.

Merrill Lynch, the largest U.S. brokerage firm, is also active in commercial lending and offers consumers a "cash management" account that combines checking, investment, overdraft, and credit card features. Through subsidiaries, Merrill Lynch can give customers a full range of brokerage, real estate, mortgage banking, insurance, and commercial paper services.[2]

The American Express Company is perhaps best known for its traveler's checks and credit cards; yet its ownership of various subsidiaries has also made it a major force in insurance, brokerage activities, global banking, and personal financial planning.[3]

General Motors Acceptance Corporation was originally formed to finance the purchases of General Motors automobiles. The corporation has since diversified into commercial lending, has become the nation's second largest mortgage banking company, and generates an annual net income of over $1 billion.[4]

The Ford Motor Company, through its subsidiaries, is engaged in leasing, automobile financing, insurance, and a broad range of home improvement, personal, home equity, and commercial and industrial loans. Ford owns First Nationwide Financial, the eighth largest thrift institution, which serves two million customers and has branches in New York, California, Florida, and Hawaii.[5]

MEETING THE COMPETITION

It has often been said that no vacuum is allowed to continue for very long in the financial services industry. If one type of financial institution does not offer certain services, or if one category of customers is denied access to certain services, the void is soon filled. Through much of their history, many U.S. banks neglected the consumer market and concentrated on dealing with businesses, agencies of government, and correspondent banks. They showed little interest in offering personal checking accounts or personal loans. The banks' competitors capitalized on that lack of interest and offered as many financial services as possible to individuals. Savings and loan associations, savings banks, credit unions, and money market funds all came into existence and grew by meeting the financial needs that commercial banks had ignored.

To compete today, banks have adopted new approaches to marketing. However, the quest for new deposits carries with it a serious problem. Establishing a relationship with a new customer may now require more care and skill on the bank's part than was needed in the past. As banks try to expand their services to businesses, individuals, and governments, the desire to attract deposits must never cause banks to relax their standards. There are many fundamental precautions that should be taken at the very beginning of a customer relationship and maintained throughout the life of that relationship. If faithfully observed, these precautions lessen risk and assure that all laws and regulations are being complied with. In addition, they guarantee that both parties—bank and customer—are fully aware of the obligations they are undertaking.

Any bank employee who is involved in opening new accounts must be ready to deal with completely unknown individuals. These individuals may not be aware of the banking laws that apply to each type of account, the policies of the individual bank, or even the type of relationship they want to establish or that best meets their needs and objectives. The customers may have a whole series of "what if?" questions. It is essential that customers be informed about what they and the bank can or cannot do in each type of deposit relationship. Ensuring a complete understanding at the time an account is opened will prevent many future problems.

Full-Service Banking

Even banks that have adopted a policy of never attempting to "be all things to all people" have necessarily expanded their range of deposit services in recent years. Traditionally, commercial banks lived up to their name by developing a customer base of correspondent banks, businesses, units of government, and institutions while serving as the nation's prime reservoir of demand deposits. Especially in the case of the major banks in money-center cities, they left the entire field of savings and time deposits to the thrift institutions.

For many years this general policy worked well. After World War II, however, the demand for bank credit increased steadily as the U.S. economy and the population grew. Banks needed new sources of funds to make the loans that fueled economic growth and to meet the needs of the 10 million men and women who had returned to civilian life at the end of the war. Individuals required automobile and home mortgage loans, and companies responding to the increased consumer demands of a peacetime economy required bank loans to expand and modernize their facilities. Deposit growth at banks lagged behind the demand for credit because of competition from other types of financial institutions—especially those that met the needs of consumers. Banks had to develop new techniques for bringing in deposits. New areas of bank marketing opened up, and many new types of relationships with customers were introduced.

Today commercial banks remain the principal depositories for checking account funds, but the nation's deposit structure shows far more in time and savings deposits than in demand deposits. Customers of every type tend to watch their balance positions closely and to keep non-interest-bearing deposits to a minimum. The introduction of automatic transfer services and NOW, Super-NOW, and money market accounts has given customers the best of both worlds; they can benefit from interest on balances and at the same time have check-writing privileges. Transaction deposits (including NOW and Super-NOW accounts) grew from 28 percent to 34 percent of total deposits in commercial banks during 1986 (table 5.1).

Interest paid to depositors has become the largest, fastest-growing, and least controllable expense category for U.S. banks. Interest expense typically exceeds the total of all other operating costs in a bank, including salaries and wages, taxes, occupancy and equipment costs, and miscellaneous expenses (table 5.2). For this reason, banks must now carefully watch the margin of difference between their total costs of funds (interest paid on all types of accounts) and the yield derived from putting those funds to work as loans and investments. That margin of difference is called the *spread*.

The lines of demarcation that formerly separated commercial banks from thrift institutions have largely disappeared. Similarly, the distinctions between the two basic types of deposit relationships have become blurred in many cases. The NOW account is the most common example; however, other combinations of account features exist at many banks,

TABLE 5.1
DEPOSIT STRUCTURE OF COMMERCIAL BANKS, 1986

Month	Type of Deposit (in billions of dollars)			Total Deposits	Transaction Deposits as a Percentage of Total
	Transaction	Savings	Time		
February	492	457	797	1,746	28
March	503	462	798	1,763	28
April	541	468	790	1,798	30
May	543	477	788	1,807	30
June	523	482	786	1,792	29
July	540	491	789	1,820	29
August	544	498	792	1,834	30
September	537	504	789	1,831	29
October	548	515	781	1,844	30
November	595	522	780	1,897	31
December	690	534	792	2,015	34

Source: Adapted from *Federal Reserve Bulletin* (March 1987), p. A18.

TABLE 5.2
EXPENSES, INSURED COMMERCIAL BANKS, 1979–86

Year	Expenses (in billions of dollars)		Interest Expense as a Percentage of Total Operating Expenses
	Total Operating	Interest	
1979	132	72	54
1980	171	98	58
1981	228	139	61
1982	238	141	59
1983	220	143	65
1984	254	167	66
1985	252	154	61
1986	250	140	56

Sources: 1979 through 1983 figures, Deborah J. Danker and Mary M. McLaughlin, "Profitability of Insured Commercial Banks," *Federal Reserve Bulletin* (November 1984), p. 512; 1984 through 1986 figures, same authors, "The Profitability of U.S.-Chartered Insured Commercial Banks in 1986," *Federal Reserve Bulletin* (July 1987), p. 551.

allowing customers to issue checks against balances that provide some form of interest or yield. For example, in 1986 the nation's largest commercial bank, Citibank, N.A., introduced a "financial account." This account offers the customer check-writing privileges, high-yield savings, overdraft protection, and certificates of deposit in a single relationship. It was marketed as "the only account you need."[6] In March 1987 the Chase Manhattan Bank, N.A., began offering a form of CD called the "market index investment," for which the interest rate was tied directly to changes in the Standard & Poor's composite index of per-share prices of 500 common stocks.[7]

Other banks in various parts of the country also have taken steps to combine the features of different deposit relationships in order to attract customers. For example, many banks issue bank cards linked to deposit accounts, thus giving access to ATMs for deposits and withdrawals.

Within the two basic categories—demand deposits and time and savings deposits—banks now offer a wide range of accounts to suit the needs and objectives of every category of customer. Checking accounts can be opened for one or more individuals, for every type of business, for agencies of federal, state, or local government, for unincorporated or not-for-profit associations and societies, for correspondent banks, and for trust relationships. The range of time and savings deposits includes the basic savings account, NOW, Super-NOW, and money market accounts, Keogh and IRA accounts, various types of CDs and savings certificates, and club (Christmas, Vacation, and Hanukkah) accounts. While a bank may not attempt to be "all things to all people," it may try to be all things to *some* people, offering various combinations of accounts and services to meet the needs of a particular market segment.

ESTABLISHING IDENTITY, CAPACITY, AND LEGAL RIGHT

A bank must obtain a charter—essentially, legal permission to conduct a banking business—before it can offer any banking services. The charter is obtained either from the Office of the Comptroller of the Currency (if it is a national bank) or from the state banking authorities. The charter authorizes the bank to enter into contractual arrangements with customers. A contract is a legal agreement that can be enforced; a bilateral contract is one in which both parties agree to certain terms and conditions.

Regardless of whether a checking, savings, or time deposit relationship is being established, one standard principle applies in every instance. The bank staff member who opens the account is presumed to be acting on behalf of the institution (the bank), which is entering into a contract. At the same time, the new customer is agreeing to the terms of that contract. The bank *must* satisfactorily identify the party or parties with whom it is dealing. It *must* know in what capacity the party is acting. Finally, it *must* verify the customer's legal right to enter into a contract with it. *Authority*

Identification

How can a bank determine that the individual who wishes to open an account is the person he or she claims to be and is one with whom the bank would normally want to do business? There is no way to be absolutely sure. In most cases an individual will produce a driver's license, auto registration, credit card, or other form of identification—yet a forger could counterfeit all of these, and the fact that a person presents three or four pieces of information instead of merely one may not of itself prove identity. The bank staff member must simply use his or her best judgment in evaluating whether the identification can properly be accepted.

References from another bank or thrift institution, or from the individual's employer, may be used as an additional form of identification. Some banks have also required customers opening an account to have their fingerprints taken to be placed on file. This practice sometimes has been effective in turning away individuals who have reasons to object to it.

Bank personnel who open accounts must be especially wary of customers who take exception to any of the methods of establishing proper identification. The bank must know its customer and must be satisfied that it is opening an account for a party with whom it can deal in confidence.

Consider a hypothetical situation. A man of whom the bank has no prior knowledge whatever approaches a bank representative and asks to open a personal account with a large amount of cash. When he is asked to produce identification and furnish bank or business references, he loudly objects, claiming that this is an invasion of privacy and that his personal affairs are none of the bank's business. He says that he is giving the bank a substantial amount of genuine currency as evidence of his own good faith, and threatens to go to another bank unless the new account is opened on his terms.

An inexperienced staff member easily could be intimidated by this. Faced with the loss of a potential new account, he or she might yield to the stranger's demands and open the account without following standard policy and procedures. Could there be serious consequences for the bank as a result? Any number of unpleasant and costly situations could subsequently occur.

The initial cash deposit might consist of money obtained illegally; in this case the bank could become the subject of unfavorable publicity and become involved in claims and lawsuits. The individual might have created problems at some other bank which make him an undesirable customer. He might deposit stolen checks that he has endorsed; as a holder in due course, the bank would rely on the endorser to make good on any problem checks—but in this case the endorser might have been able to withdraw the funds and leave town.

Banks can and must be selective in opening accounts. They are under no compulsion to establish relationships with persons who fail to meet their normal criteria. "Know your customer" is an unfailing rule that bank employees should follow.

Capacity

Assuming that the question of identification is settled to the satisfaction of the bank, the matter of *capacity* must be addressed. For whom is this new customer acting? Is Jane Smith acting on her own behalf, or does she represent other parties? Perhaps she wishes to establish an account for a partnership or corporation, or as the executor of an estate, or the agent for a musician or athlete, or as the treasurer of an association or society. It is essential that the bank determine at the outset whose interests and funds are at stake and with whom it will be dealing in the future.

Authority

Once the bank determines the capacity in which the individual is acting, it must establish that person's *authority* to enter into a binding contract. John Smith may produce a satisfactory set of documents that establish his identity, but if he claims to be a corporate officer, an executor or trustee, or the legal representative of someone else, the bank must obtain legal proof that he can act on behalf of the other party or parties. The forms and documents that establish proper authority vary depending on the requirements of each situation. The bank employee must be familiar with the types of documents that grant legal authority in order to obtain the appropriate forms at the time the account is opened.

DEMAND DEPOSIT RELATIONSHIPS

Checking accounts primarily are used to pay business or personal expenses and bills. The checking-account customer does not intend to have the balance of funds accumulate; rather, the customer wants the convenience and safety of a deposit relationship that will allow for regular, frequent inflows and outflows of funds. The simplest of these is the personal checking account.

Individual Accounts

In opening a checking account for the use of one person alone, the bank is less concerned about capacity and authority than it is about identity. If an individual produces documents and references that meet the bank's standards, the bank usually may assume that the person has the authority to enter into a contractual agreement.

Each new depositor should execute a set of signature cards (exhibit 5.1). These usually outline the general rules and regulations of the bank, and are kept on file to verify signatures on checks, loan applications, requests for funds transfers, and correspondence.

A person who is opening a checking account might ask the bank to provide a supply of checks immediately so that he or she can begin using

EXHIBIT 5.1
SIGNATURE CARD WITH TYPICAL BANK DEPOSIT CONTRACT

(Front)

(Name of Bank)	Acccount Number			Type	

ACCOUNT NAMES				TIN	SOCIAL SECURITY NO.
1.					
2.					
3.					

CHEX OK by	Opened by	Contact Off.	Approv. Off.	Branch	Mother's maiden name	DATE

☐ Subject to ☐ Not subject to backup withholding per IRS code, Section 3406 (a) (1) (c).

I/we have read, understand and agree to the information on the back of this card. Under the penalties of perjury, I/we certify that the taxpayer information provided on this form is true, correct and complete.

CLIENT SIGNATURE	IDENTIFICATION (2)
1.	
2.	
3.	

SIGNATURE CARD

(Back)

Agreements for each account signer.
I agree that all transactions between the Bank and signers of this form shall be governed by   (BANK'S NAME)   Terms and Agreements, which I have received.
For clients opening interest-earning accounts.
I have received for my information a copy of "Payer's Request for Taxpayer Identification Number" (IRS Form W-9).
Certification for clients applying for a taxpayer identification number or tax-exempt clients. (Please check appropriate box and sign.)
☐ I have applied for (or I will apply for) a taxpayer identification number from the appropriate Internal Revenue or Social Security Administration Office. I understand that if I do not provide a taxpayer identification number to the Bank within 60 days, the Bank is required to withhold 20% of all reportable payments thereafter made to me until I provide a number.
☐ I am tax-exempt because I am not a citizen nor a resident of the United States. I am a citizen of_____ and hold passport no._____

Under penalty of perjury, I certify that the taxpayer information provided on this form is true, correct and complete.

Client Signature_____

93

them. To comply with this request could cause serious problems at a future date unless adequate identification and references have been obtained. It is far more prudent to advise the individual that the initial supply of checks must be printed and will be available in a few days. By that time the necessary investigation should have been completed. The bank may, for example, wish to contact an information agency that keeps records of individuals who, because other banks have had difficulties with them in the past, cannot be considered as desirable new customers. The enforced waiting period also gives the bank an opportunity to complete the check processing on the initial deposit, thereby ensuring that any deposited checks have been honored. The Competitive Equality Banking Act of 1987 requires banks to expedite the availability to the new depositor of the funds that made up the opening deposit. This act is discussed further in chapter 15.

Since an individual depositor has the legal right to issue instructions to the bank on all matters pertaining to his or her account, that depositor also has the right to authorize someone else to act on his or her behalf. This is done through a legal document called a *power of attorney* (exhibit 5.2). When the form that grants power of attorney has been properly completed and signed, the authorized party (called the *attorney-in-fact*) can do anything that the principal would do. The attorney-in-fact may sign checks, apply for credit, and authorize transfers of funds. If a power of attorney has been properly executed and filed with the bank, the signature cards on the account must indicate that the attorney-in-fact has signing powers.

The rights of an attorney-in-fact continue in effect until the principal either cancels them or dies. Mental incompetency of either party also makes the power of attorney invalid.

Joint Accounts

Two or more depositors may share a single checking account. In such a case, the depositors usually are referred to as *joint tenants*. The most common example involves a husband and wife. Legally, neither party has exclusive rights to the account; both are considered to have equal rights to it. Therefore, in most cases either party may issue checks and otherwise issue instructions to the bank. Again, the signature cards must clearly show the legal arrangement.

Joint accounts generally carry *rights of survivorship*. Unfortunately, this term is frequently misunderstood. It does *not* always mean that, upon the death of one party, the other has a complete claim, free of any complications, to the balance of the account. Both the bank and the parties to the account should understand that state laws may apply to this relationship; for example, in some states the survivor must pay taxes on the balance in the account before the bank can allow withdrawals from it.

EXHIBIT 5.2
POWER OF ATTORNEY FORM

	DEMAND ACCOUNT
	SAVINGS ACCOUNT

ACCEPTED BY	OFFICE
	17

Know all Men by these Presents

THAT _I, TERRENCE O'NEIL_

do make, constitute and appoint _GABRIEL ROMERO_

_____ true and lawful attorney for _me_ and in _my_

name:

1. To withdraw all or any part of the balance in _my_

account number _2345678_ in
THE INSTITUTE NATIONAL BANK
by drawing checks, if a demand account; or, by giving the required prior notice and by executing the proper withdrawal order or receipt if a savings account.

2. To endorse notes, checks, drafts or bills of exchange which may require _my_ endorsement for deposit as cash in, or for collection by said bank.

3. To do all lawful acts requisite for effecting any of the above premises; hereby ratifying and confirming all that the said attorney shall do therein by virtue of these presents.

This power of attorney shall continue in force until due notice of the revocation thereof shall be given in writing.

In witness whereof _I_ have hereunto set _my_ hand and seal this _10th_ day of _April_ , one thousand nine hundred and _eighty-eight_

SIGNED, SEALED AND DELIVERED
IN THE PRESENCE OF

George Williams _Terrance O'Neil_

95

It is also possible to establish a joint account that does not carry rights of survivorship. These accounts may involve two or more tenants, and are called *tenants-in-common* relationships. This kind of account generally requires that no party may act alone; all checks or other documents must contain the combination of signatures that was specified at the time the account was opened. The combination of signatures may be changed if done in compliance with bank policy and regulatory statutes.

Some states have community property laws. Banks in those states are governed by the community property laws as they apply to joint accounts. The foregoing general information must then be modified accordingly.

Proprietorship Accounts and Fictitious Names

It is common for individuals to own and operate businesses under names other than their own. To identify the nature of his business in the minds of his customers, Harry Cole may devise some easily remembered, eye-catching trade name—or he may simply choose to have the business known as Harry's Travel Agency. Susan Jackson, operating a stationery store and newsstand, may elect to have it known as Village News and Office Supplies. Any individual who operates a business as a sole owner is a *proprietor*. The business itself is known as a *proprietorship*.

If the proprietorship is operated under the individual's own name, a bank would require identification, references, and signature cards in order to open the account. However, when any name is used other than the individual's own name, it is essential that the connection between the owner and that "fictitious" trade name be legally established.

For this reason, many states require that a proprietor who uses a fictitious name register it with state or county authorities. The bank should obtain a copy of the form used for this purpose. The form usually is called a *business certificate* or certificate of registration of trade name (see exhibit 5.3). Also, the term "DBA" (doing business as) often is used in connection with this type of business venture. The implication is that (for example) Harry Cole *is* Harry's Travel Agency, conducting a business under the trade name. Harry Cole, therefore, can sign checks on an account in the business name, can endorse checks on that account, can enter into legal contracts using the fictitious name, and can sue or be sued as a business entity.

Partnership Accounts

When two or more individuals enter into a business venture together, they may form a *partnership*. The business may operate under the names of the individual partners (for example, Mitchell and Wilson; Brown, Walker, and Brown) or it may use a trade name. Partnerships are widely

EXHIBIT 5.3
BUSINESS CERTIFICATE

Business Certificate

I HEREBY CERTIFY *that I am conducting or transacting business under the name or designation* of PRIDE INSTALLERS

at 4200 Trinity Place
City or Town of   New York   *County of* New York   *State of New York*

My full name is Solomon S. Miller
and I reside at 6200 Riverdale Avenue, Bronx, New York 10471

I FURTHER CERTIFY *that I am the successor in interest to*

the person or persons heretofore using such name or names to carry on or conduct or transact business.

IN WITNESS WHEREOF, *I have this* tenth *day of* June *19XX*, *made and signed this certificate.*

COUNTY
CLERK'S
SEAL

Solomon S. Miller

- Print or type name
- If under 21 years of age, state "I am _____ years of age."

STATE OF NEW YORK
COUNTY OF   New York   } *ss.:*

On this tenth *day of* June *19XX* , *before me personally appeared*

Solomon S. Miller

to me known to me to be the individual described in and who executed the foregoing certificate, and he
thereupon has duly acknowledged to me that he executed the same.

NOTARY
STAMP

J. Smith

_____
Notary Public

used in American business. Many law firms, accounting firms, and brokerage houses are partnerships. Most states have adopted laws pertaining to the conduct of this type of business and the rights and obligations of each partner. These laws have a direct bearing on the bank-partnership relationship.

Typically, a legal document called a *partnership agreement* is drawn up at the time the partnership is established. The agreement states the contributions each partner has made to the business, the nature of the business, and the proportions in which each partner will share in profits or losses. Any one member of the partnership may be empowered to act for all the others, so that the actions of that partner are legally binding on all the other partners.

In opening an account for a partnership, a bank should obtain completed signature cards for all partners who will be authorized to issue checks, apply for loans for the partnership, and otherwise deal with the bank. The bank also should obtain a copy of the partnership agreement. This agreement may be recorded on a standard bank form or on a form drawn up and executed by the partners. If the partnership operates under a trade name, the bank should have in its files a copy of the registration certificate.

Partnership law generally states that the death of any partner automatically terminates the partnership. However, it is recognized that enforcement of such laws would create unreasonable hardship if a business had to be dissolved immediately. Therefore, provision is made for the surviving partners to reorganize the partnership. The rights of those survivors include the authority to handle all assets of the partnership, including bank balances. The estate of a deceased partner cannot take control of a partnership bank account. When the death of a partner occurs, the bank must obtain new documents that reflect the reorganization of the business.

Corporate Accounts

The third type of business venture for which a bank may open a checking account is the *corporation*. This is an entirely different form of legal entity. Regardless of its size, a corporation is owned by its stockholders, who have contributed their capital and have received shares of stock in exchange. A corporation legally cannot exist without stockholders. It may be a small, husband-and-wife business, or a large industrial giant with annual sales of billions of dollars, but the same principle applies: In the first example, the husband and wife are the only stockholders; in the second example there may be thousands of stockholders.

Most commercial banks in the United States operate under charters as legal corporations. The incorporators of a new bank contribute their capital, apply for a charter, issue shares of stock, and establish a legal entity.

In recent years, virtually all the largest banks have converted from simple corporate ownership, forming bank holding companies in order to expand their business activities into areas the banks as such could not legally enter into. A holding company is a legal entity formed to hold a controlling stock interest in other companies. In the case of a bank holding company, the holding company controls one or more banks through stock ownership.

In opening business accounts, banks recognize that a corporation has essential differences from other types of business entities. While the stockholders of a corporation are its legal owners, they usually are not liable for its debts. A corporation is unaffected by the deaths of any of its stockholders or officers; legally, it can exist forever. In addition to having stockholders, a corporation must have a board of directors, who are elected by the stockholders, and officers, who are designated by the directors. Proprietorships and partnerships do not have stockholders, directors, or officers. A corporation has the same legal status as a person in that it can sue or be sued.

The directors constitute the active, governing body of the corporation and are responsible for the conduct of the business. They can be held legally responsible for negligence and for all that they have done or failed to do. Directors of a corporation can be sued individually or as a group.

It is only through the directors of a corporation that the legal right to open and operate a bank account can be established. Therefore, the basis for all corporate accounts is a form known as a *corporate resolution* (exhibit 5.4), a certified copy of which is filed with the bank. This legal document, signed by the corporate secretary, gives evidence that the directors met on a specified date, approved the opening of a bank account, and authorized certain corporate officers to sign checks, to borrow on behalf of the corporation, or otherwise to issue instructions to the bank.

Many banks have their own standard corporate resolution forms, and supply these to customers to be executed and signed. Where legally required, the resolution also must carry the corporate seal. If a corporation wishes to use its own form instead of the bank's, the document must meet all of the bank's legal requirements.

Every corporation operates under the terms of a charter granted by the state that gives it the legal right to conduct business. A set of bylaws usually supplements the charter. The bylaws are adopted by the corporate stockholders and describe the purposes and nature of the business, the duties of individually titled officers, and other business matters. In opening an account for a corporation, a bank may ask for copies of the charter and bylaws.

As mentioned earlier, a corporation may be formed by only two people, who serve simultaneously as the stockholders, officers, and directors. On the other hand, a large industrial firm may have hundreds of corporate officers: a chairman, a president, executive and senior vice

EXHIBIT 5.4
CORPORATE RESOLUTION

CORPORATE RESOLUTION

Anchor Broadcasting Co. Inc.
(account title)

ACCOUNT NUMBER 7964625
OFFICE 20
ACCEPTED BY (JM)
DATE 5-17-19XX

"RESOLVED, that an account in the name of this Corporation be established or maintained with the INSTITUTE NATIONAL BANK and that all checks, drafts, notes, or other orders for the payment of money drawn on or payable against said account shall be signed by any **two (2)** (indicate number) person or persons from time to time holding the following offices of this Corporation.

President   Treasurer   _____

Secretary   _____   _____

Indicate title only; not individual's name.

FURTHER RESOLVED, that said INSTITUTE NATIONAL BANK is hereby authorized and directed to pay all checks, drafts, notes and orders so signed whether payable to bearer, or to the order of any person, firm or corporation, or to the order of any person signing the same.

The undersigned Secretary of **Anchor Broadcasting Co. Inc.** (name of corporation) hereby certifies that the above is a true and correct copy of a resolution regularly adopted by the Board of Directors of the Corporation at a duly called meeting of the Board held on **5-10-19XX** (date), at which a quorum was present and voting throughout; and that said resolution is presently in full force and effect.

I further certify that the persons named below are those duly elected or appointed to the Corporate Office or capacity set forth opposite their respective names.

NAME	TITLE
John Little	President
Arthur Burnstein	Secretary
Rose Mary Forest	Treasurer

In Witness Whereof, I have hereunto set my hand and affixed hereto the Corporate Seal of this Corporation

(Corporate Seal)

Arthur Burnstein
Secretary

Dated: May 15, 19XX

---

presidents, vice presidents, a treasurer, a secretary, a controller, and numerous assistants to those titles. An official title does not necessarily give an individual the right to transact business with the bank on behalf of the corporation. *Only* those individuals authorized by the directors can do so. Therefore, whenever the corporate resolution or bylaws mention official titles, the bank must have on file the names and signatures of the people who hold those titles and who are authorized to deal with the bank on the corporation's behalf.

The signature cards filed by the bank for every corporate account must show the title and signature of each designated officer or other authorized signer. If the corporation names new officers who are authorized to deal with the bank, or if an existing signer dies, retires, or resigns, new signature cards must be obtained. An official notice of the election of new officers should be executed by the corporate secretary and filed with the bank.

Through mergers or acquisitions, corporations often change their official names to reflect new or expanded activities. The XYZ Machine Tool Company, for example, may amend its existing corporate charter (with the approval of its stockholders) or apply for a new charter so that its name becomes XYZ Industries, Inc. In this way, it publicizes the fact that it is no longer merely a manufacturer of tools. Documentary evidence of the new corporate name must be certified by state authorities and furnished to the bank.

A corporation can be identified by its legal name. When it obtains its charter it is legally required to use Inc., Corporation, Incorporated, or Limited as part of its official title. For this reason, every corporation is considered to be operating under a fictitious name. If Harry Cole were to change the nature of his business and apply for a corporate charter, the name would have to reflect that change; for example, it might become Harry's Travel Agency, Inc.

The laws of many states now allow individuals in certain professions to obtain charters under a corporate type of organization. For example, a doctor named William Hamilton might form a professional corporation (P.C.). The legal name of the business would be William Hamilton, M.D., P.C. By forming a corporation, Dr. Hamilton gains certain legal advantages. In opening an account for him, the bank must recognize the special nature of his corporation and obtain the appropriate documentation.

In addition to the standard checking account, a corporation may wish to open a money market account in order to gain interest on excess funds that are not immediately needed. Money market accounts for corporations legally are permitted under the terms of the Garn-St Germain Act and are paid interest at competitive rates. The bank may establish a minimum requirement for the account balance, and must impose certain restrictions on the number of withdrawals that the corporation can make during a month.

Fiduciary Accounts

The word *fiduciary* comes from the Latin word meaning faith or trust. It is used in banking to cover a variety of relationships in which one party is handling property for the benefit of another. These relationships may be very simple and relatively informal, or they may be extremely complex. An account established in trust for a minor child will usually involve only a basic document and may not maintain large balances; on the other hand, an account established for the executor or administrator of a substantial estate is far more complicated, requires more documentation, and may carry large balances until the estate is finally settled. The duties of executors and administrators are explained in detail in chapter 12.

Fiduciary accounts must be opened and handled with the same degree of care as checking accounts for other customers. Suppose that Matilda Henderson presents herself to the bank as the relative of a newborn child, and wishes to open an account on the child's behalf, with herself as trustee. Her identity is subject to the usual checking by the bank. Her legal authority, however, is self-established: she is voluntarily creating a relationship for the infant's benefit. The child obviously cannot execute any documents giving her the right to do so. The tendency among banks is to handle these informal ("Totten") trusts with a minimum of documentation.

On the other hand, if James Wilson, according to the terms of the will of a deceased person, has been made the executor of an estate, legally he is responsible for actions affecting that estate. The bank's approach to opening an account for him in that capacity will be quite different from its approach in Ms. Henderson's case. As executor, Mr. Wilson is responsible for determining the total value of the estate, paying all taxes, debts, and claims, and then distributing the remainder according to the terms of the will. In addition to obtaining signature cards, the bank must acquire some proof of Wilson's right to act for the estate. Similarly, if an individual has been appointed by a court or by a legal agreement as an *administrator, trustee, conservator,* or *guardian,* the bank would require all the necessary documents establishing his or her authority. Again, signature cards would be necessary.

The questions of identity, capacity, and authority as they apply to fiduciary accounts clearly depend on the type of account being opened. Many states have adopted the Uniform Fiduciaries Act. This act contains provisions that apply to fiduciary accounts and contains guidelines for banks on the type and extent of documentation that should be obtained. It also outlines the steps that banks should take to maintain and police fiduciary accounts.

The documents a bank might need in the case of complex, formal fiduciary relationships would include a certified copy of the court decree that appointed the fiduciary, testamentary letters, or a copy of the agreement that gave one party the right to handle the property of another.

Public Funds Accounts

Thousands of government agencies receive and disburse funds on behalf of the communities and citizens they serve. The Internal Revenue Service collects taxes for the federal government and issues refund checks; an individual state collects revenues and pays expenses; a turnpike authority collects tolls, pays suppliers, and issues checks for its employees' payroll; a city or town receives revenue-sharing payments from the federal government, collects real estate and other taxes, and makes its own disbursements. Government entities have debt service, payroll, and public assistance payments to make. All these activities require bank accounts. Because in most instances the funds involved are considered public funds to be used for the public's benefit, the general term *public funds accounts* is used to describe relationships opened for any department, agency, authority, or other entity of any federal, state, or local government or political subdivision.

The unit of government must officially appoint the banks with which it wishes to open accounts. State and local laws usually prescribe the procedures that must be followed in each case. The bank that opens a public funds account must be guided by these laws.

Generally speaking, all such accounts must be secured by segregated, specific assets in the bank's possession; that is, the bank must set aside U.S. government obligations or other assets of unquestioned value as a form of collateral, protecting the deposited funds. This provides an additional guarantee that public funds never will be lost. If a bank does not possess or cannot obtain enough government securities or other satisfactory assets to be pledged, it must decline to accept a new public funds account.

Informal Relationships

Accounts established for social or fraternal groups, not-for-profit and unincorporated associations and societies, and other informal types of entities constitute the final, broad category of checking accounts. A bowling league opens an account to handle the funds it accumulates during the year through members' dues payments; public contributions for the assistance of victims of some tragedy or disaster are put in another account; an employee group raises money to hold a testimonial or retirement dinner; members of a group or society affiliated with a religious denomination deposit money collected at charitable events and then make disbursements from the account. In instances such as these, the organization opening the account can hardly be expected to provide the bank with legal, formal documents and agreements.

Because such organizations are not listed in state or local government records, the bank that establishes an *informal account* must rely largely on its knowledge of the parties with whom it will be dealing. Signature cards are always needed; beyond that, each situation will dictate what additional letters, forms, agreements, or special documents should be obtained. The bank's legal staff should be consulted if necessary.

SAVINGS AND TIME DEPOSITS

Two essential characteristics differentiate demand deposits from savings and time deposits. The first of these pertains to the intention of the depositor. Funds placed in a demand deposit obviously are intended for near-term use and in most cases will be used to pay current bills and expenses. The second characteristic relates to the laws that permit the payment of interest on savings and time deposits. Since the passage of the Glass-Steagall Act, banks have been prohibited from paying interest on checking accounts as such, and Federal Reserve Board Regulation Q historically has limited the amount of interest that member banks could pay on various types of time and savings deposits. For banks that were not Fed members, state or FDIC laws established similar limits.

Obviously, the distinctions between the two categories of deposits have blurred in recent years—just as the traditional lines of separation between commercial banks and thrift institutions have become less clear-cut. For many years, it was an inflexible principle that savings and time deposits were not payable on demand; today, the NOW account has abolished that principle.

Although the intention of the savings or time depositor is different from that of the checking account customer, and while the impact on the bank of savings and time deposits—especially from the standpoint of interest expense—is different, the bank still must establish beyond reasonable doubt the identity, capacity, and authority of the parties with whom it is dealing. Basic requirements cannot be relaxed or ignored in opening a savings account or issuing a CD. Many frauds perpetrated on banks began with the opening of a modest savings account that was taken for granted and on which standard procedures were not followed.

Like its demand deposit counterpart, the savings account or time deposit creates a contractual agreement between customer and bank. The bank must be satisfied with the agreement and it must know who is authorized to withdraw or otherwise handle funds. The customer also must be made aware of the terms and conditions of the relationship.

Savings Accounts

Savings accounts are part of the "retail" side of banking that most commercial banks traditionally neglected. The funds represented by individual savings traditionally have been deposited almost exclusively with thrift institutions. Money that consumers accumulated and set aside for some future purpose, with the objective of steady growth and regular interest, did not represent the type of deposit that commercial banks sought to attract.

Many savings banks opened in New England in the late seventeenth and early eighteenth centuries to encourage thrift and provide depositories for the small saver. These thrifts operated side-by-side with the commercial banks of that period. Some of these savings banks included words such as "dime" or "dollar" in their titles to indicate that they accepted deposits of extremely small amounts. Similarly, the savings and loan associations came into being to fill needs that commercial banks had neglected; S&Ls accepted deposits from individuals of modest means and used those funds to extend home mortgage credit.

Since World War II, the emphasis on savings accounts at commercial banks has increased as those institutions have come to realize that such accounts represent a valuable source of funds and give the individual depositor added convenience. Savings accounts also are far more stable deposit relationships; that is, their balances do not fluctuate as widely or as rapidly as demand deposits do. Because they are less volatile and can be expected to stay with the banks for longer periods of time, savings accounts traditionally have been used as the funding source for longer-term loans.

While the banks recently have emphasized attracting savings deposits, the thrift institutions have moved in the opposite direction, using their expanded powers to attract various types of business accounts. Because of this, depositors today have far greater freedom of choice in determining where to place their funds, and may have difficulty in differentiating one type of financial institution from another.

Savings accounts typically are opened by or for individuals, jointly for two or more depositors (usually with rights of survivorship and allowing any party to make withdrawals at any time), for fiduciaries, and for not-for-profit or unincorporated associations, societies, and the like. The Federal Reserve changed its regulations in 1975 to allow corporations to open savings accounts at Fed member banks, with a limit of $150,000 on these corporate savings accounts. This action was taken by the Fed to make commercial banks more competitive with thrifts, which had been permitted to offer savings accounts to corporations for many years.

In every case, at the time the savings account is opened the identity of the customer(s) must be clearly established, signature cards must be obtained so that all requests for payment of funds can be authenticated, and any necessary supporting documents must be filed. As an additional safeguard, many banks ask a depositor to supply some highly personal piece of identifying data, such as his or her mother's maiden name.

The "scrambled signature" system has become widely used as a security measure. This system builds a special pattern into a camera lens, so that the depositor's signature is distorted and cannot be read by the naked eye. When a withdrawal slip or other document is presented, the signature is compared to that on the bank's signature card using this type of lens.

Traditionally, the identifying characteristic of a savings account was a passbook. Many customers still insist on having a passbook as proof of the existence of the account and as evidence of their deposits, withdrawals, and the posting of interest. It is gratifying to a customer to see the growth of an account displayed in print in a passbook and to have the feeling of security that a passbook provides. Nevertheless, with modern technology the passbook has become completely obsolete, and the expense and effort on the bank's part in posting entries to it can be avoided through automation.

Modern methods make it possible for banks to eliminate passbooks and to place the entire savings function on computer. On-line systems enable tellers at any location to have access to information on the status of an account. Instead of passbooks, customers receive quarterly statements that show every transaction, including interest postings. "Combination" statements, most often generated monthly, include this data along with activity on the customer's checking account. Combination statements may also show a customer's loan outstandings and bank card usage and outstandings.

Many of the safeguards and procedures discussed earlier regarding checking accounts apply to savings accounts. In accepting deposits to savings accounts, tellers must watch for noncash items, examine currency to detect any counterfeits, and insist on proper endorsement of all checks so that the bank is protected as a holder in due course.

Signature cards govern the operation of savings accounts. The signature card actually constitutes the contract between the bank and its depositor.

Some banks now make it possible for the depositor to have the benefits of money market rates on savings accounts. Automatic transfer services provide for regular movements of funds from a customer's demand deposit balances into a savings account. A bank may also link the two (checking and savings) accounts so that the customer who issues checks for amounts larger than the balance in the checking account in effect authorizes the bank to use the savings account as an offset.

Certificates of Deposit

As competition from other financial institutions has intensified, federal regulators have attempted to help banks by allowing them to offer a wider range of time deposits. Remember the basic difference between these deposits and savings accounts: every time deposit must carry a specific term, while savings deposits have no maturity date and theoretically could be maintained forever. Time deposits now represent by far the largest single component in the banks' total deposit structure.

As mentioned earlier, the introduction in 1961 of the large-denomination ($100,000 or more), negotiable CD helped to change that deposit structure. Their size exempted them from interest rate restrictions; thus, banks could compete freely for deposits to these CDs. However, many other types of CDs had long been used as convenient instruments for business or personal investment.

All CDs are official receipts, issued by a bank, stating that a specified sum of money has been left with the bank for a fixed length of time at a certain rate of interest. If the CD is issued in negotiable form, the holder can easily transfer his or her rights to it through the secondary market.

A new form of time deposit, the *money market certificate,* was introduced in 1978. These certificates required a minimum investment of $10,000 and were issued in non-negotiable form, with interest rates that changed according to the rates on each issue of 6-month U.S. Treasury bills.

Other Time Deposits

In their competitive efforts to attract and retain funds, many banks now offer other types of time deposits. Some offer fixed interest rates while others have variable rates. The fixed rate category includes time deposits for periods that may range from 7 days to 8 years. Banks may specify minimum deposits for time deposits.

Non-Interest-Bearing Time Deposits

Customers traditionally were required to compensate their banks with demand deposits in exchange for credit facilities or services rendered. For many of these customers, direct fee payments have become a much more attractive option in recent years. By paying fees, or borrowing on an "all-in-the-rate" basis and ignoring compensating balances, these customers have freed their funds to be used for other purposes. In some situations, a third option exists: the non-interest-bearing (NIB) time deposit.

NIB deposits carry no direct interest cost to the bank. Because Federal Reserve requirements on all forms of time deposits are significantly lower than on demand deposits, each dollar left in a NIB relationship generates a larger portion of usable funds for the bank. For example, a NIB of $100,000 gives the bank loanable and investable funds of $97,000. At the same time, it gives the customer value as a basis for earnings credits that offset the bank's expenses in providing services or extending credit.

Keogh and IRA Relationships

Since the Great Depression, U.S. society has emphasized the need for some form of retirement security to protect workers. The introduction of the Social Security program is an example of this emphasis; in addition, millions of American workers have enjoyed the benefits of pension plans operated by their employers. Until 1962, however, millions of other workers were at a serious disadvantage. Self-employed individuals (such as lawyers, doctors, accountants, authors, and consultants) had no form of pension coverage, and many workers were employed by companies that did not operate a pension plan. To enable all employed and self-employed persons to make provisions for their retirement and financial security, Congress enacted the Employee Retirement Security Act in 1962 and the Employee Retirement Income Security Act (ERISA) in 1974. These acts allowed qualified individuals to establish their own tax-sheltered plans with banks or other financial institutions. As a result, *Keogh* accounts for the self-employed and *Individual Retirement Accounts* (IRAs) for other workers became possible. Both have become extremely important types of deposit relationships for banks, brokerage firms, insurance companies, and thrift institutions.

The Tax Reform Act of 1986 made significant changes in previous legislation. The act affects retirement accounts in the following significant ways:[8]

- Self-employed individuals may establish and contribute to Keogh plans. The maximum annual contribution to a Keogh is 13.0435 percent of net earnings after certain deductions.
- The minimum age for withdrawals from a Keogh plan is fifty-nine and one-half years. Withdrawals *must* begin during the year when the individual attains the age of seventy and one-half years.
- All money contributed to a Keogh is deductible for federal tax purposes. Interest accruing on all contributions is also exempt from taxes until withdrawn.
- Individuals who are employed by others may establish and contribute to Individual Retirement Accounts (IRAs) under certain conditions.
- Workers who are not covered by employer retirement plans and who are not married to someone who is covered may contribute $2,000 per year ($2,250 for married couples with one income) to IRAs, regardless of earnings. These contributions are fully tax deductible.
- Persons with an adjusted gross income under $25,000 ($40,000 on a joint return) can make fully deductible IRA contributions ($2,000 or $2,250) even if they are covered by employer plans.
- Individuals who are covered by a pension plan and have adjusted gross incomes between $25,000 and $35,000 (or $40,000 and $50,000 on a joint return) can get a partial taxable write-off for their IRA contributions. These individuals lose $1 of IRA deduction for every $5 of adjusted gross income above the threshold.
- Individuals covered by a company pension plan who have adjusted gross incomes of over $35,000 ($50,000 on a joint return) may make IRA contributions up to $2,000 per year; however, their contributions are *not* tax deductible.
- In all cases, interest accruing on Keogh and IRA contributions is non-taxable until withdrawn. Withdrawals *must* begin during the calendar

year in which the individual reaches the age of seventy and one-half years.

As a result of the Tax Reform Act, the 1986 IRA contribution was the last one that was fully deductible for all taxpayers. The impact of this change on commercial banks is severe because, despite intense competition, banks have attracted substantial deposits in IRA plans. At year-end 1986, Merrill Lynch alone held $20 billion in IRA accounts for 1.6 million customers; commercial banks as a group held $72.8 billion, or 40.5 percent of the nationwide total; and thrift institutions as a group were the largest holders, with $96.2 billion in IRAs.[9] The changes mandated by the Tax Reform Act may limit further growth.[10]

Club Accounts

Banks offer various types of club accounts to assist individuals who wish to set aside funds on a regular basis throughout the year. The purpose may be to provide funds for the holiday season (for example, Christmas Club and Hanukkah Club accounts), for a vacation, or for educational expenses. These club accounts are relatively simple and informal.

Club account customers usually execute a signature card and agree to make regular deposits. At the end of the specified period, the bank mails or delivers a check to the depositor or simply credits his or her account. At the option of the bank, interest *may* be paid on all club deposits. The flow of money from banks to consumers during the Christmas-Hanukkah season contributes to the vast increase in spending that occurs at that time of the year.

may pay int or not pay int.

Lifeline Accounts

To encourage thrift among minors, and to ease the financial burden on senior citizens or others who cannot obtain access to financial services because of cost factors, many banks now offer so-called "lifeline" accounts. These are basic accounts on which standard fees and service charges are waived. In the case of younger customers, the balances will accumulate more rapidly; for senior citizens or other individuals who otherwise would be deprived of bank services, concerns over monthly minimum balances or service charges may be avoided.

LEGAL RESTRICTIONS ON DEPOSITS

As part of the overall pattern of regulation and supervision of banking, federal and state authorities customarily have restricted payments of interest to customers and kept the time deposit function separate from the demand deposit function. Although many restrictions have been eliminated during the era of banking deregulation, many remain—and in some cases new restrictions have been imposed.

Prior to the Great Depression, banks commonly paid interest on demand deposits. This practice led to aggressive competition and "bidding wars." While savings and time deposits represented only a small portion of the banks' deposit accounts, banks found their interest expense steadily increasing. This expense could be offset only by making as many loans and investments as possible, in order to maximize income. The greater the emphasis on increased income, the more likely it was that normal credit standards would be lowered and loans of lesser quality approved.

When the Depression occurred, banks found themselves holding quantities of worthless promissory notes representing substandard loans. This was a major factor in the closing of many banks in the early 1930s. The federal and state agencies concerned with this problem reacted by establishing various regulations on interest payments.

The Glass-Steagall Act prohibited interest payments on demand deposits, while Federal Reserve Regulation Q established maximum rates of interest on savings and time deposits. As mentioned earlier, however, Regulation Q was gradually phased out following passage of the Monetary Control Act of 1980. The federal and state regulations remaining in effect are summarized as follows:

- With the exception of NOW accounts, no savings or time deposit is payable on demand.
- Any bank has a legal right to insist on advance notice of a withdrawal from a savings account. This preserves the nature of the relationship as not being payable on demand. Of course, banks do not regularly exercise their right to advance notice, and as a matter of daily practice they allow withdrawals from savings accounts whenever requested. The important point, however, is that they *could* require advance notice at any time as long as they applied the same rules to all depositors, without discrimination of any kind.
- All time deposits exist under a contract that includes a maturity date. If the customer finds it necessary to withdraw funds before that date, a substantial penalty must be charged. Exhibit 5.5 shows the type of statement that makes this clear to customers. A bank also has the legal right to refuse payment of any time deposit before the maturity date if it wishes to make this a matter of policy.
- As a result of the Interest and Dividend Tax Compliance Act of 1983, a Taxpayer Identification Number (TIN) must be assigned for all accounts that are opened for individuals and for all interest-bearing accounts opened for nonindividuals. For an individual, the TIN is his or her Social Security number; if the individual is self-employed or operates a business, the TIN is an Employer Identification Number; and in the case of a corporation, the TIN is an identifying corporate

identification number. If a bank does not comply with the requirements for obtaining TINs from customers, a fine of $50 per account can be levied against it.

- The Bank Secrecy Act requires that all large ($10,000 or more) currency transactions be reported to the Internal Revenue Service. This requirement applies in the case of multiple, same-day currency transactions as well as to single transactions. Records of these large currency transactions must be retained for 5 years. Banks are required to list on the transaction reports the form of identification used by the customer— for example, a credit card number, driver's license, or account number. The simple notation "known customer" is not sufficient. Each currency transaction report must be filed by the bank within 15 days of the event.[11] Congress passed this legislation as a result of allegations of large sums of "laundered" (concealed and made to appear legitimate) money passing through banks and obtained from illegal sources. Many violations of the act by banks have been reported in recent years, and substantial penalties have been imposed on the violators.

Tax Reporting

As the amount of interest paid to depositors has steadily increased, the Internal Revenue Service has become concerned over the reporting of this interest as income to the recipients. All commercial banks, thrift institutions, credit unions, and other organizations that pay interest of $10 or more to any recipient during a calendar year must report that payment to the IRS. Payments must be identified by the recipient's Social Security number, TIN, or corporate identification number. The dollar amount of interest must be reported on Form 1099, and a copy of the form must be sent to the recipient as a reminder that the interest constitutes income to be included on tax returns. Brokerage firms also are required to file Form 1099s on dividend and interest payments to their clients and to report all sales of stock executed for clients during the year.

In connection with the Interest and Dividend Tax Compliance Act, banks paying interest to customers and corporate payers of dividends must impose 20 percent backup withholding before making the actual disbursements unless the recipient has filed a certificate of exemption from withholding.

CROSS-SELLING

Satisfied customers represent the most attractive market for additional selling. In establishing any new account relationship, many banks now complete a profile sheet that describes the new customer and makes him or her a candidate for future marketing efforts. The new checking or savings account customer may also need safe deposit, bank card, automobile or personal loan, IRA or Keogh, or traveler's check services. A

EXHIBIT 5.5
SAMPLE CUSTOMER DISCLOSURE

RULES AND REGULATIONS FOR

STATEMENT SAVINGS ACCOUNTS

A minimum of $100 is required to open. Interest is compounded daily on Collected Balance, and credited to the account as of the close of business the last day of March, June, September and December. A statement is sent to the Depositor at the end of the interest quarter, or monthly when any Electronic Funds Transfers have occurred. Personal Statement Savings accounts are not transferable.

Withdrawals payable to the Depositor, account transfers to the same Depositor through the bank's ATMs, and automatic payments to the Depositor's loan with the Bank are unlimited. All pre-authorized transfers (including automatic and telephone transfers) are limited to 3 per month. If the account has excessive transfers on more than an occasional basis, the Bank will cease payment of interest, as required by federal regulations.

Depositor has the right to withdraw funds at any time; but the Bank reserves the right to require written notice of at least 30 days before paying all or any portion of a deposit.

Service charges on Statement Savings Accounts include $10 if the account closes early (less than 3 months); $6 per quarter for accounts inactive for one year with Ledger Balances less than $300; and when quarterly average Collected Balance is less than $500, $6 per quarter and $2 for each withdrawal in excess of 3 per quarter. Three free pre-authorized electronic debit transactions per quarter are also allowed.

Additional provisions are applicable to all accounts, as stated in the **Rules and Regulations** for personal deposit accounts.

Member:
FDIC EQUAL HOUSING LENDER

homeowner may need a home improvement or home equity loan. The opportunities for cross-selling of bank services are limited only by the extent to which staff members are motivated and willing to identify and use them. From its files of existing customers, a bank easily can develop mailing lists so that new and more attractive interest rates, new types of accounts, and enhanced investment and loan services can be brought to the customers' attention. The convenience of conducting various financial transactions under a single roof, with a bank that has already delivered satisfactory service and demonstrated its capabilities, is a strong selling point. Chapter 14, on bank marketing, will discuss this further.

DISCLOSURES TO CUSTOMERS

Just as the Fed's truth-in-lending regulations require that specific information be disclosed to consumers regarding loan rates, terms, and the like, so several states have enacted legislation that may be called "truth-in-savings." Upon request by a consumer opening an account, these states now call for banks to provide full information on

- the effective annual yield on the account
- the annual rate of simple interest
- the frequency with which interest is compounded and credited
- the amount of interest per year on a balance of $100 and the formula used for interest-rate calculations
- the grace periods that may apply to both deposits and withdrawals
- the service charges and fees that the bank has imposed on each savings account and time deposit

In early 1987, Congress was contemplating legislation that might apply on a nationwide basis, embracing some or all of the above provisions.

SUMMARY

The initial meeting between a representative of the bank and a new customer sets the tone for all their future dealings. A favorable initial impression enhances the image of the bank. The new customer not only becomes a candidate for additional banking services, but is also more likely to recommend the bank to others. If the initial encounter leaves a poor impression in the customer's mind, however, the damage is probably irreparable. In today's financial marketplace, comparable services can be obtained at many institutions other than banks; people who are badly treated during the first contact easily can take their business elsewhere.

Nonetheless, the bank can never lose sight of the fact that a legal contract is usually the end result of the first meeting with a customer. The desire to make a good impression must be secondary to taking appropriate steps to protect the bank and comply with bank policy and federal and state regulations.

The identity of the customer, the nature of the relationship, the legal right of the customer to enter into a contract, and the restrictions that apply to each account must be established and clearly understood when an account is opened. The bank always must know with whom it is dealing and from whom it can properly accept instructions pertaining to the handling of the account. At the same time, the customer must be made aware of the terms and conditions that apply. Banks can avoid a great deal of trouble by exercising diligence and care at the start of an account relationship, as well as throughout its life.

Thrifts, insurance companies, brokerage firms, and a host of non-bank entities compete with banks in today's financial marketplace. While banks are anxious to attract new depositors and maintain existing relationships, they cannot relax their standards.

To meet the needs and objectives of their customers, banks now offer a broad spectrum of checking accounts, savings accounts, and time deposits. Banks remain the dominant group in the financial marketplace.

QUESTIONS FOR DISCUSSION

1. What advantages do bank competitors such as Merrill Lynch and Sears, Roebuck enjoy?

2. How can a bank justify requesting identification and references from a person who merely wants to deposit cash to open an account?

3. What is the difference between the principle of identity and the principle of legal right or authority?

4. What is the importance of interest expense to commercial banks?

5. What rights does an attorney-in-fact possess in handling the account of a principal? What document conveys those rights? How long do the rights last?

6. What is the difference between a proprietorship and a partnership?

7. Identify the three groups involved in operating a corporation.

8. What forms or documents should a bank obtain in connection with the opening of an account for a partnership, a corporation, a "doing-business-as" proprietorship, and a government agency?

9. What is the difference between savings deposits and time deposits?

10. What benefits or advantages do NOW accounts offer to customers?

11. What is the difference between Keogh accounts and IRAs?

12. What problems of tax reporting do interest-bearing relationships create for banks?

NOTES

1. "The Top 300 Commercial Banks," *American Banker*, March 19, 1987, p. 41.

2. Carol J. Loomis, "The Fight for Financial Turf," *Fortune* (December 28, 1981), p. 57.

3. Laura Gross, "The American Express Banker," *American Banker*, June 11, 1986, p. 1.

4. Paul A. Eisenstein, "Here Come the Auto Companies," *United States Banker* (March 1986), p. 32.

5. Christine Pavel and Harvey Rosenblum, "Financial Darwinism," *Staff Memorandum 1985–86,* Federal Reserve Bank of Chicago, p. 5.

6. Laura Gross, "Citicorp to Rethink National Strategy," *American Banker*, March 27, 1987, p. 1.

7. Laura Gross, "New Chase Account Ties CDs to Stocks," *American Banker*, March 23, 1987, p. 1.

8. Robert A. Bennett, "An Ambitious Savings Experiment Comes to an End," *The New York Times*, February 15, 1987, p. F8.

9. "IRA and Keogh Account Growth," *American Banker*, March 30, 1987, p. 27.

10. Robert M. Garsson, "'86 in Washington: Banking Industry Has Had Better Years in the Capital," *American Banker*, February 4, 1987, p. 1.

11. Jay Rosenstein, "Treasury Issues New Rules on Cash Reporting," *American Banker*, April 7, 1987, p. 1.

For More Information

American Bankers Association. *Bank Fact Book.* Washington, D.C., 1983.

Aspinwall, Richard C., and Robert A. Eisenbeis. *Handbook for Banking Strategy.* New York: John Wiley & Sons, Inc., 1985.

Bank Administration Institute. *Opening New Accounts.* Rolling Meadows, Ill., 1975.

Compton, Eric N. *The New World of Commercial Banking.* Lexington, Mass.: D.C. Heath and Company/Lexington Books, 1987.

Federal Reserve Bank of Richmond. *Instruments of the Money Market.* 5th ed. Richmond, Va., 1981.

6.

PAYING
TELLER
FUNCTIONS

LEARNING OBJECTIVES

After completing this chapter, you will be able to

●

distinguish between *paying* and *cashing* checks

●

explain why checks presented for payment must pass certain tests

●

list some of the risks a teller assumes in cashing checks

●

describe the actions tellers should take during holdup attempts

●

explain how tellers are important as the bank's prime contact with individuals who present checks

When a teller is handed a check and is asked to give coin and currency in exchange for it, two delicate factors are involved: customer goodwill, and sound banking practices and policies. Customers expect every teller to be fast and accurate, particularly on those hectic days when lines are long and tempers short. The individual who presents a check to a teller only to be told that there is some problem that requires time and effort to resolve is likely to complain about being needlessly questioned and delayed.

Too often, that individual does not understand why his or her check cannot immediately be converted into legal tender and why it requires the approval of an officer or some other authorized person. Many people believe that any check can be presented to any bank for cash.

To enhance its public image, a bank may do everything possible to shorten the lines of waiting customers and to hand over currency and coin, in exchange for checks, with a minimum of delay and inconvenience. However, if the bank neglects any of the basic steps in the decision-making process and fails to appreciate the risks that may be involved, losses inevitably will result. All tellers must understand the responsibilities they assume whenever they pay or cash checks.

✦ PAYING AND CASHING CHECKS ✦

Note that two verbs, *pay* and *cash*, are used. To the general public, the second verb alone would suffice; if asked why they are going to the bank, people generally answer that they want to have a check *cashed*. Few, if any, would answer that they want to have a check *paid*. Nonetheless, every teller must recognize at all times that there is a world of technical and legal difference between the two functions.

Paying a check is a legal obligation of the drawee bank if all requirements and tests are met. *Cashing* a check, on the other hand, is a service that banks perform as an accommodation or courtesy. Banks legally are required to *pay* checks unless there is a valid reason for their refusing to do so; they are not required to *cash* checks. Legislation passed by the U.S. Senate in March 1987—but still pending a decision by the House at the time this textbook went to press—may require banks to give cash for all U.S. government checks to customers who present a bank-issued identification card. The terms *pay* and *cash* may be misunderstood by the public, but they should never be confused by a bank employee. Each involves different rules and different risks.

Paying Checks

One of the significant changes in banking in recent years has increased the attractiveness of checking accounts to consumers. In January 1985 the regulatory minimum balance requirement for Super-NOW accounts (which offer unlimited check-writing privileges and pay an unregulated market interest rate) was lowered from $2,500 to $1,000. In January 1986 this requirement was eliminated, as was the 5.25 percent ceiling on regular NOW account interest rates. As a result, families in 1986 found it more convenient to use interest-bearing accounts that carried check-writing privileges.

Modern technology such as the automated teller machine (ATM) makes it possible for ever-increasing numbers of individuals to obtain cash at locations other than tellers' windows. Nevertheless, a 1986 survey conducted under Federal Reserve auspices showed that only 13 percent of the consumer population used ATMs to acquire cash. Sixty-one percent either presented a check to a bank teller in order to obtain coin and currency, or made a withdrawal from a savings account. In 1986 an estimated 550 million checks per month were used to obtain cash.[1] The percentage of that volume that was presented directly to the drawee banks by the drawers is not available, but in most cases the banks involved probably were *paying* rather than *cashing* the checks.

As mentioned earlier, a check is not money; it is a claim to money, an order to a drawee to make payment. In chapter 8, which deals with bookkeeping in banks, nine tests will be described that can be applied by a drawee to determine whether a check should be honored and charged to the drawer's account. At a teller's window, an on-us check can be subjected to the same nine tests. If the answers to the questions raised by those tests are satisfactory, the drawee *must* honor the instructions given to it and, upon request, convert the check into coin and currency. The Uniform Commercial Code specifically states that under these circumstances the check has been legally *paid*, just as if it had been presented to the drawee's bookkeeping department, examined, and posted to an account. The process of paying a check is equivalent to debiting it to an account.

This type of situation commonly involves a personal checking account. Depositors regard the funds on deposit as immediately convertible into cash. When the need for coin and currency arises, they issue checks payable to "cash" or to themselves and present them to tellers. A similar understanding supports the like treatment of demand deposits and coin and currency when the national money supply is calculated.

In examining an on-us check made payable to cash or to the named party presenting it, a teller easily can

- ascertain whether the check is drawn on an open account
- determine that the account has a sufficient and available balance

- verify that the drawer's signature is both genuine and authorized
- verify that the check is properly dated and not altered
- find out whether a stop-payment order is on file against the check
- find out if there is a "hold" on the account that would prevent payment of the check
- obtain a proper endorsement

The teller in this case has access to all the necessary data, and decisions are relatively easy to make. On-line terminal systems, which directly connect tellers' stations to the bank's computer, can simplify and expedite the verification process.

Paying checks is further streamlined if the bank provides customers with personalized identification cards. These usually contain the depositor's signature and account number, and may include a photograph. The cards are particularly valuable at banks that operate a network of branches. A customer who maintains a personal account at one branch can obtain cash using personal checks drawn on that account at any other branch without having to obtain official approval. Customers also may use the identification cards to facilitate purchases from local merchants.

Legally, checks payable to cash are *bearer instruments* and are presumed to belong to the person who presents them for encashment. A teller to whom this type of check is presented should ask that it be endorsed at the window. The endorsement provides the only valid trail showing where the funds went.

When a teller pays a check, his or her bank is the drawee and all necessary information is available so that a decision can be made. In paying the check, the teller follows the drawer's exact, written instructions. This is not the case in *cashing* checks.

Cashing Checks

On any business day, large volumes of payroll and dividend checks, public assistance and tax refund checks, and simple personal checks are presented to tellers to be *cashed*. The term *cashed* is used when the checks are drawn on other banks. Tellers assume a far greater risk in giving coin and currency in exchange for items drawn on other banks. The risk is greater because the necessary information about the items is not readily available. The teller has no way of determining if the account on which the check is drawn is open, and cannot verify the drawer's signature. He or she has no knowledge whether a stop-payment order has been placed on the check, or if any "hold" affects the account. Perhaps most important, the teller is entirely unaware of the balance in the drawer's account. The balance may be insufficient or uncollected, in which case the drawee bank may return the check long after the payee has left with the funds. In cashing checks, a teller can examine *only* for correct date, alteration, and proper endorsement.

Because of this lack of information, banks cash checks only when there is a valid reason for doing so and when the teller is satisfied that the amount of the check can be recovered if necessary. The payee's endorsement is of prime importance: it makes the paying bank a holder in due course. A teller who cashes a check should make sure that it has been endorsed exactly as payable. The teller may also note, under the endorsement, the identification that was presented.

If the risk in cashing checks is far greater than that incurred in paying them, why do banks cash checks at all? Banks must provide services. The risks of cashing checks are assumed because there is sufficient reason for providing this service.

Assume, for example, that XYZ Corporation carries its main corporate account at Bank *A* but also maintains a payroll account with Bank *B*. The corporation asks Bank *A* to cash payroll checks presented to it with proper employee identification, and signs an agreement indemnifying Bank *A* against any losses. The corporation's employees are told that they can, if they wish, cash their payroll checks at Bank *A*. Had Bank *A* refused the corporation's request for check-cashing services, it would have placed the entire business relationship in jeopardy. This conceivably could have led to the loss of the corporate account.

In another everyday situation, a depositor, well known to the teller and maintaining a satisfactory account with the bank, presents a check drawn on another bank and asks that it be cashed. Discretion, tact, and good judgment are the keys to this situation. Technically, the teller has every right to insist that the customer deposit the check and wait to draw against it until the funds have become collected and available. Or, the teller might insist that the customer simply deposit the check and issue a new check drawn against his or her own account. That legal right, however, need not be exercised in every case. A teller may be handed a dividend check for $50, payable to an individual who has had an account with the teller's bank for many years. If the teller curtly refuses to cash the check on the grounds that it is drawn on another bank, his or her refusal can destroy all the goodwill that has been built up over a period of years. As a service to the depositor, the teller should cash the check, noting the customer's account number on the back as an audit trail. The key here is knowing the customer.

Many depositors believe that their possession of a bank account automatically means that they can cash checks against it. Obviously, from the bank's standpoint this is not true. A bank may be willing to cash checks because the individual presenting them is a depositor, but even in these cases the bank may place a hold on the depositor's account for the amount of the check(s). The hold is a means of protecting the bank. A bank account should be considered a vehicle for depositing and issuing checks, not an automatic justification for cashing.

Tellers' authority to cash checks is determined by bank policy. Generally, the latitude given to tellers in check cashing reflects their experience and possibly their record of past performance. Dollar limits can be established for new tellers and subsequently raised if their performance warrants it. Inevitably, however, situations arise in which a person presenting a check for encashment must be referred to a customer service representative, an officer, or some other authority. If this is done tactfully, so that the individual is made aware of the reason for the referral, no ill will need be created.

Tellers should explain to the party presenting the check that it is not necessarily the "goodness" of the check that is in question. Rather, it is a question of whether a bank should hand over coin and currency in exchange for a check about which it knows virtually nothing, drawn on another bank. The bank must protect itself against the risks of providing check-cashing services. A letter of indemnification from a business to which check-cashing privileges have been extended, or the placing of a hold on the account of a depositor for whom a check has been cashed are reasonable means of protection for a bank to require in rendering this service.

In many states, nonbank "check-cashing services" will, under specified conditions, give currency and coin in exchange for payroll or other checks. They charge a fee for doing so, typically a percentage of the dollar amount of the check. In most cases, these services are licensed by the state in which they function. The fees they collect reflect the risk they are willing to assume for this service.

In the Minneapolis-St. Paul area, for example, many banks refuse to cash checks for individuals who do not have accounts with them. As a result, approximately 10 entities with names such as Money Express, Easy Money, and UnBank offer check-cashing services and charge fees as high as 10 percent of the face amount of the check.[2]

HOLDUPS

When the famous bank robber Willie Sutton was asked why he chose banks as his target on so many occasions, he replied, "Because that's where the money is." In the annual crime statistics published by the Federal Bureau of Investigation, one of the most distressing figures shows regular increases in the number of bank holdups. Despite all that banks have done to make holdups difficult to commit and unprofitable to the perpetrators, the frequency of robberies continues to grow.

Every banking office is a source of temptation to the would-be robber. This temptation is compounded when the bank has not taken the proper measures to keep tellers' supplies of cash to a workable minimum or when some other lack of proper security measures is obvious. Law enforcement agencies repeatedly have said that certain banks virtually invited holdups by ignoring the essentials of internal security.

Even when banks rigorously control supplies of cash, holdup attempts still occur with alarming regularity. Robbers may target days when banks are known to have large amounts of cash on hand—for example, during the Christmas shopping season, on active payroll days, or on days when direct deposit of Social Security or other checks has taken place.

Banks have a basic responsibility to protect depositors' funds, but that protection is not the personal responsibility of each teller when lives are at stake. During holdups, individual displays of heroism by tellers are *not* expected and should *not* be contemplated or encouraged. Bank robbers are always unpredictable, often irrational, and frequently desperate. Tellers who put up a show of resistance or who try to use force to prevent a holdup are risking not only their own personal safety, but the safety of other bank personnel and customers who happen to be on the premises at the time.

Most banks are required by law to equip their premises with cameras and burglar alarms. In addition, many have installed bullet-proof plastic shields in front of each teller's station and have armed guards on duty. Nevertheless, in a robbery attempt the teller is always the first line of defense, and no type of security system can be more effective than the actions he or she takes during a holdup. While stressing that physical resistance is unwise, every teller-training program should emphasize the positive actions that tellers can take. Bank robbery is a federal offense, and tellers can help the authorities in apprehending the criminals by following certain basic procedures.

For example, during a holdup attempt, tellers should make every effort to remain calm and take note of the bandit's physical characteristics. Tellers should try to observe the robber's height and weight, scars, and any other identifying features (see exhibit 6.1). Tellers can activate silent alarms by using a foot pedal or device in the cash drawer. Decoy or marked money can be handed over during a holdup, in the hope that it can be traced to the perpetrator. Some banks even prepare special bundles of money that contain an exploding device filled with a conspicuous dye. Anything given to the teller, such as a holdup note, should be kept so that fingerprints or other identifying evidence can be checked.

Every holdup is a traumatic experience for the bank personnel involved. Thorough training in the recommended procedures to be followed in holdups is absolutely necessary. Even though there is no way of predicting the reactions of either the teller or the robber, the importance of remaining calm cannot be overemphasized. There are many recorded instances in which a simple, calm approach completely thwarted the holdup attempt.

In one incident, a person who had staged a holdup earlier in the day returned to the same teller in the same bank for a second attempt. Law enforcement officials happened to be questioning the teller when the robber made his second appearance. She was able, calmly and quietly, to point him out, and he was apprehended at once. In other situations,

EXHIBIT 6.1
PHYSICAL DESCRIPTION FORM

COLOR CAUCASIAN SEX MALE NATIONALITY EUROPEAN (NORTH) AGE 25-30 HEIGHT 6' WEIGHT 170

BUILD HUSKY - WELL- BUILT COMPLEXION LIGHT HAIR BLONDE - WAVY EYES GREEN - LARGE
(THIN, STOCKY, ETC.) (LIGHT, DARK, RUDDY, ETC) (COLOR, WAVY, STRAIGHT, LONG, SHORT, HOW COMBED, ETC.) (COLOR, SMALL, LARGE, ETC.)

NOSE MEDIUM EARS MEDIUM GLASSES NONE MUSTACHE OR BEARD SMALL MUSTACHE
(LARGE, SMALL, BROAD, PUG, ETC.) (PROMINET, SMALL ETC.) (DESCRIBE FRAMES) (COLOR, SHAPE, ETC.)

MASK OR FALSEFACE NONE SCARS OR MARKS SMALL MOLE ON LEFT CHEEK
(TYPE, COLOR, ETC.) (TATOOS, BIRTHMARKS, FACIAL BLEMISHES, ETC.)

DISTINGUISHING CHARACTERISTICS CONFIDENT MANNERISMS: WELL- DRESSED: PROFESSIONAL
(HOW WOULD YOU PICK THIS PERSON OUT OF A CROWD?)

MISCELLANEOUS

WEAPON EXHIBITED SATURDAY NIGHT
(REVOLVER, AUTOMATIC, KNIFE, ETC.)
SPECIAL - CHROME COLOR

SPEECH EDUCATED: CLEAR -
VERY PRECISE IN DIRECTIONS

ANY NAMES USED NONE

MANNERISMS LEFT HANDED
(RIGHT OR LEFT HANDED, UNUSUAL WALK OR CARRIAGE
CHEWING ON TOOTHPICK
NERVOUS HABIT, ETC.)

CLOTHING
(DESCRIBE COLOR, TYPE OF MATERIAL, STYLE, ETC.)

HAT NONE

OVERCOAT NONE

RAINCOAT NONE

JACKET BLUE BLAZER

SUIT NONE

TROUSERS BLACK

SHIRT LIGHT BLUE

TIE NONE- OPEN COLLAR

SHOES BLACK

OTHER CLOTHING NONE

PROMPTLY FILL OUT THIS FORM AS ACCURATELY AND AS COMPLETELY AS POSSIBLE AND GIVE IT TO BRANCH MANAGER.

125

tellers have kept their poise and, while questioning the bandit on the details of a note, have attracted the attention of bank guards who then captured the robber on the spot.

By endeavoring to remain calm, by avoiding the use of physical force, and by following procedures that will help authorities to apprehend the criminal, every teller can help protect the bank, its staff, and its customers.

FRAUDULENT SCHEMES AND PRACTICES

The very nature of banking provides swindlers, thieves, and confidence men and women with opportunities for their fraudulent practices. The criminals who seek to defraud banks often are highly skilled, constantly are developing new methods to deceive banks or to frustrate the banks' security measures, and may be thoroughly familiar with a particular bank's procedures. Therefore, teller training cannot simply end with graduation from the bank's formal program; it must be continuous.

As discussed earlier, the split deposit is one of the most frequently used methods of illegally obtaining funds. Another technique consists of forging a bank officer's initials on the back of a check to show that it has been approved for cashing; the teller who does not verify this, or the bank that does not use a special code along with the officer's initials, assumes a real risk. Frequently, an individual who is trying to push through a fraudulent check will try to engage the teller in a steady stream of conversation in the hope of creating a distraction. Telephone calls may be used to give a teller false instructions on a check that will be presented for cashing or a payroll that is to be prepared. Tellers must constantly be on the alert. Unfortunately, this is particularly true in the case of young, relatively inexperienced tellers, who are often singled out by criminals as likely victims.

Bank customers may be the unwitting victims of other forms of bank frauds. For example, individuals claiming to be bank examiners sometimes have contacted depositors. Explaining that they are attempting to apprehend a dishonest teller, these "bank examiners" ask for the depositor's help. The customer is asked to withdraw a substantial sum of money and to turn it over to the "examiners," who then substitute newspaper for it and return it in a sealed envelope to the depositor. By the time the customer discovers the substitution, the thieves have long since fled. The bank's best defense against such a scheme is to announce to its depositors that any contact by individuals who claim to be conducting an examination is suspect and should be reported to the bank and to police at once.

Regular bulletins to the tellers and other bank personnel, mentioning recent instances of fraud and identifying the thieves' specific methods of operation, also can help to reduce losses.

SUMMARY

Years ago, the work of tellers was subdivided. One group, the "receiving tellers," handled only deposits; the other group, the "paying tellers," were responsible for all paying and cashing functions. Today, it is far more common to find "unit tellers," who combine both paying and receiving functions. Unit tellers have a far more diversified set of tasks to perform each day. The steady increases in banking activity, plus the unification of teller functions, intensify the need for comprehensive teller training.

Any list of required teller attributes must include accuracy, total honesty, courtesy, and the ability to work well under pressure. Tellers must be able to handle a variety of transactions and make decisions promptly and efficiently. They are the "front line" of banking, and customers often judge banks entirely on the basis of the professionalism and attitude that their tellers display.

Each teller must understand the distinctions between paying and cashing checks. He or she must be able to balance the need for establishing and maintaining customers' good will with the simultaneous need for protecting the bank's assets and the funds deposited by customers. The manner in which a teller treats a customer's request to convert a check into money is vitally important. A curt refusal and an inflexible attitude can alienate the customer; however, an overemphasis on not offending anyone can result in substantial losses to the bank.

Banks always will be natural targets for larceny. It is only through on-going education that constant vigilance can be established and maintained.

QUESTIONS FOR DISCUSSION

1. Why are banks legally required to pay checks presented to them?

2. What tests can a teller apply to checks that are presented for cashing? What risks does the teller assume in cashing checks?

3. Should banks be willing to cash every check presented by their own depositors?

4. If a check has been made payable to "cash," why should a teller ask that it be endorsed by the individual presenting it?

5. What actions should a teller take during a holdup attempt?

NOTES

1. Robert B. Avery, Gregory E. Elliehausen, Arthur B. Kennickell, and Paul A. Spindt, "Changes in the Use of Transaction Accounts and Cash from 1984 to 1986," *Federal Reserve Bulletin* (March 1987), p. 187.

2. See Jim McCartney, "Check-Cashing Stores Fill Void Left by Banks in Twin Cities," *American Banker*, April 21, 1987, p. 6.

For More Information

Chamness, Robert P., and Cliff E. Cook. *A Guide to the Bank Secrecy Act*. Washington, D.C.: American Bankers Association, 1987.

Federal Reserve Board of Governors, *Regulation H: Procedures for Monitoring Bank Secrecy Act Compliance*.

7.

CHECK PROCESSING AND COLLECTION

LEARNING OBJECTIVES

After completing this chapter, you will be able to

●

explain why speed and cost are important in the routing and
collecting of checks

●

name the objectives of check processing systems

●

explain why transit numbers and check routing symbols are important

●

describe the techniques that can be used for presenting local checks

●

list the advantages of membership in a clearing house association

●

describe the role of correspondent banks in collecting transit checks

●

explain the significance of check truncation

●

explain the concepts of Fed availability versus bank availability

●

define such terms as cash letter, explicit pricing, and RCPCs

No business venture of any kind can succeed for any length of time if it offers the public certain goods or services and then finds itself unable to cope with the volume of business that its marketing efforts have generated. In no industry does this apply more than in commercial banking. The advertising campaigns, promotions for new branch openings, offers of new and more attractive forms of deposit relationships, and other techniques used by banks since World War II have brought a tremendous increase in the number of depositors and the volume of paper that must be handled. While governments, businesses, and consumers increasingly accept various forms of electronic funds transfer systems (EFTS), check usage continues to grow. It would be ironic and tragic if the banks, having attracted so many customers and encouraged the use of checks as a payment medium, found themselves incapable of promptly, efficiently, and inexpensively handling this activity and consequently lost their share of the business. The techniques involved in the rapid and accurate processing of checks are aimed at resolving this problem.

Many customers today take advantage of ATMs; others use their plastic cards at point-of-sale (POS) terminals to pay for goods and services; others take advantage of bank-by-phone systems, authorizing their banks to pay bills for them by direct debiting; still others authorize their banks to make periodic payments for them automatically. All of these uses of EFTS have helped to move the United States toward a *less-check* society, but the original concept of a *checkless* society now appears unattainable. Checks, and the processing problems they create, will remain the cornerstone of the payments system, and in the face of steadily escalating labor costs, banks must be ready to cope with the daily volume.

CREDIT BALANCES AND CHECK PROCESSING

In simple terms, a bank's existence depends on its ability to attract and retain funds through deposits and to put those funds to work in loans and investments to generate profits. However, as mentioned earlier, daily deposit activity consists chiefly of checks. Before the deposited items can be converted into loanable or investable funds for the bank (or usable funds for the customers), they must undergo a process based on the concept of *credit balances* discussed in chapter 3.

A bank named as a drawee on a check is obliged to follow the exact orders for payment given to it by the drawer. In strict legal terminology, one who issues a promise to pay (a note) is a *maker* and one who issues an order to pay (a check) is a *drawer*. The issuer of a check actually is drawing a demand draft on a bank. However, in common usage, the issuer of a check also is called the *maker*. The bank can pay out funds against accounts *only* in exact compliance with the instructions given to it. It can pay no more and no less. In some circumstances, however, the drawee cannot honor a specific check. Whenever this happens and a check must be returned unpaid to the presenting bank (the bank that accepted it on deposit or gave cash for it), the drawee must act promptly. To delay the process renders a disservice both to the presenting bank and to the person who deposited or cashed the check.

If a drawee were allowed to take as much time as it wished in deciding if it should honor checks sent to it, the amount of daily float in the banking system would rise to entirely unacceptable levels. Customers who had deposited checks drawn on other banks would never be exactly sure of their collected balances. Banks also would suffer from these delays; the increase in float would restrict their ability to make loans and investments, and therefore decrease their income and profits.

Federal Reserve regulations, the Uniform Commercial Code, and the rules of local clearing houses all contain specific provisions concerning the time frame within which a drawee must act on all checks presented to it. If a drawee violates these rules and tries to return a check unpaid to the presenting bank after the stated time limit, the drawee may find that the presenting bank will not accept it and that its right to dishonor the check has been lost.

Banks are willing to give depositors immediate but provisional credit for deposited checks because they assume that most items will be honored by the drawees. The entire system operates on an exception basis. Notification on cash items is sent to customers only when a check has been dishonored. If banks were to notify every depositor each time a deposited check had been presented to a drawee and honored, the volume of daily paperwork would become totally impossible. Both the presenting bank and its depositors are anxious to use the funds represented by deposited checks. Therefore, in the absence of contrary information, both assume that the process of presenting and collecting those checks has been completed satisfactorily.

A related principle in banking states that the more quickly a check is presented to the drawee, the more likely it is to be honored. At the time it was issued, funds may have been on deposit to cover it; given a delay, however, other checks may have been presented in the meantime and paid against the account, thus leaving insufficient funds.

All these points emphasize the need for *speed* in the check collection process. However, speed cannot be the sole determinant; it always must be balanced against *cost*. These two factors together determine the method or channel that will be used to collect checks. Unfortunately, the fastest method is often the most expensive, whereas the cheapest method is usually the slowest.

Assume that a bank in Vermont accepts on deposit a check drawn on a bank in Missouri. If speed alone were being considered, the Vermont bank could have a messenger fly to Missouri, physically present the check to the drawee, obtain some form of acceptable settlement for it, and fly back to Vermont. This might well be the quickest method, but the expense involved could not be justified unless the large size of the check made it advisable.

Now assume that a Los Angeles bank has accepted a check drawn on a bank in Boston. The Los Angeles bank could, if it wished, simply send the check to the drawee by regular mail. Because postage is the only expense incurred, costs are kept to an absolute minimum. The time required under this method, however, makes it unacceptable to both the California bank and its depositor. Neither party could afford the luxury of waiting several days to find out if the check had been honored.

All banks analyze speed and cost together to find a system that achieves maximum speed without incurring excessive expense.

FLOAT AND BALANCES

As mentioned earlier, the term *balance* can be misleading. More specific terminology is needed to provide both the bank and its customers with an accurate picture of the status of an account.

The *book* (ledger) balance is the amount that the bank's books show as being on deposit on any given day. Because deposited checks receive immediate credit, the book balance at any time may include a substantial amount of float. When the total amount of float has been subtracted from the book balance, a *collected* balance figure results. The customer's *available* balance consists of the funds that the bank would allow to be withdrawn if the account were to close out on that date. Depending on federal regulations, state regulations, and individual bank policy, the available balance at any time may be lower than the collected balance.

THE OBJECTIVES OF CHECK PROCESSING

When a bank negotiates with a customer regarding the level of balances in an account as compensation for credit or services, and when a bank calculates its own daily funds position, the bank always must identify the amount of float. Uncollected funds have no value to the bank because they cannot be put to profitable use in loans and investments. Similarly, they have no value to the customers, who usually are not allowed to draw against them. For these reasons, successful check processing and collection systems are designed to meet two basic objectives:

- They must ensure that all deposited or cashed checks will be presented to drawees with speed and accuracy. Every drawee must then decide whether to honor the checks sent to it, and must return any unpaid items within strict time limits.
- They must reduce the daily amount of uncollected funds in the banking system, so that both the banks of deposit and their customers can have available working capital.

CHECK SORTING AIDS

Before 1910 many of the larger banks in money-market centers, serving networks of correspondents, had developed their own systems to identify the other banks to which they sent checks most frequently. Early in the twentieth century, however, the growth of the banking system and the corresponding increase in check volume created a need for a uniform, nationwide program of bank identification so that the process of sorting checks according to drawees could be expedited.

The American Bankers Association resolved the problem by developing and implementing a national numerical system, identifying every commercial bank in the United States. In 1911 the ABA published the first "Key Book." This reference book lists the *national numerical system number* (also known as the *transit number*) assigned to every bank. Formally titled *Key to Routing Numbers 19XX*, it is the most frequently used reference work for identifying a bank or determining its geographic location. The Key Book is updated annually as new banks are formed and others go out of existence. The Key Book now lists the transit numbers assigned to thrift institutions and credit unions, as well as those assigned to commercial banks. Checks or share drafts drawn against these institutions thus can be identified quickly for sorting and routing.

The Transit Number

The ABA plan specified that the transit number for each bank would be shown in the upper right-hand corner of all checks drawn on that bank. The transit number always consists of two parts, separated by a hyphen. The prefix (preceding the hyphen) uses numbers 1 through 49 to identify cities, 50 through 99 to identify states, and 101 to identify territories and dependencies. Prefix numbers for cities originally were assigned on the basis of population; thus, all New York banks have prefix number 1, Chicago, 2, and so forth. The suffix (following the hyphen) identifies the individual bank in that city, state, or territory.

If a check has been mutilated in processing and the drawee's name is no longer legible, the Key Book immediately identifies the drawee through its transit number. A check drawn on a small, rural bank can be identified as readily as a check drawn on a large, big-city bank. Some banks train tellers to enter the transit number of all deposited checks directly on the customer's deposit slip. This allows the bank accepting the deposit to trace a specific check, if necessary.

The Check Routing Symbol

Until 1945, the transit number was the sole means of identifying drawees, aside from their printed names on each check. However, as check usage continued to grow, it became apparent that an additional sorting aid was needed. Subsequently, the ABA, with the aid of the Federal Reserve Committee on Check Collections, introduced the *check routing symbol.*

The check routing symbol is not intended to identify a particular bank. Rather, it gives information as to the Federal Reserve district facility to which the check can be sent, and indicates the availability given by the Fed if the check is sent to the Fed according to a specific timetable. Federal Reserve availability is discussed in detail later in this chapter.

The ABA plan combined the transit number and check routing symbol in fractional form in the upper right-hand corner of each check. The check routing symbol is the denominator (lower portion) of the fraction; the transit number is the numerator (upper portion). The routing symbol may consist of either three or four digits that designate the Federal Reserve district and the bank or branch that serves the drawee bank (exhibit 7.1).

The United States is divided into 12 Federal Reserve districts. The first one or two digits of the routing symbol identify the drawee bank's district. For example, all drawee banks in Ohio are in District 4; therefore, these banks have a symbol beginning with a 4. Banks in Oregon are in District 12, and the check routing symbol therefore begins with those two digits.

EXHIBIT 7.1
PARTS OF THE CHECK ROUTING SYMBOL

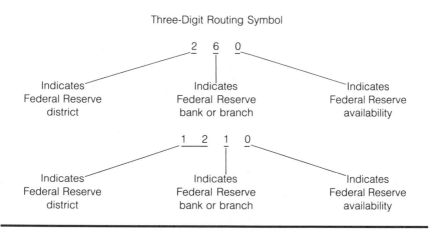

Three-Digit Routing Symbol

2 6 0

Indicates Federal Reserve district

Indicates Federal Reserve bank or branch

Indicates Federal Reserve availability

1 2 1 0

Indicates Federal Reserve district

Indicates Federal Reserve bank or branch

Indicates Federal Reserve availability

The next digit in the check routing symbol shows the Federal Reserve bank or branch in the district that serves the drawee bank. The final digit shows the availability; if it is a zero, the check is given immediate credit by the Fed. Any other number here indicates deferred (delayed) credit.

Magnetic Ink Character Recognition

While the use of transit numbers and check routing symbols helps speed check processing, both require reading by the human eye. Steady growth in check volume, combined with increases in labor costs, soon made further improvements necessary. Collaborating with check printing firms, equipment manufacturers, and other specialists, the ABA set out to develop a machine-readable code.

In 1956 the ABA Bank Management Commission announced the development of a common machine language using *magnetic ink character recognition* (MICR). The MICR system made it possible for checks and other encoded documents to be read directly by high-speed equipment. Each numeral from 0 through 9 was designed to contain a unique quantity of magnetized ink particles; thus, the machines used to read the information could never mistake one numeral for another (exhibit 7.2). The ABA also specified the placement of MICR information on all checks and required that all checks be within a specified size range (exhibit 7.3).

The acceptance and implementation of the MICR program eventually brought about a Federal Reserve regulation that unencoded checks would not be accepted by the Fed as cash items.

Every financial institution today uses its own system of assigning account numbers to customers. New checks issued to depositors already contain MICR codes showing the bank's combined transit number and routing symbol, and the customer's account number. The sequential check number also may be encoded; this is useful in preparing computer-generated statements and for the customer's own bookkeeping system.

The MICR-encoded routing symbol and transit number combination contains nine digits (see exhibit 7.3). The first eight digits contain the essentials of the two sorting aids: the routing symbol, followed by the bank's institutional identifier. The ninth digit enables the data processing equipment to verify that the first eight have been properly encoded. The ninth digit is called a "check" digit.

The *first* bank to accept a check on deposit or give cash for it usually is responsible for encoding its dollar amount in magnetic ink in the lower right-hand area of the check. Once this has been done, any bank that has modern check processing equipment can use the encoded data for sorting, processing, proving, and posting. If a check cannot be read by a bank's equipment, it becomes a reject (sometimes called a nonmachinable) item and must receive special handling.

Using the MICR system, banks could begin supplying customers with deposit slips on which their individual account numbers were pre-

EXHIBIT 7.2
MAGNETIC INK CHARACTERS

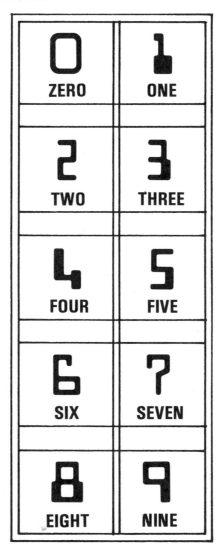

encoded. When debit and credit tickets are prepared by various departments within the bank, they must also be encoded so that these documents can be electronically processed for posting to accounts.

Electronic Sorting

In previous generations, when a bank accepted a check on deposit it usually recorded all necessary information on handwritten ledger sheets.

EXHIBIT 7.3
PLACEMENT OF MICR DATA ON CHECKS

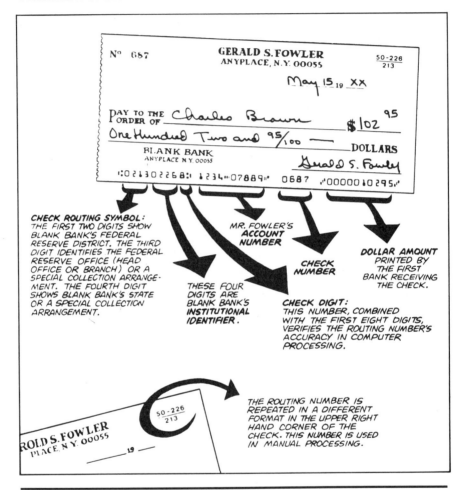

Source: Federal Reserve Bank of New York, 1981.

Today, the sheer volume of daily work obviously makes this method obsolete. It is only through automation that the banking system can process 100 million checks daily with speed and accuracy while keeping handling costs to acceptable levels.

Most banks today send batches of deposited or cashed checks to a central processing department. A copy of each deposit slip accompanies the checks. If currency made up part or all of the deposit, a cash substitution ticket is used for proof purposes. The first step in check processing is to make sure that every item is fully and correctly encoded with all the necessary MICR data.

Once all of the encoding work has been completed, high-speed sorter-reader machines can handle over 1,000 checks per minute using predetermined programs. For example, every deposited check is either (1) an on-us item, (2) a clearing item (according to the depository's definition of that term), or (3) a transit check. Sorter-readers can be programmed to read the transit-routing field, sort checks into the three groups, and then fine-sort them. The fine-sorting process can batch checks by individual drawee, by Federal Reserve district, or in some other grouping, according to the depository bank's needs.

The MICR program has not eliminated all previous check-sorting methods; it has supplemented them and made electronic processing possible for those banks wishing to use it. Some banks, instead of buying or leasing their own data processing equipment, rely on correspondent banks to perform the work for them. Other banks use proof machines that sort and batch items without the use of MICR data. Proof machine operators actually read the information on all checks and use manual keys to sort the checks and prove the totals.

PRESENTING LOCAL CHECKS

During each business day, tellers and departments accumulate local checks. These items then are proved and sorted either by proof-machine operators or by MICR sorter-readers. Every check is then endorsed by the presenting bank and listed according to its drawee bank destination. This endorsement is important, since by placing its stamp on all outgoing items a bank guarantees all previous endorsements and makes the next bank a holder in due course. Banks commonly use the term *prior endorsements guaranteed* (P.E.G.) for this purpose. During the listing process, the dollar amount of checks for each individual drawee is compared to the dollar total for the entire sorted batch.

Local checks then may be presented to the drawees in one of three ways:

- by messenger (*direct presenting*)
- through a correspondent bank
- through the facilities of a local clearing house

The order of this listing is important. Direct presenting of local checks by bank messengers was the first system used. With the passage of time and the increased check volume, however, banks began to use correspondent banks more often. Today, most major banks in money-center communities use local clearing houses to handle the largest volume of checks.

Presenting by Messenger

Messenger presentation is an excellent system when check volume is low and the community has relatively few banks. Using a messenger also may

139

be justified when an especially large check has been taken on deposit and messenger service provides the fastest means of presenting that item to the drawee. As always, speed and cost are considered together to determine if this method of presentation is desirable in a particular case.

Presenting Through Correspondents

Correspondent banks offer a variety of services, of which check collection is the most traditional and perhaps the most widely used. A bank that maintains a relationship with a larger correspondent often relies on the correspondent to present and collect checks. Thrift institutions similarly use their commercial bank correspondents to present and collect checks.

In processing and collecting checks, correspondent banks simply accept the day's deposited items and treat them as they do all other deposits; that is, they credit the sending bank's account, sort the items, and present them to drawees.

Presenting Through a Clearing House

Membership in a clearing house association is entirely voluntary. No federal or state laws or banking regulations require that such an association be formed, or that any particular bank join one. Because of the benefits they offer to members, however, clearing houses are very popular and have been implemented in many cities throughout the country. Use of a clearing house has proved to be the quickest and most economical way to present local checks and obtain settlement for those checks from the drawees.

The New York City Clearing House provides a useful example. In the mid-nineteenth century, New York was the site of 57 commercial banks. Each bank used messengers to present checks to local drawees and obtain some form of settlement for them. As the volume of checks grew and the importance of timely presenting increased, each bank found that more messengers—making more individual trips—were required to complete the day's work.

The establishment of the New York Clearing House in 1853 eliminated the need for a continual stream of messengers traveling between banks. The clearing house provided a central meeting place at which presentation of checks and settlement among the banks could be quickly and conveniently performed. Today, 12 of New York City's largest banks daily process billions of dollars of checks through the clearing house with a degree of speed and efficiency that could not otherwise be achieved.

In a typical clearing house operation, each member bank sends a messenger and a settlement clerk to the daily settlement clearing. The messenger delivers batches of sorted, listed, and endorsed checks to each of the other members; similarly, the settlement clerk records the dollar amount of checks presented to his or her bank by each of the others. The total dollar amount of the checks taken to the clearing house by any one bank is proved against the dollar totals for each of the batches it is delivering to the other banks.

Members in a clearing house *do not* settle with one another individually, nor is cash used as a means of settlement. Rather, each bank typically maintains a settlement account with the local Federal Reserve bank or with a correspondent.

If a bank delivers to the clearing house a dollar amount of checks larger than the dollar amount of checks presented to it by other banks, it is owed money. If it is presented with a dollar amount of checks larger than the total it presents to the other members, it owes money.

When the daily volume is very high, a clearing house may provide for members to deliver checks and noncash items several times during the business day. At the New York City Clearing House, for example, four exchanges of checks, one of return items, one of matured bonds and coupons, and three of stock certificates occur each day. The settlement clearing takes place at 10:00 a.m. At that time all the transactions for the preceding 24 hours are brought into proof and the final calculation of each bank's credit or debit is made.

Clearing house members in each community establish their own agreements on times of exchanges, methods of settlement, and the amount that each member annually pays to support operating expenses.

Banks that do not belong to a clearing house generally use the services of clearing house-member correspondents to present and collect local checks.

PRESENTING TRANSIT CHECKS

The problems of presenting transit (out-of-town) checks are far more complicated. In the United States a bank may cash or accept on deposit checks drawn on banks thousands of miles away. Also, transit checks may be drawn on thousands of other banks, whereas the drawees of local checks generally amount to a relatively few local institutions. For a bank in Washington, D.C., one transit item may be drawn on a bank a few miles away across the District line, while others may be drawn on banks in Texas, Florida, or Arizona. The bank in Washington must be prepared to deal with *all* types of transit items. The two governing factors of speed and cost become even more critical in view of the distances and the number of possible drawees involved.

As in the case of local items, three methods are available for the presenting and collecting of transit checks. Again, these are listed in order of historical development and relative importance. Transit items may be collected (1) by direct presenting to drawees, (2) through correspondent banks, or (3) through the facilities of the Federal Reserve. Exhibit 7.4 summarizes the basic check processing steps for on-us, local, and transit checks.

EXHIBIT 7.4
CHECK PROCESSING DEPARTMENT

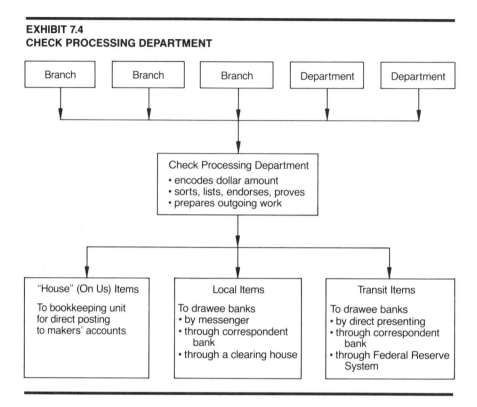

Direct Presenting

Although direct presenting of transit checks was the earliest method, it is the least used today. Sometimes it is still the quickest method; however, it is also likely to be the most costly. Banks today generally present transit checks directly only when the expense can be justified by a particular need. Direct presenting might be used when

- a particularly large check has been received and the increase in available funds through using the quickest method offsets the expense involved
- an item includes special instructions from the depositor, who agrees to accept the expense of direct presenting
- the sending bank finds that it cannot meet the local Fed schedule for delivery of checks to a specific destination, and direct presenting will therefore be quicker

Presenting Through Correspondent Banks

Correspondent banks still handle a significant portion of the daily transit check volume, and before the Federal Reserve's check collection system was established they were the most widely used agency for this purpose.

In many cases the correspondent arrangement is reciprocal; that is, each bank has an account with the other, and each uses the other to collect transit work for it. For example, a bank in St. Louis might have a mutual correspondent agreement with a bank in Richmond. The St. Louis bank sends all checks drawn on banks in the Richmond area to its correspondent and is given account credit just as any other depositor would. At the same time, the Richmond bank batches all checks drawn on banks in the St. Louis area and forwards them to its correspondent there.

In other cases, a unilateral agreement may exist. A bank that has already implemented sophisticated, rapid systems for check collection may actively market that service and act as a collection agent, handling transit work for various correspondents throughout the country. For example, one Chicago bank prides itself on the flexibility and speed of its collection system. This bank receives checks from other banks and presents them at the clearing house in Chicago, and even uses helicopters to deliver checks to drawees in the Chicago area and outlying sections of Illinois.

Banks wishing to expand their correspondent network often stress their check collection capabilities to motivate other banks to establish account relationships with them. In many cases, their prompt and efficient transit operations give the presenting banks better availability than could be gained through the Federal Reserve.

Presenting Through the Federal Reserve System

The Federal Reserve established the first nationwide check collection system. Recent figures indicate that the Fed handles some 50 million checks (about one-half of the nation's check volume) each day, with a dollar volume of $25 billion.[1] Each of the 12 Fed district banks serves as a center for check collection in its area so that transit work flows quickly and efficiently among all 12 districts. Each district bank has branches within its district. Fed banks pay each other for the dollar amounts of each day's processing by settling net balances through the Interdistrict Settlement Fund. The fund is maintained at Federal Reserve headquarters in Washington.

A bank with a modest volume of transit work might present all of it through the Federal Reserve. To do so, the bank simply would forward unsorted work, destined for any or all of the 12 districts, to its local Fed branch. Banks with large volumes of transit work must sort the items by district before sending the checks to the local Fed. As previously noted, all transit checks sent to the Fed must be fully encoded in magnetic ink if the checks are to be treated as cash items.

Assume, for example, that a woman living in Dallas buys some merchandise from a dealer in Sacramento and pays for it with a check drawn on her Dallas bank. The merchant deposits her check in his local bank, which sends it to the San Francisco Fed; the latter, in turn, forwards it to the Fed in Dallas. From that point, the check is delivered to the drawee so that it can be examined and, if honored, charged to the drawer's account. The drawee bank pays the Dallas Fed for the check, the Dallas Fed reimburses the San Francisco Fed, and the latter credits the account of the Sacramento bank.

FEDERAL RESERVE AVAILABILITY

The reserve accounts that member banks keep with their district Fed banks serve many purposes. They provide access to supplies of currency, money transfers, and Fed funds transactions. Perhaps most important, reserve accounts are used to credit sending banks for the transit checks they have sent to the Fed for collection.

Each of the 12 district Federal Reserve banks prepares and publishes a check *availability schedule* applicable to the sending banks in its district. This schedule tells the sending bank how soon its account(s) at the Fed will be credited for transit work *if* checks are sent out in accordance with a detailed timetable. All transit items sent to the Fed are classified as having *zero-day, 1-day,* or *2-day* availability.

A zero-day item sent to the Fed is classified as immediately available to the sending bank. In other words, the sending bank's reserve account is credited on the day the Fed receives the check. This, of course, assumes that the check has been received by the Fed within the limits of the abovementioned timetable. If a bank fails to meet the timetable and delivers the check to the district Fed after the deadline, it loses the benefit of zero-day availability.

The Fed immediately credits all zero-day items to the reserve accounts of the appropriate banks. Since they are drawn on the Fed, all federal government checks are zero-day items. The zero that is part of the check routing symbol on all such checks indicates this.

For check collection purposes, the Fed also carries on its books a *deferred account* for each sending bank. All 1-day and 2-day items are posted to this account when received by the Fed. Each day, the Fed automatically moves the dollar amount of these items from one category to the next; that is, today's 1-day item becomes available tomorrow, when the Fed transfers its dollar amount from the sending bank's deferred account to its reserve account. The 2-day item posted to the sending bank's deferred account today becomes a 1-day item tomorrow—and will be moved to the sending bank's reserve account on the next business day. Every day, the Fed performs the immensely complex bookkeeping for moving funds among these reserve and deferred accounts.

The fact that the Fed gives credit to sending banks for all transit items in 2 days or less creates a float position for the Fed. This is similar to the float position created when a bank gives credit to its depositors. It is physically impossible for the Fed to present every transit check to its drawee, and have that drawee examine the item, honor or return it, and settle with the Fed, in 2 days or less. Just as the depository banks credit their customers' accounts before they know whether the deposited checks will be honored, so the Fed acts on the assumption that most of the check volume is "good" and credits the sending banks.

There is one important difference between these types of floats, however: A local bank can restrict its depositor from drawing against uncollected funds, even though that depositor's book balance has been increased as a result of deposited checks. The bank—within legal limits— can establish its own availability schedule and refuse to honor checks that are drawn on it and presented "early." The Fed does not have this restrictive capability. Every transit check sent to the Fed generates account credit for the sending bank within 2 days; when the dollar amount is credited it immediately becomes part of the sending bank's reserve account and can be put to work at once.

Before passage of the Monetary Control Act in 1980, the Fed's float position averaged over $6 billion per day. The Monetary Control Act ordered both the Fed and the sending banks to make every effort to reduce that figure, and directed the Fed to levy charges against sending banks that did not comply. As a result, the average figure for Fed float has been reduced to less than $2 billion. Eliminating all float is, at this time, impossible because at any given time there will be checks that have not yet been presented and honored. An airline strike, a blizzard, or some other emergency that delays the presenting of checks by the Fed to the drawees automatically increases the Fed's float figure. Depending on the geographic locations of the sending banks and the drawees, 3, 4, or even more days may be required for the Fed to complete the presenting and collection process for certain checks.

Many major corporate customers of banks have tried to take advantage of the Fed clearing system by issuing checks drawn on banks in remote locations so that the actual presenting of those checks to the drawees will require extra time. For example, large corporations headquartered in major cities often draw checks on banks in distant cities and towns that do not receive checks quickly. While the Fed gives the sending bank credit in a maximum of 2 days, the actual time to complete presentation and collection often takes longer. The corporation (the drawer of the check) thus enjoys the benefits of positive float and can put the funds to work in investments.

In an effort to reduce its daily float position, the Fed has implemented three significant changes in its check processing systems and regulations. The first of these reduced the amount of time allowed to a drawee to decide whether a check should be honored. Under the revised schedule, a drawee bank presented by the Fed with checks must either pay for those checks or return them within 24 hours. Payment is most commonly made by a debit to the bank's own account at its district Fed.

The second major revision took into account the large geographic areas that many Fed districts embrace and the number of potential drawees in each district. For example, the Sixth Federal Reserve District has its headquarters in Atlanta, Georgia. This district bank has branches in Jacksonville and Miami, Florida; New Orleans, Louisiana; Birmingham, Alabama; and Nashville, Tennessee. Each branch must serve a great many widely separated drawee banks in the six states that make up the district. To speed up check collection and reduce Fed float, the Fed has established new facilities, known as Regional Check Processing Centers (RCPCs), in each of the 12 districts. RCPCs are strategically located check processing units to which banks can send transit checks directly for prompt handling. Each RCPC, in turn, sorts the checks sent to it and delivers them to drawees in its area. When the nationwide network of approximately 40 RCPCs has been fully implemented, the time required for presenting checks to local drawees will be significantly reduced.

The original format of the check routing symbol has been revised to accommodate the new system of RCPCs. Check routing symbols now show the RCPC nearest to the drawee bank. Through its standard sorting procedures, a sending bank thus can determine the RCPC to be used and can send transit checks directly to that facility. In areas not yet served by RCPCs, the routing symbol continues to designate the Fed district facility.

The third revision in the Fed check processing and collection system has been implemented on an experimental basis. To reduce the huge daily flow of paper, the Fed has modified the traditional idea that every check must be physically presented to the drawee to be examined and honored. The Fed forwards electronic information about certain checks to the drawees instead of routing the checks themselves. Obviously, checks for the largest dollar amounts are also those on which immediate decisions are sought; electronic presentation helps to meet this objective.

For example, an Atlanta vendor might receive a check for $100,000 from a Minneapolis corporation. The Atlanta vendor deposits the item in an Atlanta bank (see exhibit 7.5). That bank converts the information from the check to magnetic tape—and does the same for other large checks received on the same day. The tape is sent to the Atlanta Fed, which sorts the payment instructions by destination and forwards the data to the appropriate Fed district or RCPC. The Federal Reserve banks in each district then instruct the drawees to create debits to the accounts of the original drawers. This system of electronic presentation virtually eliminates float. It is one example of check *truncation*. Chapter 8 will cite additional examples of systems designed to reduce the physical flow of paper checks among banks and customers.

The long-standing concept that every check had to be physically presented to its drawee also is affected by new systems of photocopy transmission. In some major cities, experiments have taken place in which banks send digitized information about deposited checks over telephone lines to a special copy-producing machine in the offices of the drawee. Again, this system can eliminate float; the drawee can make an

EXHIBIT 7.5
MOVEMENT OF TRANSIT CHECKS THROUGH THE
FEDERAL RESERVE SYSTEM

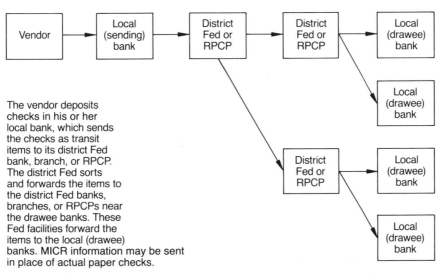

The vendor deposits checks in his or her local bank, which sends the checks as transit items to its district Fed bank, branch, or RPCP. The district Fed sorts and forwards the items to the district Fed banks, branches, or RPCPs near the drawee banks. These Fed facilities forward the items to the local (drawee) banks. MICR information may be sent in place of actual paper checks.

immediate decision on whether to honor the item, and the bank of deposit can be guided accordingly.

These systems of electronic presentation and photocopy transmission create real benefits for the recipient of a check and for the bank at which it was deposited. They expedite decision making and often can reduce or eliminate the problem of "uncollected funds." The drawers of checks resist these systems, however, because they are not anxious to have their bank accounts debited immediately.

BANK AVAILABILITY SCHEDULES

Bank customers frequently complain about the waiting period imposed on them by their banks before they can draw against deposited checks. A person who banks in New Orleans, for example, and deposits a check drawn on a bank in Utah may be aware that the Fed will credit his or her bank in a maximum of 2 days; yet the New Orleans bank may add several days to the Fed figure and tell the depositor that the funds are not available for use for 6 or more days.

In the past, every commercial bank established its own availability schedule for the funds customers deposited using transit checks. Large corporate customers of unquestioned creditworthiness might receive the same availability as the bank received from the Fed; smaller corporate customers had to wait for a longer period. Individual accounts often received the poorest availability.

The banks' rationale for implementing these availability schedules was based on two premises. In the first place, they had to consider the possibility that the deposited check might be returned by its drawee for some reason. The Fed cannot physically present and collect every check in 2 days or less, despite the fact that it gives the sending bank credit on that basis. If a check is returned, the Fed will reverse the provisional credit it gave to the sending bank and return the item to it. The sending bank, in turn, must then charge the item back to the depositor's account. Recovery of the funds may be difficult or impossible if the bank has already allowed the customer to withdraw them. Therefore, banks traditionally have added some time to the Fed schedule.

The second premise reflected the banks' desire to have the use of *collected* funds for their own profit purposes, before classifying those same funds as *available* to depositors. As mentioned earlier, float is of no value to a bank for loan and investment purposes. By giving customers deferred (delayed) availability, the banks were able to maximize their benefits from loans and investments.

However, the banks' latitude in delaying availability to customers has been severely limited under the Competitive Equality Banking Act of 1987, which was signed into law by President Ronald Reagan on August 10, 1987. That act, which will be discussed in chapter 15, sets maximum time frames for availability of funds.[2]

EXPLICIT PRICING

Until 1981, with the single exception of loans, Fed services were provided free of charge to member banks. For example, all the tasks of presenting checks to drawees, obtaining settlement, and transferring funds from deferred to reserve accounts each day were handled as a free service for member banks. At the same time, member banks were required to maintain substantial interest-free reserves with the Fed.

The Monetary Control Act of 1980 changed all of this. It made all financial institutions that offered transaction accounts subject to reserve requirements, and reduced the percentage of required reserves. At the same time, it placed *all* Fed services on a direct-charge basis. Under the terms of the act, the Fed was required to implement a system of explicit pricing for every check sent to it for collection. The sending bank must pay those charges. In turn, the banks recover these costs from their depositors either through a level of compensating balances or through direct fees.

RETURN ITEMS

Although most checks are, in fact, honored when presented to drawees, there will always be a small percentage that the drawee cannot or will not honor. The most common reason for a refusal to pay is "insufficient funds." All dishonored checks are called *return items.* By law and tradition, any such check must be returned promptly to the sending bank so that the credit originally given to it can be reversed and the depositor notified. Return items generally flow back to the presenting banks by the same method that was used to forward them in the first place: either the Fed, a correspondent, or a clearing house. The drawee must clearly identify the reason for dishonor of a check. Usually this is done using a "return slip" that is attached to the item, specifying the nature of the problem.

When a check for $2,500 or more is returned by a drawee for any reason, that drawee must advise the presenting bank of its dishonor within 24 hours.

CASH LETTER

A *cash letter* resembles a deposit slip and is used to list outgoing batches of checks sent to a drawee, correspondent, Federal Reserve bank or branch, or RCPC. It lists every check in each batch and shows the dollar total. Cash letters are used for proof purposes, by both the sending bank and the receiving bank or Fed facility.

It has become standard practice for sending banks to prepare and keep a *microfilm* record of all cash letters sent out and of the individual checks contained in each shipment. If the checks themselves are destroyed or lost, microfilming makes it possible to reconstruct the shipment. Copies of the checks and cash letters can be made from the microfilm. Drawee banks and the Federal Reserve both accept copies properly made from microfilm records.

SUMMARY

By implementing the concept of cash items, banks have provided a major service to their customers. They have also created for themselves the monumental task of processing some 100 million checks per day and routing those checks to the proper drawees—who, in turn, must decide promptly whether to honor or return each item.

Although various applications of electronic funds transfer systems have reduced check volume to some extent, it remains true that over 90 percent of all payments in the United States still are made by check. Many efforts have been made to cope with this volume on a more efficient and cost-effective basis. The creation of transit numbers, check routing symbols, MICR programs, and systems of electronic presentation represent ongoing efforts to sort, route, and collect deposited items with the proper combination of speed and cost.

Checks may be presented to drawee banks directly or through correspondents, clearing houses, or the Fed. Each bank of deposit must analyze its daily check volume and determine which method of presentation will provide the best solution.

The bank that forwards transit work to the Fed receives credit in a maximum of 2 days, even though the Fed is incapable of physically presenting and obtaining settlement for all checks within that time. The bank that accepted the check on deposit may, within certain regulated limits, defer the availability of deposited funds to the customer, over and above the Fed schedule.

The Monetary Control Act directly affects the check collection system, since it requires that the Fed impose a system of explicit pricing and collect a direct charge from the sending banks for every check it handles.

QUESTIONS FOR DISCUSSION

1. What is the relationship between a bank's daily float position and its income and profits?

2. What two factors must be considered in choosing the channel or method to be used for collecting deposited checks?

3. What information, useful to the sending bank, is found in the check routing symbol?

4. Why should the first bank to accept a check on deposit or give cash for it be responsible for encoding its dollar amount?

5. What advantages or benefits would a bank gain through membership in a clearing house association?

6. Identify two situations in which a bank might choose to present a transit check directly to a drawee.

7. If a bank sends transit checks to the Fed for collection, how and when does the bank receive credit at the Fed?

8. Should banks allow all customers to draw against deposited checks on the exact same basis as the Fed's availability schedule?

9. Why is there some resistance to electronic funds transfer systems from the issuers of checks?

10. What three changes in check processing and regulations has the Fed implemented in order to reduce its daily float position?

NOTES

1. David H. Friedman, *Deposit Operations* (Washington, D.C.: American Bankers Association, 1987), p. 77.

2. Robert M. Garsson, "How Bill Would Affect Check Holds," *American Banker*, January 29, 1987, p. 14.

For More Information

Friedman, David H. *Deposit Operations.* Washington, D.C.: American Bankers Association, 1987.

Oliver, Richard R. *Fundamentals of Bank Data Processing.* Washington, D.C.: American Bankers Association, 1983.

8.

BANK
BOOKKEEPING

LEARNING OBJECTIVES

After completing this chapter, you will be able to

•

distinguish between a bank's bookkeeping unit and its general ledger department

•

name the sources from which the bookkeeping unit receives its daily work

•

describe the visual and nonvisual tests applied to checks in the examining process

•

list the advantages and disadvantages of dual posting systems

•

explain the purpose of the daily transaction tape

•

distinguish between genuine and authorized signatures

•

name the advantages of the cycle statement system

•

list the benefits of check truncation

When the system of credit balances first was substituted for the physical exchange of money or other articles of value, the goldsmith or merchant who held those balances had to maintain accurate and timely records of every transaction. He was responsible for carrying out the *exact* orders given him by his client; that is, making the specified payments. As banks replaced merchants and goldsmiths as the holders of credit balances, they had to assume responsibility for keeping accurate records, for knowing the status of each account relationship at all times, for giving customers periodic reports on each transaction, and for carrying out the client's orders in exact detail.

A bank must handle the deposit and payment functions efficiently and promptly, and at the same time guarantee that each depositor's debits and credits will be properly recorded. The end product of this entire function, the bank statement, is vital to the customer's image of the bank. Errors, misposts, delays, or other problems in the bank statement create strong and immediate customer dissatisfaction and detract from the bank's ability to maintain the volume of business it has tried to attract through marketing.

WHAT IS "BOOKKEEPING"?

The term "bookkeeping" is directly traceable to the original system of credit balances. The holder of those balances carefully recorded all transactions for each client in some form of "book" or ledger. Today, the word bookkeeping may conjure an image of a person wearing a green eyeshade and seated on a high stool, whose job it was to enter in pen-and-ink script each day's activity. Indeed, in the early days of American banking, that image was accurate. Banks maintained staffs to literally "keep the books." These employees performed all the tasks that had originally been the responsibility of the merchants and goldsmiths in holding credit balances.

As the number of bank customers (and the volume of daily work) increased, the work of posting and maintaining detailed, accurate sets of books demanded new and improved technology. Just as the *manner* in which the work was done was revised to meet the increased requirements of both the banks and their customers, so the *name* given to the function was changed. Many banks today no longer have or refer to a *bookkeeping department*; far more often, the term *demand deposit accounting* (DDA) is used to describe the system and the department responsible for examining debits and credits, posting them to accounts, and rendering statements. However, for purposes of uniformity the traditional term, bookkeeping, will be used throughout this chapter.

A distinction must be made between the bookkeeping unit and the bank department commonly called *general ledger* or *general books*. The latter is the department that consolidates the figures supplied by every department and branch within the bank and prepares the institution's daily financial statement, showing all assets and liabilities. Included in that statement is an entry for *demand deposits*; that figure results from the work done in the bookkeeping department, which has posted all the transactions affecting customers' accounts and has arrived at a closing balance for each account. The sum total of those closing balances appears as a single entry on the bank's balance sheet or statement of condition.

For banks that no longer use passbooks for savings accounts and that combine customers' savings and checking account reports, the task is more complicated. However, relatively few institutions as yet follow that course of action. This chapter will limit itself to a discussion of the processing given to demand deposits only.

SOURCES OF BOOKKEEPING WORK

Every instrument that affects a customer's balance in any way must be processed through the bank's bookkeeping department. Checks must be examined to determine if they should be honored and then posted to reduce the balance. Data from the bank's ATMs and input from automated clearing houses (such as direct deposit of payroll) must also be examined and posted. The *posting* process can also be referred to as the *paying* of checks. Remember, the net effect on a customer's balance is identical, whether he or she has obtained cash from a teller or has issued checks that will be charged to an account.

Bookkeepers receive items every day from a variety of sources. Deposit slips originate with tellers; debit and credit tickets are prepared by other bank departments such as the loan, trust, securities, and collection departments. The bulk of the work consists of checks presented by clearing houses, the Federal Reserve, directly by other banks, and tellers who have taken the checks on deposit or given cash for them.

Although it is true that posting involves the entering to accounts of both credits and debits, the stress in this chapter is on the drawee bank's debit activity; that is, the reducing of account balances. Commercial banks settle with one another every day for billions of dollars on the basis of the authority and instructions contained in checks. The most important single function of bookkeepers involves examining the checks presented. Checks that meet all the examining tests are debited to accounts; those that fail to meet the tests should not be charged to accounts and must be returned promptly to the presenters.

BASIC BOOKKEEPING FUNCTIONS

When all checks and other instruments have reached the bookkeeping unit, the essential daily functions can be performed. To prepare and maintain up-to-date, accurate records on every checking account, a typical bookkeeping department must

- examine all work presented to it to assure that proper account numbers and dollar amounts appear
- post all debits and credits to the proper account
- arrive at a new closing balance for each account
- return items that are dishonored
- render statements to customers
- generate internal reports for the information of other units within the bank

Depending on the bank's size and organizational structure, bookkeepers also may be responsible for answering outside inquiries regarding the status of accounts.

Preliminary Examination

It is not the purpose here to suggest that every bank should adopt a fully automated system of demand deposit accounting. One of the important functions of bank management is to determine how much money and effort should be spent on automation. Many banks find it unnecessary to install the expensive and highly sophisticated computer systems that are found at larger, more active institutions. These banks are not behind the times; rather, they have chosen the type of bookkeeping operation that meets their objectives while keeping expenses within budgeted figures.

Regardless of the degree of automation that a particular bank elects to provide, certain basic procedures can be followed. Checks can be examined visually or by machine to determine whether all the necessary MICR data have been properly encoded. If information is missing, it can be encoded before the items proceed further. Similarly, all checks presented to a bank can be visually examined to assure that they actually belong to that bank. *Missorts* can and do occur. Items received by the wrong bank must be screened out at once and returned to the presenting bank. Debit and credit tickets also must be examined for complete and accurate encoding.

Posting and Computing New Balances

For banks whose bookkeeping systems are not automated, a typical procedure might entail sorting all debits and credits by account number, obtaining (from a file of statements or ledger cards) those that must be posted, posting the entries, calculating the new balances in each case, and proving the work. If all these functions are performed by one person, there are many possibilities for error. A bookkeeper might fail to detect a sorting error and post a false debit or credit. A ledger card for John Smith might be pulled from the file and erroneously posted with work intended for James Smith's account.

The *dual posting system* was developed to reduce error and improve bookkeeping accuracy. This system requires that a ledger file (for the bank's use) and a statement file (for the customer's use) be prepared and maintained on each account. Two operators post all work and prove all changes to each other. One operator posts all debits and credits to the ledger, while the other posts to the statement. Since two people are unlikely to make the same mistake, dual posting provides greater accuracy. However, since every item must be posted twice, it is also far slower and more expensive. The benefits of this system must be weighed against the costs.

Partially automated systems attempt to achieve the accuracy of dual posting while reducing expenses. These systems combine nonautomated with partially automated features. Each checking account must have its own identifying number. Special equipment is used to "read" information encoded in magnetic strips on the back of each ledger sheet. Several firms have marketed this technology to banks, using various trade names. The common feature is an ability to compare the information encoded on the ledger sheet with the information encoded on the posting work. This technology eliminates many common types of human error. Some equipment even can "read" an account's previous closing balance and compute a new balance after debits and credits have been posted.

Fully *automated systems* require a fully implemented MICR program. If the work to be posted has been encoded with the account number and the dollar amount in magnetic ink, computerized bookkeeping systems can perform not only the basic bookkeeping functions but also a host of other tasks that would have been impossible with older, less sophisticated systems.

The amount of data that can be stored in the memory of a modern computer is virtually limitless. Every type of relevant data on an account can be entered and readily accessed. For example, the master file on the ABC Corporation payroll account might show the account number, the fact that the company maintains other related accounts with the bank, the industry code assigned by the government to identify ABC's type of business, the employer identification number, the branch or other area of the bank in which the account is domiciled, the identity of the bank officer assigned to the ABC relationship, and other useful information. Depending on the capabilities of their computers, banks can design programs containing any or all of this information. The master file may be on disks, magnetic tape, or other computer media.

In fully automated bookkeeping, all debits and credits typically are passed through a MICR sorter-reader, which captures the information encoded on each item and prepares a magnetic tape called the *daily transaction tape* or *entry run*. This tape is prepared in account-number sequence. It contains the account number, the dollar amount of every transaction, and a code to show the type of debit or credit.

Depending on the bank's size and its volume of daily activity, the tape may be prepared in a single run after the close of business or consist of several separate entries. For example, a large bank may receive a substantial number of checks through the morning exchanges in the local clearing house and may make the initial tape entries as soon as those checks have been examined. Later the same day, the same bank may receive additional checks from the Fed, from tellers, or from other banks. The entry run can be adjusted as these batches of work reach the book-keeping department. If the bank has many departments and branches that originate debit and credit tickets, the final entry run may be made very late in the day to reflect all these transactions.

When all entries to the daily transaction tape have been made, the next step, called *merging* or *updating*, takes place. This process combines the transaction tape for that day with the *master file* that resulted from the previous day's posting. Each account's balance at close of business on the previous day is adjusted to reflect the new debits and credits.

This procedure accomplishes two closely related objectives: (1) it creates a new master file, and (2) it creates a new summary figure showing the closing balance in each account. The summary figure provides a demand deposit total for use by the bank's general ledger unit. The new master file that results from each day's posting becomes the basis for the next day's bookkeeping work, and the process continues on a daily basis.

Examining Checks

Examining checks is one of the most important elements in every drawee's daily bookkeeping. Each check is a set of written instructions to the drawee; the bank has an inescapable duty to comply with those instructions if the item meets certain examining tests.

Traditionally, bookkeeping procedures called for the examination of all checks *before* they were actually posted to accounts. If a check met all the tests, the amount was then debited to an account. Questionable items were referred to a bank officer, who decided whether they should be posted. Based on that officer's judgment, a check was either debited to the drawer's account or returned unpaid.

Today's automated bookkeeping systems have reversed this procedure. Examinations take place *after* the checks have been posted to accounts by the computer. There is a sound, logical reason for this. The percentage of checks to be returned is relatively small, and it is far simpler for the drawee to post every item without first examining it. Any necessary adjustments can be made at a later point in time.

Just as the concept of cash items created *provisional credits*, whereby deposited items increased a customer's balance at once but could be charged back later if necessary, so the system of fully automated bookkeeping has created *provisional debits*. Checks are posted to accounts automatically; if an item must be returned to the presenting bank for any reason, the original debit is reversed and a credit is posted. Automated bookkeeping does not change the drawee's obligation to examine checks; it merely changes the stage of the bookkeeping cycle at which the examination takes place.

As noted earlier, nine distinct tests are applied to a check to determine whether it should be charged to an account. If the check fails to pass any one of the nine tests, it *may* be returned unpaid. Many banks assume a calculated risk by eliminating some of these tests, particularly in the case of checks that are issued for small dollar amounts. In doing so, the banks recognize that there is a potential for loss whenever they honor a check that should have been returned. However, they accept this risk in exchange for a reduction in processing costs.

The nine tests are subdivided into five *visual* tests, performed through an examination of the check without reference to any other sources of information, and four *nonvisual* tests, for which other files or records must be consulted. The five visual tests answer the following questions:

- Is the item an actual check, drawn on an open account with this bank?
- Is the drawer's signature genuine and authorized?
- Has the check been altered?
- Is the check properly dated?
- Has the check been properly endorsed?

Visual examination is all that is needed for these five tests. Even the determination of genuine *and authorized* signatures may fall into this category, since some banks have personnel who are so familiar with the signature files that they can tell at a glance whether the check "passes the test."

The four nonvisual tests answer the following questions:

- Has a stop-payment order been placed on the check?
- Has a hold been placed on the account?
- Is there a sufficient balance to cover the check amount?
- Is the account balance available to the drawer?

At its discretion, a drawee *may* elect to honor a check even if it does not meet all nine tests. If it does so, the bank should always have a valid reason for its action. Generally speaking, however, a check should meet all nine conditions if it is to be charged to an account.

The first visual test is designed to ensure that the item is a valid check on which the bank is the drawee and that it is drawn on an account that permits check withdrawal. Missorts occur; in other cases, an instrument is presented that purports to be a check drawn on a demand deposit or NOW account, but actually is drawn on some other type of relationship. A check also may be presented that is drawn against a closed account. While any such items *should* have been eliminated from the batch during the entry run, visual examination of all checks helps detect any that have slipped through to the bookkeeping department.

Every signature on a check must be *both* genuine *and* authorized. If the account's signature card shows that more than one signature is required on checks, all checks presented on that account must meet this test.

A genuine signature is not forged; it is an actual, valid signature of the drawer. However, a genuine signature is not necessarily an authorized signature. The bank must verify whether the signer has a legal right to issue instructions to it.

John Jones may sign his name on a check drawn on the account of the Morrison Trading Company. His signature is genuine, but he may not have been given the authority to sign checks on the company's behalf. The same rules apply to personal accounts. Kevin Wilson may have opened a checking account in his name only. If his wife, Lucy Wilson, signs a check drawn on that account, her signature *is* genuine but *is not* authorized, and the check cannot be honored. Drawees can honor *only* those checks signed by parties who have the right to instruct that payments be made.

Businesses that use large quantities of checks often find it convenient to use facsimile (rubber-stamped or machine-generated) signatures. This saves the time-consuming, burdensome task of having every check signed by some authorized person. If a bank is to honor facsimile signatures, it must have on file a properly executed authorization from the account holder.

The test for *alteration* reflects the principle that drawees are authorized *only* to follow the drawer's exact instructions. If the drawer issues a check for $10 and someone raises the amount to $100, the drawee is expected to detect the alteration and to reject the item because it fails to conform to the drawer's original instructions and intention. If the drawee fails to do so and the account is charged for the altered amount, the drawee is liable for its error.

However, there is one exception to this general rule. If the drawer's own lack of diligence and care in issuing the check made it easy for alteration to take place, the bank *may* be able to escape its normal liability. The burden of proof would then be on the bank to show that it exercised its proper role in examining the check and that the alteration was due to the drawer's negligence.

Checking the *date* on each item is an important part of the drawee's examining process, since a check may be dishonored if it is either stale dated or postdated. *Stale-dated* checks are items that are no longer current. Under the Uniform Commercial Code, a bank is not obligated to pay a check presented 6 months or more after its issue date. Any such check *may* be returned unpaid. *Postdated* checks bear a date in the future; the drawee has neither the authority nor a valid reason to honor them.

Exceptions often occur in the handling of stale-dated checks. For example, in January of each year, the drawers of checks often erroneously continue to use the previous year as part of the date. This common error generally is overlooked, and the checks in question are honored even though technically they are one year old. A corporation may issue dividend checks to its stockholders and find that many are not negotiated promptly, because stockholders prefer to hold the checks and accumulate them. In these cases the drawee may simply assume in good faith that the checks are to be honored, or it may have on file an authorization from the corporation that waives the general rule on stale-dated items. The drawee also may contact the drawer of any stale-dated check to obtain permission to pay it.

Many checks bear the printed legend, "Not Good After __ Days." This is an attempt by the issuer to assure that the items will be negotiated promptly. In examining these checks, the drawee is expected to identify any items presented after the stated time frame and to return them unpaid in accordance with the drawer's wishes.

Examining for proper *endorsement* is an integral part of the drawee's responsibility. Whenever a check is issued, the obvious intention is that payment be made to a specific party, and the drawee is obliged to prove to the drawer that the named payee endorsed the item. If someone else received the funds—for example, if the payee's endorsement is forged or if someone endorses the check without proper authority—the drawee can be held liable. In such a case, the drawee can try to recover payment from the party who obtained the funds through the unauthorized or forged endorsement.

Endorsement is the formal act that transfers rights to an instrument. An unqualified endorsement obligates the endorser to pay the item should it be dishonored for any reason. As was mentioned in discussing the principle of holder in due course, without an endorsement there is no similar legal liability. To be effective, an endorsement must be on the instrument itself, or on a paper so firmly affixed to the instrument that it legally becomes a part of it.[1]

A depositor who receives a bank statement containing a check that he or she determines has been paid on the basis of an unauthorized or forged endorsement may enter a claim for reimbursement against the drawee, provided this is done within a legally established time frame.

Banks encounter many situations in which the endorsement on a particular check is vitally important. For example, checks issued by an insurance company or a bank trust department specifically require a written endorsement or mark. The endorsement proves that the beneficiary of an insurance policy, the recipient of an annuity payment, or the payee of a trust fund was alive when the check was received, negotiated it, and received the stated amount. A drawee has every right to return unpaid any check that has not been properly endorsed.

A check payable to two parties *must* be endorsed by both. This is true even if one of the parties wishes to deposit the item into his or her personal account. A common example involves an income tax refund check, made payable jointly to a husband and wife. The funds are payable to both, and *only* endorsement by both will suffice to avoid future claims and litigation.

The first nonvisual test reflects the legal right of a drawer to issue a *stop-payment order*; that is, to countermand the original written instructions contained in a check, and to direct the drawee to dishonor the item. A drawer might issue a stop-payment order if a dispute has arisen between the drawer and the payee, if a proposed business transaction has fallen through, or if a customer's checkbook has been lost or stolen.

The quickest means of notifying a drawee of a stop-payment order is by telephone. If the drawer places a stop-payment order by telephone and the bank accepts the request, the depositor's verbal instructions are binding and valid for a period of 14 days under the Uniform Commercial Code. The drawee always should request a written confirmation order for its files.

The UCC provides that stop-payment orders, confirmed in writing, are valid and binding upon the drawee for 6 months. After that time, the check would become a stale-dated item and could be rejected for that reason. Written stop-payment orders can be renewed by the depositor as an additional form of protection.

The UCC also stipulates that the drawer's stop-payment order on a check must meet certain conditions. The drawee must be given a reasonable amount of time to act on the request; for example, if the drawer telephones the order to the drawee and the check in question is paid at a teller's window within a few minutes thereafter, the bank clearly did not have an opportunity to comply with the order.

Through human error and unintentional oversight, a drawee may fail to honor a drawer's stop-payment order and pay a specific check. If this happens, the depositor may bring suit against the bank for its alleged negligence. In an effort to avoid this type of litigation, the stop-payment form that many banks provide to their depositors contains an "escape clause." This clause states that the drawer will not sue the bank if the check in question is inadvertently paid.

The "escape clause," however, does *not* always provide automatic protection for the drawee. Some court decisions have been in favor of the bank; others have favored the depositor. Nevertheless, the burden of establishing the fact and amount of loss resulting from payment of a check despite a stop-payment order is on the depositor.[2] Article 4 of the UCC outlines the rights and protection afforded to a depositor and to a drawee in the case of stop-payment orders.

A *hold* may be placed on an account to limit or prohibit payments against an account for a variety of reasons: The death of a depositor, certification of a check against the account, a legal notification of the depositor's bankruptcy or incompetence, a court order, an Internal Revenue Service levy, or the giving of cash by a teller may justify a hold. The depositing of checks drawn on out-of-town banks also may justify a hold on the account. Part or all of the balance in the account may be restricted. As part of the examining process, a drawee should determine whether a hold exists that would prevent the honoring of a particular check.

The two final nonvisual tests involve determining the status of an account balance at the time checks are presented against it. These tests question (1) the amount of the balance, and (2) its availability for the depositor's use.

As mentioned earlier, fully automated bookkeeping systems post all checks *before* they are examined. If this procedure creates a negative (minus) balance in the account, the bank must decide whether this *overdraft* can be permitted. Overdrafts exist when checks are *paid* for an amount larger than the actual balance. If the drawee decides to allow the overdraft, the posting that created it is permitted to stand; in other cases, the check or checks that created the overdraft are returned and the posted debit can be reversed.

Banks without fully automated bookkeeping systems can make their decisions on overdrafts *before* posting, since their bookkeepers can compare the total amounts of checks presented for each account with the amounts of the balances shown on the ledger sheets. Any checks that would cause an overdraft can be rejected at that point.

The most common single reason for returned checks in the United States is "insufficient funds." When permitted, overdrafts actually represent a type of loan; customers are using the bank's funds to make payments instead of using their own. Many banks extend overdraft privileges to their customers. The depositor is allowed to issue checks even when no funds to cover them exist in the account. Essentially, the bank thus gives a personal line of credit to the depositor. In other cases, where the depositor maintains more than one deposit account, the bank considers the overall relationship and may use an automatic transfer of funds from the depositor's other account(s) to offset the overdraft.

"Daylight" overdrafts have become an issue for banks in recent years. In these cases, a bank allows a depositor to create a large outflow of funds because an equally large (or larger) inflow of funds is expected from another bank in the form of a money transfer on the same day. If, for any reason, the transfer does not take place, the loss could be substantial. The Federal Reserve has issued warnings to banks about daylight overdrafts.

The nonvisual examining process also questions the availability of funds. As cash items, deposited checks increase the book balance at once; however, this does not make the funds immediately available for the customer's use. Within a legal time frame, the drawee has the right to return unpaid any checks that are drawn against uncollected funds, since to honor them would create potential risk.

Returning checks drawn against insufficient or uncollected funds calls for a great deal of tact and discretion on the drawee's part. Very few actions a bank can take will antagonize customers and jeopardize relationships as severely as a refusal to honor checks. The credit standing of a business or an individual may be severely damaged by the bank's action. When a drawee returns checks unpaid, it must use all its knowledge of the size and importance of the account relationship, the length of time during which the account has been maintained, the creditworthiness of the drawer, and the possible adverse consequences. On the other hand, the bank must be careful not to treat the matter casually and thus to give the impression that customers can issue checks without being concerned over the status of their account balances.

STATEMENTS

An inherent part of the bank's relationship with every checking account customer is the periodic issuing of statements that furnish a record of all the transactions posted to accounts (exhibit 8.1). While this is a burdensome task for a bank with thousands of depositors, it is necessary for the protection of both parties. The customer who receives a bank statement is legally obliged to examine it and to notify the bank if any discrepancy is found.

Under the standard version of the UCC, a customer has one year from the time a statement and accompanying checks are made available to discover and report any alterations or checks that were paid with unauthorized signatures. In all states except California (which has a 1-year rule), customers are allowed 3 years to discover and report any unauthorized endorsements. Other types of errors, such as those resulting from electronic transfers of funds, must be reported within shorter time frames. Regardless of the care exercised, the customer who fails to act within stated time limits cannot file a claim against the bank.

Cycle Statements

Depending on the number of statements that must be rendered and the wishes of customers, it may be convenient for a drawee to prepare and send out statements on the same day. This is usually done at month's-

EXHIBIT 8.1
BANK STATEMENT

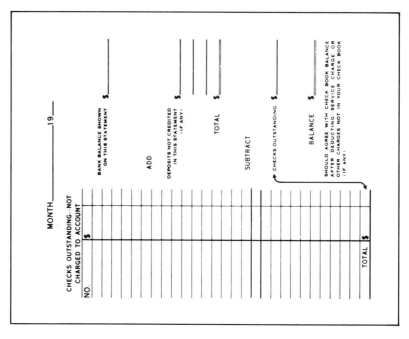

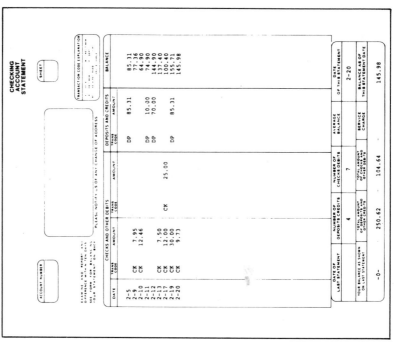

end, since business customers maintain their accounting records on a monthly basis.

However, banks with large numbers of customers may find it impossible to complete all the statement work in a single day. Instead, they use the system of *cycle statements* to reduce the workload and the overtime expense that would otherwise be required.

This system divides all checking accounts into groups and designates the days of the month on which statements will be rendered to each group. The bank may define the groups on the basis of type of account (business, personal, and so forth), alphabetically, or according to any other classification method. Ideally, 20 categories of accounts are created, so that one batch of statements is mailed out on each of the 20 business days in a typical month.

Under the cycle statement system, every customer receives the same *number* of statements per year; it is the *timing* that distinguishes this system from others. Utilities, major businesses (such as department stores), credit card issuers, and others who must work with large-volume mailings have used a similar method for many years. An added benefit of the system is increased accuracy, since the employees who prepare the statements are under less pressure and are less likely to make errors.

Bulk Filing

The bookkeeping and check processing systems in use at most banks usually entail a system called *in-filing* of paid checks. This refers to a manual method in which clerks verify and file checks according to account numbers. The checks are then manually pulled from the files for mailing out with customers' statements.

In an effort to increase productivity and improve efficiency, many banks that use the cycle statement system and have high-speed sorting operations recently have introduced a method called *bulk filing*. Reader-sorters automatically file checks according to the customer's statement cycle, rather than by account number. Bulk filing generally is faster, requires less labor, and uses less floor space than in-filing.

Closely associated with the rendering of bank statements are the tasks of *sorting* canceled checks and *returning* them to customers. Every paid check should be prominently canceled by stamping or perforation, as a proof of payment and to prevent any possible re-use. Banks must use extreme care in matching checks with statements, so that all items are properly listed and so that every customer receives only his or her own checks.

Fully automated bookkeeping systems have made the preparation of statements quicker, simpler, less costly, and more efficient. The magnetic tapes or disks that contain all relevant information can be coupled with high-speed printers to produce complete statements at any time during the month. As mentioned earlier, some banks have combined many features of a customer's banking relationship into a single statement, so that checking account, savings account, and other transactions are all consolidated through the computer.

As an extra service to customers, many banks now encode the sequential number of each check in magnetic ink. This enables them to list paid items on the statement in check-number order, so that customers can prove and reconcile their statements far more quickly and easily.

Banks always have included in their marketing of checking accounts the argument that every canceled check, returned to the depositor, would serve as conclusive proof of payment. However, as check volume has increased and as the costs (including postage) of sending billions of paid checks back to customers have steadily grown, many banks have turned to *check truncation*, convincing customers that it is not necessary to return *all* paid checks with statements.

Under this system, regular statements are sent to customers, but the paid checks are microfilmed and retained by the drawee. The customer may, upon reviewing a statement, request that any check (or all the checks) be sent. After a period of time (typically 90 days), the bank destroys the retained checks, but keeps the microfilm record on file. A front-and-back copy of any particular paid item can be prepared from the microfilm and sent to the customer if necessary.[3] This form of check truncation has been accepted by the Internal Revenue Service and the legal and accounting professions.

Banks have significantly reduced their handling costs through check truncation. The depositors—particularly commercial accounts that generate large volumes of checks each month—also benefit by avoiding the expense and effort of receiving and storing paid checks.

Internal and External Reports

The bookkeeping department is in an ideal position to provide valuable information to other bank departments every day. The more extensive and sophisticated the bank's computer installation, the greater its ability to supply customized reports that can be used for many purposes.

The most common example, of course, involves the on-line computer systems that make account information immediately available to tellers. Other internal reports may include

- trial balance or daily journal reports, showing the debits and credits posted on the previous business day and the closing account balance for each depositor
- listings of all drawings against insufficient or uncollected funds
- reports on all opened and closed accounts, and on all accounts that have shown large increases or decreases in balances
- stop-payment and hold reports
- listings of dormant accounts that have shown no activity for a period of time and have therefore been segregated and placed under dual control

The computer program may also allow authorized bank personnel to enter their decisions on whether checks should be honored or returned directly on the computer sheets, showing drawings against insufficient or uncollected funds. If a bank has a large network of branches, all of the above information can be transmitted directly to each branch.

The bookkeeping department also can help supply account information to external sources. Banks are logically called on to act as references for their customers; however, banks must exercise a high degree of caution in answering inquiries and furnishing information. Every customer rightly expects his or her account relationships to be treated confidentially. The bank must satisfy itself that an inquiry is legitimate, and must be extremely careful to give no information beyond what is absolutely necessary for the inquirer's purposes.

Inquiries about bank customers' accounts often are called "credit inquiries." Depending on the bank's policy, they may be handled directly by the staff of the *credit department*, which can obtain the necessary information from the bookkeeping unit. At other banks, the bookkeeping department handles these inquiries. In either case, certain basic principles must be observed.

The identity of the inquirer and the purpose of the inquiry should be clearly established before any reply is made. A simple inquiry may originate with a merchant who has been offered a check and is contacting the drawee to ask if it is "good." In this case, the prudent answer is to state that the check is "good at present." This tells the merchant that there are funds on deposit to cover the check at that point in time. The bank provides no guarantee that the check will be honored when it is physically presented, however; the customer may have issued other checks which reach the drawee first and thereby reduce the balance.

An inquiry from another bank is treated differently from an inquiry from a business or individual. It is a long-standing and entirely ethical practice for banks to accept legitimate inquiries from other institutions and to exchange appropriate information with them. For example, assume that two banks share a loan to the same corporation. Periodically, they will check with each other regarding approximate balance size, financial statement data, and general credit information on their mutual customer.

In another common example, a merchant may contemplate doing business with a customer of whom she has no prior knowledge. She determines that the prospective customer banks with Bank *A*, while she herself maintains an account with Bank *B*. It is perfectly proper for her to ask Bank *B* to obtain credit information on the customer from Bank *A*. Since Bank *A* knows the source of the inquiry (Bank *B*), the reason, the size of the business transaction that the merchant is considering, and the right of the customer to give its name as a reference, Bank *A* may reply by indicating how long the account has been maintained with it, the level of balances, and whether the relationship has been satisfactory. Again, care and diligence must be used in handling these inquiries, and no information should be volunteered over and above that which is essential and relevant.

One type of report prepared by the bookkeeping unit identifies accounts that have been classified as *dormant*. Every bank, at one time or another, finds that some accounts have had no activity for a period of time; that is, no deposits have been made and no checks have been issued. Once a stipulated period (defined by bank policy) has elapsed, these accounts are separated from all others and are placed under dual control. Several reasons exist for doing this.

In the first place, inactive accounts automatically constitute a source of temptation to any dishonest bank personnel who might be in a position to tamper with them. By placing dormant accounts under dual control, the bank assures itself that any sudden activity will be noted and verified. Secondly, by segregating these accounts the bank removes them from the work that must be handled every day, thus reducing bookkeepers' processing tasks. Finally, state laws often require that dormant account balances be turned over to state authorities after a specified amount of time has elapsed. Under the legal principle of *escheat*, a state has the right to claim all balances in dormant accounts. By segregating these accounts, the bank expedites the process, since it knows at all times exactly what funds have remained on an inactive basis through each calendar period.

Bookkeeping by Correspondent Banks

As a service to their smaller correspondents, many commercial banks offer to perform the entire bookkeeping function on a compensating-balance or direct-fee basis. In this way a small bank that cannot justify the expenses of automation can obtain all the benefits of the latest technology through the facilities of its correspondent. Obviously, this requires establishing complete schedules for delivery of all the necessary input and output. The smaller bank may have its couriers deliver all the debits and credits for its customers' accounts to the larger bank at a certain time each business day. It also must arrange to have the messengers pick up all reports generated by the correspondent's bookkeeping unit as soon as possible so that it will have timely information on the status of each account.

Account Analysis

In a period when interest expense and operating costs are increasing, it is critical for a bank to have systems that determine exactly how much an account is worth to it and how well it is being compensated for the services it renders. This is usually done through a system of account analysis, in which all the income from an account is calculated for the month and all the expenses are shown as an offset to that income. The bookkeeping department, again, is in an ideal position to supply the data necessary for this analysis. An example of the detailed account analysis that a bank can provide to its customers is found in chapter 11.

SUMMARY

The bookkeeping department is one of the most sensitive operating units of any bank. Regardless of which type of bookkeeping system the bank elects to use, its basic responsibility is to exercise the highest degree of care in every phase of the bookkeeping process. Accuracy is of paramount importance. Although modern automation has revolutionized traditional forms of bookkeeping, this new technology cannot reduce or eliminate the need for every drawee to protect itself and its depositor at all times.

The drawer of a check issues a set of detailed instructions to the drawee. The latter must be aware of its liability if it is negligent in any way in complying with those instructions. Similarly, to avoid risk, the drawee must apply to all orders for payment the validity tests designed to assure correct posting.

In addition to examining and posting checks, the bookkeeping department is responsible at most banks for rendering periodic statements to customers and providing the daily input for many internal reports. It may also serve as the bank's contact point in supplying information to legitimate inquirers regarding accounts. Accuracy and confidentiality are important elements of the bookkeeping department's task.

QUESTIONS FOR DISCUSSION

1. What is the difference between a bank's bookkeeping department and its general ledger department?

2. From what sources does the bookkeeping department receive its daily work?

3. What are the advantages and disadvantages of the dual posting system?

4. In fully automated bookkeeping, what information is contained in the daily transaction tape? In what sequence? How is this tape used?

5. In fully automated bookkeeping, when are checks examined?

6. What five visual tests are applied to checks in the examining process?

7. Distinguish between genuine signatures and authorized signatures.

8. Why is a drawee liable if it pays an altered check?

9. List three reasons for placing a hold on an account.

10. Distinguish between overdrafts and drawing against uncollected funds.

11. What is the advantage or benefit to a bank of the cycle statement system?

12. What is the advantage or benefit to a bank resulting from check truncation in the bookkeeping department?

13. Give three examples of internal reports that can be generated by the bank's bookkeeping department.

14. What precautions must bookkeepers take if they are called on to answer credit inquiries from outside sources?

NOTES

1. *Uniform Commercial Code* 3-202(2).

2. *Uniform Commercial Code* 4-403(3).

3. Theodore J. Gage, "Check Truncation," *Cash Flow* (February 1987), p. 2.

For More Information

Frankston, Fred M., Charles D. Mecimore and Michael F. Cornick. *Bank Accounting*. Washington, D.C.: American Bankers Association, 1984.

Friedman, David H. *Deposit Operations*. Washington, D.C.: American Bankers Association, 1987.

9.

BANK
LOANS

LEARNING OBJECTIVES

After completing this chapter, you will be able to

•

outline a bank's three objectives in its program of funds management

•

explain the need for liquidity in banking and how liquidity needs
are estimated

•

describe the interrelationship of the deposit and credit functions
and the importance of the credit function

•

list the four basic categories of bank loans

•

distinguish among mortgage loans, home equity loans, and
the various forms of consumer loans

•

explain the distinction between time loans and demand loans

•

explain the role of bank directors in the credit function

•

list some of the legal restrictions affecting bank loans

•

outline the credit analysis process

•

define such banking terms as discount rate and prime rate,
amortization, liability management, line of credit, and participations

I n manufacturing industries, profits result because some type of raw material has been purchased, processed, converted into saleable products, and sold at a price that exceeds all the cost factors involved. Making a profit in commercial banking is a similar process. The banks' raw material is the deposit; their finished products—in addition to the range of services they offer customers—are the loans they make to every segment of the American economy.

The deposit and payment functions are the foundations of banking. The third basic function, the credit function, is the most important source of bank income. The credit function

- represents 60 percent to 70 percent of total bank revenues, through interest on loans
- is legally required for an institution to meet the legal definition of a bank
- is the most traditional element in the bank-customer relationship
- must exist in banking (under the terms of the Community Reinvestment Act of 1978) so that the legitimate credit needs of communities can be met

As mentioned earlier, commercial banks provide credit to governments, businesses, and consumers. As a group, they are by far the largest holders of U.S. government obligations, and their purchases of the debt issues of state, city, and county agencies and authorities of local government enable those entities to function for the public good.

At year-end 1986, commercial banks had total loans outstanding of $1.6 trillion. Of that amount, $563 billion were commercial and industrial (including agricultural) loans, while $319 billion represented loans to individuals. The banks at that time also held $291 billion in various U.S. government issues and $183 billion in the debt issues of state, city, and county units of government.[1]

In addition to the credit facilities they make available to businesses and governments, banks provide personal, home mortgage, automobile, home equity, and home improvement loans to consumers. Bank credit and debit cards have helped make money accessible to individuals throughout the country. Our society operates largely on credit, and banks are the traditional and most important suppliers of that credit.

COMPETITION FROM OTHER LENDERS

Despite their preeminent position as suppliers of credit, banks face increasing and aggressive competition from many other types of lenders. For example, General Electric Credit Corporation, originally formed as a finance company for sales of General Electric appliances, has become a $21 billion organization that makes large commercial loans, finances real estate, and has receivables outstanding of over $15 billion.[2] General Motors Acceptance Corporation (GMAC) engages in several types of lending in addition to its major function as the financing source for General Motors automobiles, and contributes a net profit of over $1 billion per year to the parent corporation.[3]

As mentioned earlier, savings banks and savings and loan associations have always been the principal home mortgage lenders. At year-end 1986, these two types of thrift institutions showed total mortgage loans outstanding of $772 billion.[4] In addition, many thrifts have taken advantage of the expanded powers granted to them by the Monetary Control and Garn-St Germain Acts and have become active in commercial lending. During 1986 commercial loans at all FSLIC-insured thrifts increased 51.7 percent, and at the end of that year totaled $22 billion.[5]

In mid-1986 over 17,300 credit unions were in operation throughout the United States. Of these associations, 91 percent offered second mortgage loans, 65 percent extended first mortgage loans, 59 percent made loans on a "home equity" basis, and 10 percent engaged in commercial lending.[6] These activities were all additions to the credit unions' fundamental consumer lending, the original reason for their existence.

The nation's major insurance companies and many consumer finance companies also compete with banks in extending credit. However, as noted in chapter 1, the commercial banks as a group are unique in their ability to meet *every* type of loan request. All other lenders are limited in the type or types of credit they can extend. For example, insurance companies primarily extend large amounts of long-term real estate financing, particularly on commercial buildings and developments and also make direct loans to policyholders. Consumer finance companies are limited in the scope of their credit activities. Commercial banks are the *only* lenders that can provide *all* types of credit, dealing with every category of customer.

MANAGEMENT OF BANK FUNDS

It is a widely held misconception that commercial banks hold huge pools of money belonging only to themselves and that they can lend and invest as they see fit. If this were true, a bank would be risking only its own funds when it made loans. Out of every $10 loaned by banks, $9 actually come from deposits—not from the banks' own funds. Every loan is an effort by a bank to put deposited money to work at a profit, while simultaneously meeting the needs of a borrower.

Because loans generally are made with funds entrusted to banks by customers, a program must exist for the management of those funds. That program must constantly address three objectives: *liquidity, safety, and income*. Successful bank management calls for the proper balancing of all three. Any overemphasis on one at the expense of the other two, or any neglect of them, inevitably leads to very serious problems.

LIQUIDITY — most important

Every business, individual, agency of government, and institution continually faces the problem of meeting everyday obligations. If this can be done with cash or the equivalent of cash, a *liquid* financial position is said to exist. An individual who holds sufficient currency, demand deposits, or other assets that can be quickly converted into cash to cover debts, taxes, and other expenses, or a business that can pay its suppliers and creditors without difficulty, is considered to have a high degree of liquidity.

On the other hand, an individual or a business may have assets that cannot be readily converted into cash. In this case, the position is *illiquid*.

For a bank, the term liquidity has a particular application. No depositor leaves funds with a bank without expecting, at some future time, to recover the funds personally or to direct that they be paid to other parties. Demand deposits can be withdrawn at any time simply by issuing checks. Unless a bank exercises its right to demand advance notice of intent to withdraw, a savings account customer has access to part or all of the balance at any time. Time deposits mature at specified dates, when the bank must be prepared to pay back the principal plus interest. No bank can remain in business for any length of time if it rejects customers' requests for withdrawal or payment of funds on the grounds that the bank does not have the wherewithal to meet those requests. For a bank, then, liquidity chiefly applies to the bank's ability to meet its deposit liabilities; that is, to meet demands for payments of funds at any time.

The need for liquidity is not only based on the deposit function, but also is closely tied to the credit function. Every bank has customers who have dealt with it for years and who, from time to time, have a real and legitimate need for credit. They expect their banks to meet that need and to make funds available to them. Liquidity enables banks to provide for the loan demands of long-established customers who enjoy good credit standing.

The depositors' understanding of liquidity is implicit in their making their deposits in the first place. Every deposit demonstrates a customer's confidence that the bank will protect the funds and will be able to repay the funds when called upon to do so. If that public confidence is lost, a run on the bank and a state of panic may result. When this happens, all usual patterns of inflows and outflows of funds change. New deposits no longer flow into a bank that is suspected of being illiquid. At the same time, depositors will hurry to withdraw funds in an effort to protect themselves. The wave of bank failures during the 1930s was at least partly caused by this type of panic reaction.

For the American public, federal deposit insurance has brought a degree of confidence. The existence of federal deposit insurance does nothing, however, to diminish the banks' obligation to have sufficient liquidity to meet estimated outflows of funds.

Every bank bases its daily operations on a variation of the law of averages. It is theoretically possible that every depositor will want to withdraw funds at the same time, but there is very little likelihood that this will ever actually occur. It is far more likely that new deposits will arrive at the bank every day while checks are being honored and orders for withdrawal are being accepted and paid. Only when this law of averages is distorted does a problem take place.

When a manufacturer encounters a sudden, unforeseen increase in demand for its product, it usually can cope with the situation by assuring customers that the assembly lines are doing everything possible to catch up with the demand and by promising delivery of the finished goods as soon as possible. Banks have no such option. Customers cannot be asked to wait patiently until the bank solves its liquidity problem and obtains the necessary funds. Every demand for payment or withdrawal of funds *must* be honored unless there is a compelling reason to refuse it. Therefore, liquidity is an absolute must. It is always listed as the first of the three basic objectives in a bank's program for management of funds.

The Deposit/Loan Relationship

The relationship between a bank's credit function and its daily liquidity position has an additional facet. Typically, bank loans are made to existing customers and credited to accounts, or the proceeds of a loan are used to open an account. New loans generate additional deposits, and after the bank makes provision for reserves, those deposits can be put to work in the form of further loans.

A bank may overemphasize liquidity at the expense of the other two objectives in the management of funds. Such a bank might keep large supplies of coin and currency available in its vaults as a protection against possible increases in customers' demands for withdrawals. However, by doing so it reduces the percentage of its deposits available for lending. The bank's credit function is thus impaired, reducing its income flow. At the same time, the bank neglects safety requirements, because keeping large quantities of coin and currency on hand makes the bank more vulnerable to thefts and losses.

Thus, while always recognizing the paramount importance of liquidity, a bank must keep in mind that there are other inescapable obligations in its program for management of funds.

Calculating Liquidity Needs

To determine its liquidity needs, a bank usually tries to estimate its projected deposit "floor" and its loan "ceiling." The deposit floor is the low point that deposits can reasonably be expected to reach within a stated time frame. For example, if current deposits are $50 million and all available information (including past experience, seasonal factors, and maturity dates for time deposits) indicates that they will drop to $40 million, the bank needs $10 million of liquidity to meet the withdrawals. By the same token, if the loan portfolio now shows $29 million in outstandings and all seasonal and money market conditions, coupled with information from customers as to their borrowing plans, indicate an increase to a ceiling of $33 million, the bank requires an additional $4 million. The combination of the projected low point for deposits and the high point for loans yields the total estimated liquidity need for the period: $14 million.

When demand for credit is extremely high, the ratio of total loans to total deposits changes greatly, and a credit crunch may occur. The banks then find themselves hard-pressed to meet the legitimate credit needs of their markets. Conversely, when the demand for commercial bank credit decreases, the ratio moves in the other direction, and liquidity projections change accordingly. Tables 9.1 and 9.2 show the ratios of loans to gross deposits at all U.S. commercial banks in selected years. For purposes of comparison, it may be noted that at year-end 1986 the ratio of loans to deposits was 89.5 percent.[7]

Meeting Liquidity Needs

Liquidity needs at commercial banks usually are met through a combination of various types of _reserves_. Primary reserves consist of cash on hand, demand deposit balances held by correspondent banks, and reserves kept at the Fed. Secondary reserves consist of high-quality investments that can be converted into cash on very short notice.

In the strict sense of the word, primary reserves offer more liquidity, since they are immediately available. On the other hand, they produce no income, whereas secondary reserves earn interest. For example, a demand deposit at a correspondent bank does not produce interest income but is immediately available for use. A secondary reserve such as a short-term U.S. government obligation provides interest income, but must be sold in order to raise cash.

SAFETY

Just as banks must provide for liquidity in order to meet anticipated demands for withdrawals of funds and for loans, so must they address the second objective in the management of funds: _safety_. By avoiding undue risk, banks meet their responsibility to protect the deposits

TABLE 9.1

RATIO OF TOTAL LOANS TO GROSS DEPOSITS, ALL U.S. COMMERCIAL BANKS, SELECTED YEARS

Year	Ratio
1950	33.7
1960	51.2
1970	65.2
1980	82.6

Source: *Federal Reserve Bulletin*, various issues.

TABLE 9.2

RATIO OF TOTAL LOANS TO GROSS DEPOSITS, ALL U.S. COMMERCIAL BANKS, 1985

Month	Ratio
February	90.5
March	90.7
April	91.0
May	90.0
June	91.1
July	91.0
August	91.5
September	91.9
October	91.3
November	91.2
December	91.5

Source: Derived from data presented in *Federal Reserve Bulletin* (March 1986), p. A18.

entrusted to them. Customer confidence in the safety of the banks is essential, and every depositor must be made to feel that his or her funds are being fully protected. Confidence in the banking system can be weakened or lost as easily by any indication of improper or imprudent loans as by any actual or rumored difficulty in meeting requests for withdrawals.

The need for creating a climate of customer confidence became extremely urgent in the late 1980s as the number of bank failures—most of which were attributed to loan chargeoffs—steadily increased each year. The depositor who becomes aware that 144 banks were declared insolvent in 1986, that loan chargeoffs in that year exceeded $16 billion, or that 2,784 commercial banks (almost 20 percent of the total number) reported net losses rather than profits is rightly concerned over the safety of his or her funds.[8] Anything that the banks can do to bolster confidence is to their advantage, and creating an image of care and prudence in lending is essential.

Again, balancing the three objectives of funds management is important. If a bank tries to provide the absolute maximum of safety, it will never assume any risk in putting deposits to profitable use. As a result, it makes no loans or investments in which there is any potential for loss. By attempting to eliminate all risks, a bank may become so overly protective of deposited funds that it neglects the legitimate credit needs of its customers and community and inevitably stagnates.

INCOME

The third objective that must always be part of a bank's program for funds management is *income*. If liquidity and safety were the only factors a bank had to consider, it could build the largest and strongest vault imaginable, keep as much cash as possible under maximum security, and make only those loans and investments that carried an absolute minimum of risk. There would always be an adequate supply of coin and currency on hand to meet demands for withdrawals and payments of funds, and losses that resulted from loans and investments would be held to an irreducible minimum. This course of action, however, neglects the third essential element, which is the need for *income*.

Unlike their counterparts in other countries, American banks are not owned by or subsidized by the government. They are organized for profit, and their obligations to the shareholders who have invested in their future must be considered together with all other obligations to customers and communities. A bank that does not demonstrate adequate growth in its annual net income soon loses the confidence of its depositors, its stockholders, and the public.

Like the other two factors in the management of bank funds, income can never be considered alone. An overemphasis on profits, neglecting both liquidity and safety, can be disastrous. It is unfortunately true that many banks in the nation's financial history chose to stress short-term income at the expense of the other two factors, and were forced out of business as a result.

Interest on loans represents by far the largest portion of a bank's annual income. Therefore, any bank that identifies improvement in earnings as its essential goal would have to expand its loan portfolio to build up interest income. This expansion would involve aggressive efforts to attract new borrowers. Experience shows that this course of action invariably leads to a lowering of normal credit standards. The bank then approves loans that would not otherwise be made, accepting risks far beyond prudent norms.

Interest is simply money paid for the use of money. A borrower who is especially in need of funds will pay a higher interest rate. A bank that seeks to improve its earnings at the expense of safety considerations will charge higher rates as a reflection of the increased risks it is assuming. There may be an immediate short-term gain in profit, but in the long run the policy will prove fatal to the bank.

Banks always attempt to increase income, but they cannot do so if at the same time they ignore the requirements of liquidity and safety.

Priorities in Funds Management

A program for the management of bank funds must create and sustain a balance among all three objectives. This requires establishing a schedule of actual priorities, and since the most fundamental obligation is to meet all foreseeable demands for withdrawals of funds, the *primary* focus must be on liquidity. A bank's deposit base is highly volatile—demand deposits even more so than savings and time deposits—and a bank must be prepared for a shrinkage of that base at any time.

Because banks also have an obligation to try to satisfy the legitimate credit requirements of their depositors and the community, their estimate of liquidity needs must also consider loan demand. By law and as a practical matter, a bank cannot remain in business if it neglects the credit function. The U.S. economy relies on banks to supply loans and make investments, and every discussion of liquidity must reflect that basic fact.

When, and *only* when, a bank has devoted sufficient attention to all its estimated liquidity needs, can it then concentrate on investments and nonloan products and services that will contribute to its profit objectives. Every commercial bank is under simultaneous pressures from its depositors and its stockholders. Customers deposit funds with those banks that meet their requests for credit; stockholders look for growth and profits. A high degree of management skill is required to reconcile the two. Again, the demands placed on banks differentiate them from other types of lenders. If a small loan company or commercial financing firm rejects a request for credit, it loses only the interest income it could have received. On the other hand, a bank that refuses to lend to a long-standing depositor faces the loss of a valued account as well as the interest income.

BASIC TYPES OF BANK LOANS

For purposes of reporting to government agencies and for their internal management purposes in planning and monitoring, commercial banks divide their loan portfolios into four basic categories:

- real estate loans
- interbank loans
- consumer loans
- commercial and industrial loans

In areas where loans to farmers form a significant part of banks' portfolios, a fifth category, agricultural loans, may also be included. Table 9.3 shows the dollar amounts of outstanding loans in the above four categories at U.S. commercial banks at year-end 1986.

Real Estate Loans

In many areas of the United States, banks in recent years have become heavily involved in various types of real estate financing. They have

TABLE 9.3
LOAN CLASSIFICATION, ALL COMMERCIAL BANKS, DECEMBER 1986

Category	Loans Outstanding (in billions of dollars)
Real estate loans	496.4
Interbank loans	172.8
Consumer loans	319.9
Commercial and industrial loans	562.7

Source: *Federal Reserve Bulletin* (March 1987), p. A18.

supplied the funds needed for new office buildings, shopping centers, cooperatives and condominiums, and other residential developments. Their involvement takes two forms: construction loans and mortgage loans.

A real estate developer often requires funds at the very outset of a project, in order to purchase, demolish, and clear existing property and proceed with the erection of a new structure—for example, an office skyscraper or an apartment complex. A bank accommodates the developer by providing a *construction loan.*

Construction loans generally are unsecured and are short-term credits that will be repaid out of the long-term mortgage financing arranged by the builder. The proceeds of the loans are used to pay architects and contractors for their services, to meet payrolls, and to purchase needed materials. It is a common practice for a commercial bank to extend the construction loan and for another lender or combination of lenders (for example, insurance companies, pension funds, institutions and foundations, and syndicates of foreign interests) to provide the long-term mortgage when the project is completed. However, the commercial bank may fill both of these lending roles if it so desires.

Real estate *mortgage loans* are invariably long term, and the property itself serves as the collateral (security) for the loan. Commercial banks may extend mortgage loans on office buildings, apartment houses, and shopping centers if there is sufficient evidence that the regular income from rents in the project will be more than adequate to meet a schedule of regular payments. The scheduled payments provide the amortization (the gradual reduction) of the mortgage loan.

For many years, commercial banks were inactive in the home mortgage field. People who sought funds to finance home purchases generally obtained their mortgages from savings banks or savings and loan associations. More recently, however, the commercial banks have turned their attention to this type of consumer-oriented loan. The introduction of variable rate and adjustable rate mortgage loans, in which the lender can adjust the interest rate as conditions change in the money markets, has been an important factor contributing to this policy change. Table 9.4 shows the mortgage debt held by various types of lenders at year-end 1986.

TABLE 9.4
MORTGAGE DEBT OUTSTANDING, 1986

Holders	Loans Outstanding (in millions of dollars)
Commercial banks	474,724
Savings banks	214,156
Savings and loan associations	558,409
Life insurance companies	185,269
Finance companies	33,771

Source: *Federal Reserve Bulletin* (March 1987), p. A39.

Residential mortgage loans are based on the appraised value of the home and the borrower's income and creditworthiness. If the borrower defaults, the lender can foreclose on the home and sell it in an effort to recover the unpaid balance. Since the end of World War II, the number of home mortgage loans has consistently grown, partly because of the assistance of such federal agencies as the Veterans Administration (VA) and the Federal Housing Administration (FHA). These agencies provide guarantees to the lenders in case the borrower defaults.

Commercial mortgage loans are based on the projected cash flow that will result from rental income generated by the property. Again, the lender has the right to foreclose on the property in the event of loan default.

A fundamental principle in bank lending states that there should be a match between the type of loan and the type of deposit used to fund it. Obviously, every loan cannot be directly and exactly matched in this manner. As a general rule, however, time and savings deposits (which are more stable than demand deposits and tend to remain with banks for longer periods of time) are used to make long-term mortgage loans. The traditional concentration of these types of deposits at thrift institutions, which also traditionally lead lending for home mortgages, reflects this principle.

Government Mortgage Agencies

Three agencies, affiliated with the federal government, have been created to develop the secondary mortgage market and thereby help to provide funds for mortgage loans for the nation's home buyers. Because their activities involve hundreds of billions of dollars each year, these agencies directly affect the real estate lending functions of commercial banks and thrifts.

The first of these, the Federal National Mortgage Association (commonly known as "Fannie Mae"), was founded in 1938 as a result of the Depression-era housing crisis. In 1970 it became a publicly held company whose shares of stock are traded on the New York Stock Exchange.

Fannie Mae buys home mortgage loans from banks, savings and loan associations, and mortgage companies to hold in its own portfolio and issues mortgage-backed securities, guaranteeing timely payment of principal and interest to investors. Fannie Mae's 1986 loan portfolio amounted to $95 billion.[9]

The Government National Mortgage Association ("Ginnie Mae") was established by Congress in 1968 to stimulate mortgage credit. It is a government corporation within the Department of Housing and Urban Development. By providing federally backed guarantees, Ginnie Mae enables housing lenders to raise cash. The mortgages issued by those lenders serve as collateral for the agency's securities, which are sold to investors.[10]

The third agency is the Federal Home Loan Mortgage Corporation ("Freddie Mac"), authorized by Congress in 1971 and owned by the thrift institutions. By issuing bonds, it obtains funds that are used to buy the loans originated by mortgage lenders. In 1986 Freddie Mac purchased $103 billion of mortgage loans and sold $102 billion in securities.[11]

Home Equity Loans

A combination of two factors had a major impact on the real estate lending functions of commercial banks during the late 1970s. While home equity loans can be classified under the heading of "consumer borrowings," they merit special attention here because they are tied to the first category of bank loans.

The Tax Reform Act of 1986 required a phase-out of consumer deductions for interest paid to lenders on personal and automobile loans and credit card outstandings. At the same time, the act allowed taxpayers to deduct, within certain limits, interest paid on second mortgages and home equity loans. The total debt on which such interest is deductible is limited to the purchase price of the residence plus the cost of improvements; however, if the debt was incurred prior to August 16, 1986 or for qualified medical or educational purposes, the debt ceiling becomes the fair market value of the residence.

At the same time, homeowners who found that their residences had increased substantially in value had an equity in those properties far in excess of their outstanding mortgages. The residences, therefore, had substantial collateral value for borrowing purposes, and banks in large numbers began to extend credit based on those values. Homeowners use the loans for all types of personal purposes. In 1986 lenders granted $75 billion in home equity loans, bringing total outstandings to $150 billion.[12]

Home equity loans are offered in four basic forms. The loan may have either a fixed or a variable interest rate, and may be made on the basis of a single lump-sum payout to the borrower or, more commonly, as a type of revolving line of credit against which the borrower can draw (using checks or a credit card) at any time. Some banks have extended home equity loans on a basis which calls for the borrower to repay interest only until such time as a single large "balloon" payment retires the debt. In these cases, the bank retains the option to call for full repayment at any time.[13]

Interest on residentially secured credit up to the original cost of a home plus improvements remains tax deductible. Because of this, recent evidence indicates a change in the borrowing habits of consumers. Instead of using credit cards, the interest on which is being phased out as a deduction, consumers are issuing checks on lines of credit based on their home equity. One survey in 1987 projected an annual increase of 250 million in check volume as a result.[14]

INTERBANK LOANS

The second category used in classifying bank loans refers to direct extensions of credit by one bank to another, often on the basis of a correspondent relationship. Included in this grouping would be loans made by commercial banks to their thrift institution customers and *Fed funds* borrowings.

As mentioned in chapter 2, all institutions offering transaction accounts must maintain reserves with the Fed. Banks that happen to have excess reserves at any time can lend those funds to other institutions and thereby generate interest income.

CONSUMER LOANS

For much of their history, commercial banks in the United States paid little or no attention to the credit needs of individuals. Banks were a source of funds for corporations, governments, and other banks, and not for the average working person. As a result, the consumer was forced to go to other lenders such as thrift institutions for a mortgage, to a small loan company for other personal needs, or to an automobile finance agency to obtain funds for the purchase of a car.

Today, this banking attitude has changed completely. Commercial banks have shifted much of their emphasis to retail business, and the needs and wants of consumers have become extremely important in the overall banking picture.

Consumer credit today includes both the familiar installment loan, the bank card, and various types of revolving credit arrangements in which the individual has access to part or all of a predetermined amount at any time. As indicated earlier, many home equity loans are made on this basis. Payments made to a revolving credit account decrease the borrower's outstanding debt, but the borrower can subsequently borrow again to bring the credit back to the original figure.

Installment Loans

As the name implies, installment loans carry a schedule of fixed monthly payments. The bank typically provides the borrower with a coupon book for use in making payments. Alternatively, the payments may be directly deducted from the borrower's account. Generally, installment loans are unsecured (the auto loan, on which the financed automobile is the security, is an exception). The bank relies on the borrower's signed promissory note. The applicant's job, annual income, outstanding debts, length of employment, and general credit history are evaluated by the bank. If a joint application is submitted by a two-income family, the earnings and debts of both parties are taken into consideration.

Installment loans are made for every type of personal need and want. Borrowers may apply for loans to pay for home appliances, automobiles, vacations, educational expenses, and even medical and dental bills. By making these loans, the commercial banks have helped the U.S. population achieve a higher standard of living. Especially during periods of inflation, consumers are more than willing to take advantage of the banks' credit facilities, on the grounds that eventual repayment will be made with "less expensive" dollars and will come from steadily increasing personal income. However, federal government statistics indicate that in the late 1980s installment debt grew at a faster rate than personal income. In 1986 the ratio of consumer installment debt to income reached an all-time high of almost 20 percent. This increase has been shadowed by a steady increase in personal bankruptcies (exhibit 9.1). There is some concern that the ready availability of consumer credit has made it extremely easy for individuals to incur debt beyond their ability to repay.

Government regulations require that the lending bank explain clearly to each borrower the *true* annual percentage rate (APR) charged on loans. In many cases, installment loans are *discounted*; that is, the bank deducts the full amount of interest for the life of the loan before giving the borrower the net proceeds. This, of course, is advantageous to the bank because it receives all the interest at once. On a 12-month loan, the true APR is approximately twice the quoted discounted rate, and the lending bank must indicate clearly on all its notes and other loan forms the actual interest cost to the borrower.

As part of their overall installment loan operations, many banks work directly with automobile and appliance dealers and obtain loan applications from them. These dealers can be an important source of new business for the banks. In other cases, banks enter into what is known as *floor plan financing* by extending credit directly to the dealer, allowing the latter to carry an adequate inventory of cars or appliances for display and sale.

Consumer loans have proved extremely attractive to banks for many reasons. They enable the banks to compete on a broader scale with other

EXHIBIT 9.1
CONSUMER INSTALLMENT DEBT AS A PERCENTAGE OF
DISPOSABLE PERSONAL INCOME

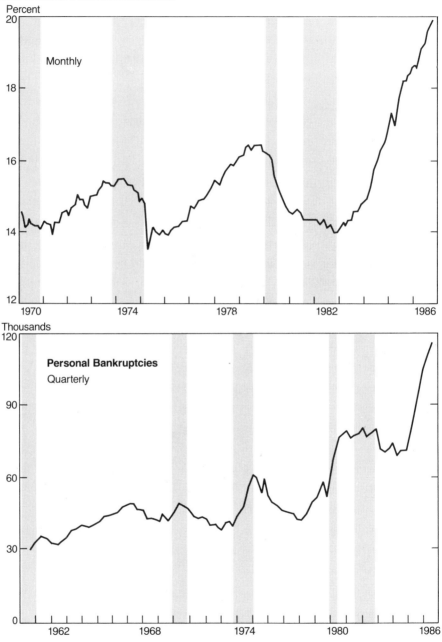

Source: Board of Governors of the Federal Reserve System, *Monetary Policy Report to Congress Pursuant to the Full Employment and Balanced Growth Act of 1978* (Washington, D.C., 1987), p. 37.

types of financial institutions and nonbank lenders. The interest income makes an important contribution to annual profits. Installment loans may be a source of new accounts for the bank. Finally, the mass of historical evidence shows that most such loans are repaid as agreed. The loss experience of banks in this area indicates that the average working individual can be trusted to meet his or her obligations and repay his or her debts.

Bank Cards

No discussion of consumer lending would be complete without mention of the pieces of plastic that have become so important and so common in everyday life in the United States. When they were first introduced on a large scale, these were known as "credit cards," because the user was able to travel, entertain, or purchase merchandise on a credit basis and make payment at a later date. Today, it is far more appropriate to use the term "bank cards," because they are now put to a far wider range of uses. In many cases, as in the point-of-sale terminal, the card actually acts as a *debit* card which transfers funds by debiting the cardholder's account and moving funds to the seller's account.

No development in consumer lending since the 1950s has had as permanent and dramatic an effect as the bank card. Plastic has become part of the way of life for the majority of Americans. In 1986 cardholders included 80 percent of families earning $20,000 to $20,999; 83 percent of those earning $30,000 to $49,999; and 97 percent of those earning over $50,000 per year. The number of cards per family in each of those three groups averaged 5, 7, and 8, respectively.[15] Over 2 million merchants now accept bank cards, annual usage is in the $82 billion range, and Visa and MasterCard have approximately 140 million cardholders.[16]

Instead of obtaining a personal installment loan to acquire the goods and services they want, many individuals simply use their bank cards as payment vehicles. Recent evidence, however, indicates that card usage may decrease—again, because of the gradual removal of interest on card outstandings from the list of tax-deductible items. As mentioned earlier, home equity lines of credit may be substituted for bank cards by many consumers. In February 1987 a survey of 2,855 households disclosed that 37 percent planned to reduce their use of bank cards and 36 percent planned to borrow through home equity facilities.[17]

COMMERCIAL AND INDUSTRIAL LOANS

Commercial and industrial loans make up the largest category of bank loans. This is in keeping with the commercial bank's traditional emphasis on doing business with companies of every type and size. Some commercial loans are made for relatively small dollar amounts, while others may be for many millions of dollars. A bank may simultaneously lend $25,000 to a company to finance the purchase of raw materials, and lend millions of dollars to an airline to purchase new jet planes. Some loans are made for terms longer than one year; most are made for shorter periods, and the most common maturity period is 90 days. The latter statistic reflects the fact that these loans are made on the basis of highly volatile demand deposits. Quick turnover of loans is desirable because it provides for liquidity and returns the borrowed funds to the bank so that they can be used again. Many commercial loans are made on a *demand* basis; the bank can call for repayment at any time, or the borrower can repay the face amount whenever convenient. Other commercial loans are made on a *time* basis, with a specific maturity date. From the bank's standpoint, both demand and time loans have advantages and disadvantages.

For example, a demand loan requires considerable attention from the bank; the bank must ensure that regular interest is paid and must also have some agreement with the borrower that the loan will not stay on the bank's books indefinitely. On the other hand, demand loans permit the bank to make any changes in interest rates that it feels are necessary at any time. Time loans, like the original concept of the home mortgage, traditionally have been made with fixed interest rates that remain constant until the loan is repaid.

In addition to being short term, most commercial loans are unsecured. Credit is extended on the basis of an analysis of all available information regarding the borrower and the bank's confidence in the borrower's willingness and ability to repay. As additional protection for the bank, the personal guarantees of the principals in the business often are made part of the commercial loan.

Many commercial loans are called *participations,* because a loan to a single borrower is shared by two or more banks. These shared loans exist for many reasons. For example, a corporation that maintains accounts at several banks and that requires a substantial loan may divide the loan among its various banks. A single loan may legally be too large for one bank to assume. For practical (rather than legal) reasons, one bank may decide that a loan is too large for it to handle alone. Banks often refer loan proposals to their correspondent banks and invite the latter to participate with them.

Agricultural Loans

As mentioned in chapter 2, archaeological evidence testifies that lending to agricultural enterprises is as old as civilization itself. The farmer in America today requires financing just as his predecessor in ancient Babylon did. Farm equipment must be financed, supplies purchased, and workers paid. For many banks in the United States the four categories of loans that have been discussed in this chapter are less important than a fifth category, farm credit. In the late 1980s the widespread problems of farmers have resulted in severe problems for the lending banks; the value of farm property and the farmer's return on investment have shown steady decreases, and many banks that had a high concentration of loans to farmers have experienced losses or have actually been liquidated as a result.

LOAN CLASSIFICATION

Although the four basic categories of loans offer a convenient method of classifying the components of a bank's portfolio and meet federal requirements for reporting outstandings, many loans could easily be placed under more than one heading. A major credit to a large corporation, shared by several banks, is both a commercial loan and a participation at the same time. A home mortgage loan obviously is a real estate credit—yet it is also a loan made to a consumer. In classifying its loans, a bank must be careful to avoid any duplications so that the total picture is accurate.

Many banks also classify loans on an industry basis. The information is used internally, to help the bank track concentrations of its loan funds in certain segments of the economy, such as the automobile, petroleum, tobacco, or aerospace industries. Then, if a particular industry begins to show problems, the bank is aware of the loans that may be affected and is better able to take whatever action may be needed.

BANK LENDING POLICIES

The typical bank is a corporate entity, of which the board of directors is the active, governing body. Policymaking therefore begins at the board level. Directors of a bank are actively involved in the credit function. They must review the bank's portfolio of outstanding loans to ensure that the institution is truly meeting the credit needs of its customers and the community. They must assign credit authority in varying amounts to the bank's lending officers, so that each officer knows the maximum loan amount he or she can individually approve and what combinations of higher authority are needed for larger amounts. Directors must conduct periodic reviews (audits) of the bank's entire credit function to ensure that proper procedures are being followed in all cases and that undue risks are not being taken. Finally, as a matter of policy, directors have the ultimate loan authority on all loans above a stipulated amount.

All the information staff members require as to organization of the bank's credit function, lending objectives and standards, level of loan authority, review and charge-off procedures, and loans to the bank's own officers and directors may be published in a comprehensive credit policy guide.

LEGAL RESTRICTIONS ON BANK LOANS

The importance of the credit function to a bank's success or failure, the impact that bank loans have on the nation's economy, and the emphasis on consumer protection in today's society have led to the imposition of many federal and state restrictions on bank loans. All lending officers must be familiar with these restrictions.

The maximum dollar amount of an unsecured loan to any single borrower is legally restricted. The general rule is that a bank may lend no more than 15 percent of its capital and surplus to any one borrower on an unsecured basis; if the loan is secured, the limit becomes 25 percent. In this way, banks are forced to diversify their loans, avoiding the problem of "too many eggs in one basket." Many participations result from this restriction on a bank's legal lending limit.

The sizes and maturities of real estate loans are restricted by the laws of various states. For national banks, these restrictions are contained in regulations issued by the Comptroller of the Currency.

Many state laws restrict the maximum interest rates that can be charged on various types of loans (for example, home mortgages, bank card outstandings, and personal installment loans). *Usury* is the legal term for excessive and punitive interest, and a bank that is found guilty of usury is subject to heavy civil and criminal penalties.

In addition, the following Federal Reserve regulations affect loans made by member banks:

- Regulation B prohibits any discrimination by a lender on the basis of age, race, color, national origin, sex, marital status, or receipt of income from public assistance programs.
- Regulation O limits the amount that a member bank may lend to any of its own executive officers and requires that officers report their borrowings to the board of directors.
- Regulation U limits the dollar amount a bank may lend when the loan is secured by stock market collateral and the proceeds are used to buy listed securities or pay for securities already bought.
- Regulation Z ("Truth in Lending") applies to all credit extended by member banks for personal, household, family, or agricultural purposes. It requires banks to make full disclosure of actual loan costs to the borrower, to meet certain standards in advertising credit facilities, and to answer any complaints within a specified time period.
- Regulation BB implements the Community Reinvestment Act (CRA), passed by Congress in 1978.

The CRA resulted from complaints that some banks were guilty of a practice known as *redlining.* The banks were alleged to have drawn red lines around the borders of certain parts of their communities to indicate areas where loans would not be considered. Federal examinations of banks now must include assessments of the extent to which the credit needs of the community have been met. Individuals who feel that a bank's record has been unsatisfactory may register their complaints, and federal authorities may refuse to approve a bank's request for additional branches or services if its constituents have criticized its credit policies.

Aside from these restrictions, the extending of credit is left largely to the judgment and prudence of each individual bank.

INTEREST RATES

Within the legal limits established by various laws, the interest rates that banks charge reflect the fact that money is essentially nothing more than a supply-and-demand commodity, the price of which fluctuates widely. The rate charged on a specific loan usually represents a combination of factors, including

- the cost of funds to the bank — *Primarily*
- the availability of funds
- the degree of risk perceived by the bank
- the term of the loan

The funds that a bank uses to make loans generally come from the bank's deposit base. Obtaining that deposit base carries a *cost* to the bank in the form of interest paid to depositors. Given that the largest portion of a bank's deposit base consists of interest-earning time and savings deposits, the bank must ensure that its earnings from interest on loans is greater than its payments of interest on deposits. The spread between the two is known as *net interest income*. *cost of dep & loan int income*

If business activity increases, loan demand rises with it. However, the amount of funds available for loans is limited at any given time. Banks may be forced to revise their lending policies, allocating loanable funds to those customers who appear to have the most valid claims. From time to time, because of economic conditions, banks also may find themselves with a larger supply of loanable funds. They will then become more aggressive in seeking borrowing customers and in offering new types of loans.

Interest rates may be affected by the degree of *risk* as perceived by the bank. Other lenders (for example, finance companies) legally are allowed to charge even higher rates than banks because they assume risks that are not acceptable to banks. Banks assess the creditworthiness of the borrower and the various risks that enter into that borrower's business operations and set the rate accordingly, within legal limits.

The *time frame* during which a loan will be outstanding also affects the interest rate charged. The longer the term of the loan, the greater the uncertainty of repayment and the more likely that some unforeseen event will cause the borrower's credit standing to deteriorate. Adjustable rate loans help to address this problem.

The Federal Reserve plays a major role in controlling the nation's supply of money and credit by raising or lowering reserve requirements and the discount rate. More importantly, through the decisions of the Open Market Committee, the Fed directly impacts the availability of credit at member banks.

ASSET AND LIABILITY MANAGEMENT

The simplest definition of assets and liabilities states that an asset is anything of value that is *owned*, while a liability represents anything that is *owed*. Historically, U.S. banks chiefly concerned themselves with *asset management*. Demand deposits flowed in steadily on an interest-free basis, and the banker's task was simply to put those funds to profitable use. To the bank, its loans and investments are assets. While asset management is still important, *liability management* now must receive at least equal attention. Changes in the banks' deposit base require that each bank make decisions about how much it needs in working funds and how much it is willing to pay for them in a competitive marketplace. Deposits are a liability to the bank because the funds are owed to depositors. Interest paid to depositors remains the largest, fastest-growing, and least controllable bank expense. Interest paid to depositors must be offset by interest received on loans.

In bank lending, every effort is made to match loans with the kinds of deposits best suited to fund them. For example, increased requests for loans from creditworthy customers may require that the bank increase its efforts to acquire funds in the CD market. The rates that must be paid to obtain those deposits will directly affect the rates charged on loans. The principle of "matched funding" applies to every component of the bank's portfolio.

THE DISCOUNT AND PRIME RATES

Regulation A of the Federal Reserve allows each Federal Reserve bank to extend short-term seasonal or emergency credit to financial institutions. In making loans, the Fed charges the borrower the *discount rate*, reflecting the money market conditions prevailing at the time.

The discount rate paid by banks is lower than the rate of interest paid by a bank's own customers, since the credit rating of the bank is considered to be higher than that of depositors.

The *prime rate* is a base or reference rate that a bank establishes and uses to compute appropriate rates of interest for its loan contracts. The prime rate is typically 1 percent to 2 percent higher than the discount rate.

The prime rate, however, is only one reference device among several used by banks to price loans. The interest rate actually charged to a customer for a specific loan may be above or below a bank's prime rate. For example, a major corporation that has maintained an account with the bank for many years, has left good balances with the bank, and enjoys excellent credit standing may pay interest at this preferential rate. A borrower of more modest size may be charged at a rate lower than prime, if other factors warrant making the loan. Typically, however, commercial loans are made at rates higher than the base or reference rate, as a reflection of the risk factors. The prime rate set by the bank also fluctuates in relationship to the overall economic climate.

LOAN STRUCTURING

In addition to establishing pricing mechanisms, banks also devote attention to the actual structuring of each loan as regards the time frame for payment. The purpose of the loan influences that time frame. A loan made to a manufacturer so that he can buy raw material to meet a seasonal need usually is a short-term loan, generally unsecured; a loan made to a corporation so that it can make a major addition to its factory is a longer term credit. Wherever possible, the bank seeks a definite schedule of amortization; that is, of reduction of the principal through periodic payments. Installment loans have always been made on this basis, but the concept also can be applied to other credits. A schedule of amortization prevents a commercial loan from staying on the bank's books indefinitely, and also contributes to liquidity for the bank.

Some loans are structured on the basis of a so-called *balloon* payment. In such cases the borrower makes a specified number of smaller, regular reductions to the loan's principal and then makes a large final payment.

BASIC CREDIT PRINCIPLES

The generic term *borrower* may refer to a consumer who has obtained a small installment loan or to a nationally known corporation that has borrowed the bank's legal limit. In either case, the borrower should be subject to a standard set of guidelines and principles. Regardless of the size or type of credit, if these basic credit principles are always followed they will help protect the bank against losses; if they are ignored, the bank's risk immediately increases.

No set of principles and rules for lending will completely eliminate loan losses. No absolute formula or system exists that will positively guarantee that every loan will be repaid in full, with interest. Credit principles are *preventive;* they cannot provide total protection.

From time to time, a bank may lend against a savings account, a CD, or a quantity of U.S. government obligations. If the borrower defaults, the bank can immediately charge the loan balance to the account, apply the CD to repayment, or sell the securities. For these loans, the bank's risk is minimal. Loans of these types, however, constitute only a small fraction of the total portfolio. The vast majority of bank loans involve credit risk, and losses may take place even if all precautions are taken.

With the exception of loans that are completely secured by cash or its equivalent, each extension of bank credit carries with it the risk that some unexpected event will convert a "good" loan into a problem situation. An individual who has met all the criteria for a consumer loan may suddenly be forced out of work by the collapse of an employer's business. A client company that previously displayed a strong financial condition may become the victim of new competition or a change in public taste. Loans that seemed perfectly sound at the outset may have to be written off. These things happen not because the lender's judgment was poor but because the borrower has been hurt by conditions that could not be controlled.

In making a credit decision, the bank should be guided by the traditional "Cs" of credit: the *capacity* of the borrower to repay, the *character* of the borrower, the *conditions* that prompt the borrower to request credit, the *capital* that the borrower posseses, and any *collateral* that comes with the loan. Yet unforeseen events can always take place to create problems for the lenders. Despite years of training and experience, loan officers never become infallible; losses are a necessary part of the business of lending. The best that can be hoped for, in the face of the many demands for credit that are made on banks every day, is that basic credit principles will always be observed.

Credit Analysis

The key to credit analysis is making the decision as to where the bank can *best* place the funds it has available for lending. Ideally, funds will be placed where they will generate maximum profits and minimum losses. Credit analysis involves gathering all available information about the borrower, evaluating it, and using it to make a credit judgment. Information about the past and present is used to project what is likely to happen in the future. The question "What could go wrong?" is essential to credit analysis. To help answer that question, the loan officer should obtain some fundamental information during the initial interview with the borrower. The loan officer should ask the following questions:

- What is the requested amount?
- What is the purpose of the loan? Is it legal and in conformity with bank policy?
- For what length of time will the funds be needed?
- What will be the source of repayment?
- Is any type of collateral available?

Sources of Repayment

Regardless of the size or type of loan requested, a bank should make every effort to identify the source of funds from which the borrower will make repayment. A farmer who needs to borrow until harvest time should establish that repayment of this loan will come from the sale of the crops. An applicant for a home mortgage or other consumer loan should be able to show that his or her regular income will allow for regular monthly payments. A real estate developer must demonstrate that income from tenants in a new shopping center or office building will generate sufficient cash flow to meet the bank's repayment schedule. A toy manufacturer who borrows funds to produce and distribute products in time for the Christmas season must satisfy the bank that profits from sales should be sufficient to repay the loan.

Collateral

Lenders always have sought to protect themselves by obtaining some form of security that could be attached to a loan and used in case of default. *Collateral* is property pledged by a borrower to secure a loan. A farmer may pledge the value of land or equipment; the buyer of a new automobile may give the bank a security interest in the car; or a business may give the bank a *lien*, or *chattel mortgage*, on certain assets. The test of all collateral is its marketability. How easily can the collateral be sold? What will it yield if it is sold?

Whenever a bank accepts as collateral government obligations or other securities, savings account passbooks, life insurance policies with a cash surrender value, or merchandise stored in a warehouse, the bank believes that the assigned property *could* be readily sold, if necessary, and that the proceeds of the sale would reduce or pay off the loan. If it takes physical possession of the collateral (as may be done with stocks and bonds), the bank must provide for its safekeeping and control. Under the UCC in most states, the lender is required to register its security interest in collateral with the appropriate authorities.

Collateral may strengthen a borrowing situation, but it should never be the *only* reason for approving a loan. Borrowers should be able to repay from income and profits, and a bank should not look to the collateral alone as the justification for extending credit. The business of banking does not succeed through foreclosing on real estate, repossessing cars, or seizing a borrower's assets. These steps are taken only when normal payment procedures have not been followed. In addition, the bank usually incurs additional costs associated with foreclosures or repossessions, and a long period of time may elapse before the process is completed. During that time, the bank classifies the loan as *nonperforming* and as a *nonearning asset*.

In lending against collateral, a bank must protect itself against any possible fluctuations in the value of the assigned property. For example, stocks and bonds listed on a national exchange often are used as collateral. The bank assigns a loan value to those securities that is lower than the market value. The spread between the loan value and the market value is known as the *margin*. The bank may calculate the market value of the security at the time the loan is made and lend on 70 percent of it; the 30 percent margin is designed to protect the bank against changes in market prices. If the market declines, the borrower is asked to reduce the outstanding loan or to furnish additional collateral.

Credit Investigation

There can never be any excuse for a bank's negligence in obtaining all available information in order to make a credit decision. Information on businesses and individuals is readily available from a number of sources. Any failure to acquire and use it increases the bank's risk and creates the potential for future losses.

In the case of consumer credit, investigation usually consists of verifying the applicant's job, income, past credit history, and outstanding debts. In many cities, banks subscribe to credit bureaus (central information sources that maintain records of consumer borrowings). Each subscribing bank provides the credit agency with daily input on new applications and loans, repayments, rejected requests, and delinquencies. The information supplied by the applicant can be checked against the central data file. Recent laws stipulate that if a bank declines a loan on the basis of unfavorable credit information, it must make that fact known to the applicant and furnish him or her with a copy of the report if asked to do so.

The investigative process for businesses is far more detailed, and the sources of information are far more numerous. The logical starting point is the bank's own credit department, where credit files are maintained on each account and borrower. These files provide a complete history of the bank's relationships with its customers. They contain correspondence; reports of interviews; data on average balances, previous loans, and overdrafts; and internal memos.

Credit information also is available from other banks, provided there is a specific and ethical reason for requesting it. It is entirely proper for banks to exchange appropriate information with one another.

Various credit agencies publish regular reports on business firms. Most commercial banks subscribe to one or more of these agencies (for example, Dun & Bradstreet, Inc.) and can obtain updated financial information on a business.

In lending to businesses, banks rely heavily on financial information supplied by the borrower. The figures on submitted balance sheets, income statements, supplementary schedules, and projections should be thoroughly analyzed to detect trends in the business, compare the borrower with others in its industry, and help assess the borrower's ability to repay the loan through the normal operations of the firm.

Trade references also may be part of the investigation of a business borrower. The bank contacts a company's suppliers and asks what their experience has been in selling to it on credit terms. Their responses indicate how well the firm has been able to meet its trade obligations. In many situations a bank uses its knowledge of a customer to make an advance judgment as to the amount of credit it feels it can prudently extend. This amount represents the customer's _line of credit_, and is available in part or whole at any time. If the existence of the line is confirmed in writing to the customer by the bank, it is called an _advised_ line; if it is used only for internal purposes and the customer is not made aware of it, it is called a _guidance_ line.

A line of credit is an expression of a bank's willingness to lend up to a specified amount. A major corporation of unquestioned credit standing may be granted a line of credit as large as the bank's legal lending limit. A smaller business may have a more modest line, and an individual may be extended overdraft privileges, or be allowed to have bank card outstandings up to a certain dollar figure. As mentioned earlier, revolving credit lines are common. The borrower typically uses part or all of the line, repays part of it, uses the line again, and so on.

A line of credit is converted into an actual loan through the signing of a note, the issuing of checks, or the use of a bank card. Lines of credit must be taken into consideration when the bank computes its liquidity needs.

Compensating Balances

It is a basic truth of banking that customers deposit funds with those institutions that make credit available to them and that banks lend to those customers who provide it with deposits. This is nothing more than an acknowledgment of the interrelationship of the deposit and credit functions. Traditionally, banks have expected business borrowers to maintain noninterest-bearing balances that are proportionate to the size of each line of credit or loan. Depending on money market conditions and competition, a formula might require balances equal to 10 percent of a business's line of credit and 20 percent of an actual loan. Therefore, a corporation with a $100,000 line of credit would have to keep balances of $10,000 to support the line and would have to increase its balances to $20,000 whenever the line actually was used. The cost of the compensating balances to the borrower is over and above the direct interest expense.

In recent years, this traditional practice has been replaced at many banks by a willingness to quote _all-in-the-rate pricing_ to borrowers, without any consideration of balances. Business borrowers prefer this method for several reasons. It eliminates the need for maintaining interest-free deposits, so that the company can put additional funds to profitable use. All-in-the-rate pricing also avoids the need for repeated negotiations between bank and borrower as to the level of balances.

Loan Review

The recent experiences of many banks support the idea that losses often result from a lack of attention to information that develops during the life of a loan. Changes in business circumstances are frequent, and loans that were considered of good quality when they were made can deteriorate later. Loan officers need to maintain close contact with borrowing customers. Loan officers must be alert for any new conditions that affect the credit, and do everything to ensure that the quality of the loan does not diminish. The loan officer's concerns over each loan do not end when the loan has been approved and placed on the bank's books; rather, they are only beginning.

Many banks provide for a system of loan review, so that a staff of specialists will examine all loans that have been made and will give an early warning of potential problems. Loan losses always present a source of real concern to banks. Loan review units can prevent losses by taking timely action where it is warranted and, in some cases, by arranging for a restructuring of the loan for the benefit of both parties.

The system of loan reviews gives management some assurance that loan officers have stayed within their authorities, that policies have been followed, and that all necessary documentation on each credit has been obtained. If the size of the portfolio warrants it, the review process may include both secured and unsecured loans, and existing loans as well as new ones. It may assign a rating or grade—excellent, satisfactory, or substandard risk, or imminent workout situation—to every credit. Charged with the responsibility for examining each loan, identifying existing or possible problems, and recommending corrective action, this impartial unit can make a real contribution to any bank's bottom-line profits.

SUMMARY

In American society today individuals, businesses, units of government, and institutions all use credit—and there are many sources from which funds can be borrowed. Thrift institutions, for example, increased their commercial loan portfolios by 43 percent in 1986, to $16 billion.[18] Non-bank corporations such as General Motors Acceptance Corporation also have become increasingly active in various areas of lending. Nevertheless, the commercial banks continue to dominate the market, providing every type of loan to every category of borrower.

In providing loans, banks basically use depositors' funds rather than their own. Therefore, banks must maintain a delicate balance at all times among the three objectives of liquidity, safety, and income. Overemphasis on any one of the three, at the expense of the other two, can have unfortunate results.

The four basic categories of bank loans constitute the major source of bank income, yet each extension of credit carries with it a degree of risk. No absolute, foolproof formula has ever been devised to eliminate losses. The objective of prudent bank lending is to keep losses to a minimum. In real estate, interbank, consumer, and commercial lending, banks follow a set of systematic procedures that are designed to keep losses to acceptable levels. These procedures help protect depositors' funds, from which 90 percent of loans are made.

Based on the availability and cost of funds, and on its own decisions as to the types of loans it is willing to make, each bank sets policies regarding loans and gives its loan officers stated amounts of credit authority within which to work. Banks function, however, under the constraints of the legal restrictions that have been imposed by federal and state governments. Whenever a bank considers a loan, it should follow an established set of credit principles to ensure that all necessary information has been gathered and evaluated.

Detailed and ongoing knowledge—about the borrower, the industry of which the borrower's business is a part, the impact of the economy on that business, the competition the borrower faces, and the "Cs" of credit as reflected in the borrower's financial operations—is the key to success in lending.

QUESTIONS FOR DISCUSSION

1. Why is liquidity so essential for a commercial bank?

2. What would be the consequences if a bank chose to overemphasize liquidity, safety, or income?

3. What two factors are considered when a bank estimates its liquidity needs?

4. Why have home equity loans assumed greater importance in recent years?

5. Distinguish between construction loans and mortgage loans.

6. On what basis are consumer installment loans generally made?

7. Why are most commercial and industrial loans made on a short-term basis?

8. What role do the bank's directors play in the overall credit function?

9. Identify three Federal Reserve restrictions on bank loans.

10. What is meant by usury?

11. Distinguish between the discount rate and the prime rate.

12. What test is applied to all collateral? Does collateral alone justify the granting of a requested loan?

13. From the information published by your bank, identify the amount of credit it has extended in each category of loans.

NOTES

1. *Federal Reserve Bulletin* (March 1987), p. A18.

2. General Electric Credit Corporation, *1984 Annual Report*, p. 31.

3. Paul A. Eisenstein, "Here Come the Auto Companies," *United States Banker* (March 1986), pp. 32–33.

4. *Federal Reserve Bulletin* (March 1987), p. A39.

5. Kenneth J. Hicks, "Commercial Loan Growth Slows at Top Thrifts," *American Banker*, May 8, 1987, p. 1.

6. Jeffrey Kutler, "Firm Foresees 30% Fewer Credit Unions by 1990," *American Banker*, May 13, 1987, p. 1.

7. *Federal Reserve Bulletin* (March 1987), p. A18.

8. John G. Medlin, "More Than Ever, Banks Must Adhere to Basics," *American Banker*, May 14, 1987, p. 4.

9. Phil Roosevelt, "Fannie Mae Has Gone Far," *American Banker*, May 15, 1987, p. 14.

10. Jim McTague, "America's Dream Girl of the Mortgage Market," *American Banker*, May 15, 1987, pp. 15–16.

11. *Ibid.*, pp. 12–13.

12. Daniel M. Clark, "Home Equity Taps the American Dream," *ABA Banking Journal* (April 1987), p. 50.

13. Robert M. Garsson, "Home Equity Safeguards Sought," *American Banker*, April 27, 1987, p. 22.

14. Jeffrey Kutler, "Home Equity Accounts Mean More Checks," *American Banker*, April 27, 1987, p. 23.

15. Robert B. Avery, Gregory E. Elliehausen, Arthur B. Kennickell, and Paul A. Spindt, "Changes in the Use of Transaction Accounts and Cash from 1984 to 1986," *Federal Reserve Bulletin* (March 1987), p. 184.

16. *Federal Reserve Bulletin* (March 1987), p. A40, and Eric N. Compton, *The New World of Commercial Banking* (Lexington, Mass.: Lexington Books, 1987), p. 148.

17. Jeffrey Kutler, "Consumers Say Tax Reform Will Alter Habits," *American Banker*, April 27, 1987, p. 1.

18. Hicks, "Commercial Loan Growth," p. 1.

For More Information

American Bankers Association. *Bank Investments and Funds Management.* Washington, D.C., 1987.

Beares, Paul. *Consumer Lending.* Washington, D.C.: American Bankers Association, 1987.

Buchanan, Michael, and Ronald D. Johnson. *Real Estate Finance.* Washington, D.C.: American Bankers Association, 1988.

Cole, Robert H. *Consumer and Commercial Credit Management.* 7th ed. Homewood, Ill.: Richard D. Irwin, 1984.

Compton, Eric N. *The New World of Commercial Banking.* Lexington, Mass.: Lexington Books, 1987.

Frey, Thomas L., and Robert H. Behrens. *Lending to Agricultural Enterprises.* Boston: Bankers Publishing Company, 1981.

Hale, Roger H. *Credit Analysis: A Complete Guide.* New York: John Wiley & Sons, Inc., 1983.

Hayes, Douglas. *Bank Lending Policies, Domestic and International.* Ann Arbor: University of Michigan, 1977.

Hoffman, Margaret A., and Gerald C. Fischer. *Credit Department Management.* Philadelphia: Robert Morris Associates, 1980.

Krumme, Dwane. *Banking and the Plastic Card.* Washington, D.C.: American Bankers Association, 1987.

Mason, John M. *Financial Management of Commercial Banks.* Boston: Warren, Gorham, & Lamont, 1979.

McKinley, John E., and others. *Analyzing Financial Statements.* Washington, D.C.: American Bankers Association, 1988.

Ruth, George E. *Commercial Lending.* Washington, D.C.: American Bankers Association, 1987.

10.

BANK
INVESTMENTS

LEARNING OBJECTIVES

After completing this chapter, you will be able to
•
rank bank priorities in funds management
•
list some of the risks banks face in making investments
•
explain the principle of diversification in investments
•
cite the legal restrictions on bank investments
•
determine the investments that banks legally are required to make
•
list the components of a bank's investment portfolio
•
describe the meaning and importance of municipals
•
analyze the effect of tax legislation on bank investment strategies
•
name the securities-related activities that banks legally are permitted
to provide

The credit function of commercial banks is not confined purely to direct lending to customers. It also includes the investments that banks make. Both loans and investments put the bank's available funds to profitable use; however, there are two basic differences between loans and investments.

The first difference involves the bank's purposes and priorities. The fundamental business of banking is the lending of money to individuals, businesses, units of government, and other banks. It is expected that banks will fulfill their community obligations by supplying the funds that customers in those communities legitimately wish to borrow. In turn, this lending process helps the communities to prosper and grow. As mentioned earlier, the Community Reinvestment Act requires that banks work to meet the credit needs of the towns and cities they serve. Moreover, an institution that does not make commercial loans fails to meet the legal definition of a bank. Banks are not required, however, to make investments.

In allocating funds, banks must give first priority to customers' credit needs. Investments have a lower priority and are usually made only after the demand for loans has been met.

The second difference between loans and investments reflects the relationships between the parties. In making a loan, a bank negotiates directly with the borrower regarding the amount, purpose, maturity, rate, and other factors of the loan. In most cases, the bank is dealing with a party known to it through a deposit relationship.

When a bank makes an investment, on the other hand, it does so indirectly; that is, through a dealer or underwriter. The bank relies on investment rating services to determine the quality of the investment and the risk involved. Local issues of securities may not be rated by agencies such as Moody's or Standard & Poor's, and the bank may have to conduct its own inquiries and have its own analysts rate the issues before an investment is made. Still, the bank does not negotiate directly with the issuer in most cases, and the issuer may have no knowledge of who the purchaser is.

Interest on loans and income from investments both contribute to bank earnings, but the *purpose* of each is different. Banks do not make loans primarily for the sake of the income they generate. Rather, loans reflect the bank's obligation to meet the credit needs of its customer base. On the other hand, investments *are* made chiefly for income purposes.

207

The fact that a bank is contributing to the general well-being of a community by buying that community's notes or bonds is secondary to the income objective. When loan demand increases, the bank's investment portfolio usually decreases. In keeping with its schedule of priorities, the bank will sell off part of its investments to obtain the funds with which to make loans.

TYPES OF RISK

Risk enters into investments as it does in the case of loans; however, there is more than one type of risk that banks face in each case. In loans, the chief concern is *credit risk*, which concerns whether the borrower will be able to repay as scheduled. Investments also carry credit risk concerning whether the issuer of securities will be able to raise the funds necessary to pay principal and interest. Investments also carry *market risk*. If the holder of an investment wishes to sell it at any time, market conditions and the overall desirability of the security will determine the market value, and the seller cannot control these conditions.

As interest rates fluctuate, the appeal of a bond issue paying a certain rate of coupon interest may increase or decrease in the eyes of potential buyers. U.S. government obligations carry *no* credit risk because there is no doubt as to the ability of the federal government to honor them. U.S. government obligations *do carry market risk*, however, because interest rates on many types of money market instruments change frequently. A bank wishing to sell a government bond issued several years previously with a 5 percent coupon may find that the bond is unattractive to investors—not because of credit risk, but because other bonds, with higher coupon rates, are readily available. Under these conditions, sale of the bond will create a direct loss for the bank.

In any given year, a bank may show profits or losses on sales of securities, depending on the market conditions that existed at various times during the 12 months. In certain cases, a bank will deliberately sell some of its investments at a loss in order to raise funds and use the proceeds for loans that carry a higher rate or return. Taking such losses can also work to the bank's advantage if the institution has a substantial amount of net taxable income against which the losses can be offset.

Diversification

For both legal and practical reasons, banks invest their funds in various types of issues. The legal reasons are twofold:

- Banks are prohibited from investing in any common stock.
- Banks are limited as to the percentage of their capital and surplus they can invest in the securities of any one issuer, *except* for investments in U.S. government obligations.

208

The first of these restrictions traces back to thousands of bank failures that accompanied the Great Depression. Before 1933, banks actively invested in corporate stock issues; in many cases, they were considered to have done so simply in the expectation of making a quick profit. In this respect, their optimism reflected that of the general public, which believed that stock prices would continue on an unending upward spiral. However, this type of investment was not and is not considered a legitimate use of deposited funds. The Glass-Steagall Act of 1933 restricted the investment opportunities for banks, limited their ability to become involved in merchant banking, and prohibited them from underwriting certain types of debt issues.

The Comptroller of the Currency has expanded on Glass-Steagall by defining as "investment securities" those that are *not* distinctly or predominantly speculative.

The second legal restriction resembles the limit placed on unsecured bank lending to a single borrower. It prevents banks from placing excessive amounts of depositors' funds in the securities of a single issuer (other than the U.S. government) and therefore forces them to diversify.

Every institution's practical investment policies will reflect its own changing priorities. A bank makes investments *only* after liquidity needs have been met and loan demand satisified. If all available funds have been used for those two purposes, investment activity temporarily ceases.

Required Investments

Many banks make investments because they are required to do so by law. Many states, to ensure further protection for bank deposits over and above the coverage provided by FDIC, require that banks hold and segregate a quantity of federal or state obligations. For the same reason, since the trust operations of banks have a significant impact on retired persons, widows, minors, and the beneficiaries of estates, the trust powers granted to banks by individual states require that federal and state debt issues be set aside to protect the pension, trust, and profit-sharing funds they manage.

Aside from required holdings, a bank's investment portfolio usually is divided into two parts. The actual investment account consists of the securities held to generate income for the bank. The second part may be called the trading account, in which the banks "make a market" by holding a certain amount of federal and state or local (city, county, authority, or agency) obligations as a means of serving their customers who may wish to invest in them.

Two exceptions to the provisions of the Glass-Steagall Act allow for bank investments in common stock: Member banks in the Fed are legally required to buy and hold stock in their district Federal Reserve bank, and bank holding companies are allowed to own stock in their various subsidiaries.

209

TYPES OF BANK INVESTMENTS

A typical bank's investment portfolio consists almost exclusively of four types of holdings. These holdings are

- direct obligations of the U.S. government: bills (short-term, 91-day or 180-day issues); notes (usually with 1- to 5-year maturities); and bonds (long-term, larger-denomination obligations)
- obligations of various U.S. government agencies
- various municipal issues (to be defined and discussed later in this chapter)
- miscellaneous investments that meet the risk criteria, such as bankers' acceptances, certificates of deposit issued by other institutions, or highest-quality commercial paper

As mentioned earlier, U.S. Treasury bills offer the investing bank a dual advantage. Because they are immediately marketable, they provide liquidity and therefore are part of the bank's secondary reserves. At the same time, they are a source of investment income. At year-end 1986 the total investment accounts of all U.S. commercial banks amounted to $474.5 billion, of which $291.3 billion (61.4 percent) were U.S. government issues. Banks' trading account assets totaled $29.3 billion.[1]

Municipals

Municipals is a generic term that describes the bonds issued by any government or agency of government other than the federal. A state, city, county, town, public authority, school district, or sewer district issues bonds to raise funds over and above its income from taxes. Some municipals are backed by the full taxing power of the issuer and are known as "full faith and credit" obligations. Commercial banks are allowed to underwrite these general obligation bonds; that is, they are permitted to purchase them directly from the issuer and distribute them by reselling them to investors. Other municipals, called revenue bonds, are *not* backed by the taxing power of the issuer. Revenue bonds are supported only by the direct income that is anticipated to result from a specific project. For example, a local government may issue revenue bonds to raise funds to construct a new toll road. Each bondholder depends on the profit from the new turnpike's operations to provide a source of repayment. With very few exceptions, commercial banks are not allowed to underwrite revenue bonds.

Unlike U.S. government obligations, which are considered entirely free of credit risk, municipal bonds involve both credit risk and market risk. Their credit risk reflects the fact that the credit standing of a municipal issuer cannot be as high as that of the federal government. Their market risk is greater for the same reason. For example, publicity about

210

the financial problems of a city or state may make municipal issues unattractive to many investors.

Given the credit and market risk that municipals carry, why have banks considered them to be worthwhile investments? There have been two basic reasons. The first of these was the tax advantage that municipal issues traditionally gave to investors. Income from municipals is completely exempt from federal income taxes, and may also be exempt from state and local taxes. For example, an investor in California who purchases bonds issued by a California government unit enjoys exemption from both federal and local taxes on the income. The higher the tax bracket of the bank or other investor, the greater the advantage of deriving tax-free income from municipals.

However, the Tax Reform Act of 1986 significantly reduced this advantage. By lowering the tax brackets into which banks generally fall, it made investments in municipals less attractive. In 1985, for example, a 5-year, 5 percent municipal bond generated a tax-equivalent yield of 8.49 percent when the bank's effective tax rate was 46 percent. With a reduction in the effective tax rate to 34 percent (as called for by the Tax Reform Act) the bank's tax-equivalent yield drops to 5.33 percent, leading the bank to look for other investments with a higher rate of return.[2]

The Tax Reform Act had an additional impact on bank strategies regarding investment in municipals. The act denies to banks any deduction for the interest expense they may incur in borrowing funds for the purpose of buying or carrying tax-exempt obligations, except when the obligations are issued by communities or authorities (excluding states) that sell less than $10 million of obligations per year.[3] This provision of the act eliminates what had been a dual advantage for the banks. Before the Tax Reform Act was passed, banks were allowed to deduct that interest expense in calculating their tax liability at the same time that the income derived from the municipal issues was exempt from taxation.

In 1985 the nation's 1,000 largest commercial banks increased their municipal holdings by 45 percent to a total of $104.4 billion. Ten of those banks reported holdings of $1 billion or more. In 1986 the same 1,000 banks, anticipating the effects of the Tax Reform Act, reduced their municipal portfolios by 13 percent.[4]

The second reason for bank investments in municipals lies in the commitment that banks make to their communities. Banks recognize that their own well-being, growth, and profitability are closely tied to conditions in their own communities, from which they draw part or all of their income. If a city or town is unable to raise the funds it needs and its economy deteriorates, its banks inevitably will suffer as well. Every bank investment in municipal issues represents a vote of confidence in the ability of the municipality to maintain a healthy economy and to eventually repay its debts. By investing in municipals, banks act as corporate citizens that *give* to their communities as well as *take* from them.

Spacing of Maturities

In attempting to achieve the proper combination of liquidity, safety, and income, banks not only diversify their investment portfolios among various issues, but also ensure that their holdings carry a range of maturities. Table 10.1 shows the various components and maturity ranges of the investment securities portfolio of a major money-center commercial bank. The securities with the shortest maturities provide the bank with a high degree of liquidity; at the same time, their interest rates may be lower than those shown by the longer-term issues.

SECURITIES ACTIVITIES AND SERVICES AT BANKS

Commercial banks are financial intermediaries whose raw material is deposits. Deposited funds are loaned or invested in order to generate profits. Investment banks, on the other hand, raise funds directly from savers by underwriting and distributing securities. Investment banks are not investors themselves; except for brief periods while the securities are part of their inventory, they do not own or hold those issues. Commercial banks, on the other hand, are major investors who buy and hold the securities originated by others. The Glass-Steagall Act of 1933 is largely responsible for the separation of the two types of banking. In recent years, commercial banks have actively sought greater freedom in their securities activities and services as a means of serving their customers better in an environment of aggressive competition.

Glass-Steagall originally prohibited Fed member banks from under-writing, distributing, and dealing in stocks and bonds, with the exceptions of federal government issues and general obligation municipals. The act also limited the purchase of securities for a bank's own account to certain specified issues, and prohibited Fed member banks from affiliating with investment banks.

Today, commercial banks are important entities in the secondary markets for federal government and federal agency obligations. As deal-

TABLE 10.1
COMPOSITION AND MATURITY OF AN INVESTMENT PORTFOLIO
(in millions of dollars)

Type of Security	Within 1 Year	1–5 Years	6–10 Years	Over 10 Years	Total
U.S. Government	$ 5	$1,363	$1,130	$ 472	$2,970
Municipals	328	81	254	948	1,611
Other Securities	116	471	37	219	843
Totals	$449	$1,915	$1,421	$1,639	$5,424

Source: Chemical New York Corporation, *Annual Report*, 1985.

ers, the banks buy for their own accounts and sell from inventory; as brokers, they collect commissions on each sale. In addition, they underwrite and distribute the permitted issues of state and local governments. Banks also may trade in futures contracts, which provide for the delivery of a security or asset at a specific future date at a fixed price, determined at the time the contract is executed.

In their trust departments, the operations of which will be detailed in chapter 12, over 4,000 commercial banks manage assets totaling some $689 billion. The banks purchase and sell securities for customers of their trust departments. Usually the bank acts as directed by the customer but in some cases banks may act at their own discretion. They offer investment, financial, and economic advice to individual investors, business firms, agencies of government, and investment companies.

Many banks have sought permission to expand their activities in actual brokerage services. In 1981 BankAmerica Corporation began proceedings to acquire Charles Schwab, a brokerage firm that traded securities at very low commissions, extended stock market credit on margin, and offered custody services. Since that time, other major banks have acquired brokerage firms or have entered into cooperative arrangements with nonbank brokers and dealers. In this way, banks have become much more competitive with the nation's brokerage firms and have been able to provide a broader range of services to their customers. The Federal Deposit Insurance Corporation has ruled that banks that are *not* Fed members are not restricted by the Glass-Steagall Act, and therefore are free to have affiliates engaged in securities-related activities.

SUMMARY

Bank investments contribute to the overall credit function, but occupy a lower priority in the management of funds than loans. As a group, commercial banks are the largest holders of U.S. government obligations. Banks also have made substantial investments in the debt issues of state and local governments, authorities, and agencies; however, the Tax Reform Act of 1986 has made municipal issues less attractive to banks. The total portfolio of a commercial bank usually consists of both a trading account, in which an inventory of securities is held for resale to customers, and a larger investment account, in which the bank may place its own funds (within legal limits).

Bank opportunities to underwrite and invest in various securities are restricted by federal laws. In addition, the banks themselves have been careful to protect their liquidity, safety, and income by diversifying their holdings and by spacing the maturities of the issues they hold.

In recent years, many banks have been granted regulatory approval to engage in a wider range of securities-related activities in order to provide more complete services to their customers.

QUESTIONS FOR DISCUSSION

1. Why do investments occupy a lower priority in the management of bank funds than loans?

2. How can bank investments contribute to liquidity?

3. Distinguish between credit risk and market risk.

4. What risk does a bank incur when it invests in U.S. government obligations?

5. Identify two restrictions that affect bank investments.

6. Explain the differences among U.S. Treasury bills, notes, and bonds.

7. Define the term *municipals*.

8. Give two reasons why banks invest in municipal issues.

9. Distinguish between commercial banks and investment banks.

10. Identify some of the securities-related activities in which banks in your community are now engaged.

NOTES

1. *Federal Reserve Bulletin* (March 1987), p. A18.

2. "Bank Investment Report," *ABA Banking Journal* (February 1987), p. 35.

3. Matthew Kreps, "Uncertainty About Taxes Spurred Banks to Buy Municipal Bonds in '85," *American Banker*, June 10, 1986, p. 6, and "Big Banks Trimmed Municipal Bond Portfolios in '86," *American Banker*, May 13, 1987, p. 42.

4. Donald Yacoe, "Banks Look for New Investments Under Tax Reform," *American Banker*, February 24, 1987, p. 6.

For More Information

American Bankers Association. *Bank Investments and Funds Management*. Washington, D.C., 1987.

Aspinwall, Richard C., and Robert A. Eisenbeis, eds. *Handbook for Banking Strategy*. New York: John Wiley & Sons, Inc., 1985.

Crosse, Howard D., and George H. Hempel. *Management Policies for Commercial Banks*. 2d ed. Englewood Cliffs, N.J.: Prentice-Hall, Inc., 1973.

Johnson, Frank P., and Richard D. Johnson. *Commercial Bank Management*. New York: Dryden Press, 1986.

11.

BANK
ACCOUNTING,
PRICING,
AND
PROFITABILITY

LEARNING OBJECTIVES

After completing this chapter, you will be able to

•

describe double-entry bookkeeping and
how debits and credits are used in posting

•

name the two basic reports that banks prepare to show
the details of their financial condition

•

distinguish between the cash and accrual methods of accounting

•

list the major asset and liability accounts that appear on a bank's
balance sheet

•

list the major income and expense accounts that appear on a bank's
income statement

•

name the four major ratios that are used as measures of bank
profitability

•

explain the importance of loan-loss reserves

•

explain why account analysis is valuable to both banks and customers

Accounting has often been called "the language of business." Through accounting, all the transactions affecting a business—the facts and events, translated into figures—are gathered, classified, and reported in accordance with specified principles, procedures, and terms. When considering a request for a commercial loan, a bank expects the applicant to supply it with detailed financial statements prepared in conformity with generally accepted accounting standards. Any absence of information concerning the business's assets and liabilities, income, or expenses immediately tells the bank that the applicant simply does not know how the business is operating. To state that a business showed a profit for the year is a simple matter; to find the reasons for that profit is a more complex task. Accounting answers the basic questions regarding what happens to make a business successful or unsuccessful.

With respect to accounting, banks must be prepared to do even more than they expect from their borrowers. Even the smallest banks are under greater pressure than their customers to develop and use accounting systems that will record, present, and interpret the many transactions that occur every day.

The information developed through a bank's accounting systems is important to many individuals and agencies that are vitally concerned about the financial strength and profitability of the institution. These individuals and agencies include

- federal and state regulatory authorities
- the bank's directors and managers
- the bank's customers
- the bank's stockholders

Every examination of a bank by federal and state authorities includes a determination of the bank's true financial condition. The Comptroller of the Currency, the Federal Reserve, the Federal Deposit Insurance Corporation, and the state banking departments each require that the banks under their jurisdiction file periodic *call reports*. These contain not only financial data, but also a certification by management that the figures are accurate and up to date. National banks must file their call reports, whenever requested, with the Comptroller. State-chartered member banks file their reports with the Federal Reserve and the state. State-chartered, insured nonmembers file with the FDIC. All others file their call reports with the state banking authorities.

For internal management purposes, each bank must systematically update all its asset, liability, income, expense, and capital accounts. For the directors and senior officers, bank accounting identifies the branches, departments, and services that are directly generating profits or losses. These directors and officers depend on the management information supplied by accounting to make planning decisions.

Customers demand timely and accurate bank statements, showing all the transactions that have affected their accounts and providing their current status. Many customers also scrutinize published data showing the bank's financial condition and its profitability. Depositors have an on-going interest in the strength of the bank.

Finally, like those in any corporation, the bank's stockholders clearly are entitled to information. The value of the stockholders' investment is directly related to the financial information that shows where and how the bank acquired funds, how the funds were put to work, and what the results were.

In summary, no bank can operate without an efficient system for recording all transactions and summarizing their effects on the bank's books.

Accounting and the Planning Function

Banks now operate in an environment of increasingly numerous and more aggressive competition. The banks that have recognized this have placed far greater emphasis on planning than ever before. They realize that senior management and the board of directors *must* determine the overall mission and the major objectives of the organization and must develop policies and strategies to use the bank's resources to best advantage. Planning is intended to lead to managerial decision making by tying together all the component parts of the bank. The annual budgeting process and the effort to forecast future conditions and events are important parts of the overall planning process.

Through the bank's accounting systems, management can decide what needs to be done in the areas of asset and liability management. In deciding whether to eliminate certain unprofitable branches or services, or to reduce expenses in certain areas and commit additional resources to another, managers rely on a detailed examination of the financial data. The published figures clearly indicate the current status of the bank and are used to help management develop goals and policies. The policies, in turn, lead to the practices that staff members follow every day—and that contribute to future growth and profitability. Accounting forms the basis for the entire planning exercise.

TYPES OF ACCOUNTING RECORDS

Many daily bank transactions are entered on temporary records, such as adding machine tapes. These temporary records are used for proof purposes; they lose their value as the transactions are completed in other areas of the bank and the figures are posted to "permanent" records.

Permanent bank records may include summaries of temporary records or the originals or microfilm copies of documents.

A third category of records is essentially archival. This category includes records that must be kept for longer periods of time as required by law or by bank policy.

In bank accounting, a *journal* is a book of *original entry*. Each processing area in a bank usually has some form of journal into which daily transactions are posted. Eventually, entries are transferred from journals to the bank's *ledgers*, which are records of *final entry*. For example, the loan department in a branch of a bank makes daily entries of loans "made and paid." These original journal entries eventually will become part of the bank's ledger records. The typical bank maintains a *general ledger* department, in which all financial information from every department and branch is consolidated so that the daily financial condition of the bank can be determined. In addition to the general ledger, *subsidiary ledgers* normally are maintained for specific types of accounts. For example, demand deposit accounts, savings accounts, loans, and fixed assets each might have a subsidiary ledger.

Double-Entry Bookkeeping

The fundamental technique used in bank accounting requires that each transaction affect two accounts and be recorded by a balanced set of entries. This is known as *double-entry bookkeeping*. Every *debit* must have an equal, offsetting *credit*. Total debits must equal total credits.

The posting of *debits* increases an asset or expense account, or decreases a liability, income, or capital account. The posting of *credits* accomplishes the reverse. Credits increase a liability, income, or capital account and decrease an asset or expense account.

For example, assume that a customer deposits $100 in a checking account. The transaction is recorded by (1) a debit, which increases the cash account, and (2) a credit, which increases the demand deposits account. The cash account is an *asset* of the bank because it represents something of value that the bank owns or that is owed to it; the demand deposit account is a *liability* of the bank because it represents money owed to a customer.

Unless a bank is insolvent, its total assets will always be greater than its total liabilities. The excess of assets over liabilities is the *net worth* of the bank and is shown in its capital accounts. A fundamental equation in bank and corporate accounting states that total assets must always equal total liabilities plus net worth.

Basic Reports

Two basic reports convey all the essential information regarding a bank's current condition and the results it has achieved. The *statement of condi-*

tion, also called the *balance sheet*, is prepared as of a specific date. For example, a balance sheet can be prepared for December 31, 1987. The *income statement*, also called the *profit and loss (P & L) statement*, covers a period of time. The P&L statement might, for example, cover the year ended December 31, 1987. The balance sheet lists all the asset, liability, and capital accounts of the bank; the profit and loss statement shows all revenues and expenses and the net profit or loss for the period.

A bank's total portfolio of loans is its largest asset; total deposits are always a bank's largest liability. Asset, liability, income, and expense accounts are the most common account categories into which the bank's activities are grouped (see table 11.1).

Accrual Accounting

Because of the nature of their operations, many businesses use a system of *cash accounting*. Under this system, entries to the firm's records are made *only* when cash actually is received as income or paid out as an expense. If banks were to follow this method, their income figures would be so severely distorted as to become meaningless.

As an example, consider the interest that must be paid to the holders of CDs at maturity and to savings account customers at the end of the quarter. Using the cash method, no entries would be made on the bank's books until the actual payouts to depositors took place. This would ignore the fact that the interest expense actually was incurred at an earlier date. As another example, consider that a customer borrows $25,000 from the bank and agrees to repay it with interest 90 days later. The cash method

TABLE 11.1
ACCOUNT CATEGORIES

Category	Definition	Subdivisions
Asset accounts	Items owned by or owed to the bank, having commercial or exchange value. May consist of specific property, claims against property, or items such as cash, drafts, and loans.	Loans and securities Cash and due from banks Float Income earned but not collected Fixed and other assets
Liability accounts	Funds entrusted to the bank by depositors and/or obligations incurred through operations.	Demand and time deposits Loan commitments Accrued and other liabilities
Income accounts	Accounts that classify and segregate actual and accrued revenues.	Interest on loans Interest on investments
Expense accounts	Accounts that classify and segregate actual and accrued expenses.	Interest expense Salaries and wages

of accounting gives no recognition to the fact that the bank actually earns interest each day throughout the life of the loan.

Because of the nature of *their* business, banks generally use the *accrual* method of accounting. This system records expenses at the time they are incurred (regardless of when they are paid) and records income at the time it is earned (regardless of when it is actually received). Thus, in table 11.2, "accrued interest receivable" is an asset account; "accrued taxes" and "other liabilities" are liability accounts.

Statement-of-Condition Assets

The following items commonly are listed as assets on the bank's balance sheet:

- Cash on hand and due from banks: the currency and coin held in the bank's vaults, plus checks that are in the process of collection and balances maintained with correspondents.
- Investments: direct obligations of the U.S. government, obligations of other agencies of the federal government, and municipals.
- Loans: all indebtedness to the bank, usually subdivided by loan category and/or by domestic and global loans.
- Fixed assets: real estate owned by the bank, furniture, fixtures, and equipment.

Member banks also list under "Investments" their stock in the Federal Reserve.

Statement-of-Condition Liabilities

The following items commonly are listed as liabilities on the balance sheet:

- Deposits: all money owed to depositors, subdivided as to demand, savings, and time deposits.
- Taxes payable: all taxes (federal, state, and local) that must be paid.
- Dividends payable: if the board of directors has approved payment of a quarterly dividend to stockholders but the actual disbursement has not been made as of the date of the statement, this entry will show the bank's liability.

Correspondent bank balances also are included under "Deposits." If the scope of the bank's operations warrants it, deposits may be subdivided between those held in the United States and those at foreign branches.

Income-Statement Entries

In order of size and importance, the sources of bank income typically include

TABLE 11.2
CONSOLIDATED STATEMENT OF CONDITION: ASSETS, LIABILITIES AND STOCKHOLDERS' EQUITY

	Assets		
	December 31		
(In thousands of dollars)	19XX	19XX	Change
Cash and due from banks	$ 1,649,334	$ 1,332,586	$ 316,748
Overseas deposits	458,313	460,396	(2,083)
Investment securities:			
U.S. Treasury securities	881,081	982,654	(101,573)
Securities of other U.S. government agencies and corporations	199,318	243,420	(44,102)
Obligations of states and political subdivisions	738,813	396,948	341,865
Other securities	88,278	92,032	(3,754)
Total investment securities	1,907,490	1,715,054	192,436
Trading account securities	14,846	66,140	(51,294)
Funds sold	168,600	108,450	60,150
Loans (net of reserve for loan losses and unearned discount)	9,715,728	8,074,132	1,641,596
Direct lease financing	147,860	134,472	13,388
Premises and equipment, net	133,506	132,320	1,186
Customers' acceptance liability	372,835	248,271	124,564
Accrued interest receivable	133,840	123,719	10,121
Other real estate owned	34,332	13,668	20,664
Other assets	103,939	131,711	(27,772)
Total assets	$14,840,623	$12,540,919	$ 2,299,704

- interest on loans
- interest and dividends on investments
- fees, commissions, and service charges

Expenses, again in the order of their size and importance, would include

- interest paid to customers
- salaries, wages, and benefits
- taxes

The bank's income statement produces a *net* (revenues less expenses) figure, which usually is translated into earnings per share. In

TABLE 11.2
CONSOLIDATED STATEMENT OF CONDITION, (CONTINUED)

Liabilities and Stockholders' Equity

(In thousands of dollars)	December 31 19XX	December 31 19XX	Change
Demand deposits	$ 3,543,141	$ 2,937,065	$ 606,076
Savings deposits	3,585,808	3,485,886	99,922
Savings certificates	1,635,215	1,391,107	244,108
Certificates of deposit	1,827,420	1,601,707	225,713
Other time deposits	424,592	313,811	110,781
Deposits in overseas offices	1,468,003	722,950	745,053
Total deposits	12,484,179	10,452,526	2,031,653
Funds borrowed	897,189	924,501	(27,312)
Long-term debt	44,556	43,766	790
Acceptances outstanding	373,022	249,088	123,934
Accrued taxes and other expenses	142,756	122,064	20,692
Other liabilities	171,904	122,890	49,014
Total liabilities (excluding subordinated notes)	14,113,606	11,914,835	2,198,771
Subordinated notes:			
8¼% capital note to Wells Fargo & Company, due 1998	25,000	25,000	—
4½% capital notes due 1989	50,000	50,000	—
Total subordinated notes	75,000	75,000	—
Stockholders' equity:			
Capital stock	94,461	94,461	—
Surplus	300,036	251,512	48,524
Surplus representing convertible capital note obligation assumed by parent corporation	10,065	14,589	(4,524)
Undivided profits	247,455	190,522	56,933
Total stockholders' equity	652,017	551,084	100,933
Total liabilities and stockholders' equity	$14,840,623	$12,540,919	$ 2,299,704

this way, stockholders know how much each share of outstanding stock earned during the period. If the bank's total expenses for the period are greater than its income, the net figure will be a negative one, recording the actual loss for that period.

On the bank's balance sheet, assets and liabilities always are listed in order of liquidity. Therefore, "Cash and due from banks," is the first asset shown, while "Deposits (subdivided)" is the first liability shown.

Tables 11.2 and 11.3 present specimens of a major bank's statement of condition and income statement. In examining the tables you will find additional categories of financial data that have not been mentioned in this discussion of the basic concepts in bank accounting. It is not the

TABLE 11.3
CONSOLIDATED STATEMENT OF INCOME

	Year ended December 31	
(In thousands of dollars, except per share data)	19XX	19XX
Interest income:		
Interest and fees on loans	$ 823,415	$693,463
Interest on funds sold	6,429	3,496
Interest and dividends on investment securities:		
U.S. Treasury securities	69,938	59,883
Securities of other U.S. government agencies and corporations	16,520	25,228
Obligations of states and political subdivisions	22,504	15,846
Other securities	7,067	7,268
Interest on overseas deposits	24,394	37,658
Interest on trading accounts securities	4,419	3,478
Direct lease financing income	33,371	32,560
Total interest income	1,008,057	878,880
Interest expense:		
Interest on deposits	463,733	414,832
Interest on federal funds borrowed and repurchase agreements	35,193	33,019
Interest on other borrowed money	17,751	12,882
Interest on long-term debt	21,232	19,079
Total interest expense	537,909	479,812
Net interest income	470,148	399,068
Provision for loan losses	41,028	46,379
Net interest income after provision for loan losses	429,120	352,689
Other operating income:		
Trust income	21,635	19,649
Service charges on deposit accounts	25,511	24,254
Trading account profits and commissions	(268)	1,690
Other income	43,797	23,324
Total other operating income	90,675	68,917

purpose of this text to try to present a comprehensive study of the principles and techniques of bank accounting. The American Institute of Banking and many other educational institutions offer courses entirely devoted to this topic. However, one important point deserves mention here regarding the listing for *loans* on the bank's balance sheet. Regulatory authorities and the Internal Revenue Service agree that it is appropriate for a bank to recognize that not all its outstanding loans will be repaid as scheduled. Therefore, based on the institution's past experience, the quality of its portfolio, and all the economic and political considerations that affect that portfolio, each bank is permitted to *reduce* the total loan amount by a reserve for possible loan losses. This reserve is *not* an advance admission by the bank that the full amount of the loan-loss

TABLE 11.3
CONSOLIDATED STATEMENT OF INCOME, (CONTINUED)

	Year ended December 31	
(In thousands of dollars, except per share data)	**19XX**	**19XX**
Other operating expense:		
Salaries	168,085	145,746
Employee benefits	41,028	32,126
Net occupancy expense	34,919	31,636
Equipment expense	20,648	19,234
Other expense	94,331	68,317
Total other operating expense	359,011	297,059
Income before income taxes and securities transactions	160,784	124,547
Less applicable income taxes	73,484	61,076
Income before securities transactions	87,300	63,471
Securities gains (losses), net of income tax effect of $(1,233) in 1977 and $48 in 1976	(1,020)	40
Net income	$ 86,280	$ 63,511
Income per share (based on average number of common shares outstanding):		
Income before securities transactions	$4.03	$3.16
Securities transactions, net of income tax effect	(.05)	—
Net income	$3.98	$3.16

reserve will always be used for charge offs. Rather, it is a prudent expression of the possibilities and serves as protection for events that may take place in the future.

All yearly additions to the loan-loss reserve come out of the bank's income. This accounting principle received wide publicity in 1987, when Citicorp and Chase Manhattan announced huge increases ($3 billion and $1.6 billion, respectively) in their reserves for possible loan losses. Although it was evident that these actions would cause both banks to show large net losses for the year, the increased reserves were considered to be a reflection of the banks' concern over the status of their international loan portfolios.[1] International banking will be discussed further in chapter 12.

PRICING

Banks recently have placed new emphasis on specialized accounting to arrive at a better understanding of what the true expenses are in each day's operations. This increased emphasis reflects the basic changes that have taken place in the overall deposit structure, the labor costs that affect so many functions, and the banks' efforts to counter new, aggressive competition from other entities in the financial services industry.

When banks enjoyed the benefits of large, relatively inactive demand deposits, the need for detailed cost accounting was relatively small. The size of these interest-free balances virtually guaranteed profits, and as asset managers the bankers simply concentrated on putting those deposits to work. The general philosophy held that companies that maintained large checking accounts were entitled to services, without serious concern by either party as to the cost of those services.

Today, consideration of true costs—and for the recovery of those costs plus profit from customers—is an essential part of bank operations.

The excess demand deposits that bankers formerly depended on have been replaced by expensive forms of savings and time deposits. Banks have introduced many new services in an effort to compete with other financial intermediaries. Labor costs in an inflationary economy have escalated steadily. *Knowing* the costs of each service or product and *recovering* those costs at a profit through appropriate pricing mechanisms are vital not merely for the banks' profitability but, in many cases, for their actual survival in the marketplace.

The Monetary Control Act of 1980 directed the Fed to implement a system of explicit pricing for all its services to banks. Since 1913, with the sole exception of loans, the Fed had been providing free services to the banks in exchange for the interest-free reserve balances they kept with it. In this respect, the Fed's position was like that of the banks themselves. The Fed's new pricing for such essential functions as check collection and money transfers further stimulated the banks to revise their own thinking regarding pricing.

If justification ever existed for banks to give away their services, it has disappeared in the face of interest expense, increased labor costs, and cost factors that are imposed externally. Today's banking requires an integrated cost accounting system that can analyze job functions to determine exactly what expenses are incurred in each task, recognize all the indirect costs (for example, overhead and administrative expenses) that must be added on, compute a total, add the appropriate profit margin, present the final price figure to the customer, and recover it through compensating balances, fees, or a combination of the two.

Consider, for example, an operation as basic as a teller's handling of a customer deposit. The first step in a complete system of cost accounting and pricing analyzes all the components of the teller's tasks and the time needed for each. The teller's hourly salary then forms a base for determining the direct expense incurred in the work performed. Branch and administrative overhead, and a profit margin, then are added in to arrive at a final price.

Cost analysis gives recognition to the cost of the funds used for loans and investments. This is one of the factors banks use to determine the rate of interest that should be charged on any given loan. Thus, cost analysis assists the credit function.

As mentioned earlier, banks traditionally have used two methods of obtaining compensation for services rendered. Corporate customers may maintain compensating balances at their banks as a way to support their borrowings. The banks have benefited from this method because the balances provided the raw material needed to fund ongoing operations. More recently, however, banks have begun to charge direct fees in full or partial compensation for services. For example, if the customer's balances (as valued by the bank) do not cover the expenses created by a service, a balance deficiency fee is used to make up the difference.

Many corporate loan customers today request an "all-in-the-rate" system that completely ignores balances. The interest rates these customers pay are all-inclusive, reflecting the bank's cost of funds and all other risk, expense, and profit factors. For other services such as lock box, payroll preparation, and money transfers, these customers expect to be given specific price schedules and to pay the bank a monthly fee.

There are several reasons for this trend. A corporation may find it possible to free its balances and put those funds to profitable use (perhaps at a yield higher than the bank's allowance rate on balances). The fees paid to the bank in lieu of balances are a tax-deductible, direct business expense. From the bank's standpoint, the trend away from balances and toward fees is acceptable as long as the fee income offsets the loss of compensating balances. From one or the other source, the bank still needs funds for daily operations. The trend toward direct fees is strengthened when interest rates are declining or when loan demand is low, because the fee income offsets a decrease in loan interest.

The Federal Reserve publishes *comparison schedules* that show the pricing and cost structures used by banks throughout the country in connection with various services. Through these schedules, one bank can compare its prices and costs with those quoted by others (averaged, nationwide). Similarly, corporate financial officers who must deal with several banks often wish to make comparisons among these institutions by analyzing the prices quoted for the same services.

Pricing of Consumer Deposits

The pricing and recovery of costs in retail banking are especially complicated because consumers now can choose from among so many types of interest-bearing relationships. In a 1987 study conducted by the Federal Reserve Bank of New York, most of the responding banks indicated that their rate decisions in pricing consumer deposits began with estimates of the wholesale cost of funds; that is, with the rates on large-denomination CDs. Those rates are influenced by maturities (the longer-term CDs naturally carry higher rates). However, the NOW, money market deposit, and savings accounts favored by so many consumers have no specific maturity. Whatever rates are established at the start of the process must be adjusted to accommodate that difference and to reflect competitive factors.[2]

Passbook savings accounts cost more to maintain and process than statement savings accounts. In recognition of this, banks that provide both types of accounts often set lower interest rates on all their passbook accounts.

Another study, prepared at year-end 1985, analyzed data from 195 banks in various parts of the country. Each such bank had at least $500 million in total deposits, and as a group they held almost 30 percent of the total domestic deposits nationwide. These banks responded to questions as to the minimum balances they required to pay interest on money market deposit accounts (MMDAs), NOW, and Super-NOW accounts; the monthly fees they charged if required balance levels were not maintained; and their policies regarding per-check charges. In each case, the majority of banks agreed on the following:

- Minimum balances required to earn interest were $1,000 on MMDAs and $2,500 on Super-NOW accounts; NOW accounts had no required minimums.
- If balances fell below the required minimums, 96 percent of the banks charged fees on NOW and Super-NOW accounts, while 68 percent charged fees on MMDAs; the monthly fees were usually in the $4 to $6 range.
- Most banks did not impose any charges for checks issued by customers against the three types of accounts, regardless of balances.[3]

PROFITABILITY

Any discussion of banking in the United States must recognize the fact that commercial banks, savings banks, and savings and loan associations here are organized as profit-making institutions. In many other countries, banks are nationalized; their governments absorb the banks' expenses and retain any profits. Under the U.S. system, the profitability of each institution is important to stockholders, depositors, government regulators, management, and the general public. The concept of *profitability* shows how well the institution has managed its resources and how effectively it has performed. High or increasing profitability constitutes the only way that a bank can expand its operations on a long-term basis and induce investors to purchase new offerings of its stock or debt issues.

For internal management purposes and for use by investment analysts and state and federal regulatory authorities, various ratios have been developed to show how profitably a bank is operating. The measures most widely used are

- return on assets
- return on equity
- capital ratio
- earnings per share

The *return on assets* (ROA) is calculated by dividing a bank's earnings before securities gains or losses by its average total assets during a period. Table 11.4 shows the ROA ratios for two major commercial banks in selected years from 1974 through 1982. (These figures are used merely to illustrate the principle and concept.)

Analysis of these ratios shows that the ROA for Bank *A* steadily declined. Even in years when its earnings increased, its ROA decreased because Bank *A's* assets grew at an even faster rate. Evidently, Bank *A* was not using its assets in the most profitable way. If you look only at the reported growth in assets, you might conclude that the bank's performance was excellent; however, despite the fact that its assets increased 132 percent during the period, analysis of the ROAs produces a very different conclusion.

TABLE 11.4
RETURN ON ASSETS

Year	Earnings Before Securities Transactions (millions of dollars)	Average Total Assets (millions of dollars)	Return on Assets (percent)
		Bank *A*	
1974	35.0	3,580	0.98
1976	41.6	4,411	0.94
1978	42.1	5,341	0.79
1980	55.5	8,577	0.65
1982	42.9	8,332	0.51
		Bank *B*	
1974	10.7	1,566	0.68
1976	12.7	1,668	0.76
1978	16.7	2,018	0.83
1980	23.3	2,573	0.91
1982	29.5	2,978	0.99

The performance of Bank *B* during the same years is far more impressive. Its earnings increased by 176 percent, despite the fact that its assets grew by only 90 percent. Bank *B* consistently employed its assets in such a way that the return, or *yield*, on them grew far more rapidly and meaningfully.

The average ROA in 1986 for all commercial U.S. banks was 0.50 percent. It was 0.63 percent in 1985. The impact of loan losses for banks with a concentration of agricultural loans in the Chicago, St. Louis, Kansas City, and Minneapolis Federal Reserve districts was evident; their ROAs were 0.07 percent in 1986 and 0.20 percent in 1985.[4]

A 1985 study analyzed the ROA figures for the nation's 345 largest *bank holding companies* for the years 1980 through 1984 (table 11.5). Again, while the analysis is not current, it is used to illustrate the trend in ROAs. Table 11.6 also shows comparative figures for a selected group of major banks in 1986 and 1985. Bank holding companies will be discussed further in chapter 13.

The second key measure of bank profitability is *return on equity* (ROE). This is calculated by dividing a bank's earnings before securities transactions by the average dollar amount of total equity during a period. The term *equity* is used to describe the ownership interest represented by stockholders' investment in the bank, plus retained earnings. Because a bank's total assets are always far larger than its equity, the ROE is always

TABLE 11.5
ROAs AND ROEs FOR 345 BANK HOLDING COMPANIES, 1980–84

	Return on Average Assets				
			Percentage in		
Size Class[a]	1980	1981	1982	1983	1984
Average for entire group	0.63	0.62	0.61	0.62	0.55
$100 million–$1 billion	0.80	0.76	0.67	0.75	0.74
$1 billion–$5 billion	0.87	0.78	0.76	0.78	0.82
$5 billion or more	0.59	0.59	0.58	0.58	0.49

	Return on Average Equity				
			Percentage in		
Size Class[a]	1980	1981	1982	1983	1984
Average for entire group	13.89	13.37	12.71	12.21	10.50
$100 million–$1 billion	12.51	11.78	10.33	11.83	11.78
$1 billion–$5 billion	14.00	12.57	12.26	12.55	13.30
$5 billion or more	13.95	13.66	12.96	12.15	9.78

Source: Martin H. Wolfson, "Financial Developments of Bank Holding Companies in 1984," *Federal Reserve Bulletin*, December 1985, p. 926.
a. *Size class* refers to total assets for these 345 bank holding companies.

TABLE 11.6
COMPARATIVE FIGURES, 1986 v. 1985

	Return on Assets (percentages)		Return on Equity (percentages)	
	1986	1985	1986	1985
14 major money center banks (New York, Chicago, Boston, Pittsburgh)	0.70	0.65	13.32	13.16
Banks with assets over $10 billion	0.89	0.81	15.68	14.90
Banks with assets of $5 to $10 billion	0.89	0.88	14.24	14.37

Source: "1986 Performance of Top U.S. Banking Companies," *American Banker* (June 17, 1987), p. 18.

significantly higher than the ROA. ROE, in effect, measures the rate of return a bank has achieved in relation to the funds invested in it. The data in table 11.7 is taken from the same period and represents the same two commercial banks used in table 11.4.

For the year ended December 31, 1985, Morgan Guaranty Trust Company (New York) led the nation's commercial banks in reported ROE, with 18.06 percent. The average at the nation's 14 largest money-center banks (table 11.6) was approximately 13 percent; and General Motors Acceptance Corporation (a major nonbank competitor) reported an ROE of 22.30 percent while that of the Ford Motor Company was 19.30 percent.[5]

TABLE 11.7
RETURN ON EQUITY

Year	Earnings Before Securities Transactions (millions of dollars)	Average Shareholders' Equity (millions of dollars)	Return on Equity (percent)
		Bank *A*	
1974	35.0	316	11.1
1976	41.6	347	12.0
1978	42.1	398	10.6
1980	55.5	467	11.9
1982	42.9	513	8.4
		Bank *B*	
1974	10.7	100	9.4
1976	12.7	111	11.4
1978	16.7	128	13.1
1980	23.3	153	15.2
1982	29.5	187	15.8

231

When a prospective bank submits its charter application, regulatory authorities question the dollar amount of capital that has been contributed by the incorporators. The bank's original capital consists of the number of shares they have purchased multiplied by the price per share. When the bank begins to operate and generate profits, retained earnings are added to the original capital. The bank may also sell additional shares of its stock, thereby increasing its capital base.

Every examination of a bank by federal or state authorities tries to determine whether its capital is adequate to support its operations. The third measure of bank profitability, then, is the *capital ratio*. This ratio is obtained by dividing the bank's total capital by its total assets.

The stronger a bank's capital position, and therefore its capital ratio, the greater the appearance of strength and solidity it projects. Capital serves as a cushion against temporary losses. It also helps protect uninsured depositors, depositors whose balances exceed the insurance coverage limit, and holders of liabilities in the event the bank is liquidated. Nationwide, the capital ratios for banks generally range between 5 percent and 9 percent. This means that 91 percent to 95 percent of total assets are financed through various liabilities. For this reason, banking is often referred to as an industry that is highly *leveraged*. In other words, banking is highly dependent on debt in order to function.

In 1985 reports of actual or potential loan losses at many banks led the Comptroller of the Currency, the Federal Reserve, and the FDIC to rule jointly that all commercial banks must maintain a capital ratio of at least 6 percent.[6]

The final measure of bank profitability, *earnings per share* (EPS), simply divides the bank's net bottom-line income by the average number of shares of its stock outstanding during a period. Growth in EPS commonly is regarded as a key indicator of bank performance. EPS figures also provide a means of determining how highly the bank's stock is regarded in the marketplace. For example, if a bank's earnings per share for 1987 are $5 and a share of its stock is being traded at $25, the price-to-earnings ratio is 5. The bank's earnings per share can be compared with the figures for other banks and corporations. Because of investors' concerns over the financial strength of the banks, the price-to-earnings ratios for commercial banks generally are far lower than those for major corporations, whose shares of stock commonly are traded at 10, 15, or 20 times their annual EPS.

A complete analysis of a bank's profitability requires detailed attention to each of these four ratios over a period of several years, rather than a focus on any one ratio for a single year. For example, a bank's board of directors and senior management may have made a heavy commitment of resources in one particular year in order to enter a new service area or expand the bank's branch system. A very substantial addition to the bank's reserve for possible loan losses in a single year likewise will be considered a one-time aberration. ROA, ROE, capital ratios, and EPS all must be measured over time to identify trends.

Information for Customers

The information systems that have been designed to give bank management data on the profitability of account relationships are also important and valuable to customers, especially those customers with major corporate accounts at more than one bank. *Account analysis* is the term used to describe the information reports that give specific details on all the elements involved in servicing an account and the profit or loss that account creates for the bank. Customers use account analysis to monitor their bank balances so that any excess interest-free demand deposits can be moved to other interest-bearing relationships. Customers also compare the earnings allowances and schedules of service charges supplied by the banks.

The following elements would be included in a full account analysis:

- Calculation of the average daily book balance for a month, *less* the average daily float. This yields the average daily collected balance, and reflects the concept that uncollected funds in an account have no value to the bank or depositor.
- Deduction from the collected balance of the required reserves that the bank must maintain against it. This yields the average daily loanable or investable balance; that is, the net balance that the bank can put to use in making loans and investments. This figure is important because it represents the bank's actual source of earnings as opposed to float and reserves.
- Application of an earnings credit to the average daily loanable balance. The earnings credit is stated in terms of an annual percentage rate that the bank calculates according to its cost of funds and conditions in the money market. The bank may adjust the earnings credit rate each month as conditions change. (It must be noted that the earnings credit allowed to a customer *cannot* be paid or construed as interest, since that would be a violation of federal regulations prohibiting payment of interest on demand deposits. Rather, the earnings credit is an offset for the customer against the total expenses the bank has incurred in rendering services on the account for the month.)
- Itemization of all the charges resulting from those services, including the cost to the bank of federal insurance coverage (for example, 1/12 of 1 percent in the case of FDIC, or $.83 per $100.00 of average collected balance).

Assume, for example, that a commercial account has had an average daily investable balance of $100,000 for the month and that the bank is using 6 percent as the earnings credit rate for that month. The actual credit would be shown as $500 ($100,000 × 0.06, divided by 12).

The analysis would then list all the activity and service charges created by the account for the month. For example, it might include

- deposit tickets
- checks deposited
- checks paid
- account maintenance (standard monthly charge)
- debit and credit memos
- coin and currency supplied
- money transfers
- Federal Reserve charges on money transfers

The total costs for all activity would then be compared with the earnings credit of $500, and a net profit or loss shown for the month. Alternatively, the analysis might translate the total costs into a level of compensating balances so that any excess or deficiency could be seen at a glance.

If the earnings credit exceeds the total charges, the account is profitable to the bank. If the opposite is true, the account operated at a loss, and the officer responsible for the account would be expected to ask the customer for additional balances or to charge the account directly for the deficiency.

It must be noted that this system of detailed account analysis has been outlined by way of explanation. It cannot and should not be applied to *every* checking account at every bank. However, it is extremely useful for the large, active commercial accounts. It helps both the bank and its customers arrive at a mutual understanding of all the factors that make an account relationship profitable or unprofitable.

In the case of personal checking accounts, commercial banks in general have found that these have become far more expensive to maintain. At the same time, the shrinkage in demand deposits among the large corporate accounts has caused a corresponding decline in bank income. As a result, there has been a trend toward significantly higher bank charges on all types of consumer accounts—for example, increased monthly maintenance charges, charges for returned checks, fees on credit cards, and charges for overdrafts.

The Income Statement

In analyzing bank profitability, one must pay as much attention to all the components of the income statement as to the basic ratios that measure performance. This is the same logic that is applied in credit analysis. The figures themselves are meaningful, but the underlying reasons for those figures and the factors that created them are even more important.

In analyzing a bank's income statement the primary focus must be placed on net interest income. This figure identifies the *spread* (profit margin) between interest income from investments and loans and interest paid to depositors; that is, net interest income relates the direct cost of funds to the earnings produced from use of those funds. As the ratio of time and savings deposits to demand deposits continues to change, this spread will assume increasing importance.

Analysis of the income statement also provides information as to how well the bank is keeping its direct operating costs (such as salaries and wages) under control. Annual expenses inevitably increase during periods of inflation, but the percentages of these increases must be related to the bank's productivity and the actual growth in its volume of business.

The income statement can be subdivided into far greater detail to show every component of income and expenses. At banks that have introduced *product management*, an individual is made responsible for the profitability of his or her specific product (for example, a letter of credit, a custody account, or a money transfer). That individual is held accountable by senior management for all matters pertaining to the product.

Account officers, also called relationship managers, use detailed statements showing the profitability of all the relationships assigned to them: the balances maintained, the income derived from use of those balances, the expenses created by services rendered, and the other expenses that result from administering the accounts. If a branch network is not meeting management's profit objectives, a detailed analysis of the income statement will disclose this and management can be guided accordingly.

Relationship Management

During the 1980s the term *relationship management* has become widely used in banking. It identifies an approach wherein a bank considers a customer's actual or potential use of *all* the bank's services. The bank officer who handles the account of ABC Corporation is expected to know the company's operations and future plans in sufficient detail to identify additional services that could be sold to it, and he or she is expected to be able to work with the customer in providing those services. The ABC Corporation may maintain several accounts with the same bank; the officer assigned to that corporation looks at the entire banking relationship rather than at a single account. The bank officer can be compared to a senior consultant selected to develop a group of related projects and who calls in specialists as needed to accomplish the various tasks.

Cross-selling has become an important part of relationship management and bank marketing. A satisfied client generally is the best source of additional business, and selling an additional service to that client is far less expensive than marketing the same service to new prospects. Customer profile forms can identify all the bank's services that the client is presently using and those that might effectively be marketed. Checking accounts, interest-bearing accounts, and card usage can be shown on the profile sheet of an individual, and that person's probable future needs—home equity loans, safe deposit boxes, and trust opportunities—can be targeted for future cross-selling.

SUMMARY

Bank accounting systems are designed to present, record, and interpret all the information that results from each day's transactions. The figures are vital for the bank's management planning, are required by federal and state regulatory authorities, and are expected by stockholders and customers. The public cannot be expected to place its faith and confidence in a bank that cannot provide information on the profitability of its operations and the various factors that contribute to that profitability.

Bank accounting systems generally use double-entry bookkeeping as a proof and control technique and always develop two basic reports, known as the balance sheet (statement of condition) and income statement. Call reports showing the bank's financial condition are submitted whenever required by authorities; quarterly balance sheets and income statements are made public; and far more detailed accounting information is used internally for a variety of purposes. Through the application of cost accounting, the accounting systems enable a bank to recognize how its expenses are connected with each phase of its operations. The profitability of each service or product can be identified. All this information helps bank management develop effective strategies to recover costs and generate profits.

Through several critical ratios, the degree of success a bank has had in putting its assets to profitable use and generating an adequate rate of return on its stockholders' equity can be measured. These ratios enable one to assess the bank's profitability over a period of time.

In an era when the basic deposit structure of commercial banking has changed so drastically and the costs of doing business have increased dramatically, banks must become knowledgeable about the factors that influence their revenues and expenses and gain expertise in knowing, controlling, and recovering their costs.

QUESTIONS FOR DISCUSSION

1. What is the difference between journals and ledgers in bank accounting? What purpose does the bank's general ledger serve?

2. What effect would the posting of debits have on an asset or expense account? How could credits affect a liability account?

3. What term is used to describe the excess of a bank's assets over its liabilities?

4. Identify the two basic reports that are produced through bank accounting.

5. Explain the difference between the cash and accrual methods of bank accounting. Which system is generally used by banks? Why?

6. What is a bank's largest asset? What is its largest liability? What are the largest income and expense items?

7. How did the Monetary Control Act of 1980 affect the need for banks to price their services more effectively and recover their costs?

8. Why might a corporate customer prefer to compensate the bank with direct fees rather than balances?

9. Identify the four major ratios that are used in determining a bank's profitability.

10. What is the importance to a bank of cross-selling?

11. From your bank's most recent published figures, calculate its ROA and ROE.

NOTES

1. Bart Fraust, "Citicorp's Debt Move Lifts Stock," *American Banker*, May 21, 1987, p. 1.

2. Richard G. Davis, Leon Korobow, and John Wenninger, "Bankers on Pricing Consumer Deposits," Federal Reserve Bank of New York, *Quarterly Review* (Winter 1987), pp. 6–13.

3. Richard G. Davis and Leon Korobow, "The Pricing of Consumer Deposit Products—The Non-Rate Dimensions," Federal Reserve Bank of New York, *Quarterly Review* (Winter 1987), pp. 14–18.

4. "Midwest Banks Improve Performance," *American Banker*, June 10, 1987, p. 7.

5. "1985 Performance of Top U.S. Banking Companies," *American Banker*, June 20, 1986, pp. 22–24; *see also* Robert M. Garsson, "Big 3 Automakers' Lending Units Post Record Earnings for '85," *American Banker*, February 18, 1986, p. 31.

6. "New Rule for Banks," *The New York Times*, February 11, 1985, p. D17.

For More Information

Frankston, Fred M., Charles D. Mecimore, and Michael F. Cornick. *Bank Accounting*. Washington, D.C.: American Bankers Association, 1984.

Johnson, Frank P., and Richard D. Johnson. *Commercial Bank Management*. New York: Dryden Press, 1986.

Moebs, G. Michael and Eva Moebs. *Pricing Financial Services*. Homewood, Ill.: Dow Jones-Irwin, 1986.

12.

SPECIALIZED
BANK
SERVICES

LEARNING OBJECTIVES

After completing this chapter, you will be able to

•

define the terms *banker's acceptances, trust receipts,* and *Eurodollars*

•

list the steps in a letter of credit transaction and
the benefits letters of credit provide to the involved parties

•

describe the importance—and the problems—of global banking and
country risk analysis

•

define the most important terms used in trust operations

•

name the steps involved in settling estates

•

distinguish between the functions of a trustee and those of an agent

•

list the duties and responsibilities of a bank acting as
transfer agent, registrar, paying agent, or trustee under indenture

•

describe the legal restrictions that affect bank trust operations

•

explain the deposit, disbursement, and information services banks
offer in their cash management programs,
and the safeguards banks employ in their safe deposit operations

S ince 1945, banks have responded to the wants and needs of their customers and to the steady increase in competition from other financial service organizations by developing specialized services. When effectively marketed, these services generate profits for the banks. All of them are over and above the basic functions of handling deposits, processing payments, and extending credit. The success or failure of a particular bank often can be measured by its ability to provide quality, cost-effective services to corporate, institutional, government, and individual customers. This chapter addresses four important and widely used service areas: international, trust, cash management, and safe deposit.

GLOBAL BANKING

In the second half of the twentieth century, global banking has become a critical factor in the profitability of many major U.S. banks. Even in those institutions whose international business does not require the facilities of an independent department, the demand for many specialized services relating to foreign trade grows each year.

Prior to World War II, many Americans believed that the United States could operate in a type of vacuum, ignoring the developments in and problems of other countries. The bankers who accepted this isolationist approach and who therefore did little to position their institutions on a global basis now appear to have been misguided in their thinking. Today countries are increasingly dependent on one another, and money knows no geographic boundaries. Electronic transfers of funds move many billions of dollars among the money centers of Hong Kong, London, Tokyo, Paris, Frankfurt, and the major cities in the United States every day. For the largest U.S. banks, the entire world has become a marketplace. Bankers and their customers have had to become familiar with Eurodollars, the debt positions of the less-developed countries, and the U.S. balance-of-payments deficit.

Of course, U.S. banks have not been alone in their efforts at global expansion. In 1987 the five largest banks in the world were non-U.S. banks. Only one U.S. bank was named among the top 15.

In expanding their international operations, our major commercial banks have simply followed the lead of their largest corporate customers, who saw the huge potential for sales and profits in foreign countries following the end of World War II and quickly began to market their products on a global basis. Companies such as IBM, General Electric, Dow Chemical, General Foods, and DuPont became suppliers to war-ravaged nations that lacked productive capacity, and today the output from these companies can be found in every corner of the globe. In many cases, banks duplicated this pattern of overseas growth.

In 1947 only 7 U.S. banks had established branches outside the United States; by 1981, 152 Federal Reserve member banks had established 787 overseas locations; and in 1983 the 924 foreign facilities of U.S. banks reported total assets of $466 billion.[1] By year-end 1986, 158 member banks were operating 952 branches in foreign countries.[2]

There has also been growth in the number of foreign banks operating branches in the United States. In 1986 countries from other parts of the world operated 978 banking facilities here.[3] Foreign-owned banks in the United States reported commercial and industrial loans outstanding of $114.2 billion, or 22.3 percent of that 1986 total.[4] The 27 Japanese banks constituted the dominant foreign group, with assets in the United States of $202 billion, deposits of $110 billion, and commercial and industrial loans of $46 billion.[5]

A principal factor in the tremendous expansion of the international services offered by U.S. banks has been the steady increase in foreign trade. For many years, the United States has been a net importer of products such as automobiles, textiles and apparel, and television sets. The inflow of goods, far in excess of the outflow, has created a steadily worsening deficit in the balance of U.S. payments. In 1986 that deficit was $148 billion, and in early 1987 it averaged $12.3 billion per month.[6] This problem has been repeatedly addressed by the president, Congress, and spokespersons for many major U.S. industries. The ongoing deficit has a significant impact on the total debt position of the United States; that debt totaled $2.2 trillion at year-end 1986.[7]

SERVICES TO IMPORTERS

Many U.S. banks do not maintain their own international divisions, but depend on their larger correspondents to provide any needed services. Many others have found it both necessary and highly profitable to create a specialized unit, often called "a bank within a bank," to deal with all the technicalities of foreign trade, the problems of each country's customs and regulations, the differences in language, and the customized processing of a huge volume of daily transactions. A large part of that daily volume results from the banks' interface with U.S. importers.

Letters of Credit

Of all the international services now offered by banks, the best known and most frequently used is the *commercial letter of credit*. A buyer of goods might require assurance that the merchandise being bought will conform exactly to specifications. A seller of goods may require an assurance of payment after the goods have been shipped. A letter of credit can minimize the risks to both parties.

A *letter of credit* (L/C) is an instrument issued by a bank, substituting the credit standing of that bank for the credit standing of the importer (the buyer) of goods. It guarantees that the exporter (the seller) will be paid if all the terms of the contract are met. At the same time, it protects the buyer by guaranteeing that no payment will be made unless and until that contract is fulfilled.

Letters of credit can be issued in *revocable* or *irrevocable* form. The revocable L/C is rare, since its terms allow it to be canceled or amended by either party without the approval of the other. An irrevocable L/C stipulates that no changes can be made without the full consent of the buyer *and* the seller. A typical application for a letter of credit (exhibit 12.1) will clearly state that the credit is irrevocable.

L/Cs may also be issued on either a *sight* or a *time* basis. The sight L/C calls for immediate payment against the documents that provide evidence of a shipment of goods; the time L/C specifies a later date by which payment must be made.

Assume, for example, that a company in San Francisco has negotiated with a firm in the Federal Republic of Germany to purchase a quantity of machine tools. The price of the total order has been agreed upon; however, the American firm wants assurance that the terms of the purchase contract will be met and the German company requires some guarantee of payment. The San Francisco buyer approaches a local bank and completes an application for an irrevocable sight L/C in favor of the exporter. If the California bank is convinced of the buyer's credit standing and financial responsibility, it will agree to the application. The letter of credit usually stipulates

- that the issuing bank maintain a security interest in all property covered by the credit
- that the issuing bank is not responsible for physically counting or otherwise examining the actual goods being ordered
- that the issuing bank is not responsible for the genuineness of any documents submitted to it

The application submitted by the California importer will specify the various documents that are required. It is understood and agreed that the bank will rely on those documents as proof that the specified shipment has been made. Commonly used documents required in connection with letters of credit include

- *commercial invoices*, listing the goods that have been ordered, and usually specifying the price and terms of the sale

EXHIBIT 12.1
COMMERCIAL LETTER OF CREDIT

NAME OF ISSUING BANK Morgan Guaranty Trust Company of N. Y.	IRREVOCABLE DOCUMENTARY CREDIT	Number 7465
Place and date of issue New York October 1, 19--	Date and place of expiry December 10, 19-- London	
Applicant Fred Downs, Inc. New York, N.Y.	Beneficiary Albert Tennyson and Sons 2347B Park Lane London N. 2, England	

Advising Bank Ref. No. Bank in London London, England	Amount ℔ 2,000 (Pounds Sterling)
	Credit available with Bank in London by
Partial shipments ☒ allowed ☐ not allowed Transhipment ☒ allowed ☐ not allowed	☒ sight payment ☐ acceptance ☐ negotiation ☐ deferred payment at against the documents detailed herein
Shipment/dispatch/ taking in charge from/at Southampton for transportation to New York	☒ and beneficiary's draft at sight on Bank in London

Commercial invoice covering wool fabric FOB Southampton.

Marine bills of lading consigned to Fred Downs, Inc.

Documents to be presented within   days after the date of issuance of the transport document(s) but within the validity of the credit.

We hereby issue this Documentary Credit in your favour. It is subject to the Uniform Customs and Practice for Documentary Credits (1983 Revision, International Chamber of Commerce, Paris, France, Publication No. 400) and engages us in accordance with the terms thereof, and especially in accordance with the terms of Article 10 thereof. The number and date of the credit and the name of our bank must be quoted on all drafts required. If the credit is available by negotiation, each presentation must be noted on the reverse of this advice by the bank where the credit is available.

This document consists of   signed page(s).

- *insurance certificates,* providing that the merchandise will be safe-guarded during transit
- *bills of lading,* issued by the carrier (steamship company, airline, trucking firm, or other transporter) handling the shipment of goods
- *consular (customs) invoices,* issued by authorized representatives of the country to which the merchandise is being shipped
- *certificates of origin,* specifying the source of the material or labor used in producing the merchandise
- *certificates of quality,* issued by recognized appraisers (individuals who have specialized knowledge regarding particular commodities)

In our example, consular invoices would be issued by U.S. Customs officials to verify the quantity, value, and nature of the shipment and to ensure that import laws are not being violated. Consular invoices also provide a basis for statistical reports on the quantity and type of imported goods. Certificates of quality may be required as evidence that the goods being shipped conform to the buyer's specifications.

The *bill of lading* is one of the most important documents because it serves three simultaneous purposes. It is a *receipt* issued by the carrier for a specific shipment of goods; it is a *title document,* proving that the carrier has legal possession of the goods; and it is a *contract,* by which the carrier agrees to transport the goods from and to specific locations.

The importer's bank in California reviews the application and approves it on a *liability basis;* that is, the bank is willing to accept the applicant's guarantee to reimburse the bank after payment has been made to the seller. The California bank thus becomes known as the *opening (issuing)* bank under the L/C. It forwards notification to a bank in the Federal Republic of Germany, showing that the L/C has been opened in favor of the beneficiary. The German bank, in turn, contacts the exporter—thus becoming known as the *advising* bank. The advising bank often is a correspondent of the issuing bank, and the applicant may specify which bank is to be used by the seller of goods in obtaining payment.

The seller has now become the *beneficiary* of the L/C, provided that all the terms and conditions of the contract are met. The required documents, for which the seller has made arrangements, provide the evidence that the contract has been fulfilled.

To obtain payment, the beneficiary draws a draft on the California bank and presents it, with all accompanying documents, to a German bank. This German bank may or may not be his or her own bank or the advising bank; it may act merely as a collection agent and send the L/C, with all documents, to the issuing bank in San Francisco. In this case, the latter will examine all the documents carefully and make payment to the German bank.

Frequently, however, the exporter will present the L/C, draft, and documents to his or her bank and request immediate payment. That bank may then examine the documents and, finding them in order, honor the draft at once. The exporter's bank can do so with full confidence, since it knows that the opening bank must reimburse it if all documents are in order.

Regardless of which method of payment is used, funds will flow from the issuing bank in California to the paying bank in Germany, and the former will then recover the funds from the buyer's account with it.

Specialized Letters of Credit

In addition to their value as instruments that finance foreign trade, L/Cs serve many other international and domestic purposes. For example, *standby* letters of credit may be used to assure payments of trade obligations, to guarantee payment of promissory notes, or to cover other debts of an obligor who uses the credit standing of a bank to reinforce his or her own.

In recent years, standby L/Cs have been widely used by municipalities in the United States in order to make their debt issues more attractive to the investors. Through these L/Cs, the issuing banks guarantee that the municipal obligations will be paid even if the issuers should default. Banks issued $15 billion in this particular type of standby L/C in 1986. Again, foreign banks with U.S. branches were aggressively competitive in this marketplace, accounting for 69 percent of that dollar volume.[8]

L/Cs also may be issued on a *performance* basis. Like standby L/Cs, the performance L/C serves as a kind of insurance policy. It may be positive or negative; that is, payment will be made by the issuing bank when the terms of a specific contract have been met, or payment will be made if the applicant (obligor) fails to live up to the terms of a contract with the beneficiary.

Banker's Acceptances

If the L/C is established on a time basis, the exporter's draft is forwarded to the issuing bank with all documents so that they can be examined and payment approved. If the exporter requests immediate payment and all documents are in order, the issuing bank (on which the draft was drawn) may opt to stamp the draft with the word *accepted*, have it officially signed and dated, and remit the funds. A draft that has been accepted in this manner is called a *banker's acceptance* (B/A). The original draft (an order to pay) has been converted into the bank's unconditional promise to pay. Every B/A is a direct, irrevocable obligation of the accepting bank. B/As are bought and sold in huge quantities every day; there is a ready market for them as investment vehicles, because the full faith and credit of the accepting bank support them. The bank *must* make payment, whether or not it obtains reimbursement from the buyer of the merchandise.

Trust Receipts

The California importer may need to take possession of the German merchandise, process it, display it to potential buyers, and sell it in order to generate income. At the same time, the California company may not have sufficient funds to permit its account to be charged for payments under the terms of the letter of credit. Often, the goods must be sold before the importer can pay the bank. This problem is solved through *trust receipts.*

These agreements allow the importer to take possession of merchandise, process it, and sell it. The proceeds of the sale generate the income that will be used to pay the bank. Trust receipt financing actually is a specialized form of secured lending, because the bank holds full legal title to the merchandise until payment is made. Under the terms of the Uniform Commercial Code, a bank extending this type of financing should record its security interest in the merchandise with state authorities as a means of protecting itself if the importer should default.

The borrower under a trust receipt agrees to keep the merchandise, and any funds received from selling it, separate and distinct from other property. The borrower agrees that the merchandise represents collateral subject to repossession by the lending bank.

Warehouse Receipts

Under certain conditions, merchandise that has been imported and stored in a bonded warehouse may be acceptable to a bank as collateral for a loan. Because a *warehouse receipt* is a legal document of title, the importer may endorse it (assuming it has been issued in negotiable form) and transfer his or her rights to the merchandise to the lending bank. The bank verifies the existence and value of the stored goods and extends a loan on that basis. As the loan is reduced or paid, the bank allows the release of part or all of the merchandise so that the borrower can use it.

Negotiable warehouse receipts are also issued in domestic business transactions. Commodities such as cotton, grain, and soy beans often are placed in bonded warehouses as soon as they have been harvested. Properly executed warehouse receipts for these commodities may be used as collateral for a bank loan that is needed to meet the customer's financial needs until the goods are sold.

Other Services to Importers

Aside from letters of credit, banker's acceptances, trust receipts, and warehouse receipts, banks may offer other specialized services to importers. A bank's foreign branches or correspondents can readily provide the importer with information about the credit standing of a foreign firm. Banks also extend direct loans to importers, following the same credit procedures as in domestic lending.

Another important bank service to importers involves *foreign exchange* contracts. For example, assume that an importer has agreed to make payment, in yen, to a Japanese exporter 90 days after agreeing to buy certain merchandise. The importer calculates the cost of the shipment in dollars at the prevailing rate of exchange when the contract is signed, and is anxious to pay no more than that amount regardless of any fluctuations that may take place in the relative values of the two currencies.

The importer's bank can enter into a contract by which it commits itself to make payment for the stated number of yen; the bank thus becomes responsible for any changes in exchange rates that may take place during the 90-day time frame. The importer has been protected; the shipment cannot cost more than the original amount in dollars.

For the convenience of customers who are required to make payments in foreign currencies or who need to convert one currency into another, many major banks maintain large holdings of important currencies and make these available as necessary. In addition, banks may actively trade in various currencies. Trading in currencies offers substantial profit opportunities, but also carries the risk of large losses. Banks manage their risks by hedging in various currencies at the same time. For example, a bank can hedge a large holding of a foreign currency by selling the same amount of the currency for future delivery at a fixed price. Banks also help customers to manage risks by guaranteeing the prices of those currencies far into the future.

Banks may profit from foreign exchange operations simply by purchasing a particular currency at a lower price and reselling it at a higher price. Banks also may collect fees for international services to customers. For example, a customer typically will pay a fee for the bank's guarantee through a foreign exchange contract.

SERVICES TO EXPORTERS

Major banks today offer a wide variety of specialized services to U.S. exporters, as follows:

- They may accept drafts drawn in foreign currencies, treat these as noncash (foreign collection) items, collect them through overseas branches or correspondent banks, and credit the net proceeds to the exporter's account.
- They may make direct loans to the exporter to assist him in producing and shipping the merchandise.
- They may provide the exporter with letters of introduction that can assist in dealings with foreign banks or companies.
- They may publish periodic economic reports on foreign countries. Such reports generally contain up-to-date information on customs restrictions, currency regulations, the stability of the government, and the overall economic condition of the country.

SERVICES TO INDIVIDUALS

To assist individual customers who are visiting foreign countries, banks may make supplies of various local currencies available. If the customer requires relatively large amounts, the bank may issue a *traveler's letter of credit*, guaranteeing payments of funds up to a stated total amount. Payments against this L/C are made in local currency by branches of the issuing bank or through its foreign correspondents. The paying bank reduces the balance representing the unused portion of the L/C each time a payment takes place.

The disadvantage of the traveler's L/C is that it must be presented to a bank. For the traveler's convenience, the L/C has largely been replaced by *traveler's checks*. These are issued both by banks and other financial institutions, such as the American Express Company. Traveler's checks have the advantage of easy negotiability throughout the world. Each check is signed at the time it is purchased and must be countersigned as it is used. Hotels, restaurants, airlines, and other parties that accept these checks are guaranteed repayment by the issuer.

Individuals also may ask their banks to provide them with *letters of introduction*, which can be used to establish their identity with foreign banks or branches, providing proof of the traveler's creditworthiness and integrity.

EURODOLLARS

When the oil-producing and exporting countries (OPEC) raised oil prices during the 1970s, they immediately became the recipients of unheard-of wealth. Much of this wealth came from the less-developed countries of the Third World. The OPEC countries found a safe haven for much of this wealth in the foreign branches of U.S. banks, into which they made large deposits.

The large-scale expansion of overseas branch systems of U.S. banks, plus the creation of "offshore" facilities (in locations such as Nassau and the Cayman Islands), provided global corporations with depositories into which they could place the funds derived from their local operations.

The term "Eurodollar" was first introduced into the language of banking in the 1960s. Eurodollars are simply dollars that have been recorded as being on deposit outside the United States. They differ from domestically deposited dollars only in terms of their technical location, and can easily be brought back to the U.S. by the banks' head offices.

Because many Eurodollars originated from the deposits made by OPEC nations the term *petrodollars* was coined to indicate their source. Eurodollars also result from the deficit in the U.S. balance of payments; as a nation, the United States must pay for many of its imports in dollars, which the sellers deposit in local banks as Eurodollars.

If a corporation deposits $1 million with a bank in the United States, the value of that deposit to the bank must be reduced by the reserve required by the Fed. On the other hand, Eurodollars recorded on the bank's books are *not* subject to reserve requirements; therefore, if deposited overseas in Eurodollars, the entire $1 million theoretically represents loanable or investable funds.

Corporations benefited from Eurodollars because such deposits were not governed by Regulation Q. A bank can pay any rate of interest it chooses in order to attract and keep such deposits. The hundreds of billions of Eurodollars that now exist constitute a major source of funds to the banks; at the same time, they have proved most attractive to corporations. The net result is that the largest U.S. banks now generally report more than half of their total deposits as "foreign," and the bulk of those foreign deposits can be found in interest-bearing relationships, such as large-denomination CDs.

It has often been pointed out that deposits, in and of themselves, have no value to a bank; they are valuable only in the sense that they provide the banks with funds that can be put to profitable use. As deposits grow, banks logically seek to lend and invest those funds. The tremendous increase in overseas deposits that began in the 1970s created a need on the part of the banks to "recycle" those deposits in the form of loans. This recycling helps to explain the huge increases in global debt that have caused so much concern in recent years.

GLOBAL CREDIT OPERATIONS

U.S. banking activities in countries throughout the world can be grouped under two major headings: The first of these comprises *basic services*—for example, accepting deposits, processing local payments, and extending credit. The customer base for these services consists of individuals, smaller businesses, and international corporations.

The second category—*global lending*—is perhaps the primary concern of the largest U.S. banks today. It includes the broad spectrum of loans made by those banks to foreign governments and corporations. Public confidence in the soundness of the U.S. banking system has been significantly weakened by the succession of newspaper and magazine articles outlining the magnitude of the debt crisis. From 1973 to 1981 the long-term debt of less-developed countries to all lenders grew from $97 billion to $425 billion; the U.S. banks alone increased their foreign loan portfolios from $105 billion in 1975 to $400 billion in 1981. As of year-end 1986, the seven largest U.S. bank lenders to less-developed countries reported outstandings of $47.7 billion. Much of this amount was concentrated in loans to countries in Latin America.[9] In response, some of these major banks have increased their loan-loss reserves.

The tremendous growth in loans to foreign governments and businesses in part resulted from the infusion of billions of dollars of new deposits into the U.S. banking system through OPEC activity during the 1970s. The banks "recycled" those petrodollars by expanding their foreign loan portfolios, possibly without giving enough consideration to all the risk factors involved.

One consequence of that expansion has been a far greater emphasis among U.S. banks on the concept of *global (country) risk analysis*. This term describes the systems that have been developed to classify and report on a bank's outstanding loans in every part of the world. In addition to the criteria that are used in domestic credit analysis, global risk analysis attempts to consider all the local factors such as stability of government, changing economic conditions, the rate of inflation, the political climate, and the steps (if any) that local governments have taken to improve their ability to repay debt. Global risk analysis also includes recognition of the fact that loans made directly to a foreign government may simply be repudiated; that is, the authorities in a debtor country may simply refuse to recognize or honor the debts at all.

The International Banking Act

In an effort to promote competitive equality between domestic and foreign banking institutions in the United States, Congress passed the International Banking Act of 1978. This act established certain restrictions on the interstate operations of branches, agencies, subsidiaries, and affiliated companies of foreign banks. Each such bank was required to designate its *home state* in the United States, and its deposit-taking activities were limited to that state. However, foreign banks operating in more than one U.S. state as of July 27, 1978 were "grandfathered" and thus were permitted to continue interstate banking. The act also allowed a foreign bank to establish *Edge Act* offices. Any foreign bank with consolidated worldwide assets of $1 billion or more was made subject to Federal Reserve requirements. U.S. offices of foreign banks accepting retail deposits of less than $100,000 must join FDIC.

The Edge Act

In 1919 Congress passed legislation intended to help U.S. commercial banks serve those customers who were actively involved in foreign trade. The Edge Act allowed banks to establish facilities across state lines to provide those services directly related to foreign trade. Edge Act offices *cannot* offer complete banking services and are not full-scale branches. A bank that establishes this type of facility in a city where foreign trade is important cannot use it for normal deposit, payment, or credit functions unrelated to international business.

TRUST DEPARTMENT SERVICES

Full-service commercial banks today, along with the many thrift institutions that have substantially increased the scope of their activities, offer a wide variety of services aimed at meeting the financial needs of all categories of customers while generating profits. Many specialized services in the domestic arena involve the bank's trust department. At some larger institutions, the trust department may be called the fiduciary division.

The basic concept of a trust can be traced to Roman history. Roman citizens were able to bequeath property to fraternities or trade unions. Later, in the Middle Ages, church representatives were authorized to safeguard the wills of deceased persons. A *trust* may be defined as a relationship in which one party holds property belonging to another, with some particular benefit in mind. A *trustee* assumes the responsibility and the problems of holding and administering some form of assets for the benefit of another, who is called the *beneficiary*. Banks, individuals, and corporations all may act as trustees.

In the early history of U.S. banking, many financial institutions were organized specifically to act as trust companies; they operated under state charters and were chiefly involved in the handling of investable funds. During the last decade of the nineteenth century, more trust companies than national banks were operating in New York City. Over the course of time, they gradually assumed some or all of the commercial banks' functions, accepting demand and time deposits and extending credit. Their origins still are reflected by the words ". . . Trust Company" in their legal titles. It was not unitl 1913 that the Federal Reserve Act allowed national banks to begin offering trust services.

Major commercial banks today offer a wide range of trust services for individuals, businesses, educational institutions, nonprofit entities, and units of government.

Banks and other financial institutions that offer trust services are said to enjoy a *fiduciary* relationship with their clients. To justify the faith and confidence implied by the Latin meaning of that term, they must always act in the clients' best interests. The function of a bank's trust department is to hold secure and administer the clients' assets in such a way as to protect those interests while generating profits for the bank.

TYPES OF TRUST SERVICES

Depending on the needs of its market and the volume of business it is able to produce, a modern bank may offer any or all of the following fiduciary services:

- settling estates
- administering trusts and guardianships
- acting as trustee under indenture
- administering employee benefit and retirement plans
- assisting in estate planning and tax counseling

In each case, the technicalities of trust operations and the legal background of fiduciary services depend largely on a specialized vocabulary. Trust department personnel must be familiar with special terminology that is not used elsewhere in the bank. Many chapters of the American Institute of Banking offer entire courses dedicated to the particular services provided by the international and trust departments of banks.

Settling Estates

The legal term for a person who has died is *decedent*. When a person dies, the sum total of that person's assets is known as his or her *estate*. If the person left a valid *will*, according to state laws, he or she is said to have died *testate*; if no will exists, or if the will is ruled invalid for any reason, the person is said to have died *intestate*.

In the decedent's will, he or she leaves specific instructions as to how the estate is to be distributed. The will designates a bank, law firm, individual, or other party as the *executor* who is to carry out those instructions. Each will must be admitted to *probate*; that is, a special court must examine and approve it, confirm that the executor is qualified to perform the duties involved in settling the estate, and confirm the process by which assets will be transferred to the heirs and beneficiaries.

If the decedent died intestate, if the will is invalid, or if the executor cannot or will not serve, the court appoints an *administrator*. The duties of executors and administrators are essentially the same; in sequence, they must take the following steps:

- An inventory must be taken to determine the exact value of the estate. Every asset of the decedent must be itemized and a specific dollar value shown for each.
- All necessary federal and state tax returns must be filed, and the necessary taxes, based on the value of the estate, must be paid. All debts and claims against the estate also must be settled.
- The remaining assets must be distributed, either according to the terms of the will or as directed by state laws.

When a bank acts as executor or administrator, it is legally liable for maintaining detailed records of all its actions and rendering an accounting to the court and to the beneficiaries.

Administering Trusts and Guardianships

Trust funds administered by banks are subdivided by specific type. The most common are *testamentary trusts, living trusts,* and *institutional trusts.*

A testamentary trust is created under the terms of a decedent's will. Here, the decedent is also called the *testator* because he or she directed that a trust fund be established with the proceeds of the estate for the benefit of named beneficiaries. As trustee under a testamentary trust, the bank's duties include managing the assets turned over to it by the executor or administrator and paying the income to the designated beneficiaries.

As the name implies, a living trust does not involve a decedent. A living trust is created by the voluntary act of an individual who has executed a trust agreement and has transferred certain property to the bank. One who establishes a trust fund in this fashion is called a *trustor* or *settlor*. Every living trust carries with it specific terms and conditions that the trustor has included in the written trust agreement, accepted by the bank.

Institutional trusts are established when a college, hospital, university, or charitable organization turns over cash and securities to a bank. The bank's duties then involve active management of the investments that have been and will continue to be made. None of the net earnings from an institutional trust may go to an individual or private shareholder.

Guardianships, sometimes called conservatorships, are established by court order for the benefit of a minor or incapacitated person. A minor is defined by state laws as one who is not of legal age; an incapacitated person is a person who has been declared incompetent because of illness or senility. A guardianship also may be established voluntarily by an individual who asks a court for assistance.

Guardianships may be *of the person* or *of the estate or property*. A guardian of the person acts in place of a parent and provides for the necessities of life for the ward, including food, clothing, shelter, and schooling. Banks generally prefer not to act in this capacity. They do, however, act as guardians or conservators of the estate or property, in which case they receive, hold, and manage certain assets for the benefit of the ward.

Agency Services

The third category of trust services includes all cases in which a bank acts as *agent* for an individual, a business, or any other customer who wishes to take advantage of the trust department's expertise and capabilities. There is a significant legal difference between the role of agent and that of trustee. Trustees assume legal title to property that is turned over to them; agents are given specific authority by a *principal*, who retains legal title to the assets.

For individuals, the most common *agency services* include safekeeping, custody, managing agent, and escrow. For corporations and agencies of government, banks provide transfer agent, registrar, paying agent, and dividend disbursing services. Large banks often subdivide agency services into personal and corporate categories.

The simplest and least expensive agency service offered to individuals is that of *safekeeping*—protecting certain property that the principal entrusts to the bank. The bank has no active duties. It merely accepts, holds, and returns upon request the stocks, bonds, or other assets that the principal has delivered to it. The bank must issue a specific receipt for the property turned over to it and maintain itemized records of all such property.

Custody services include safekeeping of assets plus the collecting of income for the principal for crediting to an account. A custodian may buy and sell securities for the principal *only* when specifically instructed to do so. The custodian also may furnish timely information to the principal on all matters affecting his or her interest, such as notices of annual meetings, stock splits, bond maturities, and special stockholder votes.

Banks often provide custody services for individuals, correspondent banks, and agencies of government.

As a *managing agent*, the bank performs all the duties of a custodian and exercises specific powers and responsibilities granted to it by the principal. For example, in handling securities for a principal, the bank will generally review his or her investments from time to time and recommend retention, sale, exchange, or conversion, or the purchase of new securities. The managing agent also may be given discretionary power; that is, the principal may authorize the agent to buy, exchange, or sell securities *without* prior written approval. As custodian, the bank could never act without such written instructions.

Discretionary accounts exist only when the bank has held a series of meetings with the principal to determine his or her investment objectives.

As managing agents, banks often handle real estate instead of securities. In these cases they collect rental income, pay the taxes on the real estate, provide for the maintenance of the property, and credit any net income to the clients' accounts.

Business transactions, particularly those that involve real estate, often require that an impartial, trusted third party be named as agent for the two principals. This third party, whom the principals approve, becomes the *escrow agent*. The agent takes possession of deeds to property or other assets and documents, and safeguards them until the business transaction is completed.

Because all parties to an escrow arrangement must be in full agreement as to the duties and responsibilities of the agent, specific signed escrow documents are always required. These agreements often are prepared by the bank itself, since as agent it is legally liable for exact compliance with the instructions given to it.

Corporate Agency Services

To assist businesses and units of government in handling the tremendous volume of detailed work that results from securities transactions, banks provide corporate agency services under several headings.

As *transfer agent*, a bank acts on behalf of a corporation and is responsible for changing the title to ownership of that corporation's shares of stock or registered bonds. It acts as agent *only* for the corporate customer, and its appointment as transfer agent must be confirmed by the corporate directors. Purchases and sales of corporate securities may require issuing new stock certificates bearing the new owner's name.

As *registrar,* a bank acts on behalf of *both* a corporation and the latter's stockholders. Every corporation is legally authorized to have a certain number of shares of stock outstanding. The registrar must maintain records of the number of shares canceled and reissued so that no over-issue can take place. In this sense, the registrar monitors the work of the transfer agent to ensure that the legal limit on the outstanding shares is not exceeded. The bank thus protects the interests of the corporation's stockholders while rendering a service to the corporation itself. This work lends itself readily to computerization.

Acting as a *paying agent,* the bank is responsible for making all periodic payments of interest or dividends to the holders of the shares of stock or bonds issued by a corporation or unit of government. The *paying agent* also is responsible for redeeming all debt issues as they mature, and is sometimes called the fiscal agent.

Banks recognize the very wide diversification of ownership that exists among many corporations, which may have hundreds of thousands of stockholders. When a corporate board of directors has voted a quarterly dividend on the outstanding shares of stock, there can be a huge amount of work involved in computing the amount of each stockholder's check, mailing those checks, posting the paid checks to an account, and reconciling the balance. As paying agent or dividend disbursing agent, a bank can assume the entire workload and can also assist both the corporation and its many shareholders by providing for automatic reinvestment of their dividends in additional shares of stock.

When a corporation issues bonds as a means of raising funds from investors, it must execute a legal agreement called an *indenture.* A bank or trust company must be named as trustee under this agreement. The *trustee under indenture* is responsible for seeing to it that all the terms of the agreement are met, thereby protecting the bondholders. The trustee guarantees that each bond is authentic, makes all payments on the bonds, and destroys them after redemption so that they can never be presented for payment a second time.

One of the fastest growing and most competitive areas of trust services involves trust funds maintained for the employees of corporations and banks. *Employee trust* funds may result from union negotiations, from a corporate or bank policy aimed at attracting and retaining employees by providing them with fringe benefits, or from an increased emphasis on the social responsibility of the employer in providing for the well-being of the employees.

A bank or business may establish a *pension* or *profit-sharing* (deferred compensation) plan and make regular contributions into a trust fund. If the employees also invest their own funds in the plan, it is called a *contributory* plan. If the employer alone makes all payments into the trust fund, it is called a *noncontributory* plan. The duties of a bank in handling pension and profit-sharing plans involve accepting all payments, investing them, maintaining detailed records to show the accrued value of the trust for each employee, making all payments, and providing detailed data on every transaction.

All employer contributions to qualified (approved by the Internal Revenue Service) pension and profit-sharing plans are business expenses, and therefore are deductible from earnings for tax purposes. Investment income and gains on the funds are likewise exempt from taxes.

Once a bank or corporation has established a pension fund to provide retired employees with a regular source of income, it is required to make regular contributions into the fund. On the other hand, an employer's contributions to a profit-sharing fund fluctuate according to each year's net profits.

Banks must publish information about the annual growth in the rate of return on pension and profit-sharing plans they administer. Employers can compare the performance of several banks and select the institution that has demonstrated the highest growth rate through its investment policies and programs.

401(K) Plans

Section 401(K) of the Internal Revenue Code allows an employer, such as a bank or corporation, to establish a trust fund into which employees can make regular contributions, on a pre-tax basis, through salary deductions. These contributions are a subtraction from the employee's taxable income, which the employer may or may not match, up to a specified amount. The terms of the 401(K) plan are subject to Internal Revenue Service approval. These plans are extremely attractive to employees, since they provide for a reduction in taxable income while at the same time establishing a source of retirement income.

Individual Retirement Plans

The scope and importance of Keogh and IRA relationships were discussed in chapter 5. Commercial banks, thrift institutions, insurance companies, and brokerage firms compete aggressively for these attractive deposits. Through their trust departments, banks now offer a wide variety of investment vehicles into which Keogh and IRA funds can be placed. These investment instruments generally earn interest at rates tied to the current rates on U.S. Treasury bills or money market certificates. Fixed or floating rates of interest, without a rate ceiling, can be offered on Keogh plans and IRA relationships.

Sweep Accounts

In the *sweep account,* all balances in an interest-free account, over and above a specified figure, automatically are "swept" each night into interest-bearing investments. This relationship allows the customer to maintain a demand deposit (with FDIC coverage) for normal purposes while at the same time generating interest on excess funds. A relatively new product for banks, sweep accounts also are aggressively sought by nonbank competitors.

Repurchase Agreements ("Repos")

For many years banks have provided their corporate and institutional clients with investment opportunities in the form of *repurchase agreements,* commonly called *repos.*

A repo is *not* a deposit. It is a form of investment in which the customer gives the bank funds for a stated period of time. The funds are used by the bank to buy federal government obligations, and under the terms of the repo agreement the bank agrees to "buy" the securities back from the customer at a specified time. The advantage of the repo to the customer lies in the interest rates that can be earned; however, the customer does not actually own the securities. If the bank for any reason does not or cannot fulfill its agreement to repurchase the securities, the customer has limited recourse.

Retail repos are not exclusively the function of a bank's trust department, although many banks handle them in that area. Depending on each bank's policy, they may be handled through the branches along with other account activity, even though they are not legally deposit relationships.

Financial Planning and Counseling

The structure of federal and local taxation is such that affluent individuals must give increased consideration to all the problems and implications of investment management and estate planning. Many banks provide a valuable service to their clients in this regard by working with them to design and implement plans that will reduce the tax burden on an estate, ensure that assets go to the survivors as desired, and thereby provide maximum benefits to the client's heirs and beneficiaries.

Counseling with clients involves first gathering information about their current financial situations, investment holdings, and needs and goals. The bank evaluates this information and recommends appropriate services to the client.

Competition in this field is both widespread and intense. Insurance companies, brokerage firms, and estate planning companies are among the entities that vie aggressively with the banks. In many cases, they are able to capitalize on existing relationships with their policyholders and customers by cross-marketing trust services.

Many skills are required to provide the various trust services. Trust departments must always be staffed by personnel with a wide range of specialized knowledge. Tax experts, attorneys, and investment analysts are among the typical members of a trust department's staff; they unite to meet the individual objectives and serve the best interests of each client.

In appointing any fiduciary, the basic purpose of the client is to obtain the benefits of expertise, maximum safety, group judgment, long experience, financial strength, and continuing accessibility. The trustee or agent always must be available to answer questions, give advice, and solve problems for the principals and/or beneficiaries. In competing against the nonbank entities that are seeking trust business, many banks either have or can acquire the skills required to provide those benefits. Their marketing task is to make that fact known to the public.

The trust departments at many banks have become an extremely important source of revenues. Table 12.1 lists the 10 largest U.S. banks and financial institutions as of year-end 1986, ranked according to the market value of their managed trust assets. (Managed trust assets are those on which the banks can make discretionary investment decisions.) The total 1986 trust income for each institution also is shown. For the top 100 banks and trust companies who offer trust services, total trust income for 1986 rose 24.4 percent, to $5.69 billion.

Bankers always have prided themselves on their professionalism and their ability to provide quality services. They have not, however, always resorted to effective marketing as a means of attracting additional trust business.

TABLE 12.1
TRUST ASSETS AND INCOME, 1986

Institution	Managed Trust Assets (in billions of dollars)	Total Trust Income (in millions of dollars)
J.P. Morgan & Co., Inc.	61.7	398.4
Bankers Trust New York Corp.	56.3	222.4
Citicorp	51.7	233.9
Wells Fargo & Co. (San Francisco)	45.2	90.1
PNC Financial Corp. (Pittsburgh)	41.1	127.6
Chase Manhattan Corp.	33.5	265.6
Northern Trust Corp. (Chicago)	28.6	148.9
Mellon Bank Corp. (Pittsburgh)	27.8	198.0
State Street Boston Corp.	26.1	176.6
Manufacturers Hanover Corp.	25.8	147.7

Source: L. Michael Cacace, "J.P. Morgan Bumps Citicorp to Take First Place as Leading Trust Manager," *American Banker*, June 30, 1987, p. 1.

Trust Marketing

An increasing number of well-to-do Americans are prime candidates for trust services. This, combined with the large volume of securities transactions that lend themselves to computer processing and the escalating number of Keogh, IRA, and "sweep" relationships, indicates that the field of trust services offers excellent potential for future growth and profits. Nonetheless, as is true with virtually every aspect of bank services, banks face intense and aggressive competition from many areas. Many of the nation's thrift institutions have taken advantage of the powers granted them by the Monetary Control Act and the Garn-St Germain Act and have begun offering trust services. Insurance companies, estate planning firms, brokerage houses, and other nonbank entities also are seeking new trust business.

Marketing trust services involves the same considerations that apply to marketing other bank services. The trust department should be considered as a profit center that contributes directly to the overall earnings of the bank; as such, it must price its services realistically and ensure that the right services are sold to the right customers in the right way. Detailed planning and market research are needed to identify opportunities and evaluate the competitors; systems of cost accounting are used to determine pricing strategies (to the extent this is permitted under various state laws that may restrict trust department fees); and new products must be developed to meet the changing needs of customers and prospects. Finally, the bank must participate in the actual selling of the various services to customers.

In marketing its many different trust products and services, the bank must be aware that customers and prospects are unconcerned with product names. Rather, the marketing effort must focus on customers' needs, wants, and goals, and any product may have to be tailored to meet a client's particular situation and objectives. Customers unfamiliar with the customized nature of financial services may be lost to the bank if the marketing program does not address this point.

In previous years, trust units in banks catered only to the very wealthy. Today the market has expanded tremendously and banks who ignore its potential must face the loss of valuable new business. In their marketing, banks should capitalize on their basic advantages: experience, convenience, accessibility, expertise, and completeness of services.

Banks have been providing trust services since the eighteenth century. No competitor has comparable experience.

A full-scale bank trust department can serve a client as banker, administrator, advisor, accountant, and investment and tax consultant— all under one roof. The client need not go to various different sources.

The bank is always available; even the best-qualified individuals in other organizations may not be. Trusts are always handled on a team basis, so that at least one individual on the bank's staff is familiar with each client's situation and can be called on at any time.

An integrated trust department makes a wide combination of specialized skills available to the client. Full-time skilled money managers have access to all the latest data so that they can provide investment, legal, tax, and accounting knowledge. The staff can demonstrate a highly personalized sensitivity to client needs and objectives, drawing up detailed proposals and implementing them to suit particular situations.

Trust departments can provide safekeeping in the bank's vaults, can collect income and pay bills, can manage property and file tax returns, can meet all legal requirements, and can make investment recommendations that provide the client with maximum benefits.

LEGAL RESTRICTIONS

The management of wealth has become an increasingly complex problem because of constantly changing laws and tax statutes imposed by federal and local governments. When a bank acts as a trustee or agent, it becomes involved directly in the process of money management and thereby incurs a serious responsibility. Many trust services are specifically intended for the protection and benefit of dependents, minors, heirs, beneficiaries of estates, corporate stockholders, and retired individuals whose entire standard of living may be determined by the pensions or other payments they receive. In all such cases, the courts apply the general legal principle that, in its fiduciary capacity, a bank is subject to heavy penalties should its actions (or its failure to act) cause any harm to a principal or beneficiary.

Aside from that general principle, several specific restrictions apply to the trust operations of banks. The first of these provides that no bank may begin offering trust services without first obtaining approval to do so from the proper authorities. For example, a national bank that wishes to establish a trust department first must apply for permission from the Comptroller of the Currency. The national bank's request also requires the approval of the Federal Reserve and FDIC.

A second legal requirement, designed to give additional protection to all principals and beneficiaries, varies among the individual states. This requirement compels the bank to set aside securities of unquestioned value, such as U.S. government obligations, as a form of collateral against the proper performance of trust duties. A bank's balance sheet will show the dollar value of the government obligations that have been segregated for this purpose. Through this restriction, all clients who are affected in any way by the trust department's operations have a measure of added safety over and above any federal insurance coverage that may apply to them.

The third legal restriction on trust operations is found in the laws of states that establish maximum limits on the fees banks can charge for certain services.

PRINCIPLES OF TRUST INSTITUTIONS

To suggest standards of operation for fiduciaries over and above all legal requirements, the American Bankers Association has published a list of the basic principles that banks should follow. This list includes

- the "prudent man" principle
- segregation of trust assets
- separate policymaking and audit
- acquisition of specialized skills
- prevention of conflicts of interest

A court opinion issued in 1830 held that a trustee must act faithfully and with sound discretion, acting as a prudent, intelligent person would act under similar circumstances. This "prudent man" principle requires that a bank act with all the skill, caution, care, diligence, and sense of responsibility that such a person would display. As part of this principle, it should be noted that a prudent person would be expected to exercise *more* care in handling someone else's property than in handling his or her own. When one is dealing only with one's own assets, certain risks may be willingly assumed, since any profit or loss affects no other party.

The property of each individual trust *must* be kept separate from that of all other trusts and from the bank's own assets. The trust departments of many banks are physically segregated from the rest of the institution and domiciled in separate buildings, with their own vaults, data processing equipment, and other facilities. An "imaginary wall" also must exist between the trust officers and their counterparts in other areas of the bank; they should never exchange information on, or participate jointly in meetings with, accounts that both units may share.

A special committee of the bank's board of directors must set the policies that will be followed concerning investments and the size and type of trust relationships that will be accepted. There also must be a separate trust audit, distinct from any audits conducted in other areas of the bank.

A bank is expected to use all its expertise *plus* all the skill that it can reasonably acquire in conducting trust operations. Banks should continually seek to improve their skills so as to render even better service to clients, and each institution should regularly review all its trust operations in an effort to identify possible areas of improvement.

The final ABA principle is specifically designed to prevent any accusation of a conflict of interest. It is aimed at the practice of self-dealing and states that a bank (1) should have no personal interest whatever in any investments bought or sold for trust funds, and (2) should not purchase for itself any property from any of its trusts. All dealings between the bank's directors, officers, and staff members and its trust funds are prohibited.

CASH MANAGEMENT SERVICES

The third area of specialized bank services can be called *cash management*. As indicated earlier, the tremendous expansion of the American economy since the end of World War II has led to the development of new, specialized financial services. Commercial banks, especially those in the money market centers and those that handle the accounts of the largest corporate customers, have identified changing needs and developed appropriate responses to those needs. In this way, banks provide benefits to the users of their services, and generate new deposits that can be used as a base for loans and investments.

Beginning in the early 1950s, many banks began offering new services to corporations and agencies of government to help them

- collect incoming payments more quickly and efficiently
- manage and reconcile outgoing payments more effectively
- obtain timely and complete information on the status of their bank accounts

Through these cash management services, major banks provide deposit, payment, and information services that have been widely accepted by corporate, government, and correspondent bank customers. They also have become extremely important to the banks as a source of both balances and direct fees.

Lock Box Service

Uncollected funds have no real value to the depositor *or* to the bank that has given immediate provisional credit for deposited checks. The corporation or unit of government that receives large volumes of checks each day has a strong interest in any procedures that will reduce the number of days otherwise required to receive checks through the mail, examine and deposit them with banks, and convert them into available funds. The first cash management service introduced to address this problem is called *lock box*.

A bank, acting as agent for a customer, will establish a post office box in that customer's name and will have its messengers pick up all mail from the box throughout the day. In the bank's central processing unit, the envelopes are opened, and checks are examined for negotiability and deposited. Some form of posting medium—a photocopy of each deposited check, or magnetic tape containing all the necessary information—is furnished to the customer.

Because incoming payments flow directly to the post office, incoming mail time is reduced. The bank's messengers make frequent pickups from the post office, so the receipt of payments is expedited. Because the bank, as agent, is making regular deposits to the customer's account and is sending deposited checks to drawees by the quickest possible means, float is reduced and the availability of funds is increased. Finally, because the bank assumes all the work of receiving, examining, endorsing, and depositing checks and supplying some form of daily information, the customer's clerical costs are reduced and an audit trail is provided on every payment.

Lock box customers at major banks vary widely. Major corporations use the service, but units of government also benefit from it as a means of collecting property, sales and income taxes, automobile registration fees, and tobacco and liquor taxes. Thrift institutions, which are the nation's primary mortgage lenders and therefore handle huge volumes of incoming monthly payments, use lock box services through their correspondents.

Large corporations whose customers are located throughout the country often establish several strategically located lock boxes so that incoming mail time is kept to a minimum. For example, a corporation may ask banks in New York, Atlanta, Chicago, Dallas, and San Francisco to provide the same service and subsequently to transfer funds to a central concentration bank. This system gives the customer maximum availability of funds. In other cases, banks may establish facilities across state lines that simply receive mail payments, or may enter into joint ventures with nonbank companies to offer processing of payments at a network of regional locations.

Depository Transfer Checks

Many corporations and government agencies receive incoming payments at widely dispersed locations—sales offices, regional lock box banks, and so forth. They require a means of rapidly and inexpensively moving each day's deposits to a central concentration bank account. The *depository transfer check* accomplishes this purpose. It is a preprinted, no-signature check that is prepared by the concentration bank and is drawn on an account at a local or regional bank. The concentration bank prepares the checks based on information reported either directly by the corporation or government agency or by the local banks. For a state government whose lottery tickets are sold at a great many locations, the concentration bank may prepare hundreds of checks in a single day in order to move funds into the concentration account; a corporation that operates five or six regional bank accounts but uses the same depository transfer check service will require far fewer prepared checks. The bank sends the customer daily reports showing the amounts drawn in from each location.

Depository transfer checks are far less expensive for the customer than wire transfers.

One improvement in the original system of depository transfer checks has been made possible through the use of electronic funds transfer systems. Debits to the customer's accounts at local or regional banks can be made electronically and processed through the facilities of automated clearing houses so that funds flow directly into the concentration bank without the creation of a volume of paperwork.

Payment Services

Although daily usage of electronic funds transfer systems continues to increase, nationwide check volume is still approximately 100 million items per day.

Disbursements for payroll, accounts payable, dividends, taxes, and freight payments create a chronic problem for the issuers of checks, who must match all paid and returned checks against check registers to determine the number and amount of checks still outstanding at statement date. In addition, unless the check issuers have agreed with their banks to adopt some form of check truncation, they must also store the paid checks and gain access to them when necessary.

Many banks provide account reconciliation and microfilm archival services as part of their cash management product line. *Account reconciliation* (or *reconcilement*) uses the MICR data encoded on a customer's checks to provide a computer-generated listing that shows all paid checks in check number sequence. If required, the paid checks can be sorted into check number order and returned with the listing. If the customer gives the bank magnetic tape or other input containing all the details of each issued check, the reconciliation can also include a complete proof sheet, showing the check number and dollar amount of all unpaid items and matching their total to the closing account balance. Through this service, the customer's time, effort, and expense in proving each bank statement can be reduced to a minimum.

Many banks recognized some time ago that their traditional system of returning every paid check to the issuer was unnecessary and expensive. Accordingly, they implemented a *microfilm archival service*. This is a system of truncation based on the assumption that a computerized listing of paid checks is, in effect, a verification by the drawee that those items have been properly charged to the drawer's account. Accounting, legal, and tax authorities generally have agreed to accept this assumption, provided the bank can provide actual proof of payment if necessary.

In microfilm archival service, paid checks are not returned to the issuer. They are retained by the drawee for a period of time after having been reduced to microfilm, and are subsequently destroyed. Copies of a check can be produced from the microfilm whenever requested.

A customer can derive substantial benefits by using these two services together. The bank also benefits by reducing its expenses in posting, proving, and mailing checks.

Controlled Disbursements

The financial officer of a corporation, unit of government, or other entity *receiving* a large number of checks naturally is anxious to reduce float on incoming payments so that the funds can be put to work. Conversely, the financial officer who *issues* a large number of checks wants to delay presenting and posting because until the drawees have received and processed the checks, no actual disbursement has taken place. Both individuals wish to make *float* work to their advantage.

To increase float on issued checks, corporations open accounts at remote locations, preferably out of the banking mainstream. It is for this reason that checks drawn on banks in Alaska, Montana, and New Mexico have begun to appear in significant numbers. The issuers recognize that the Fed cannot possibly deliver checks to these remote points in a maximum of 2 days but will always give the sending bank (at which the checks presumably have been deposited) credit within that time. Funds availability to the payee is not affected by the remoteness of the drawee bank. If presenting takes several additional days, the Fed absorbs the float.

Many banks now offer a cash management service called *controlled disbursement* accounts, emphasizing the control feature rather than the beneficial float. These banks open a check processing facility away from their head offices and give their customers morning reports on the dollar amounts of checks presented to that facility, providing an important control feature that eliminates uncertainties regarding outstanding checks. Each such check usually requires at least one extra day to reach the facility and be posted. The issuer thus gains disbursement float. If banks market these accounts on the basis of the control feature rather than on the Fed float factor, the Fed has no objections to their doing so.

INFORMATION SERVICES

A financial officer in one of America's major corporations once commented that the term "cash management" is misleading, since he never sees cash at all. Instead, he sees computer printouts, terminals, and screens, or microfilm records. All incoming payments for his firm flow to lock box banks, which supply magnetic tape that goes directly to the company's computers for daily posting. Wherever possible, the company pays through EFTS—for example, by direct deposit to accounts. In other cases, checks that the firm issues are fully reconciled and retained by the drawee on microfilm. The third application of this company's cash management program involves one of the most important services developed by banks in recent years: the supplying of daily information to customers through terminals in their offices, showing all balance data and the debits and credits that have been posted to accounts.

Just as the banks have had to develop management information systems for their own use, corporations, correspondent banks, and government agencies have identified an increasing need for timely and thorough information that will enable them to put available funds to the most profitable uses.

The basic information service allows the customer to access the bank's data base early each morning through a PC or terminal and identify the ledger, collected, and available balances in one or more accounts. Detailed debit and credit reports can be printed out as part of this service. Some banks have added a feature that enables the customer to access the system again, later in the day, to obtain updated information. A corporation, correspondent bank, or unit of government may designate a single bank to receive and consolidate balance information from all its depositories so that all data will appear on a single printout. The terminals through which information is furnished also can be used to initiate wire transfers or to provide stock market quotes and foreign exchange and money market rates.

Security is a critical element in this cash management service. Each customer must use a unique identification code and method of access. Further precautions may be built into the program so that unauthorized persons cannot obtain information or issue wire transfer instructions to the bank.

Traditionally, most banks looked for compensating balances to support their cash management services. However, customers now tend to pay direct fees for each service, just as they do for loans.

SAFE DEPOSIT SERVICES

The safe deposit facilities at banks today offer the same basic service that was provided many years ago by the goldsmiths who accepted valuables from their clients for safekeeping. Then, as now, the key word is *protection*. By their very nature, banks must have vault facilities for the protection of currency, securities, and collateral. It is logical that they should extend the use of those facilities by making them available to customers. However, safe deposit services are not offered solely because they are a traditional part of banking. In addition, they may be thought of as a new business tool to attract customers, or as a defensive measure designed to prevent existing depositors from seeking banking services elsewhere.

Upon proper identification, and with proper documentation in each case, a bank may establish a safe deposit relationship with (1) an individual; (2) an individual together with a *deputy* (agent) whom he or she appoints and whose rights are comparable to those of an attorney-in-fact; (3) two individuals jointly; (4) a sole proprietor; (5) a partnership; (6) a corporation; or (7) a fiduciary. In the case of a corporation, the bank must obtain a separate corporate resolution authorizing the safe deposit relationship.

Whenever a safe deposit box is rented, the bank must obtain appropriate signature cards. Typically, these cards include the terms of the contract between the customer and the bank. The bank then assumes responsibility for the adequate protection of the customer's property.

It is important to note the significant difference between the relationship a bank has with a depositor and with a safe deposit customer. The party renting a safe deposit box has every right to expect that the *identical* property placed in the box will be protected and can be retrieved whenever necessary. Frequently, this property is unique and cannot be replaced. Family heirlooms, valuable documents, and jewelry, for example, must remain in the same condition as when the customer placed them in the box; no change or substitution is acceptable. On the other hand, a depositor who gives the bank $100 in currency cannot expect to receive the identical currency when a withdrawal is made.

Each bank that offers safe deposit services must be fully aware of the liability it can face. It would be a tragic mistake for a bank to treat the relationship casually and to neglect any action that provides protection for the safe deposit customer.

In recent years, there have been many cases of burglaries in which highly professional thieves, using sophisticated equipment, laser technology, and the most modern tools, have been able to penetrate the steel and concrete walls of bank vaults, bypass the alarm systems, and rifle not only the bank's own cash compartments but customers' boxes as well. If a customer claims that certain valuables, allegedly placed in a safe deposit box, have been removed without his or her authorization or knowledge, the burden of proof usually is on the bank to prove that it did everything possible to provide protection. Any evidence of negligence on the bank's part in the control of its daily safe deposit operations, or any proof of defects in the vault's construction or maintenance, may convince a judge or jury that the customer is entitled to damages.

Right of Access

The safe deposit signature cards and contract clearly stipulate which persons are allowed to have access to a box. Possession of a key *does not* establish right of access. The best precaution a bank can take to avoid any future claims requires each individual desiring access to sign a slip of paper that can be compared with the cards on file. The bank may require additional identification, such as the use of a password or mother's maiden name. If a bank is proved to have been negligent in verifying the identity of any individual who sought access to a box, its defense is immediately weakened. Carelessness in any single situation can be extremely detrimental. It is not sufficient for the bank to publish procedure manuals for safe deposit personnel; employees must implement those procedures with extreme care at all times.

In addition to exercising controls over the right of access, a bank may employ many other safeguards and procedures in its daily safe deposit operations. The following are among the most common:

- Keys to unrented boxes should be under dual control at all times. By following this rule a bank can ensure that no unauthorized party could have obtained a key, made a duplicate from it, and used it after the box was rented.
- No member of the bank's staff should ever accept custody of a customer's key, for the same reason mentioned above.
- Safe deposit boxes never should be opened for a customer in the open area of the vault. Private rooms should be provided for customer use and should be searched after each occupancy. In this way the bank can attest that no observer was able to see the contents of a customer's box and thus to know if it was an attractive target for theft.
- For the same reason, no bank personnel, under normal circumstances, should have any knowledge of the contents of a box.
- When a customer terminates the safe deposit relationship and mails the keys to the bank, the box should be opened under dual control. If any property is found in the box, it should be closed and locked. The bank should then require the customer to come in to remove the contents.
- All safe deposit boxes require use of both a bank key and a customer's key to open them. The bank's key should never be referred to as a "master" key, because use of this term might give the impression that the bank has a single key that will open every box.
- In the event of a customer's death or incompetence, the bank must immediately observe all federal, state, and local laws regarding disposition of the property in the box.

Any question or doubt that arises in the daily operations of the safe deposit vault should be resolved in favor of *maximum* protection of the customer's property. The potential for claims and lawsuits is always high. The proper conduct of safe deposit operations may not generate large profits for the bank, but a single act of negligence—no matter how well-intentioned—can result in a court decision that creates a substantial loss.

Questions often arise as to the insurance that covers safe deposit operations. The contents of a customer's safe deposit box are not specifically insured, nor does federal deposit insurance apply to them. Rather, the customer is paying for the security that the bank's facilities are intended to provide, and a general-liability bank policy is usually in effect.

OTHER SPECIALIZED SERVICES

The former board chairman of one of America's largest banks stated its marketing policy in these words: "We intend to supply every useful financial service anywhere in the free world where permitted to us by law and which we can perform at a profit." His attitude is shared by many major banks, which display a willingness to discern customer wants and needs and an ability to respond to them through various services. In many cases these services do not fall into the traditional, narrow concept of "the banking business."

It is not the purpose here to suggest that every bank should begin offering all services to every category of customer. Many banks realize that it is impractical to attempt to be "all things to all people." Also, many customers do not require the entire spectrum of services that a bank in a major money market center might provide. Rather, the objective here is to list several specialized services as further evidence of the dramatic changes in commercial banking. No longer do banks merely accept deposits, process payments, and extend credit, although those three functions still represent their major contributions to the economy. In today's highly competitive marketplace, banks often find that new services represent their only means of attracting new customers and retaining existing ones.

Payroll Services

Employers today must cope with a host of payroll problems that arise from complex federal, state, and local tax requirements, labor laws, and the need for timely and completely confidential preparation of every payroll for their employees. Many banks provide a highly customized payroll service, using the same equipment and technology employed in processing their own payrolls. They can assume the entire burden of calculating each individual's gross pay, making all statutory and voluntary deductions, providing all current and year-to-date information, and computing the net pay. That amount can then be directly deposited to the employee's account with the bank, directed to another financial institution through the ACH network, or paid to the employee by check. The bank providing payroll services enters into a contract that includes responsibility for rendering all necessary tax and earnings reports to units of government.

The customer benefits resulting from this service include speed and accuracy in the preparation of each regular, bonus, and overtime or incentive payroll; complete confidentiality; and greatly reduced clerical work. The bank offering the service usually charges a direct fee based on the number of employees being paid, and may benefit from the opening of new accounts for the customer's employees and from the temporary use of the taxes that are withheld from employees' pay.

EFTS Services

Direct deposit systems are part of the total EFTS approach to today's banking. They enable any paying agency to reduce the number of checks that would otherwise be issued, or to eliminate checks entirely. Examples include the magnetic tape furnished to financial institutions by the Social Security Administration for its regular payments to recipients or provided by branches of the armed forces and by corporations for payroll disbursing.

Many banks combine the direct deposit function with automated teller machine (ATM) facilities. For example, they will credit each employee's net pay to his or her account and will install ATMs on the employer's premises to offer ready access to cash.

Point-of-sale terminals have been installed in many stores, gasoline stations, and other locations in conjunction with banks or other financial institutions. These terminals allow the purchaser of goods to pay through direct debits to an account, with a corresponding credit electronically posted to the account of the seller.

Preauthorized payment systems eliminate the need for customers to issue checks for such standard monthly payments as insurance premiums and mortgage loans. The accounts of the payees can then be electronically credited.

The information services that were described as part of the cash management product line can likewise be offered to customers who take advantage of home banking systems. An individual can use his or her PC to obtain current balance information, to authorize disbursements, and to obtain information on interest rates, stock market quotations, and foreign exchange rates.

The federal government has become extremely conscious of the need for consumer protection in the EFTS age. Federal Reserve Regulation E specifically addresses this question, as do state and local laws. Each bank offering EFTS services must initiate security measures that protect the user, and must be aware of the rights and obligations that apply both to itself and to the customer.

Services to Correspondent Banks

To expand its correspondent network and build up its deposit base, a bank must be prepared to meet the specialized needs of other institutions. Demand deposit accounting is one service offered to correspondents. Investment portfolio analysis is another, which may also be offered in conjunction with safekeeping facilities for the correspondent bank's securities. One bank may offer to prepare all Form 1099s for its correspondent, thereby providing the Internal Revenue Service with the required information on interest and dividend payments.

Thrift institutions are active users of the specialized services offered by their commercial bank correspondents. These may include lock box (for the daily collection of mortgage payments), payroll preparation, portfolio analysis, Fed funds transactions, and account reconciliation for the many money orders and teller's checks issued by the thrift institution.

Brokerage and Insurance Services

Chapter 15 will summarize the status of the financial services industry today, with particular attention to the most important contemporary issues that affect banks. However, mention may be made here of one aspect of specialized services in which banks are interested.

The Glass-Steagall Act divorced commercial banking from investment banking and restricted the ability of commercial banks to engage in the securities business. Recent years have witnessed some relaxation of that restriction, and wherever possible the banks have taken advantage of that relaxation by offering new services.

A customer using a Sears, Roebuck financial center can handle his or her insurance, brokerage, investment, real estate, and banking needs at a single location. The commercial bank obviously would like to be able to offer a similar range of services under a single roof. In some cases, banks have gained a limited degree of freedom to offer discount brokerage services to their customers.

SUMMARY

Commercial banking today involves a world-wide market. Banking activities now encompass far more than the basics of attracting deposits, processing payments, and extending credit. In this environment, innovation and an expanded range of services have become the keys to growth and profitability. Banks continually strive to identify their markets, study the wants and needs of those markets, and develop and provide new or enhanced services that will benefit customers while generating profits.

A tremendous expansion of international banking has taken place since the end of World War II, and new service opportunities continue to open up as America's imports and exports increase. Earnings from international operations make up a large part of the income of many major banks today. Similarly, through their trust departments U.S. banks manage hundreds of billions of dollars of property and generate significant income through the wide range of services they offer a growing and diversified clientele.

Cash management services have become an important income contributor for many banks. Through cash management services, banks can reduce float and clerical work, increase the availability of funds, and monitor and adjust bank balances so that idle funds can be put to profitable use.

Safe deposit services require specific security procedures for the protection of customers' property. Every appropriate measure must be taken to ensure that the bank never is negligent in the care it provides.

The increased capability of computers and the widespread acceptance of many applications of EFTS also have enabled banks to broaden the range of their specialized services. Only through service can banks compete successfully against the many other financial intermediaries in today's marketplace.

QUESTIONS FOR DISCUSSION

1. How does a letter of credit, issued by a bank, protect the interests of both the buyer and seller of goods?

2. Define the following terms in international banking:

   a) banker's acceptance
   b) bill of lading
   c) Eurodollar
   d) irrevocable letter of credit

3. What benefits does trust receipt financing offer to an American importer of goods?

4. List three international department services that would be helpful to an American exporter.

5. What legal difference exists between the role of a bank as trustee and its role as agent?

6. List, in order, the steps that must be followed in settling estates.

7. Define the following terms:

   a) executor
   b) testamentary trust
   c) indenture
   d) settlor

8. Describe the duties a bank would be required to perform in each of the following roles:

   a) escrow agent
   b) custodian
   c) registrar

9. For each of the following services, identify one benefit to the bank and one benefit to the user:

   a) lock box   d) controlled disbursements
   b) payroll preparation e) on-line information services
   c) depository transfer checks

10. List any five safeguards that a bank might use as protective measures in its daily safe deposit operations.

NOTES

1. Eric N. Compton, *The New World of Commercial Banking* (Lexington, Mass.: Lexington Books, 1987), pp. 70–71.

2. Board of Governors of the Federal Reserve System, *73rd Annual Report 1986,* p. 201.

3. "Location of Foreign Banks' U.S. Offices," *American Banker,* February 27, 1987, p. 6.

4. "Foreign Banks' Lending Share of the U.S. Market," *American Banker,* April 9, 1987, p. 7.

5. L. Michael Cacace, "Japan's U.S. Presence Grows," *American Banker,* February 27, 1987, p. 1.

6. Charles P. Thomas, "U.S. International Transactions in 1986," *Federal Reserve Bulletin* (May 1987), p. 321, and *Federal Reserve Bulletin,* June 1987, p. A54.

7. *Ibid.,* p. A30.

8. Dennis Walters, "Stunned U.S. Banks Fear Deeper Market Inroads by Foreign Firms," *American Banker,* February 26, 1987, p. 29.

9. *Newsweek,* June 1, 1987, p. 42.

For More Information

Beehler, Paul J. *Contemporary Cash Management: Principles, Practices, Perspectives.* New York: John Wiley & Sons, Inc., 1983.

Blevins, Ronald L., John M. Clarke, James Mitchell, Jack W. Zalaha, and August Zinsser, III. *The Trust Business.* Washington, D.C.: American Bankers Association, 1988.

Chorafas, Dimitris N. *Money: The Banks of the 1980s.* New York: Petrocelli Books, 1982.

Friedman, David H. *Deposit Operations.* Washington, D.C.: American Bankers Association, 1987.

Oppenheim, Peter K. *International Banking.* 5th ed. Washington, D.C.: American Bankers Association, 1987.

Roussakis, Emmanuel N., ed. *International Banking: Principles and Practices.* New York: Praeger, 1983.

13.

REGULATION, EXAMINATION, AND INTERNAL CONTROLS

LEARNING OBJECTIVES

After completing this chapter, you will be able to

•

assess the reasons for extensive federal and state regulation, supervision, and examination of banks, and the current trend toward deregulation

•

describe the chartering process

•

list the regulatory agencies involved with each type of bank

•

explain the purposes of examinations of banks by federal and state authorities

•

explain why unit banking predominates in the United States

•

outline the provisions of the Bank Secrecy Act, Regulation Y, and the Douglas Amendment

•

list the basic operating safeguards included in a bank's system of internal controls

•

describe the essential elements in auditing, including verification

•

describe the various components of an effective human resources management program

The evolution of commercial banking in the United States has been marked by confrontations and compromises between groups whose views on regulation are diametrically opposed. Colonial Americans strongly opposed the concept of centralized banking, and their attitudes continued in the new nation's formative years. The so-called "Free Banking Laws," passed by the Michigan legislature in 1837 and later adopted in other states, gave full legal sanction to this philosophy and continued a system under which virtually anyone could open a bank and operate it with a minimum of government regulation and examination. Unfortunately, widespread failures, counterfeiting of bank notes, and wildcat banking resulted, severely damaging public confidence in the strength and reliability of the banking system.

From the start, the doctrine of free-enterprise banking had some prominent opponents. Alexander Hamilton favored a strong central bank and the imposition of federal controls over banking. He reasoned that when human beings failed to do voluntarily what was just and reasonable, it was the basic function of government to take action. Although Hamilton did not succeed in his efforts to have Congress charter a federal institution modeled on the Bank of England, his influence led to the establishing of the First and Second Banks of the United States.

The confrontation between those who favored federal intervention in the banking industry and those who opposed it resulted in compromise, in the form of the National Bank Act of 1863–64. National banks, the office of the Comptroller of the Currency, and national bank notes came into existence. However, banks were not forced to seek national charters: banks could—and still can—operate under state charters. The Federal Reserve Act of 1913 also represented a compromise. State-chartered banks were allowed to remain outside the Fed system if they chose to do so. The act also allowed state-chartered members to resign from the Fed system at any time, and national banks, which were legally required to become members, could convert to state charters and then withdraw. Since 1913, fewer than one-half of U.S. commercial banks have been Fed members; at year-end 1986, Fed member banks numbered 5,954 (of which 4,866 were national banks), and nonmembers numbered 8,232.[1]

The Glass-Steagall Act, passed in 1933, also contained an element of compromise, although the need to accommodate opposing forces was less severe at this time. The wave of bank failures during the early 1930s had made the need for banking reform evident to all. Nonetheless, the act did not force every bank to join the newly formed FDIC.

The Monetary Control Act in 1980 and the Garn-St Germain Act in 1982, like the three earlier legislative landmarks, were reactions to weaknesses, problems, and crises that had been identified throughout the banking industry. In addressing the problems of attrition from the Fed system and failures and losses among thrift institutions, these acts added to the list of banking regulations.

Many observers within and outside the banking industry have characterized it as the most rigidly, frequently, and thoroughly regulated and examined of all the industries in our country. The system of external controls imposed by government agencies takes effect even before a bank is in operation; before it can accept its first deposit a bank must pass a series of qualifying tests pertaining to its charter application. Throughout its life cycle it is subjected to an unending host of controls that keep it in the harsh spotlight of detailed examinations and restrict the range of its services. Even after a bank has officially gone out of business, the system of external controls applies until the last depositor has been repaid and the final claim has been settled. Few, if any, nonbank businesses have so much regulation and so many restrictions with which to cope.

The era of confrontation regarding banking regulation continued into the 1980s. Indeed, recent controversy has been at least as strong as at any previous time in our history. Strong opinions have been voiced by many who seek a broad relaxation of at least some of the regulations affecting banking. Equally strong are the arguments of those who oppose any such deregulation. There are two broad, major areas of concern:

- Given the increasingly aggressive and intense competition that banks face in the financial services industry today, should they be allowed expanded powers so that they can compete more equitably?
- Are the existing regulations that have prevented full-scale interstate banking for over 50 years still reasonable and proper?

The question of full-scale interstate banking is a contemporary issue that will be further addressed in chapter 15. Banking deregulation, of course, relates to the number and extent of the controls and restrictions that have historically been placed on U.S. banks.

The bankers' case for deregulation intensified as a result of the events that took place in the financial services industry in 1986. During that year the General Electric Credit Corporation, already an extremely powerful force in that industry, acquired one of the nation's leading brokerage houses and investment banking units: Kidder, Peabody & Company. General Motors Acceptance Corporation, already boasting a huge portfolio of automobile-loan receivables, became the nation's second largest servicer of home mortgage portfolios and entered the direct mortgage origination business. The Ford Motor Company's First Nationwide Financial Corporation expanded its interstate network and announced plans for a nationwide branch system based in K-Mart stores. Sears, Roebuck and Company, with its network of financial centers already partially in place, began offering consumers cash rebates as incentives to use its new Discover card. The Tax Reform Act of 1986 revised the tax structure affecting banks, thereby creating an additional tax burden of as much as $10 billion for them over a 5-year period, and the interest exemption banks had previously enjoyed on debt incurred to buy municipals was removed. The Tax Reform Act also limited consumer deductions for IRAs, which had a negative impact on the banks.[2] Little wonder, then, that bankers sought various forms of relief.

Pressures on Congress to bring about legislative reform originated not only from bankers, but also received strong support from several prominent regulators.

In 1986 Comptroller of the Currency Robert L. Clarke suggested that banks must be granted greater flexibility to diversify their income sources and to restructure their products and services.[3] Later in that year, Federal Reserve Board Governor Martha R. Seger stated that "if we do not move ahead [with deregulation], we will find that banking organizations will be ever more seriously handicapped in their competition with other financial service providers. . . ." She continued, saying "Ultimately, I would hope that banks and bank holding companies would be full-line providers of financial services."[4]

In January 1987 Paul A. Volcker, then chairman of the Fed's Board of Governors, again asked Congress to permit banks to underwrite municipal revenue bonds, commercial paper, and mutual funds.[5] In the same month E. Gerald Corrigan, president of the New York Fed, presented a sweeping proposal that would lower many of the legal barriers that now prevent banks from entering certain other businesses.[6] In May 1987 Alan Greenspan, who later that year replaced Volcker as chairman of the Federal Reserve, described deregulation of banking (with certain limitations) as "essential to the health of both banking and financial services."[7]

REASONS FOR BANK REGULATION

Neither bankers nor regulators seek total freedom from regulation. Both recognize that the basic nature of the banking business justifies governmental controls. Those who resent the fact that banking is subjected to more extensive restraints and controls than any other industry must recognize the uniqueness of banking and must appreciate the fact that many of those controls came about because the banks themselves had created the need for them. Deregulation cannot be construed to mean a total absence of federal or state control over banking; rather, it is a term that indicates the desire to remove some of the existing restrictions while preserving the rights of governments to exercise a degree of regulation and supervision over the banking system.

What unique factors in banking justify the number and type of restrictions that have been placed on it? The first reason is that banking has a tremendous impact on the nation's money supply. As the holders of the largest amount of demand deposits, banks control a large part of that supply. Moreover, aside from the federal government itself (and those thrift institutions that have taken advantage of their expanded lending powers), the banks are the only institutions that have the ability to create money through the credit function. It is entirely proper that governments should have a strong interest in the soundness of the one industry whose everyday operations are so closely tied to the national money supply.

The second reason for the existence of so many and such rigorous government controls over banking was stated by Alexander Hamilton, the first U.S. secretary of the Treasury. He pointed out that governments must intervene for the general good of the public when the private sector has not met its obligations and carried out its tasks properly. In the case of banking, it is essential to the country's well-being that public confidence in the system be built up and preserved. It is a responsibility of governments to contribute to that confidence by regulating and examining banks to help assure the public that their deposits are secure and that the institutions are well managed.

A third reason exists for bank regulation. No industry daily affects as many others as does banking. The services to businesses, individuals, and governments that flow from the banks' deposit, payment, and credit functions are indispensable to the nation's total economy. It is logical that federal and state agencies should be deeply concerned about the soundness of the one American industry on which so many others depend.

Finally, government agencies recognize the high degree of interdependence between the well-being of the banks and that of the communities in which they function. The concept of social responsibility requires banks to render a service to their communities by becoming involved in local problems. Regulation of the banking industry in some cases has taken the form of legislation, such as the Community Reinvestment Act, requiring banks to take positive steps to improve their communities by giving to them in addition to taking deposits from them. In other cases, laws directly affect the relationships between banks and the individuals who live in their communities. For example, legislation prohibits any form of discrimination in lending. As each state is the sum total of all its communities and municipalities, so the nation is the sum total of the 50 states; therefore, there is a rationale for federal laws that require banks to help improve the quality of life in their geographic localities.

Criticism of existing federal and state regulation of banking intensifies whenever there is news of bank failures. Critics ask why problem areas at the banks were not identified earlier, how the failures were allowed to occur, and whether the system actually works. Often, it is suggested or assumed that the remedies for bank failures lie in adding new controls over the industry or in creating new supervisory agencies.

Criticisms, questions, and corrective measures have validity only if they lead to improvements in the present system. Deregulation—the removal of some of these controls—is another approach. Nonetheless, even the most outspoken advocates of free enterprise would find it impossible today to support the removal of all forms of government controls over banking.

REGULATORY AGENCIES

The banking legislation passed in 1863, 1913, and 1933 created different categories of banks, and various agencies of government were assigned *primary* responsibility for supervising each category. Four agencies that have regulatory authority over certain segments of the commercial banking industry will be discussed here.

The *Comptroller of the Currency* has jurisdiction over the 4,800 nationally chartered banks, which operate some 22,000 branches. The Office of the Comptroller is responsible for chartering, examining, and supervising all national banks. All requests by any of these banks for the opening of new domestic or foreign branches or for the offering of new services (for example, in the trust area), and all mergers or acquisitions involving national banks must have the approval of the Comptroller. The many functions of this agency are carried out by regional administrative offices throughout the country. The Comptroller also is an *ex officio* member of the Board of Governors of the Federal Deposit Insurance Corporation.

The *Federal Deposit Insurance Corporation* insures roughly 98 percent of all commercial and savings banks in the United States. It sets enforceable standards for its members, assesses them according to the size of their average annual deposits, can examine a member bank at any time, and may act to prevent the failure of an insured bank by bringing about its merger with or acquisition by a stronger insured institution, or by taking other positive action (for example, buying the troubled bank's assets or providing it with an infusion of fresh capital funds).

The seven members of the Board of Governors of the *Federal Reserve System* are appointed by the president, subject to confirmation by the Senate. The seven members must come from seven different Fed districts. In addition to its basic tasks in the area of national monetary policy, the Fed is responsible for regulating all member banks, examining state-chartered member banks, overseeing members' international operations, and supervising all bank holding companies (including regulating the scope of their activities).

All national banks *must* be members of the Federal Reserve System; all Fed members must also belong to FDIC. Therefore, every national bank technically is subject to three different federal regulatory agencies.

281

To ensure a sound, well-run banking system, each agency, along with the banking departments in each state, has the right to conduct an examination of the banks that fall under its jurisdiction.

Each of the 50 states has its own banking authority. This authority regulates branch banking within the state's borders, approves charter requests, sets maximum interest rates on certain loans, and otherwise supervises the actions of banks within the state.

OTHER REGULATORY BODIES

In addition to the federal and state agencies named above, many other nonbank agencies exercise some degree of control over the operations of commercial banks. For example, the Department of Justice has the right of approval on any bank merger that, in its judgment, might create a trend toward monopoly. The Securities and Exchange Commission requires banks and all other corporations that issue and sell stock to the public to file regular, detailed reports with it. The Treasury Department's Office of Law Enforcement has implemented the Bank Secrecy Act through extensive record-retention and reporting requirements. In 1986 and 1987, additional federal laws were passed regarding financial recordkeeping and the reporting of currency and foreign transactions. The regulations now require banks to secure Taxpayer Identification Numbers, retain an original (or microfilm or other copy) of most demand-deposit or savings-account records for 5 years and a record of each item (check, draft, or transfer of credit) for $10,000 or more remitted or transferred to a person, account, or place outside the United States. Foreign transactions of any type that involve $10,000 or more also must be recorded and the records held for 5 years. All currency transactions of more than $10,000 must be reported by the bank to the Internal Revenue Service.[8]

The Tax Equity and Fiscal Responsibility Act of 1982 (TEFRA) compels banks to take many additional steps in the area of tax compliance, and the 1984 Deficit Reduction Act imposed additional requirements. Banks now are required to report mortgage interest collected, IRA contributions received, and the amounts withheld on interest and dividend payments.[9]

Several states have passed truth-in-savings legislation that provides consumers with detailed information and enables them to compare accounts at various financial institutions. Examples of the information that banks are called on to supply include annual rate of simple interest, effective annual yield, the formula for interest calculations, the frequency of compounding and crediting of interest, and the grace periods for deposits and withdrawals.

An example of state regulation affecting banks is the Florida legislation that became effective on July 1, 1987. Financial institutions in that state are required to collect and remit a 5 percent tax on a wide range of services, including cashier's and traveler's checks, money orders, stop-payment orders, overdraft and returned-check charges, and safe deposit box fees.[10]

BANK CHARTERING

When Salmon P. Chase and his colleagues drafted the National Bank Act, they specifically addressed the issue of chartering. It had become apparent that the new system of national banks could not be allowed to follow the concept of free banking; the political abuses and uncontrolled activities that had resulted under that concept had created so many problems that most people agreed some method of regulating the opening of banks was absolutely necessary.

The National Bank Act specified that those wishing to establish a new national bank had to submit a charter application to the Office of the Comptroller of the Currency. The application was subjected to the following four tests:

- Is the new bank actually needed in the community?
- Is it backed by a sufficient amount of capital?
- Are the incorporators and proposed senior officers experienced, capable, and of impeccable character?
- Is the new bank likely to grow, serve the community well, and be profitable?

These four basic questions are as valid today as they were in 1863, and they remain as the fundamental considerations in the appraisal of every request for a bank charter. In addition to approval by the Comptroller of the Currency, an application for a new national bank charter must also gain approval from the Federal Reserve and the FDIC, since national banks must belong to both.

An application for a state charter is submitted to the state banking department, and must pass similar qualifying tests. If the proposed new bank desires membership in the Federal Reserve System or in the FDIC, its application must also be reviewed by those agencies.

BANK EXAMINATIONS

Periodic examinations have become an accepted part of our banking system. Every commercial bank receives at least one such examination each year, and the frequency may be increased if conditions in a particular bank seem to warrant it. It is impossible, however, for each regulatory agency to examine every bank under its jurisdiction. Even if this were physically feasible, it would involve much unnecessary duplication of effort, with a consequent increase in expense to the taxpayers. For example, if a national bank were to undergo separate annual examinations by the Comptroller's Office, the Fed, and the FDIC, its operations would be disrupted on three separate occasions—when a single, thorough examination probably would have sufficed.

To avoid duplication and waste, federal regulatory agencies have agreed on an examination format acceptable to all of them. The *primary* examining responsibility is assigned to one agency, which then transmits the results of the examination to all other interested agencies and to the bank's board of directors (see table 13.1).

This system in *no* way inhibits the right of any agency to conduct its own, separate examination of a particular bank if conditions appear to justify this. For example, if the Comptroller of the Currency identifies a problem at a national bank, on the basis of the Comptroller's report, both the Fed and the FDIC could immediately conduct their own independent examinations if they felt this was appropriate.

Purposes of Bank Examinations

The basic purpose of every bank examination by a regulatory agency is to determine certain facts about the bank. The examiners *do not* specifically try to locate fraud or embezzlement. Rather, they perform an evaluation of the bank's reporting systems for all its assets, liabilities, income, and expenses. Every bank is required to submit detailed balance-sheet and income-statement data to the authorities. The examiners verify these to ensure that all assets, liabilities, income, and expenses have been accurately recorded. They determine the bank's degree of compliance with all the laws and regulations that affect it. They assess the quality and effectiveness of the bank's management, as judged by the policies and procedures that can be noted and by the institution's track record of

TABLE 13.1
BANK REGULATORY AUTHORITIES

Type of bank	Regulatory Authority	Annual Examination Conducted By
National bank	Comptroller of the Currency Federal Reserve FDIC	Comptroller of the Currency
State member bank	Federal Reserve FDIC State banking department	Federal Reserve[a]
State nonmember insured bank	FDIC State banking department	FDIC
State nonmember noninsured bank	State banking department	State banking department

a. Examinations of state-chartered member banks are often conducted jointly by state banking department examiners working closely with Federal Reserve examiners.

performance. They measure the adequacy of the bank's capital, since adequate capital protects the stockholders and depositors by ensuring that the bank could withstand losses and adverse conditions.

In summary, every external examination of a bank must answer the following questions:

- What is the bank's true financial condition?
- Are all appropriate laws and regulations being observed?
- Is the bank's capital sufficient?
- What improvements can be made?

The fourth question suggests that a bank examination should identify changes the institution can make to operate more profitably, correct existing weaknesses, and better serve the needs of its customers and community.

The bank's board of directors constitutes the active, governing body of the bank. Therefore, the bank's board receives a copy of the examination report and is expected to take corrective action wherever needed. The examiners representing federal and state agencies also have the right to call a meeting of the bank's board to discuss specific problems.

Federal agencies periodically prepare a "warning" or "watch" list of banks at which specific weaknesses and problems have been found. Any bank that has been placed on this list can expect to receive much closer scrutiny from government regulators. In addition to more frequent or more detailed examinations, a bank in this category may be required to accept certain actions designed to keep it from failing.

In 1985, as increasing numbers of banks began reporting large losses, the Federal Reserve announced that it would increase the frequency of its bank examinations and strengthen the requirements for reporting deficiencies to bank directors and managers. The largest banks and bank holding companies, and those classified by the Fed as having significant problems, became subject to two examinations per year.[11]

BANK HOLDING COMPANIES

Holding companies have existed in the United States for many years. Holding companies come in many formats and in different sizes. However, each one is a legal corporate entity that exercises control over other companies through ownership of their stock. Historically, many holding companies have included banks among their components, and in some cases the holding companies were formed as a means of bringing together several banks—even when the institutions were located in more than one state. For example, the entity now called First Interstate Bancorp consists of 23 banks with over 950 branches in 12 states.[12]

Under pressure from the Federal Reserve on the grounds that many holding companies were being used as a means of evading restrictions on interstate and intrastate banking and branching, Congress passed the Bank Holding Company Act in 1956. This act gave the Fed primary responsibility for regulating and supervising bank holding companies. It was amended in 1966 and 1970 with two basic objectives in mind. The first objective was to control the expansion of bank holding companies to avoid monopolies and restraint of trade; the second was to maintain a separation of banking from commerce. The act defined a bank holding company as an organization that directly or indirectly controlled 25 percent or more of the voting stock of two or more banks. Each such organization was required to register with the Fed, and the Fed was empowered to regulate the formation of bank holding companies and their acquisitions or mergers.

Because the act exempted holding companies that involved only one bank from any restrictions, many of the nation's largest banks changed their corporate structure during the 1960s to form one-bank holding companies. These were free to engage in activities outside the normal business of banking.

Fears arose that large banks would achieve great concentrations of economic power and would diversify into a variety of unrelated businesses; therefore, in 1970 Congress acted to bring *all* bank holding companies under the supervision of the Fed.[13] As of year-end 1984 there were 6,146 registered bank holding companies in existence; by year-end 1986 that number had grown to 6,465 BHCs, controlling 9,409 commercial banks and holding 92 percent of the total assets of all insured commercial banks in the United States.[14]

Passed in 1966, the Douglas Amendment to the Bank Holding Company Act provided that a BHC operating in one state could not acquire a bank in a second state unless the latter specifically authorized the acquisition by statute. Recent trends toward regional and interstate banking, as permitted by various states, will be discussed in chapter 15.

Regulation Y of the Federal Reserve System implements the BHC Act as amended. It defines a bank as any institution, organized under the laws of the United States, that accepts demand deposits *and* makes commercial loans.

As an important part of its overall regulation of BHCs, the Federal Reserve Board of Governors has identified the permitted activities in which all such holding companies may engage (table 13.2). The Fed's rationale for approving these (or any activities subsequently added to its list) is based on the premise that they are closely related to banking. BHCs frequently seek permission from the Fed to engage in other activities. Each such request is evaluated on the basis of risk, competition, and the public good. In 1986 the Fed's Board of Governors amended Regulation Y so that all BHCs could engage in six additional nonbanking activities: tax preparation and planning, consumer financial counseling, commodity trading advisory services, check guarantee services, credit bureau and collection agency services, and personal property appraisal.[15] Employee benefits consulting and student loan servicing also have been approved for all BHCs.[16]

TABLE 13.2
ACTIVITIES PERMITTED FOR BHCS AS OF 1984

---

1. Making and servicing loans and other extensions of credit.
2. Operating as an industrial bank.
3. Performing trust activities.
4. Acting as an investment or financial adviser.
5. Leasing real or personal property on a full payout basis.
6. Making equity and debt investments in corporations or projects designed primarily to promote community welfare.
7. Providing financially related bookkeeping and data processing services.
8. Acting as agent or broker for certain limited forms of insurance.
9. Acting as an underwriter for certain types of insurance directly related to extensions of consumer credit.
10. Providing financially related courier services.
11. Providing management consulting advice to nonaffiliated banks and depository institutions.
12. Acting as agent or broker for the sale of money orders, savings bonds, and traveler's checks.
13. Performing real estate appraisals.
14. Arranging equity financing for commercial real estate.
15. Underwriting and dealing in government obligations.
16. Providing foreign exchange advisory and transaction services.
17. Acting as a futures commission merchant.
18. Providing discount securities brokerage services.
19. Investing in export trading companies.

Source: Board of Governors of the Federal Reserve System, *The Federal Reserve System: Purposes and Functions*, 7th ed., Washington, 1984.

BRANCH AND UNIT BANKING

If you have lived or worked in California, New Jersey, Arizona, or New York, you have probably seen the large numbers of bank branches in those states and may have believed that they are typical, and that branch banking exists throughout the country. This is not the case. Branch banks actually are in the minority; *unit* banks, which have no branches, predominate. This results from the consistent upholding of the principle of states' rights by the highest courts in our country.

The National Bank Act of 1863 contained no mention of branch banking. In 1865 the act was amended to permit a state-chartered bank that converted to a national charter to retain its existing branches. National banks had no branching power until 1927, when the McFadden Act was passed.

The McFadden Act permitted national banks to open branches, but *only* to the extent that state-chartered banks could do so under the laws of their respective states. If a state law prohibited or restricted the extent of branching within that state's borders, all banks in the state were forced to comply. The right of each state to regulate branching within its borders repeatedly has been upheld by the courts. According to recent statistics,

Unit banks out number Branch banks

seven states (Illinois, Colorado, Kansas, Missouri, North Dakota, Texas, and Wyoming) are unit banking states, while 18 states have statutes that allow restricted branching—for example, within a single county. In other words, fully half of our 50 states do not allow full-scale branch banking.

The legality of branching aside, many banks choose to operate as unit institutions simply because they find no need to incur the expense of opening and staffing branches. Many unit banks adequately serve the needs of their communities and customers, and regard branching as unnecessary.

The number of actual "brick-and-mortar" branches in the United States probably will decline as public acceptance of EFTS applications grows. Modern and sophisticated electronic terminals accept deposits, supply balance information, handle withdrawals of funds, initiate transfers between accounts, and provide cash advances to customers. The initial cost of installing these terminals is high and the technology to support them is expensive; however, over the long run they offer significant advantages to banks and can be expected to replace many of the existing branches.

Electronic Terminals

The question of whether ATMs and point-of-sale terminals can be legally considered as branches of banks—and therefore subject to federal and state restrictions on branching—is controversial. Most states hold that remote terminals are not branches, but the states have not reached a consensus on this point.

As in many other areas of the financial services industry, commercial banks today see themselves as operating at a serious competitive disadvantage with regard to remote terminals. For example, the Federal Home Loan Bank Board allows the S&Ls under its jurisdiction to establish 24-hour ATMs *anywhere* in the United States. Sears, Roebuck has established its financial centers to provide bank-related services wherever its customers are. The American Express Company's dispensing machines sell traveler's checks in airports and at other locations throughout the country. General Motors Acceptance Corporation and General Electric Credit Corporation offer their credit-related facilities in every one of the 50 states. Commercial banks enjoy no such freedom to operate competitively.

[handwritten margin note: In most states, not considered Branches]

INTERNAL CONTROLS

All of the arguments that justify the need for systems of external controls over banking apply with at least as much force to the need for a thorough, ongoing program of internal controls within each bank. The owner of an automobile may have complied with all state regulations regarding its inspection and may have obtained adequate insurance coverage, but he or she is still responsible for the day-to-day operation of the car. A corporation may have met every federal and state requirement pertaining to its business, but its management must still do all that is necessary to run the firm properly. It is the inescapable and clear duty of bank management to take any and all steps that are necessary to protect the assets of both the bank and its depositors and to see to it that all operating procedures are efficient and safe.

Because the bank's board of directors is its active governing body, the individuals who serve on that board must ensure that a system of efficient internal controls is in place and must take steps to see to it that the system is meticulously followed. Directors are elected by the stockholders, and are responsible for the proper conduct of all the bank's affairs. They can be held personally liable for what they do or what they fail to do. If their actions or their failure to act should result in the bank's liquidation, they may be subject not only to civil suits brought by the shareholders who claim that their interests were not properly protected, but also to criminal prosecution. Directors cannot adopt a passive attitude and wait for federal or state examiners to identify problems for them, nor can they point to the existence of insurance as a protection for the bank.

Generally speaking, it is impossible for directors to physically visit each branch and department of the bank and to observe every phase of its daily operations in order to satisfy themselves that everything is as it should be. The board delegates this responsibility, usually by naming one officer who will have primary responsibility for checking on the effectiveness, adequacy, and daily adherence to every aspect of the internal controls program. For purposes of uniformity and as a functional description of the job, that officer will be identified here as the bank's *auditor*.

Policy at most banks requires that the board directly appoint the auditor, and that he or she report to the board directly, bypassing other levels of management. This policy is designed to ensure the auditor's objectivity and thoroughness in reviewing the operations of the organization.

At smaller banks it may not be possible to justify the appointment of a full-time auditor. In such cases, the position may be filled by an officer who has other responsibilities. Nonetheless, there must be a complete and clear separation of duties. Auditors cannot become involved in banking transactions, such as the originating of debit and credit entries, which they themselves must subsequently review and approve.

A distinction must be made here between auditing in a bank and the federal and state examinations of the same institution. Earlier in this chapter, the point was made that external examinations do not specifically try to locate instances of fraud or embezzlement. Auditing does exactly this. Auditors try to identify and correct a bank's weaknesses and problems *before* federal and/or state examiners visit the bank.

The distinction between the terms *auditing* and *controls* is important. Controls are established first; auditing is the process by which the existence, completeness, and effectiveness of the controls are verified.

For example, a bank establishes a control over one aspect of its operations by requiring everyone who wishes to gain access to a safe deposit box to sign a signature slip. This control is designed to prevent unauthorized persons from gaining entry to boxes. In an audit, the auditors would determine whether this control procedure was being followed on every occasion. Bank policy also may state that all debit and credit tickets must bear two signatures as evidence of dual control. Auditors will determine if the policy has been followed. The examination of a bank by federal or state examiners would not focus on these points; it is the auditor's duty to do so.

Auditing

Auditing embraces a great many duties, including the design and implementation of the bank's internal controls system. The auditor is responsible for determining the accuracy of all the bank's accounting records, specifically those that affect asset, liability, income, and expense accounts. The controls that are in place or are needed play an important part in the process.

Because the auditor must certify that all figures for these categories of accounts have been properly stated and that all entries affecting them are correct, he or she has full authority to examine any and all departments and branches of the bank through which those entries originate. The auditor, reporting directly to the directors, identifies the degree of care and skill with which the program of internal controls is being put into daily practice and suggests changes and new procedures as necessary.

Every commercial bank expects to be examined at regular intervals by representatives of federal and state authorities. However, the most thorough and demanding check on all procedures invariably is the one that the bank's own auditors conduct. This is exactly as it should be. No bank can neglect the task of keeping its own house in order. Systematic and thorough auditing guarantees that all financial information is accurate and that all appropriate internal controls are in place and functioning.

Elements of Successful Auditing

If an audit program is to be successful, it must contain three fundamental elements: _independence, control_, and _surprise_. *time, staff, frequency*

The auditor's <u>independence</u> makes it possible for him or her to examine part or all of the operations of any component of the bank at any time. No one at the management level should have the authority to limit this independence. The auditor alone has the right to decide which areas should be visited and which phases of the operations in those areas should be audited.

Similarly, the auditing staff must have <u>full control</u> over every audit. The entire process would be invalidated if the officer in charge of a branch or department were allowed to tell the auditors which records would be made available to them and which would be kept private, or which aspects of operations in that branch or department could be audited.

The third element, surprise, usually is considered indispensable in any successful auditing program. One of the best-kept secrets in the bank must be the schedule that shows when and to what extent certain units will be audited. There should be no set routine or predictable timetable for this. The most efficient units in any bank are those in which the staff has performed every task and maintained every record as if everyone expected the auditors to arrive on the following day.

Verification

As part of the auditing process, it is often appropriate to send letters to the bank's customers, asking them to confirm the accuracy of the figures shown on the bank's books. Using a system of random sampling, auditors may select certain customers and ask them to verify the balance shown in a checking or savings account, the outstanding amount of a loan, or the securities that the bank is holding as collateral or in a fiduciary role. Verification may be either positive or negative.

least used → *Positive* verification requires that every customer who is contacted during an audit must sign and return a form letter, agreeing or disagreeing with the figures as shown. This is the more expensive and time-consuming of the two methods, since follow-up letters frequently are necessary and the audit cannot be considered complete until each customer has replied.

Negative verification, therefore, is the more widely used method. It calls for a reply from the customer only when there is disagreement with the figures shown. Banks commonly use negative verification with their customers. For example, when a typical checking account statement is sent to a depositor, the depositor is expected to contact the bank only if he or she finds a discrepancy between the bank's stated figures and his or her own. If the customer does not do so, the bank is allowed to assume that its figures are correct.

Verification involving thousands of customers obviously is impractical, but when a percentage of the total customer base is contacted, a useful purpose is served. If a bank employee has somehow been able to destroy or manipulate transaction records or entries, an audit might not disclose the irregularity; verification would do so at once.

SECURITY

Banks naturally are prime targets for every type of embezzlement, fraud, and robbery. In their unceasing effort to improve internal security, banks unfortunately have found that each new procedure and system they introduce has brought about corresponding attempts by criminals to find loopholes in those procedures and to frustrate those systems.

A bank may implement a set of special codes to prevent unautho-rized money transfers; an individual finds a method of penetrating those codes and initiates a fraudulent transfer of funds to a foreign bank. Another bank assigns a staff member to audit its dormant accounts; that person identifies a weakness in the system of controls and embezzles a seven-figure sum by manipulating those accounts. Banks consistently update their vault facilities and alarm systems in an effort to provide maximum security; robbers use new laser technology and electronic equipment to bypass the alarms, gain entry to the vault, and steal the contents of safe deposit boxes as well as the bank's supply of cash. In some cases thieves have carefully studied the daily opening procedures used by banks and have taken advantage of a moment's inattention or negligence to enter the premises and stage robberies. Computer "hackers" throughout the country try to penetrate the banks' data bases to gain confidential information about accounts or to effect bogus transac-tions. Many banks have installed protective plastic shields in front of tellers' windows; robbers then threaten personnel with alleged dynamite or bombs. A bank places cameras in its branches to film transactions; a member of a holdup team simply covers the camera lenses with black paint to frustrate the system. The list is endless.

The cost of insurance protecting banks against holdups and embez-zlement has become prohibitively high. As a result, many banks have dropped this coverage and canceled their policies, thereby assuming the risks and losses themselves.

Officials of the Federal Reserve Board and the Federal Deposit Insur-ance Corporation estimated that the U.S. banking industry lost $1.1 bil-lion in 1986 through fraud and embezzlement and stated that about one-third of the bank failures in recent years had been caused by serious insider abuse, fraud, or other apparent criminal activity. In 1986 the Federal Bureau of Investigation investigated 7,286 cases of bank fraud and embezzlement. Of these, about one-third involved thefts of more than $100,000.[17]

Discouraging though the preceding statistics may be, none of them should be construed to mean that the number of embezzlements and robberies makes security programs useless. These exceptions create headlines and draw attention to the banks; the millions of transactions that each day are handled safely and efficiently are ignored. Security must always be a prime concern of banks, and the controls designed to protect each institution's assets and those of its customers can never be neglected. Bank management personnel always must remember that it is far better to *prevent* a loss than to recover one. The need for vigilance is unending. The principles underlying all systems of internal controls are to (1) reduce temptation, (2) minimize opportunities for theft, and (3) protect innocent people.

It is unfortunately true that one major responsibility of a bank's officers and directors is to address the problem of losses through employee dishonesty. The very nature of banking makes large quantities of money accessible to staff members every day. In an inflationary and materialistic era, economic and social pressures and temptations can prove overpowering to an employee. Just as banks recognize the need for external controls, so should every bank employee accept the systems of internal controls and auditing as a form of protection, rather than as an indication of management's lack of faith in their honesty. The measures that banks take in the area of internal security actually provide employees with both physical and psychological support.

Internal Controls

Many banks appoint individuals to act as security officers, responsible for deriving maximum benefits from the system of internal controls. A bank also may designate a compliance officer to be in charge of filing all the necessary reports to federal and state authorities regarding the bank's conformity to legal requirements. There are various protective procedures that banks have found it prudent to implement. The following examples are by no means all-inclusive; they merely identify some common security procedures.

Every bank should follow a policy of *mandatory vacations* for all employees, specifically including all bank officers. The pressures of business should not be accepted as an excuse for ignoring this requirement. The policy is based on the premise that individuals who refuse to take annual vacations may have something to hide, and are afraid that a replacement might uncover evidence of this during their absence.

The Comptroller of the Currency, and some state banking regulators, have issued guidelines recommending adoption of this policy. When a bank is examined by representatives of either agency, personnel records may be audited to determine if officers have complied with the policy.

The value of *dual control* was mentioned earlier in the context of accounting. Wherever possible, work is divided among two parties, and the individual who originates an entry affecting the bank's books should not be the same individual who posts or approves it.

For banks that have installed automated systems, *data security* becomes one of the most important aspects of the internal controls system. Access to computer facilities must be restricted, and controls must be implemented to prevent unauthorized persons from obtaining information from the data base or initiating entries to it. The bank's records of demand deposit balances, credit card usage and outstandings, and investment holdings are but a few of the primary areas that require constant attention to prevent manipulation.

Rotation of duties among personnel can be another method of effective internal control. A clerk who has become familiar with one aspect of a particular operation may be rotated to another part of the same department. For example, a teller who has been assigned to savings accounts for a period of time may be moved to duties involving the paying and receiving functions on checking accounts. This type of rotation offers advantages besides security; it provides management with flexibility in filling vacancies and contributes to the individual's overall training and mastery of different job skills.

Unannounced cash counts are an integral part of internal controls programs. Supervisory personnel conduct these without any predictable scheduling, so as to ensure the accuracy of tellers' proofs. When an audit is being conducted, the bank's auditors usually make a cash count the first item on their agenda.

Prenumbered forms commonly are used in banking. These provide an operating safeguard because every form—whether used or voided—must be accounted for. The ledgers in which prenumbered forms are recorded can be placed under dual control, and the forms themselves may be designed with an additional copy for auditors' use.

Cameras and alarm systems are required under the terms of the 1968 Bank Protection Act. The act specifies that one individual in each bank must be designated to supervise the installing and testing of devices that discourage robberies and assist in the identification and apprehension of persons who commit such acts. The Bank Protection Act also sets specific requirements for control of coin and currency and for other internal controls.

Efficiency controls grow increasingly important as the growing number of forms, the variety of systems of work flow, and the annual increases in labor costs impact on each bank. It has been claimed that banks lose more money through simple inefficiencies than through any other single cause. Simplifying a form or rearranging the work flow in a department can reduce operating costs and improve accuracy. Systems reviews should be conducted periodically to ensure that the most modern techniques are being used and that management is obtaining all the information it needs on each day's operations. Work measurement and standards of productivity make it possible for management to establish reasonable goals. Many banks publicize their successes in improving a particular operation, reorganizing a department, or reducing costly errors and time-consuming processes. Other banks can learn from these success stories.

Employee suggestions can be an important way to improve efficiency controls. Suggestion awards, which have become commonplace in banks, reflect a recognition that the individuals directly involved in tasks are often the ones who can best identify necessary improvements. This form of participatory management can not only bring direct rewards to those whose suggestions are accepted and the units whose productivity is improved, it also contributes to employee morale as individuals see that their own on-the-job experience helps management achieve the overall goals of the institution.

PERSONNEL IN BANKING

No discussion of internal controls in banking would be worthwhile if it ignored the fact that banking always has been, is now, and always will be a people-based industry. The emphasis on automation and the increased usage of EFTS by customers sometimes leads to unnecessary questions about the "obsolescence" of personnel. Regardless of the extent to which new technology is introduced, banking always will depend on the interpersonal relationships of staff members with the public and with one another.

Banking remains a service industry. In general, service industries have replaced manufacturing industries as the leaders in the United States economy, and will become even more important in the future. A steadily growing population and an expanding economy will demand even more services from banks. No degree of automation will, of itself, meet those demands. So far, automation has not eliminated jobs in banking. Instead, it has created new ones, and has provided many opportunities for employees to change from monotonous, assembly-line work to more challenging and interesting jobs, often requiring new skills.

The term *human resources* often is used to describe the unit of a bank that performs all the functions connected with selecting and hiring, training and developing, evaluating, and retaining employees. Similarly, bank annual reports frequently attribute the success of the organization to its human resources. This new terminology reflects the recognition that employees constitute a resource for the bank.

Banks in the United States still employ more than one million workers. The future of the industry is limited only by the imagination and creativity of those workers and their commitment to professionalism. New services will require the productive efforts of personnel who are trained and ready to help their banks prosper and grow. The challenges are great, but so are the opportunities. The importance of qualified employees can only increase. The future belongs to those who believe in it, can adjust to change, can recognize their own role in it, and can prepare to cope with its problems and take advantage of the potential for personal growth that it offers.

OBJECTIVES OF PERSONNEL MANAGEMENT

Every bank strives to render services and manage its assets in the best interests of its stockholders, depositors, regulatory authorities, and community. At the same time, the bank tries to generate adequate profits. To achieve these objectives, the bank must provide leadership to the diverse individuals it employs. Human resources management embraces all the functions that are involved in that daily process.

Personnel policies form the foundation of this area of management, and it must be recognized at the outset that employees are the instruments of policy and not its object. The long-range objectives of all bank policies will only be produced by and through people.

Effective personnel policies have certain characteristics and are implemented in a certain way. A successful policy

- must be based on the goals of the organization
- must originate with senior levels of management
- must establish ground rules that support the effective operation of the bank
- must be clearly written, definite in content, and widely and effectively communicated to the staff
- must indicate what individuals in the bank will do and why they will act in a certain way

The following are some brief examples of effective policy statements:

- The bank will provide equal employment opportunities to every worker, without regard to race, creed, color, sex, age, or national origin.
- Employees have a right to expect evaluations of their performance by their superiors at least once each year. Salary increases and promotions will *not* be automatic, but will be based entirely on performance as measured against objectives.
- All new employees will serve a probationary period, normally lasting 90 days. This period may be extended if doubt exists as to the individual's capability.
- Certain specific actions, if committed by a member of the bank's staff, will constitute cause for immediate termination.
- Wherever possible, vacancies on the staff will be filled from within.

PROCEDURES AND PROGRAMS

After policies have been approved by senior management (often with the concurrence of the directors), they usually are disseminated in the form of detailed manuals. Manuals must be updated promptly to reflect any changes in policy. Staff meetings may be necessary for officers and supervisors as a means of making employees aware of changes that affect them and ensuring that policies are clearly understood.

Policies are translated into daily procedures and programs. For example, a system of job posting may be implemented to meet a policy regarding filling vacancies from within the bank. A job posting describes the nature and location of the vacant position, the grade level (and possibly salary range), and the qualifications an applicant should have. Employees who are interested are encouraged to apply for the vacant positions.

SELECTION AND HIRING PROCESSES

The standards a bank uses to choose its employees may well be the most important factor in determining its future success. The salary expenses incurred in hiring the right individuals for the right positions are easily justified if the candidates bring to the bank the qualities and skills it needs. No individual can be expected to prove reliable, loyal, and dedicated if he or she has been made to feel underpaid at the time of hiring. In most communities, banks must compete in hiring, and cannot ignore the prevailing wage scales and costs of living.

Many banks recruit management trainees from colleges and universities. Individuals who seem to have potential for future positions of responsibility may be interviewed on the campus and then brought to the bank for further screening. Recruiting programs also may be conducted at local high schools. Many bank employees who are alumni or alumnae of a particular college or school serve as their bank's spokespersons in recruiting at that institution. Banks sometimes use public advertising and the services of employment agencies, and employees can be encouraged to refer friends or acquaintances when openings occur.

The selection and hiring process is fruitless if the bank does not correlate an applicant's experience, education, skills, and interests with the position for which he or she is being considered. Skilled members of the human resources staff try to select the candidate who will best match the needs of the job. Employing overqualified people can be as big an error as hiring underqualified people.

The hiring process must be oriented to future as well as present needs. For example, a need to hire number of clerks and tellers to fill current vacancies is obvious; what may be less obvious is the problem of management succession. How many of the bank's existing officers and supervisors can be expected to leave the bank within a specified time frame? How many lending, trust, international, or other specialized officers must be trained and developed to meet projected staffing needs 2, 5, or 10 years in the future?

As an essential part of the hiring process, it is incumbent on the bank to verify all the information the candidate for employment has supplied. There can be no excuse for failure to check on educational and employment credentials. Did the individual actually attend the schools as claimed? What was his or her academic record? Are the periods listed for prior employment correct? Are there unexplained gaps in the chronology of past employment? What impression did the person make on previous employers?

While commonly requested, personal references are less valuable in hiring. Obviously the candidate will supply only the names of those individuals who are most likely to report favorably.

For certain sensitive areas in the bank, the hiring process may involve administration of a lie detector (polygraph) test. The staff in the human resources unit who decide that such testing is advisable must be thoroughly familiar with local laws on the subject, and must be completely satisfied that the polygraph operators can interpret results correctly.

JOB DESCRIPTIONS AND EVALUATION

No bank employee should be at a loss to know how well or how poorly he or she is doing. Similarly, no employee at any level should be unsure about the tasks his or her job requires, the lines of reporting, and the results that are expected. The first step in ensuring that employees are well informed about their own positions is providing detailed job descriptions.

Job descriptions help employees perform efficiently. They also enable the bank to develop equitable programs of salary compensation and to assist personnel officers in filling vacancies as they occur. Federal, state, and local laws pertaining to affirmative action and equal opportunity demand that each bank's hiring and placement procedures be based on completely objective criteria, such as matching the applicant's qualifications against the requirements as stated in the job description.

Maintaining current job descriptions for every staff position also provides a tool for conducting periodic performance evaluations and for personal interaction with the person who is being reviewed. The employee's accomplishments can be compared with the requirements and objectives of the position. This review process should not be a one-way street. The individual who is evaluated should be given every opportunity to agree or disagree with the review. Many banks require that the staff member initial or sign the evaluation as a permanent record that he or she has seen it and has discussed it with the reviewer. The signature does not necessarily indicate that the employee agrees with the contents; it simply attests to the fact that the evaluation did take place and that the employee was made aware of it.

SALARY ADMINISTRATION

For many years, banking had a reputation for paying its employees relatively poorly. Only if banks pay competitive salaries for comparable work and responsibility can they overcome this stigma. One test of the effectiveness of a bank's salary administration program is the frequency with which its staff members resign to accept better-paying positions elsewhere.

It is an unavoidable cliché to state that salary administration programs in banking must reward those who are productive and penalize those who do not meet standards; yet experience indicates that banks have not always translated this truth into practice. If an employee has displayed outstanding performance and an unusually large salary increase seems warranted, the bank should have no reluctance to grant it. Conversely, no bank can afford the luxury of a program that automatically grants increases simply because an individual has completed another year of service. Each increase should reflect the results the employee has achieved and the contributions he or she has made to productivity and profitability.

Enlightened human resources management today reviews the demands of each department and branch and measures the tasks performed in it. If areas in the bank appear to be overstaffed, it is likely that the bank is paying for employees' poor productivity.

Compensation for bank employees is not confined to actual salary and wage payments; it also includes the fringe benefits that are common throughout industry today. Medical and surgical insurance, non-contributory pension plans, deferred compensation plans based on profit-sharing, and other indirect expenses for the bank must be considered as parts of an overall package that the candidate for employment will match against those offered elsewhere.

CAREER PATHS

In bygone years, progressing through a career in banking was usually slow, and often painful. Individuals accepted the fact that they would remain in the same job for long periods of time and would be promoted only when a senior employee retired or died. In today's work environment, employees have other avenues in which to pursue financial careers; if they do not perceive opportunities in the banks, they can go elsewhere. Individuals not only want to know how well they are doing in their current positions; they are also anxious to learn whether they will be considered for advancement and, if so, how long the waiting period will be.

Many banks now include a specific mention of career paths as part of their employees' periodic evaluations. For what positions, and in what areas of the bank, can this person be considered? Assuming continuing qualifying performance, within what time frame is promotion possible or likely? Are the employees—and the bank's—interests best served by keeping the individual in one area, or by transferring him or her to another area?

A basic function of human resources administration is to bring the objectives of the bank into harmony with those of the individual. It is a sound management concept, *and* one that is helpful to the employee, for banks to identify and notify workers who have the potential for promotion. As part of the regular performance review, a frank discussion that spells out management's projected career path for the employee is a valuable part of the overall process.

Again, the benefits extend in both directions. Employees must be told what they are expected to do in order to become promotable. It is not simply a matter of having managers indicate what plans the bank has for staff members; the opportunity to move ahead carries with it an obligation for the employee to demonstrate efforts toward self-improvement.

TRAINING AND DEVELOPMENT

Mere increases in staff size, while often a necessary part of a bank's growth and its expansion of services, cannot meet and satisfy all the institution's future needs. Banking steadily becomes more and more complex, and skills that were never required in the past are now essential. Changes in the basic deposit structure, the new emphasis on liability management, the increasing importance of electronic funds transfer systems, and all the other innovations that have been mentioned in this text support this view. In the human resources area itself, a far more enlightened approach exists today; the autocratic methods of the past, which led banks to be criticized for their lack of a people-oriented attitude, are disappearing.

Many banks have instituted systems that use employee-profile forms. These are detailed documents, often generated and updated through the computer, that give a complete picture of an individual's educational background, job experience, special aptitudes, hobbies and interests, and performance evaluations to date. Through these profiles, management can determine what training and development programs might help the individual progress to the desired level. The profiles also indicate any areas of deficiency that must be remedied to make the employee more productive and better prepared to meet the bank's future needs.

The word *needs* applies to the individual worker as well as to the bank. Human resources management can identify programs that can meet those needs. For example, performance reviews can indicate a specific problem area that can be resolved through training. Perhaps a manager's own performance displays a lack of sensitivity to his or her subordinates' attitudes and aspirations. Perhaps an individual is unaware of the cross-selling opportunities inherent in his or her current position, or is not entirely comfortable in a marketing role. Perhaps the employee can be taught new techniques directly related to the job. Most basic of all, it may be that the individual simply does not feel part of the overall institution and cannot relate to its objectives.

Banks today offer many internal training programs designed to enhance employees' skills, prepare them for additional future responsibilities, and give them the knowledge they need in a rapidly changing industry. Teller training, credit training, marketing training, and communications training are but a few of these. The number and content of the programs must be revised regularly to meet new organizational and individual needs.

The difference between training and development should be highlighted here. Training is intended to increase a person's knowledge and skills. It may help him or her to make better decisions, but it will seldom result in his or her wanting to do so. On the other hand, development describes personal growth and motivation. Development may be said to come from within, since the individual has been conditioned to want to change.

For example, a bank's program designed to provide the nucleus of its future officer cadre will include both credit *training*, which teaches the person the necessary judgmental skills and shows the steps in evaluating a loan request, and management *development*, which gives the candidate the necessary encouragement to assume responsibility and make full use of his or her talents.

Consider the following cross-section of personnel in a typical bank. The tellers require training not only in the functional skills of the job, but in the provisions of the Bank Secrecy Act that affect them and in the new regulations regarding check holds. Individuals responsible for opening new accounts not only must be familiar with documentation and procedures; they must also be trained in the sections of Regulation E that pertain to disclosures, authorizations, and liabilities. All personnel involved in any form of lending need extensive training so that they become aware of all the ramifications of Regulation B (Fair Credit Reporting), Regulation U (Stock Market Credit), Regulation Z (Truth in Lending), and the Community Reinvestment Act.

External programs for the training and development of bank personnel are at least as numerous and comprehensive as those that banks provide internally. At the forefront of these must be listed the curricula of the American Institute of Banking. No industry-sponsored adult-educational institution can equal AIB in the breadth of job-oriented courses it offers each year through hundreds of chapters in every part of the country. There are also many graduate and undergraduate schools of banking that offer both basic and advanced banking-related education. Few other industries offer employees so many opportunities for improving their job-related knowledge. Tuition refund plans at many banks enable employees to be reimbursed for their educational expenses. After-hours education is widely supported and encouraged by banks because it provides a means of supplementing internal programs, thereby helping to prepare workers for the new opportunities that are part of the industry today.

SUMMARY

The banking industry in the United States has evolved from colonial times, when little meaningful supervision was exercised over the chartering and operating of banks, to the present day, when every bank is subject to a host of federal and state laws that affect virtually every aspect of its daily functions. External controls over a bank are imposed even before it can open its doors. These controls continue throughout the bank's existence, and apply until the last depositor has been repaid and the final claim disposed of. Many bankers, and some regulatory authorities, feel that these restrictions are excessive, particularly since nonbank competitors are not governed by them. Many of the restrictions, however, result from the perception that uncontrolled banking is detrimental to the economy and society.

Every bank today is subject to chartering requirements and periodic examinations by federal and state regulatory authorities. These are intended to ensure that the institution is operating in a legal and prudent manner.

Most major banks today are part of bank holding companies, which were formed in order to permit subsidiaries and affiliates to engage in businesses that the banks themselves were barred from. All operations of bank holding companies are directly supervised by the Federal Reserve.

The same reasons that have been used to justify a system of external controls over banking also explain the need for thorough programs of internal controls. These programs typically are the responsibility of an auditor who is named by and reports to the bank's board of directors. Internal controls implement various safeguards to protect the assets of the bank and those of its customers.

Security is an issue that applies to many aspects of banking today. Physical security involves making the premises as safe as possible, for the protection of depositors and employees. Security must also extend to all the documents and records that are a vital part of banking. Effective management of human resources contributes to overall security by ensuring that competent and trustworthy individuals are hired, retained, and rewarded.

External and internal controls, reflecting the efforts of regulatory agencies and each bank's board of directors, combine to make the institution as secure and efficient as possible.

QUESTIONS FOR DISCUSSION

1. List three factors justifying the regulation and examination of banks by government authorities.

2. What four tests are applied to requests for new bank charters?

3. Which government agency would have primary responsibility for examining a national bank? Which other agencies might also examine it?

4. Identify the four questions that every bank examination should answer.

5. What is a bank holding company? How does the Douglas Amendment affect bank holding companies?

6. Why are there more unit banks than branch banks in the United States?

7. Who appoints a bank's chief auditor? To whom should the auditor report?

8. List the three essential elements in an audit program.

9. What two types of verification are used in auditing? Explain the difference between the two.

10. List four operating safeguards or procedures that might be part of an overall program of internal controls.

11. What three characteristics should effective personnel policies have?

12. What purposes do job descriptions serve?

NOTES

1. Board of Governors of the Federal Reserve System, *73rd Annual Report 1986*, p. 247.

2. Robert M. Garsson, "'86 in Washington: Banking Industry Has Had Better Years in the Capital," *American Banker*, February 4, 1987, p. 1.

3. "We Must Redefine What Banking Is," *ABA Banking Journal* (November 1986), p. 18.

4. Martha R. Seger, "Maintaining a Safe, Competitive Banking System," *American Banker*, December 18, 1986, p. 4.

5. Robert M. Garsson and Jay Rosenstein, "Give Banks New Powers, Volcker Asks Congress," *American Banker*, January 22, 1987, p. 1.

6. Jeffrey Kutler, "Corrigan Offers New Script for Banking," *American Banker*, February 2, 1987, p. 17.

7. Alan Greenspan, "The Case for Deregulation of the Banking Industry," *American Banker*, June 4, 1987, p. 15.

8. "Bank Secrecy Act," *Bankers Weekly*, May 19, 1987, pp. 5–8.

9. Henry Ruempler and Marjorie Penrod, "Tax Traps for the Unwary," *ABA Banking Journal* (June 1987), p. 32.

10. "Bankers Fume Over Florida's New Sales Tax," *American Banker*, July 8, 1987, p. 3.

11. Robert D. Hershey, Jr., "Fed Plans to Bolster Bank Examinations," *The New York Times*, October 8, 1985, p. D1.

12. Michael Reese and Eric Gelman, "California Dreamin'," *Newsweek* (August 4, 1986), p. 36.

13. Board of Governors of the Federal Reserve System, *The Federal Reserve System: Purposes and Functions*, 7th ed. (Washington, D.C., 1984), p. 95.

14. Martin H. Wolfson, "Financial Developments of Bank Holding Companies in 1984," *Federal Reserve Bulletin* (December 1985), p. 924, and Federal Reserve System, *73d Annual Report 1986*, p. 188.

15. Federal Reserve System, *73d Annual Report 1986*, p. 188.

16. Richard M. Whiting, "New Nonbanking Activities: A Look Back and Ahead," *American Banker*, January 8, 1986, p. 54.

17. "Banks Bilked of $1.1 Billion," *The New York Times*, June 9, 1987, p. D1.

For More Information

Golembe, Carter H. and David S. Holland. *Federal Regulation of Banking, 1986–87*. Washington, D.C.: Golembe Associates, Inc., 1986.

Haimann, Theo and Raymond L. Hilgert. *Supervision: Concepts and Practices of Management*. 4th ed. Cincinnati, Ohio: South-Western Publishing Company, 1987. (Available through the American Bankers Association or your local AIB chapter.)

Johnson, Frank P. and Richard D. Johnson. *Commercial Bank Management*. New York: Dryden Press, 1986. (Available through the American Bankers Association or your local AIB chapter.)

Summers, Donald B. *Personnel Management in Banking*. New York: McGraw-Hill Book Company, 1981.

14.

BANK
MARKETING

LEARNING OBJECTIVES

After completing this chapter, you will be able to
•
describe the importance of marketing in today's banking
•
list the key elements in bank marketing programs
•
understand the new emphasis on product management
•
recognize changes in customers' attitudes and needs
•
explain ways in which all staff members can participate in marketing
•
describe the value of cross-selling

Throughout most of their history, the nation's larger commercial banks, especially those in the money market centers, were the exclusive suppliers of many financial services. However, they offered those services only to a restricted market. The banks' focus was on their corporate, institutional, government agency, and correspondent customers. The wants and needs of "retail" customers—consumers—often were neglected.

For the most part, these banks were operating in a seller's market. They could afford to wait for customers to come seeking their services. The banker was primarily an asset manager whose task was to make selective loans and investments, using the demand deposits that steadily flowed in from the aforementioned customers. Marketing tended to be passive, not active.

Another factor has influenced this traditional passivity. The word "salesman" has had unpleasant connotations to many bankers, who believed that it applied chiefly to door-to-door peddlers and used-car vendors. Many bankers see themselves as occupying prestigious roles in their communities; the idea of aggressive selling has had little if any appeal for them.

In the years since World War II, this scenario has necessarily changed. To their dismay, commercial banks have learned that no vacuum exists for long in the financial marketplace. When one type of institution, either because of restrictive regulations or simply because of its own policies, cannot or does not act to meet the wants and needs of the market, another quickly steps in to do so. For example, thrift institutions enjoyed spectacular growth in the years immediately following World War II, chiefly by meeting the consumer demand for home mortgage loans. Credit unions likewise grew far faster than many banks by providing loans at lower cost and offering accounts with higher yields. Major auto finance companies succeeded by satisfying a consumer need—one in which many banks had little or no interest. Money market funds also enjoyed spectacular success because they responded to an unmet consumer need for attractive investment vehicles.

Sears, Merrill Lynch, General Electric Credit, American Express, General Motors Acceptance Corporation, and Ford Motor Company— and many other providers of financial services—continue to diversify, expand, and further diminish the banks' share of the marketplace. Most of these intermediaries, largely unregulated and therefore at a significant advantage in their operations throughout the country, have a long history of successful selling in retail markets. They have a great deal of expertise in marketing to consumers, an area in which most banks historically have done very little.

Nevertheless, despite the efforts of their many competitors, commercial banks have continued to grow and be profitable. As a group, their bottom-line net income for the year 1986 was $17.4 billion.[1] A new recognition of the scope, value, and importance of marketing has played an important role in the banks' continued profitability.

PLANNING AND CORPORATE CULTURE

The planning process begins with establishing goals to be reached within a certain time frame. The goals should be ambitious but attainable. Setting unrealistic goals that are beyond the reach of the staff creates nothing but frustration. On the other hand, setting goals that can be met with only minimal effort serves no real purpose. A "business as usual" approach may mean stagnation in today's marketplace. A challenging but realistic goal provides the best solution.

To survive and achieve their goals in a highly competitive environment, banks must adopt new ideas and new approaches. Passive marketing no longer is acceptable. Customers may not come to banks with requests for new or better services. Demand deposits no longer flow automatically into the banking system as they traditionally did. Competitors are capitalizing on their advantages and marketing aggressively every day. The banks, adapting to and managing change in the financial services marketplace, must adopt a new and radically different corporate culture: an attitude that permeates the entire institution and focuses on the marketing function. They must be *active*, rather than *reactive*.

THE MARKETING FUNCTION

The term *marketing* often is misunderstood. It does not refer only to selling, nor does it describe a single activity performed by a handful of bank staff members. Rather, marketing involves a full set of diverse activities that can be integrated to achieve certain goals. The entire staff of the bank can take part in these activities. A total marketing program includes

- conducting research to identify the wants and needs of the types of customers that the bank wishes to attract and retain
- selecting the most appropriate and cost-effective methods of advertising
- developing, managing, and enhancing the various products and services that will appeal to the bank's targeted markets
- training staff members in the effective sales techniques and involving the entire staff in the selling effort

- establishing officer call and staff incentive programs
- monitoring the increased business and profits that result from specific marketing efforts and revising the latter as necessary
- anticipating changes that will allow the bank to expand geographically, to increase the range of services it can offer, or both

Not every one of the nation's 14,000 commercial banks absolutely requires a full-scale, integrated marketing program. Nevertheless, many bankers today realize that some kind of consistent and effective marketing is necessary. Banks *must* devise and introduce ways of making the public aware of the products and services they can provide. The alternative is entirely unacceptable; to perpetuate the passive approach of the past simply allows competitors to seize additional opportunities to market their own services and thus attract an even large share of the available business.

MARKET RESEARCH

No bank has ever encountered problems because it compiled and interpreted too much information about its customers, marketing prospects, and competitors. Problems generally result—as they do in the exercise of the credit function—from a lack of knowledge. *Market research* is designed to remedy that lack.

Market research describes the systematic collection and analysis of all appropriate data needed to project sales volume, identify customer and merchant attitudes, and discuss the problems involved in bringing new products or services to the attention of the targeted audience.

Before market research can be conducted, senior management must identify the categories of customers it wishes to attract and keep. If the bank is following an "all things to all people" approach, it will seek to offer the widest possible range of services to every segment of the marketplace, wherever it is legally allowed to do so. Far more common, however, is a process called market segmentation, in which the bank targets specific customer groups for its marketing efforts. In connection with specific groups, market research can provide a wealth of useful information.

Assume, for example, that AIB Bank in Center City is considering submitting a request for approval from federal or state regulators to offer certain trust services. Preliminary market research indicates that affluent individuals represent the most desirable market segment for these services. The bank then seeks to determine how many affluent individuals live in the immediate area. It tries to identify the specific services that will have the greatest appeal to this group, and estimates the cost of providing these services and the benefits that will result. The bank must investigate what services its local competitors are offering, what their pricing structure is, and how well they are succeeding. AIB Bank also may use market research to learn what its existing customers perceive as the bank's strengths and weaknesses.

ADVERTISING

Banks today place a tremendous emphasis on all forms of advertising. In view of that, it may be surprising to learn that in 1950 the nation's commercial banks spent less than $2 million on advertising. By 1972, as banks' marketing efforts became more aggressive, they were spending 10 times that amount; now, they commit huge sums of money to television, radio, newspapers, magazines, trade publications, billboards, and other methods of getting their messages across. Banks also use special promotions to introduce new services or to announce acquisitions or the opening of new branches.

Each type of advertising must be carefully analyzed to measure its costs against its projected benefits. A television commercial during a prime-time news program may be extremely costly, but it will reach a far wider audience than a less-expensive radio message. The greater cost of a strategically placed billboard on a busy highway may be justified when compared with a less-expensive type of advertising that will be seen by fewer individuals. Market research in a community will disclose which categories of individuals read which newspapers; the bank can place its advertisements accordingly.

Direct Mail

A 1987 study by a Chicago-based research firm indicated that 20 percent to 30 percent of the total marketing budgets at many banks are traceable to various types of direct-response programs. At some institutions direct-response advertising accounts for 50 percent of overall marketing costs. Although telephone solicitation is part of an overall direct-response program, by far the bulk of the effort is in mailings. Direct mail may be used to address existing customers; for example, promotional material may be mailed out along with bank statements. It also may be used to saturate a selected market within the community, or to conduct promotions on a nationwide scale. For example, many banks have used nationwide mailings to expand their lists of bank card candidates. In 1986 First National Bank of Chicago distributed 83 separate offers through the mail: 23 for deposit, asset, and investment plans and 60 for bank cards. These mailings gave the bank over 90 million "exposures" to the public.[2]

Direct mail often targets a specific population group. The largest single segment of the U.S. population currently comprises people between the ages of 25 and 40 years. These people are very much aware of yield opportunities, greatly concerned about convenience and leisure time, easily motivated to move funds from one institution to another, and willing to accept innovations. Marketing programs that recognize and capitalize on the financial sophistication of these individuals can bring excellent results.[3]

PRODUCT MANAGEMENT AND DEVELOPMENT

During the 1960s some of America's largest manufacturing and sales corporations introduced a new idea. For each product, they appointed one individual to assume responsibility for everything connected with that product. This concept has since been adopted in banking. *Product managers* at many banks have become important members of the marketing staff, even when they are not technically employees of the marketing unit.

The product manager at a major bank today handles many diverse and important functions. Typically, these include the following:

- Product design: What features should the product have?
- Product development: What resources of the bank are needed to introduce and deliver a new product or enhance an existing one?
- Product enhancement: What improvements might be made in order to induce more customers or prospects to buy a product?
- Product pricing and profitability: How can the product be priced to recover costs, generate profits, and sell against competition?
- Developing product plans: What are the goals for sales of the product during the year, and what marketing strategies will help achieve those goals?
- Operations coordination: How can the bank ensure quality of performance and timeliness of delivery?

Product managers can apply market research to nearly all these functions. Market research helps reveal what customers want, like, or dislike about products; and assessments of past marketing strategies can help the manager develop the most cost-effective promotions for each product.

The product manager usually is responsible for preparing detailed profitability studies to show all the costs associated with the product and the revenues resulting from it. He or she also may become directly involved in operations and systems planning involving the product, for example, redesigning the work flow in a department or applying new technology.

In summary, a product manager must become completely familiar with every aspect of the lock box, letter of credit, coin and currency operation, money market account, or other bank product to which he or she is assigned. The product manager then coordinates the work of the various bank departments in order to make a maximum contribution to the effectiveness of the marketing program.[4]

MARKETING TRAINING

As mentioned earlier, in the minds of many bankers from past generations a "salesman" was an individual who used hard-sell, high-pressure tactics and who had little or no real concern for the well-being of the customer. These bankers felt that selling, by its very nature, was demeaning. They also believed that it was unnecessary. Their viewpoint naturally prevented them from learning, using, or disseminating effective marketing techniques.

In today's marketplace effective, aggressive marketing is absolutely necessary. Marketing training, in addition to its other values, corrects long-held misunderstandings about the nature of selling. Marketing training shows that a salesperson in banking is *not* an unscrupulous confidence artist, perpetrating a flim-flam on a gullible public. Rather, it shows that salespeople fill a creative and beneficial role by satisfying client needs. There is nothing demeaning about selling, and the bank that fails to train its staff members in effective sales principles may not survive in a highly competitive environment.

Banks can learn from the successes of the major U.S. corporations who have sold their products for many years. The old-time banker may have felt that there was no possible connection between selling gasoline, toothpaste, computers, or detergents and selling bank services; today the opposite is true. Bankers now realize that what has worked well in other industries can apply as well to banking—and that individuals *can* be taught to sell effectively.

Individuals generally *do not* buy products as such. Rather, we buy a product because we perceive some benefit in owning it. Effective advertising and selling convinces the buyer that he or she will gain the most benefits from buying a particular product. The most successful salespersons in any industry are those who understand their own motivations as consumers. These salespersons recognize the techniques that have motivated them to buy and transfer those techniques to selling situations of their own. By establishing rapport with prospective buyers and consulting with them to identify specific wants, needs, and attitudes, salespersons gather information and shape their responses accordingly. They appreciate the reasons for customer concerns and objections and answer these in such a way that the customers convince themselves of the product's benefits.

Some major banks have recruited experienced sales and marketing personnel from various industries and from marketing and advertising firms. These individuals conduct in-house training sessions, communicating their expertise to bank staff members. Other banks have retained firms that specialize in marketing training to conduct seminars. The American Bankers Association provides materials on marketing, and the courses and facilities of the American Institute of Banking can be made part of a bank's overall marketing training effort.

Bank customers tend to characterize banks in terms of their personnel rather than their brick and mortar facilities. Staff members are the key focal points in bank-customer relationships. In most cases, staff constitutes the basic reason why a particular bank is favored or is poorly regarded. A 1987 study of executives in 2,800 companies each having annual sales of $50 million to $250 million confirmed this marketing tenet.[5]

Marketing training communicates product knowledge to the audience, provides orientation on the bank's history, strengths, track record of growth, and plans for the future. It also outlines the range of services available. This process helps staff members understand that their marketing efforts must concentrate on the customer rather than on the product, helping the customer to perceive the benefits of buying the product.

Most importantly, marketing training helps staff members make more effective sales calls. Five general rules governing sales calls are listed as follows:

- No customer or prospect call should ever be made without planning, using background information from the bank's files and identifying a specific reason and purpose for the call.
- Through effective questioning, the caller should lead the customer or prospect to identify a present situation and the problems that go with it—problems that the bank's products or services can help resolve.
- The sales call should never reflect an overcommitment of the bank's resources or overstate of the benefits of a product.
- Customer objections must be handled professionally.
- Whenever a product or service is sold, the banker always should follow up with the customer after the fact to ensure satisfaction.

The customer's time, like that of the bank representative, is valuable. Preparing for the call actually *saves* time, because an informed bank representative can better anticipate and direct the conversation to a particular product or service. Often, a prospect will want to make some modification or improvement to an existing bank relationship—for example, obtaining information on account balances and transactions more quickly or decreasing processing time. The bank representative can then discuss specific products or services designed to help the customer achieve his or her goal.

The caller should never promise something that the bank cannot fulfill. It is important that the bank representative know the limits as well as the advantages of the bank's products and services. Moreover, he or she should respond to customer concerns with a cooperative, realistic approach. If the customer objects to the call—or to some aspect of the program or service being discussed—the bank representative cannot display resentment toward the objections, or treat them lightly.

After selling a product or service to a customer, it is both polite and good business to follow up with a call to be sure the customer is satisfied. An attitude of caring and of seeking to ensure that the bank is delivering the product as promised enhances the image of the bank. If a problem has arisen, the call can help restore the customer's confidence; alternatively, if the customer is satisfied, a follow-up call may lead to the sale of additional products or services.

QUALITY SERVICE AND CONTROL

The marketing director of a large midwestern bank has identified a problem that many bankers face today. His efforts are directed primarily toward improving the quality of the bank's performance in all areas of customer service. Banks face external pressures to improve services in order to remain competitive. Meanwhile, from within the bank, they face pressures to reduce expenses and increase income. To accommodate both needs, quality is critical.[6]

Banks that have emphasized quality performance have found an almost infinite number of service areas to address. How long do customers have to wait on teller lines? How promptly are complaints resolved? What is the error frequency in such departments as bookkeeping, lock box, and letter of credit? Are telephone inquiries referred at once to the proper person or unit? Are documents and correspondents proofread carefully before they are sent out? Do the bank's personnel create an image of commitment to quality?

In a 1987 survey conducted for the *American Banker*, quality of service ranked first as the factor that pleased customers the most about their financial institutions (table 14.1).[7] According to the same survey, quality of service was also the factor that the largest group of respondents *disliked* about their principal financial institutions (table 14.2).

The Customer Service Institute (in Silver Spring, MD) has drafted a "Customer's Bill of Rights" stressing the need for banks to provide courteous and considerate treatment, market their services and products truthfully and honestly, answer complaints and inquiries in a timely manner, and create a service-oriented culture within their organizations.[8]

Emphasizing service can be done in creative ways. One major bank developed a poster that conveys a message about caring for customers by alerting them to various ways in which they can protect themselves against losses and frauds (exhibit 14.1).

Every bank has a cadre of individuals—calling officers, relationship managers, account officers—whose major responsibility is the development of new business. However, no institution should perceive its total marketing effort as being the responsibility of those staff members alone. Rather, every bank employee should become involved in marketing. For example, each employee may have numerous relatives and friends who represent candidates for bank services. The employee can be an ambas-

TABLE 14.1
SOURCES OF CONSUMER SATISFACTION

Factor	Respondents Listing This Factor[a] (percent)
Service	42
Convenience	25
Product range	17
Interest rates	9

Source: Laura Gross, "Fourth Annual Consumer Survey: How Americans View the Financial Services Industry," *American Banker*, October 1987, p. 30.
a. Total number of respondents = 1,053.

TABLE 14.2
SOURCES OF CONSUMER DISSATISFACTION

Factor	Respondents Listing This Factor[a] (percent)
Service	13
Convenience	12
Interest rates	10
Fees	6

Source: Laura Gross, "Fourth Annual Consumer Survey," p. 30.
a. Total number of respondents = 1,053.

sador for his or her institution by conveying the impression that it offers cost-effective and quality service, and that it is interested in meeting consumers' wants and needs and providing benefits to those who use its services.

As in other industries, various forms of incentives can be offered to motivate staff members to sell certain services. Incentives may take the form of direct cash awards, merchandise prizes, additional vacation days, or, in the case of special promotions and contests, trips to popular resorts. Periodic meetings can be held in the bank to bestow awards on those who have displayed enthusiasm and skill in selling.[9]

In the performance evaluation process, recognition should be given to an employee who has introduced new business when doing so is not a normal part of his or her daily work. Internal newsletters and magazines also can give recognition to industrious employees.

Some banks offer direct commissions to their business development officers, thereby making these individuals the peers of salespersons in

315

EXHIBIT 14.1
BANK POSTER

HELP US PROTECT OUR MOST VALUABLE ASSET-YOU!

DO's & DON'Ts

Do count your cash at the teller window, put it away, and make sure your wallet and pocketbook are secure.

Do destroy all unused deposit/withdrawal tickets.

Do keep your money "under wraps" until you get to the teller.

Do be cautious of the revolving door team scheme, where the person ahead of you suddenly stops the door while an accomplice, who is behind you, has the opportunity to grab your belongings.

Do use the automatic teller machines and quick drop deposit box during busy hours and remember to put your receipts away.

Don't leave your money and belongings on the counter while preparing for the teller.

● **Don't** leave any personal account information behind.

● **Don't** fall for the "Look, you dropped your money on the floor" scheme where one person diverts your attention by throwing $ on the floor and asks if it's yours, while an accomplice takes off with your deposit.

● **Don't** make it easy for someone to steal your personal property.

● **Don't** be fooled by imposters dressed in business suits or guard uniforms who offer to take your cash deposit to the teller.

other industries. The yearly commissions may be based on the dollar amount of new balances introduced, the dollar value of sales of specific products, or on other measurable criteria.

Cross-selling is an integral part of bank marketing. For example, customers frequently receive some form of advertising insert with their monthly bank statements. More valuable, however, are the efforts that staff members make to cross-sell. One recognized principle of banking states that a customer who uses many services at a particular bank is far less likely to transfer to another institution. Many bank employees are in an excellent position to sell added services every day. The consumer loan representative can recommend the opening of a checking account, mentioning that the borrower will receive a lower interest rate if the payments are automatically deducted. A customer who has arranged for the purchase of securities is a logical candidate for a safe deposit box; a safe deposit attendant, in turn, can mention the availability of the bank's traveler's checks to individuals who are known to be planning trips. The bank representative who successfully sells one cash management service can use it as the introduction to another; for example, a company that has adopted lock box service is an excellent prospect for a terminal-based information service that will provide timely details on each deposit.

The daily possibilities for cross-selling are limited only by the creativity and enthusiasm of the employee. Each bank's group of satisfied customers provides it with the best opportunities for additional marketing.

Preparing for the Future

The present condition of dramatic and ongoing change in U.S. banking makes it imperative for bankers to prepare now for the future. If it appears that regulatory changes will enable an institution to offer additional services, all the units that will be involved should have everything ready so that the services can be introduced to the public as soon it is legally permissible. If the long-standing barriers to interstate mergers, acquisitions, and branching continue to disappear, management should be in a position to act quickly to capitalize on each new opportunity. Strategies to develop new business in new geographic areas should be part of a bank's forward planning.

The impetus to prepare for the future may come from one of several factors, or from a combination of them. For example, management may react to aggressive competition in its community by developing an innovative product. A change in senior management at a traditionally conservative bank may trigger a new attitude toward anticipating and managing change. Technological improvements that enable the bank to lead in its market area by providing new or enhanced services also may be part of this process. Whatever the conditions that lead up to it, planning and preparing for the future are essential components of today's banking. The bank that ignores them will find itself at a severe disadvantage in the financial marketplace, for its many competitors are not standing still.

SUMMARY

One of the most significant changes in commercial banking in the years since World War II has been a cultural change involving the approach to marketing. Much of the exclusivity that banks once possessed in providing financial services has disappeared. Competition has increased both numerically and in intensity. The banks' future growth and profitability, and in many cases their actual survival, will depend on their ability to adjust to the knowledge that attitudes that were appropriate in their industry 5, 10, or 20 years ago may be completely inappropriate today. For example, selling—an activity that many past generations of bankers refused to consider—has become a necessity. The senior vice president of a large bank in Baltimore has summarized the problem, saying that "banks, by and large, are not sales-oriented, not promotion-oriented, and not team-oriented. And today you have to be all those things in order to survive."[10]

As a group, today's bank customers are far different from those of earlier generations. Banks must adapt to this. Today's customers have many new options in obtaining financial services from other sources, and they generally display no hesitation in moving funds from one intermediary to another whenever it is to their advantage. If one type of financial institution does not meet their wants and needs and provide them with what they perceive as maximum benefits, they have no difficulty in finding another that will do so. Competition is aggressive and continuous, and much of it comes from financial intermediaries that enjoy significant inherent advantages.[11]

In reaction to this change in customer sophistication, and in response to the changing needs of their markets, many major banks have embarked on full-scale marketing programs. Banks of smaller size, while not needing such substantial programs, have abandoned their traditional opposition to marketing and have adopted techniques that are appropriate in their own communities.

Senior management first establishes the broad areas of the marketplace that the bank wishes to target. That is, it identifies the types of customers the bank hopes to attract and keep. Market research then contributes information on the wants, needs, and attitudes of customers and prospects so that the bank may begin product development and enhancement. Advertising programs are drawn up on a cost-effective basis to publicize new services or conveniences for customers. In-house seminars can be held to train staff members in product knowledge and effective selling, and these can be supplemented by using outside training specialists and the facilities of both the American Bankers Association and AIB.

Training sessions should help staff members understand what a service or product actually does, which customers and prospects are most likely to use it, the benefits that users can gain, and the sales techniques that will be most effective. Development of additional business is not the sole responsibility of designated calling officers; it can be part of the daily work of the entire staff. There is no reason why every employee cannot be motivated and encouraged to take advantage of daily opportunities for cross-selling to existing bank customers or making relatives and acquaintances aware of the institution's range of services.

For bank personnel who are directly involved in calling on customers and prospects, the bank should provide special training—possibly including role-playing, case studies, or other techniques.

QUESTIONS FOR DISCUSSION

1. Identify four elements that might be part of a bank's complete marketing program.

2. What information might market research develop about a community that would be valuable in planning?

3. What advantages does television advertising offer to a bank? What are its disadvantages?

4. List four functions that might be part of product management at a major bank.

5. What techniques or elements might be introduced into a sales call on a customer or prospect to make the call more effective?

6. From your knowledge of your own institution, what measures are taken to provide quality service?

7. Why is cross-selling an important part of many bank marketing programs today?

NOTES

1. Alex Sheshunoff, "Which Way the Bottom Line?" *ABA Banking Journal* (August 1987), p. 33.

2. Laura Gross, "Direct Marketing Gets Serious," *American Banker*, March 3, 1987, p. 1.

3. *Ibid*.

4. Robert P. Ford, "The Changing Role of Product Management," *The Bankers Magazine* (November-December 1985), p. 5.

5. "Middle Market Banking Needs," *ABA Banking Journal* (August 1987), p. 84.

6. Laura Gross and Jay Rosenstein, "Quality Service Standards Get New Attention," *American Banker*, October 5, 1987, p. 9.

7. Laura Gross, in "Fourth Annual Consumer Survey: How Americans View the Financial Services Industry," *American Banker*, October 1987, p. 30.

8. "'Customer's Bill of Rights' Sets Rules for Courtesy and Accuracy," *American Banker*, August 25, 1987, p. 16.

9. "A Banker's Advice: Try Incentive Pay," *ABA Banking Journal* (February 1985), p. 20.

10. In Dr. Thomas W. Thompson, "It's a Selling Business," *United States Banker* (December 1983), p. 6.

11. Barry Deutsch, "Banking's Striking Changes Are the Missing Ones," *American Banker*, August 12, 1987, p. 4.

For More Information

Berry, Leonard L., Charles M. Futrell, and Michael R. Bowers. *Bankers Who Sell*. Homewood, Ill.: Dow Jones-Irwin, 1985.

Pezzulo, Mary Ann. *Marketing for Bankers*. Washington, D.C.: American Bankers Association, 1988.

Richardson, Linda. *Bankers in the Selling Role*. 2d ed. New York: John Wiley & Sons, Inc., 1984.

15.

CONTEMPORARY
ISSUES

LEARNING OBJECTIVES

After completing this chapter, you will be able to
●
list the major changes that have taken place
in the financial services industry in recent years
●
define functional and geographic deregulation
●
list some of the reasons why bankers have requested deregulation
●
present arguments for and against such deregulation
●
outline the trend toward interstate banking
●
define nonbank banks and the role of these institutions as competitors
●
describe the financial services offered by
banks' competitors and the advantages these competitors enjoy
●
outline the ramifications of the 1987 Competitive Equality Banking Act

R ip Van Winkle, the fictional character created by Washington Irving, slept for 20 years and awoke to find that the entire world around him had become completely different. He was amazed at the new environment, confused by all that had taken place while he slept, and at a loss to understand how to adjust to all the changes.

If Rip Van Winkle were a banker who fell asleep in 1967 and awakened today, what changes would he find? How different would banking be for him?[1]

His first and most drastic adjustment would be accepting that banking no longer enjoys exclusivity in providing financial services. Instead, banking is an important part of a financial services industry that includes numerous and aggressive competitors.

When this imaginary banker fell asleep in 1967

- nonbank banks did not exist, and companies such as Sears, Merrill Lynch, General Electric Credit, and Ford Motor Company were not serious competitors for banks in the financial services field
- demand deposits were far larger than time and savings deposits
- most major banks operated entirely within the borders of their home states; interstate banking (with the exception of Edge Act facilities) was strictly prohibited by various laws, and intrastate branch banking was generally restricted by the laws of individual states
- personnel costs were the largest expense item for most banks and the usual legal lending limit was 10 percent of capital
- controlled disbursement accounts, Eurodollars, explicit pricing of services, money market funds, automated clearing houses, country risk analysis, debit cards, and truth in lending laws were terms that had not yet entered the bankers' vocabulary

Many other significant changes have occurred since 1967, and the end is nowhere in sight. Banking is *not* static; it is an industry in an ongoing state of transition, and each change brings with it new issues and challenges that must be faced. What may be contemporary in 1988 may be completely out-of-date 1 or 2 years later.

The issues that banks face raise immediate questions, including the following:

- Will Congress deregulate commercial banking on a geographic basis, a functional basis, or both, so that banks become better able to compete?

- Will full-scale, nationwide interstate banking become legally authorized?
- What actions will nonbank competitors take to capture an even greater share of the financial marketplace?

Many other issues undoubtedly will surface as the financial services industry evolves. The answers to these three questions are of immediate concern to bankers because they will strongly influence the role of banks in that evolution.

DEREGULATION

For many years, bankers have asked Congress to change existing laws—some of which were passed over 50 years ago—and to enact new laws relaxing the multiple restrictions that have made commercial banking the most thoroughly and frequently regulated and supervised of all our industries.

The word *deregulation*, as used by bankers, does not refer to the type of deregulation that federal authorities extended to the airlines industry during the 1980s. Nor does it mean the complete elimination of federal and state controls over banking, for such a move could lead to complete chaos. As discussed in chapter 13, many factors justify regulatory controls over banking; no industry that handles over $2 trillion of depositors' money can ever hope to be completely free from government regulation.

For commercial bankers, "deregulation" refers to a lessening of restrictions, not to their elimination. The term describes the search by the banks for additional powers so that they can compete more equitably with other suppliers of financial services. It means legislative change, similar to that which has had an impact on thrift institutions in recent years.[2]

The Depository Institutions Deregulation and Monetary Control Act of 1980 contains this word in its official title. Yet, from the commercial banker's viewpoint, the act did little to relax the rigid restrictions under which banks must operate. Instead, the act conferred expanded lending powers on thrifts and gave them the right to apply to the Fed for credit. The act did not give commercial banks the equality they seek in the competitive marketplace.

Similarly, in 1987 Congress enacted the Competitive Equality Banking Act, which President Reagan reluctantly signed into law. Congress intended to close the loopholes that had allowed "nonbank" banks (described later in this chapter) to proliferate and to compete to such a great extent with commercial banks. Instead, in its final form, the act gave "grandfather" protection to all such nonbank banks established before March 5, 1987—and prevented bank holding companies from forming their own nonbank banks. Of even greater importance, a section of the act established a moratorium on the granting of new securities, insurance, and real estate powers to bank holding companies and stand-alone banks. This was the exact opposite of the deregulation that bankers had hoped for.[3] The act specifically prohibited federal regulators from granting additional powers to banks until Congress could reconsider the entire matter.

Earlier in 1987, a federal appeals court had upheld the right of a bank to offer investment advice and securities brokerage services to customers through a single subsidiary. Litigation to prevent banks from doing so had been brought by the Securities Industry Association.[4] This was a limited step toward deregulation, following an earlier Supreme Court ruling that banks could legally offer discount brokerage services. These court actions relaxed the restrictions originally imposed under the Glass-Steagall Act; however, this small step did not give the banks the latitude that they had wanted.

Shortly after the Competitive Equality Banking Act was passed in 1987, Chairman L. William Seidman of the Federal Deposit Insurance Corporation proposed the elimination of the Glass-Steagall prohibition of securities underwriting and the repeal of the Bank Holding Company Act. He also suggested that banks be given unlimited powers as long as their securities and other activities were conducted through separate subsidiaries that had no ties or access to the bank's insured deposits.[5] At the time this book went to print, Congress was considering these proposals.

Bankers' demands for deregulation are not based on sheer greed, or on a desire simply to become bigger and more powerful. Rather, their demands reflect their serious concerns about survival in the changing financial services industry. Without deregulation, many of today's banks find it increasingly difficult to compete in the rapidly changing financial environment. They are trying to match competitors who operate under no comparable restrictions.

Robert L. Clarke, Comptroller of the Currency in 1987, described Glass-Steagall and the Bank Holding Company Act as "outmoded and restrictive" and specifically used the word survival in arguing that Congress should allow U.S. commercial banks to compete more freely.[6]

For example, 15 foreign banks in 1987 enjoyed exemption from the Glass-Steagall provisions that restrict the activities of domestic banks.[7]

Consumers today enjoy a freedom of choice in obtaining financial services that their predecessors never had. Whether for Keogh or IRA relationships, investment management, estate planning, or basic account services, many thrift institutions, brokerage firms, insurance companies, and retailers actively solicit their business. At the same time, large corporations increasingly find it easy to bypass the banks' credit function, borrowing instead from one another through the commercial paper market. From 1975 to 1985, the commercial and industrial loans at the largest banks showed a relative decline of 40 percent as borrowers turned to other sources of funds.

Arguments Against Deregulation

Deregulation of banking can take two forms: *functional*, affecting the range of activities and services permitted to banks, and *geographic*, referring to the areas of the United States into which banks are allowed to expand. The latter type of deregulation will be discussed later in this chapter in relation to interstate banking.

In the case of functional deregulation, strong opposition has immediately been voiced by representatives of the securities, real estate, and insurance industries. Additional opposition has come from those who claim that functional deregulation would allow institutions in an already-weakened industry to assume further risks, thereby creating still more problems for themselves. Opponents claim that deregulation would increase the numbers of "problem banks," of which 1,509 were on the FDIC list as of March 31, 1987, and actual or near failures, of which 54 were recorded in the first 3 months of 1987.[8] Indeed, by October 1, 1987 the Federal Deposit Insurance Corporation had closed 136 federally insured commercial banks.

It is questionable whether functional deregulation would actually cause this to happen. For example, if existing laws were repealed so that banks could underwrite municipal revenue bonds, would those banks incur greater risk than they now do by lending directly to those same municipalities or by investing in their debt issues? If banks were permitted to expand their investment portfolios by acquiring shares of stock in the nation's largest and most creditworthy corporations, would they then assume more of a risk than they now do by making direct loans to those same businesses? If banks were given the right to engage in insurance- and brokerage-related activities, would this necessarily lead to imprudent speculation and unwarranted risks?

Functional deregulation, allowing banks to expand their range of services, would take place through the subsidiaries of bank holding companies (BHCs). The Federal Reserve has complete jurisdiction over all BHCs and can immediately disapprove any application for a new service if, in its judgment, that service (1) is not directly related to banking, (2) is not in the public interest, or (3) would create an undue concentration of power. The history of the Fed clearly shows that on many occasions it has rejected BHC applications for additional services. There is no reason to believe that the Fed would begin neglecting its responsibilities if deregulation were to take place.

Some opponents claim that deregulation would lead to bank failures similar to the 1984 failure of Continental Illinois National Bank and the 1987 failure in Texas of First City Bancorporation. However, deregulation has no connection with the problems at those two giant banks. Deteriorating loan portfolios, management problems, and lack of liquidity were the major contributing factors in those and other large bank failures; deregulation was not a cause. Deregulation did not cause the energy- and agriculture-related credits at those two banks to become uncollectible. The $1 billion in aid that FDIC provided to First City in 1987 (the second largest rescue in FDIC history) was made necessary by problems entirely unrelated to deregulation.[9]

One final argument against deregulation holds that it would violate the traditional segregation in the United States of banking from commerce; that is, the separation between the major suppliers of money and the major users of money. It is true, of course, that the parts of any bank holding company are linked together, and that any problems that a non-bank component in a BHC might have would affect the financial strength of the holding company's bank or banks. Indeed, it has been suggested that there is a real obligation on the part of those banks to stand behind their affiliates, possibly lending to them when other customers cannot obtain credit.

Nevertheless, as the ultimate authority over all BHCs, the Fed would always serve as the regulator, and could take action to protect the interest of the banks' depositors and preserve the financial condition of each institution.[10] In addition, FDIC has recommended that Congress consider legislation to create regulatory barriers that would prevent any improper or unlawful dealings between the bank(s) in a BHC and the other components.[11]

Geographic Deregulation

Whenever geographic deregulation is mentioned, *interstate banking* immediately enters into the discussion. Here again, it is necessary to clarify the term. It remains true that full-scale branching across state lines is restricted by both the McFadden Act of 1927 (which gives national banks branching privileges only to the extent that state-chartered banks have the same freedom) and the Douglas Amendment to the Bank Holding Company Act (which prevents interstate acquisitions by BHCs unless the involved states agree to them). The U.S. banking system thus remains quite different from those found in other countries; in the sense of full-scale bank operations across state lines, interstate banking does not exist.[12] However, no observer of the contemporary scene can fail to notice the extent to which commercial banks have been able to expand their operations, make acquisitions, and offer certain services across state boundaries. In this sense, interstate banking *does* exist in the United States—at least in part.

The Douglas Amendment is based on *reciprocity*. The legislatures of the involved states must mutually agree to interstate acquisitions. One of the most important trends in banking during the 1980s involved takeovers of this type. In 1975 only one state had enacted laws that permitted such acquisitions; by 1987 that number had grown to 36 plus the District of Columbia, and all 37 of these jurisdictions allowed full-service banking. Other states permitted interstate acquisitions on a more limited basis. As of 1987, only nine states—Arkansas, Colorado, Hawaii, Kansas, Montana, New Hampshire, North Dakota, Vermont, and Wyoming—had not passed laws to allow some type of interstate banking on a reciprocal basis with other states.[13] Many state legislatures have set "trigger dates," allowing interstate banking at specified future points in time. For example, complete, nationwide reciprocal banking becomes possible in California on January 1, 1991.

Aside from full-scale branching and interstate acquisitions, other banking activities have been conducted across state lines for many years. Edge Act offices help customers finance foreign trade; major banks also operate separate loan-production and consumer-finance offices, leasing facilities and discount-brokerage offices. Banks also have acted under the "extraordinary acquisition" section of the Garn-St Germain Act by purchasing troubled thrift institutions in other states, in some cases subsequently converting them into commercial banks.[14] FDIC has played an active part in many of these acquisitions, acting on the grounds that an interstate takeover of a distressed thrift is preferable to allowing the institution to fail.

In June 1985 the Supreme Court ruled that individual states had the right to form regional banking zones; that is, they could pass laws that would allow acquirers from certain specified areas to enter their jurisdictions while excluding those from other states. This ruling arose from laws passed in Connecticut and Massachusetts, allowing interstate acquisitions of banks *only* within the borders of those two states.[15] Table 15.1 lists some of the largest acquisitions that have occurred since the Supreme Court issued its ruling.

Combinations such as Pennsylvania BHCs with those in New Jersey, or North Carolina BHCs with those in Georgia or Florida simply recognize that state boundaries should not constitute barriers at a time when both customers and competitors disregard them. The nation's largest corporations deal with banks throughout the country, thrift institutions have no restrictions against crossing state lines, and consumers can use their bank cards to obtain cash from ATMs wherever they go. As a result, the chief financial officer of Chemical New York Corporation, among others, has predicted that full-scale interstate banking will become a nationwide reality in the early 1990s.[16]

Arguments Against Geographic Deregulation

The trend toward full-scale nationwide banking has not developed without strong opposition. Community banks in many parts of the country successfully serve their local customers, and see no reason why greater concentrations of economic power should be allowed to take place through continuing acquisitions by the largest money center banks. Opponents claim that if left unchecked, a series of such acquisitions could

TABLE 15.1
MAJOR INTERSTATE ACQUISITIONS

Acquirer and Location	Acquired and Location	Combined Assets (in billions of dollars)	Price of Acquisition (in billions of dollars)
First Wachovia Corporation Winston-Salem, N.C.	First Atlanta Corporation Atlanta, Ga.	15.7	—a
Trust Company of Georgia[b] Atlanta, Ga.	Sun Banks, Inc. Orlando, Fla.	15.6	—
Bank of New England Corporation Boston, Mass.	CBT Corporation Hartford, Conn.	6.9	—
First Union Corporation Charlotte, N.C.	Atlantic Bancorporation Jacksonville, Fla.	6.5	—
Bank of Boston Corporation Boston, Mass.	RIHT Financial Corporation Providence, R.I.	3.8	—
Fleet Financial Group Providence, R.I.	Norstar Bancorporation Albany, N.Y.	—	1.3
Chemical New York Corporation New York, N.Y.	Texas Commerce Bancshares Houston, Tex.	—	1.2
Security Pacific Corporation Los Angeles, Calif.	Rainier Bancorporation Seattle, Wash.	—	1.2

Sources: *American Banker*, December 23, 1985, p. 14, and June 9, 1987, p. 30.
a. Not listed.
b. This was a merger of equals.

lead to monopoly. Consequently, many community banks have spoken strongly against geographic deregulation.

To counter this argument, the point may be made again that all BHC activities and acquisitions come under Fed jurisdiction. Any takeover across state lines that was found to be anticompetitive in nature, giving the acquirer too large a market share and tending to drive one or more smaller banks out of the marketplace, could be immediately rejected by the Fed. In addition, the Department of Justice automatically has the right to block a combination of banks that would tend toward monopoly.

In California and New York, the home states of many of the nation's largest banks, statewide banking has existed for many years. Smaller banks continue to operate in both states, meeting the wants and needs of their customers and competing effectively with the larger institutions.

As with functional deregulation, any geographic deregulation that Congress may approve should take place only under certain controls and restrictions. In 1985 Fed Chairman Paul Volcker urged Congress to pass laws that would permit interstate banking, but he also recommended that those laws prohibit any acquisitions involving any of the 25 largest banks and any acquisitions that would give one institution more than 15 percent to 20 percent of the banking assets in a particular state. His proposal also included a provision that any individual state should retain the right to refuse to enter into interstate agreements.[17] Similarly, Martha Seger, a member of the Fed Board of Governors, stated in 1985 that full interstate banking would, in her judgment, result in a better long-term banking structure *but* that it should not be unrestricted; rather, she would require controls over all large interstate bank mergers and acquisitions.[18]

COMPETITION IN THE FINANCIAL SERVICES INDUSTRY

The third critical contemporary issue to be discussed here addresses the size, number, and types of bank competitors and the range of services that many of them offer. Their current activities help to explain why the banks' share of the total financial marketplace has steadily decreased in recent years.

Five of the 10 U.S. corporations reporting the highest net income for the second quarter of 1987 are listed in table 15.2. These corporations are cited because of the successes they have had in providing financial services in every part of the country. Our mythical banker, awakening after 20 years, would be amazed to notice their penetration of the marketplace and the disadvantages under which his bank might operate in trying to compete with them. Both the functional and geographical deregulation that these suppliers of financial services already enjoy are envied by many bankers.

None of these competitors is constrained by federal or state laws as to where they can establish and operate facilities. None of them is required

TABLE 15.2
EARNINGS OF FIVE MAJOR CORPORATIONS
(three months ending June 30, 1987)

Name	Net Income (in millions of dollars)
Ford Motor Company	1,498
General Motors Corporation	980
General Electric Corporation	720
Chrysler Corporation	429
Sears, Roebuck & Company	390

Source: "Corporate Scoreboard," *Business Week* (August 17, 1987), p. 101.

to obtain Federal Reserve approval when it wishes to offer additional financial services. None of them is subject to periodic examination by the Fed. Therefore, each has significant advantages in competing with banks.

For example, First Nationwide Bank FSB (federal savings bank) reported $1.8 billion in consumer loans at year-end 1986, making it the largest thrift institution in that field. Its parent, First Nationwide Financial Corporation, owned by Ford Motor Company, has 210 branches in 11 states, owns a consumer finance company with 160 offices, and operates 110 minibranches in K-Mart stores.[19]

Another subsidiary of the Ford Motor Company, Ford Credit Company, is the nation's second-largest finance company. Ford Credit has net receivables of over $30 billion generated through 6,000 automobile dealerships and 142 branch offices. Directly or through subsidiaries, Ford Credit Company offers leasing, insurance, and a wide range of commercial, personal, home equity, and home improvement loans to supplement its portfolio of auto loans.[20]

General Motors Acceptance Corporation (GMAC) was organized in 1919, at a time when banks did not seek to make automobile loans. It now contributes over $1 billion annually in net income to its parent corporation. GMAC is the second-largest mortgage banker in the United States, is a major commercial lender, and plans to enter into life and homeowner insurance and money-market fund operations. With total assets of over $75 billion and net receivables of over $66 billion, if GMAC were legally classified as a bank it would rank fifth among all U.S. commercial banks.[21]

General Electric Credit Corporation is the nation's largest nonbank business-to-business lender and has total assets of over $20 billion. In addition to financing sales of its parent company's appliances, it owns an investment banking, brokerage, and underwriting firm (Kidder, Peabody and Company) and offers commercial and residential financing, aircraft leasing, and life, property, and mortgage insurance.[22]

Chrysler Corporation, like General Motors and Ford, operates its own finance company, which handles automobile, commercial, and insurance financing. In addition, through subsidiaries, it owns Chrysler

Financial and FinanceAmerica, formerly part of the BankAmerica Corporation. These units contribute to an annual net income of over $154 million and receivables of over $15 billion.

When he was chairman and president of Sears, Roebuck and Company, Edward Telling made no secret of the corporation's long-range objectives, saying "Someday every Sears outlet will be a bank, making second mortgages, selling to consumers in their homes via electronic buy-and-bank services, and more. . . ." Sears' goal, he said, was "to become the largest consumer-oriented financial service entity."[23]

Sears represents the classic combination of elements in a financial services institution that can give the consumer completely integrated "packages" of financial services in every part of the country in a way that no bank or bank holding company can match. Sears has over $14 billion in retail receivables, resulting from use of its credit cards by over 26 million active cardholders. It owns a commercial bank (Greenwood Trust Company, in Delaware), a savings bank (Sears S&L), plus one of the nation's largest insurance companies (Allstate), one of the largest brokerage firms (Dean Witter), and a major real estate firm (Coldwell Banker). The new network of financial centers positioned within Sears' 800 store locations enables the consumer to handle retail purchases, insurance, ATM transactions, mortgage payments, and investments under a single roof. The introduction of Sears' Discover card adds to the company's stature as a competitor of banks.

A senior vice president of the Sears organization stated in September 1987 that 8 million consumers already carried the Discover card, enabling them to obtain cash from 17,000 ATMs and goods and services from over 600,000 companies and merchants.[24] The statistics testify to Sears' image and its degree of acceptance among consumers, helping to explain why the company has become a prime competitor for banks. In a 1987 survey of 1,130 consumers, 31 percent of the respondents identified Sears as the provider of financial services that best met their needs; American Express placed second (8 percent), and only one bank holding company, Citicorp (7 percent), placed among the top five in popularity. In the same survey, Sears clearly led in creating an image of innovativeness and responsiveness to change; 21 percent of the respondents placed Sears first, with Citicorp a distant second (7 percent).[25]

Sears enjoys by far the highest recognition rating in the financial services industry: 96 percent of U.S. consumers have stated that they are familiar with Sears. Of the consumers in the 1987 survey who had annual incomes of over $50,000, fully 84 percent expressed awareness of Sears' services.[26] This consumer group matches the segment of the population that many banks are anxious to attract.

Competition comes from many other quarters besides the largest corporations. Merrill Lynch, with assets of over $53 billion, offers brokerage, insurance, real estate, investment, mortgage banking, and commercial paper services. Its cash management account, with investment, check-writing, and overdraft privileges, has over one million customers. Retailers such as J.C. Penney, Kroger, and K-Mart can use their networks of stores to market a range of financial services to consumers.

In reviewing the examples mentioned above, a compelling reason for the bankers' demands for some form of functional or geographic deregulation stands out: nonbank corporations repeatedly have been able to acquire and operate firms in the insurance, securities, underwriting, and real estate businesses—and, in many instances, to buy and operate banks—when banks legally are prevented from doing so. This degree of freedom even extends to companies that would never be thought of as major suppliers of financial services. For example, Tucson Electric Power Company has ownership in a California commercial finance company, a BHC in Tennessee, a Florida S&L, and a California thrift institution. Also in Arizona, Pinnacle West Capital Corporation, owner of a public utility, also owns that state's largest thrift institution. Other examples can be seen in Nevada and Florida.[27]

One final group of bank competitors is the nation's thrift institutions. As mentioned earlier, the Monetary Control and Garn-St Germain Acts gave thrifts expanded powers, and they have used these to become aggressive competitors in commercial and consumer lending. During 1986 thrifts increased their consumer loan portfolios by 12.5 percent to a total of $50.6 billion; at year-end 1986 they accounted for 8.8 percent of all outstanding consumer loans in the United States.[28] The Federal Home Loan Bank Board has given approval for all S&Ls under its jurisdiction to establish their ATMs anywhere in the country.

Nonbank Banks

While our Rip Van Winkle of banking slept, over 165 "nonbank banks" came into being. These now form yet another source of competition for commercial banks.

A nonbank bank avoids the legal definition of a bank by excluding one of the services required by the definition. A nonbank bank may elect (1) not to offer commercial loans, or (2) not to accept demand deposits. In most cases, nonbank banks elect the former option and do not offer commercial loans; they are often called consumer banks or limited-service banks.

Many nonbank banks are owned by corporations. Merrill Lynch, Sears, Roebuck, American Express, Beneficial Finance, and Dreyfus Corporation all own nonbank banks. Others are simply limited-service institutions that provide checking and savings accounts, credit cards, CDs, and personal loans.

In 1987 approximately 300 applications for the formation of additional nonbank banks were pending with federal authorities. Because they are not subject to many of the constraints that affect full-service commercial banks, nonbank banks can spread across geographic areas very quickly; some have displayed growth rates exceeding 100 percent per year.

Greenwood Trust Company of Delaware may be cited as a prototypical nonbank bank. When it was acquired by Sears, Roebuck in January 1985, its total deposits were $10.8 million and its total assets $12 million; in 1987 its deposits were $1.8 billion and its total assets $2 billion. Its CDs are sold by the Dean Witter subsidiary of Sears in the Sears Financial Centers throughout the country, and its money market deposit accounts have been marketed by mail to the millions of Discover cardholders.[29]

The Competitive Equality Banking Act

This legislation was mentioned earlier in this chapter in connection with the pressures that have been exerted on Congress to give banks and bank holding companies some measure of relief through functional or geographic deregulation or both.

During 1987 Congress, under pressure from the regulatory authorities, legislators, commercial bankers, representatives of thrift institutions, and activist groups who expressed concern over the safety of deposits in the banking system, enacted the Competitive Equality Banking Act. Its provisions have an important impact on the entire financial services industry, especially as regards the banks. While some rules and regulations stemming from the act had not yet been put in final form when this text went to press, the general provisions of the act can be summarized as follows.

The act provides "grandfather" protection to existing nonbank banks, but, effective in August 1988, limits their rate of growth to 7 percent annually. It also prohibits nonbank banks from cross-marketing products and services with their parent-company owners.

The functional deregulation sought by commercial bankers was not granted by the act. Instead, federal authorities were prevented, until March 1988, from approving new insurance, real estate, or securities activities for banks.

A newly chartered financing corporation was created to provide an infusion of $10.8 billion over 3 years into the Federal Savings and Loan Insurance Corporation, thereby improving public confidence regarding protection of deposits at insured thrifts. To bolster public confidence even further, Congress expressed its intent that deposits, up to the statutory limits at all insured depository institutions, be backed by the *full faith and credit* of the federal government.

The act authorized FDIC to arrange interstate takeovers of failing institutions with assets of over $500 million, provided that FDIC extends financial aid in such transactions. In the bidding process for such takeovers, FDIC is required to give priority to banks from states that have passed interstate banking laws.

The Competitive Equality Banking Act has raised some additional issues. For example, title IV of the act, the Expedited Funds Availability Act, establishes new regulations on check clearing. These regulations will be embodied in a new Federal Reserve Regulation, titled Regulation CC. As of September 1990, a permanent schedule of availability will become effective, requiring banks to make the following deposited items available for withdrawal on the next business day: cash deposits, wire transfers, government checks, cashier's, teller's, and certified checks, and the first $100 of all deposits. Other local checks must become available to the depositor in 2 business days, and transit checks must be made available in 4 business days following the deposit.

A temporary schedule of availability applies from August 31, 1988 to September 1, 1990; it establishes 6 business days as the maximum delay in availability. Effective September 1, 1988, cash, wire transfers, government checks, and cashier's, teller's, and certified checks, deposited into new accounts, must be given *one-day* availability when the initial deposit consisting of such items is $5,000 or less. On the excess above $5,000 there is a maximum delay of 8 business days in availability.

Regulation CC also will contain, in its final published form, rules regarding disclosure requirements, endorsement standards, and return-item procedures for checks. For example, banks wishing to take advantage of the Federal Reserve's revamped return-item services will be required to conform to standardized endorsement procedures. A special area has been designated on the back of checks for endorsement by the bank of first deposit, as have areas for subsequent endorsements in the processing chain. New standards have been established for ink colors to be used on checks.

A draft of Regulation CC was sent out for review by depository institutions throughout the United States during 1987. Comments on the regulation were to be submitted to the Fed by February 8, 1988, approximately the time this textbook went to press.

Among the issues raised by the new rules is the matter of new potential for fraud by depositors, who will have access to as much as $5,000 one business day after the initial deposit is made.

The Competitive Equality Banking Act contained a provision that the moratorium on new authorities and powers for banks not be extended beyond March 1988. The action(s) that Congress might take after that date constituted grounds for nothing more than speculation in 1987.

Restructuring the Banks

Each section of this chapter has addressed a contemporary issue in banking. The combination of all of these concerns creates one final issue: if Congress does not give banks additional powers in the securities, real estate, and insurance businesses, what courses of action might the banks then take?

One possibility calls for a bank to give up its existing charter so that it may offer all the financial services from which it is now barred. If those services represent greater opportunities for profit, the banking business as such could be dropped completely.

A second approach has been suggested by Gerald Corrigan, president of the Federal Reserve Bank of New York. He has proposed that the existing financial services industry be restructured under federal supervision into three classes of institutions. The three classes would be

- bank or thrift holding companies
- financial holding companies
- nonbank financial companies

Holding companies in the first category could have one or more nonbank financial subsidiaries and could eventually engage in securities and insurance activities in addition to banking. However, they could not engage in any nonfinancial activities and could not be owned or controlled by an "outside" corporation.

Financial holding companies would not own or control deposit-taking institutions unless the deposit-taking institutions so desired, while companies in the third group could offer nonbank financial services and nonfinancial activities but would be prohibited from ownership or control of banks or thrifts.[30]

Further discussion of these and other proposals awaited the actions of Congress when the moratorium created by the 1987 act expired in March 1988.[31]

SUMMARY

Bankers in the 1980s have witnessed a series of threatening developments. Combinations of major retailers and manufacturers with nonbank banks, securities companies, insurance companies, and thrift institutions have become commonplace, and the banks' share of the total assets held by financial institutions has steadily decreased. While the provisions of the Glass-Steagall Act still prevent banks from offering securities-related services and products and investing in corporate securities, competitors have steadily increased their share of the marketplace. Major corporations increasingly turn to the commercial paper market in order to raise funds, thereby bypassing the banking system.

Worldwide, U.S. commercial banks have continually lost ground in relation to foreign banks. Only one U.S. commercial bank in 1987 ranked among the world's 25 largest institutions, and foreign banks in the United States, often unhampered by the regulations that affect domestic banks, have assumed far more importance.

Both the commercial banks and the Federal Reserve Board of Governors urged Congress to take cognizance of the sweeping and dramatic changes in the financial services industry by expanding the powers of bank holding companies, specifically by giving banks authority to engage in securities activities.[32] However, the Competitive Equality Banking Act of 1987 had the opposite effect. Although it limited the future expansion of nonbank banks, it prevented federal authorities from granting commercial banks any additional powers until March 1988.

Comptroller of the Currency Robert L. Clarke expressed the reactions of many bankers regarding the Competitive Equality Banking Act in saying, "I think it's a terrible piece of legislation. . . . I don't think it does any real good . . . (and it) does little to eliminate or restrict the real competition that banks face. . . . I see a lot of troubling evidence that banking as it is presently structured is losing ground to all sorts of competitors."[33]

At year-end 1987 the McFadden Act and the Douglas Amendment to the Bank Holding Company Act continued to prevent bank holding companies and banks from establishing full-scale interstate operations. However, a significant number of interstate acquisitions took place with the approval of state legislators, usually on a reciprocal basis, and interstate takeovers of troubled institutions often were made possible by the intervention of federal regulators.

Therefore, at the end of 1987 many questions posed in previous years still remained unanswered; namely, whether Glass-Steagall should be repealed, whether full-scale interstate banking and branching should be legally approved, and whether banks and bank holding companies should be given more freedom to compete more effectively.

QUESTIONS FOR DISCUSSION

1. How does the Glass-Steagall Act restrict the activities of commercial banks?

2. What is meant by functional deregulation?

3. How does the Douglas Amendment prevent full-scale nationwide banking?

4. Explain the term reciprocity as it affects interstate banking.

5. Identify the advantages that nonbank competitors enjoy in offering financial services.

6. What is a nonbank bank?

7. List three important provisions of the 1987 Competitive Equality Banking Act.

NOTES

1. James M. Culberson, Jr., "Community Banking Then and Now," *ABA Banking Journal* (August 1987), pp. 18–24.

2. *Federal Reserve Bulletin* (August 1986), pp. 541–54.

3. Karen D. Shaw, "Competitive Equality Act May Disadvantage Banks," *American Banker*, September 10, 1987, p. 4.

4. Jed Horowitz, "Court Upholds Move by Banks into Brokerage," *American Banker*, July 8, 1987, p. 1.

5. Barbara A. Rehm, "Seidman Backs Increased Bank Powers," *American Banker*, August 24, 1987, p. 3.

6. In "Banks Need Greater Flexibility Just to Survive," *The New York Times*, September 9, 1987, p. A26.

7. Thomas G. Labrecque, "A Radical Approach to Banking Reform: Legalize Competition" (speech to the University of Richmond Business School, February 12, 1987, Richmond, Va.).

8. "FDIC Summarizes 1st-Quarter Banking Results," *American Banker*, August 13, 1987, p. 4.

9. Robert Trigaux, "First City Recapitalized in FDIC Bailout," *American Banker*, September 10, 1987, p. 1.

10. Paul A. Volcker, in *Federal Reserve Bulletin* (August 1986), p. 544.

11. Nathaniel C. Nash, "F.D.I.C.'s Chairman Suggests Eliminating Bank-Holding Laws," *The New York Times*, August 22, 1987, p. 1.

12. "Interstate Banking: Business as Usual?" *ABA Banking Journal* (December 1986), pp. 29–32.

13. "Trigger Dates: Rundown of Interstate Banking Laws Nationwide," *American Banker*, February 18, 1987, p. 53.

14. Thomas P. Vartanian, "If You're Thinking of Acquiring a Thrift," *ABA Banking Journal* (November 1983), p. 70.

15. Gordon Matthews, "'85 Court Decision Reshaping Industry," *American Banker*, June 9, 1987, p. 1.

16. Andrea Bennett, "Nationwide Banking at Our Doorstep . . . ," *American Banker*, August 5, 1987, p. 6.

17. In Nathaniel C. Nash, "Fed Backs Interstate Banking," *The New York Times*, April 25, 1985, p. D1.

18. In "Given Effective Legislative Controls, Interstate Access Will Help Banking," *American Banker*, January 4, 1985, p. 4.

19. L. Michael Cacace, "First Nationwide Leads in Consumer Lending," *American Banker*, August 14, 1987, p. 6.

20. Eric N. Compton, *The New World of Commercial Banking* (Lexington, Mass.: Lexington Books, 1987), pp. 225–26.

21. *Ibid.*, pp. 223–25.

22. *Ibid.*, pp. 227–29, and Andrew Albert and Robert M.Garsson, "General Electric Emerges as a Financial Power," *American Banker*, April 28, 1986, p. 3.

23. Compton, *New World*, pp. 235–39.

24. "Discover's Rolling Along," *ABA Banking Journal* (September 1987), pp. 82–84.

25. Jay Rosenstein, "Consumers Say Sears Most Responsive," *American Banker*, October 5, 1987, p. 9.

26. Jay Rosenstein, "Sears' Retail Clout Helps Launch Financial Network," *American Banker*, September 28, 1987, p. 48.

27. Nina Easton, "Cash-Rich Utilities Diversify by Acquiring Financial Firms," *American Banker*, August 12, 1987, p. 1.

28. "Consumer Lending at Thrifts," *American Banker*, August 14, 1987, p. 1.

29. Eric N. Berg, "Limited Banks' Giant Hurdle," *The New York Times*, July 2, 1987, p. 1, and Barbara A. Rehm, "Florida Challenges Fed Decision Allowing Limited-Service Banks," *American Banker*, June 23, 1987, p. 16.

30. In Federal Reserve Bank of New York, *Annual Report 1986*, pp. 34–36.

31. John J. Mingo, "'Narrow Banks' Part of Plan for Restructuring Regulatory System," *American Banker*, September 15, 1987, p. 5.

32. Board of Governors of the Federal Reserve System, *73rd Annual Report 1986*, p. 177.

33. Steve Cocheo, "No Time for Disunity," *ABA Banking Journal* (September 1987), pp. 31–32.

For More Information

Compton, Eric N. *The New World of Commercial Banking*. Lexington, Mass.: D.C. Heath and Company, 1987.

APPENDIX A

AN OVERVIEW OF THE FEDERAL RESERVE SYSTEM

I n 1913 Congress passed legislation creating the Federal Reserve System to provide a safer and more flexible banking and monetary system. The Fed's original purposes included giving the country an elastic currency, providing facilities for rapid collection of checks, and supervising the banking system.

The Fed contributes to the nation's financial and economic goals by influencing the supply of money and credit in the economy. It tries to ensure that growth in those two elements over the long run will encourage economic growth with reasonable price stability. On a short-term basis, the Fed uses its policies to combat inflationary or deflationary pressures. Finally, as a lender of last resort it can avert liquidity crises and financial panics by making funds available to depository institutions.

Although in some respects the Federal Reserve resembles the central banks in other countries, there are also major differences in the institutions. The decisions of the Fed do not have to be approved by the president, and all stock in the Fed is held by its member banks. On the other hand, all appointments to the Board of Governors of the Federal Reserve are made by the president with the consent of the Senate. The chairman of the Board of Governors, representing the Fed in policy discussions, regularly reports to Congress and meets with the secretary of the Treasury and the chairman of the Council of Economic Advisers. Members of the Fed Board of Governors frequently testify before Congress on matters of concern and also serve on the Federal Financial Institutions Examination Council, which also has representatives from all the other federal regulatory agencies.

STRUCTURE OF THE FEDERAL RESERVE

The Board of Governors is composed of seven individuals appointed to 14-year terms. The seven terms are arranged so that one term expires in each even-numbered year. The major responsibilities of the Board include setting reserve requirements, approving discount rates as a tool of monetary policy, supervising and regulating member banks and all bank holding companies, establishing and administering protective regulations in consumer finance, and overseeing the 12 district Federal Reserve banks. The members of the Board of Governors make up a majority on the Federal Open Market Committee (FOMC), which directs the open-market operations (buying and selling of government securities) that are the principal instrument of monetary policy.

Each of the 12 Federal Reserve district banks has its own board, consisting of 9 outside directors. Three of the directors are Class A (representing member banks), three are Class B (representing the public), and three are Class C (appointed by the Board of Governors, but representing the public). The Class B directors are elected by the member banks in their district.

The directors of the 12 Federal Reserve district banks oversee the operations of those banks, subject to overall supervision by the Board of Governors. They establish the discount rate for their banks, again subject to approval by the Board.

EARNINGS AND EXPENSES

The Fed derives most of its income from interest on the securities it acquires and sells through open-market operations. Other sources of income include fees charged to financial institutions for various services under the terms of the Monetary Control Act of 1980 and interest charged to financial institutions on loans made to them. For 1986 the Federal Reserve System showed a total net income of $18.0 billion. Earnings are allocated first to the payment of all expenses incurred in the operation of the System, then to the mandatory dividend of 6 percent paid to member banks on their Federal Reserve stock. All remaining earnings—$17.8 billion in 1986—are paid into the United States Treasury.[1]

MEMBERSHIP

As of June 30, 1986, there were 14,186 commercial banks in the United States; 4,866 national banks were members of the Federal Reserve System (as required by law), while 1,088 state-chartered banks had elected to become members. Therefore, at that date there were 5,954 member banks and 8,232 nonmember banks.[2] Member banks as of that date held approximately 70 percent of all commercial bank deposits and about 40 percent of the deposits at all depository institutions (commercial and savings banks, S&Ls, and credit unions).

The Monetary Control Act of 1980 makes all depository institutions subject to reserve requirements, which must be maintained against transaction-type accounts, nonpersonal time deposits, and borrowings from banking offices abroad. These institutions may maintain their reserves directly with the Federal Reserve bank in their district, or through a member bank correspondent.

MONETARY AND FISCAL POLICY

The fiscal policy of the United States involves taxation and spending, as determined by the federal government. Monetary policy, on the other hand, encompasses actions taken by the Fed that affect the availability and cost of depository institutions' reserves, that change the discount rates, and that result in purchases and sales of government obligations.

The reserve assets of depository institutions can be used to satisfy their reserve requirements. Those assets consist of vault cash and reserve balances with Federal Reserve banks.

Nonborrowed reserves consist of those reserves (such as securities holdings) that depositories obtain from the Fed through open-market operations. Borrowed reserves consist of loans made to depositories through the Fed's credit function ("discount window"). Open-market purchases of government obligations add to nonborrowed reserves; sales of government obligations reduce those reserves.

When the Fed buys securities from any seller, it pays by issuing a check on itself. This action eventually increases the reserve account of the seller's bank at the Fed. Conversely, when the Fed sells securities through open-market operations, the payment results in a reduction in the reserve account of the buyer's bank at the Fed. In this way the Fed can change the amount of reserves available to depository institutions and thus influence the rate of growth of the money supply and conditions in credit markets. After each of its meetings, the Fed's Federal Open-Market Committee (FOMC) issues a directive to the Federal Reserve Bank of New York that guides the open-market operations of that institution in the period before the next meeting. All such directives are made public, and the votes of each member are recorded.

The Discount Window

Although less important than open-market operations, the credit function of the Federal Reserve constitutes another important tool of monetary policy. Until passage of the Monetary Control Act, only member banks had the privilege of applying to the Fed for loans; since 1980, all depository institutions have been able to do so. The word privilege is appropriate here, since Regulation A of the Board of Governors of the Fed (see Appendix B) establishes the constraints that apply. Most borrowings from the Fed are for extremely short periods and are made when depositories find that their other normal sources of funds are not reasonably available.

Loans made by the Fed to depositories take the form of both *discounts* and *advances*. Discounts are loans in which the depository uses notes that are payable to it and which it has endorsed. Advances, on the other hand, are loaned to a depository on the basis of the depository's own note, secured by adequate collateral. Securities of the U.S. government and of federal agencies represent the most common type of satisfactory collateral. During 1986 Federal Reserve banks made 19,000 loans to depository institutions, amounting to $193.4 billion.[3]

The Discount Rate

As mentioned earlier, each of the 12 Federal Reserve banks establishes its own discount rate; that is, the rate of interest to be charged to all borrowers. The discount rate structure generally is uniform throughout the country, except for very short periods when one or more banks have changed the rate and the boards of other banks have not yet acted.

If a depository institution is making frequent use of the discount window, the Fed may apply a surcharge above the posted discount rate.

Reserve Requirements

As of December 30, 1986 the statutory limits on reserve requirements for all depository institutions were

- 3 percent on net transaction accounts of $36.7 million or less and 12 percent on all net transaction account balances in excess of $36.7 million
- 3 percent on all nonpersonal time deposits maturing in less than 18 months, with no reserves required on deposits with longer maturities

These statutory limits constituted the actual reserve requirements in effect on that date.[4] The Monetary Control Act allows the Board of Governors of the Fed, under extraordinary circumstances, to exceed the statutory limits. Each depository institution must maintain a given level of reserves on average over a 14-day period ending every other Wednesday.

The three tools of monetary policy—open-market operations, the discount rate, and reserve requirements—are used in combination by the Fed to produce the desired effect.

SUPERVISION AND REGULATION

The responsibilities of the Fed in supervising and regulating the banking system include:

- supervising and regulating all state-chartered member banks and all Edge Act corporations and bank holding companies
- supervising and regulating the activities in the United States of foreign banks under the International Banking Act of 1978
- regulation of the commercial banking structure through administration of the Bank Holding Company Act and the Bank Merger and Change in Bank Control Acts
- regulation of the foreign activities of all member banks

Congress also has given the Fed responsibility for consumer protection. This responsibility is carried out through Federal Reserve regulations such as B, E, Z, AA, and BB (see Appendix B).

Examinations of state-chartered member banks are conducted jointly by the Fed and the individual states. The examination entails an appraisal of the soundness of the institution's assets, an evaluation of internal operations, policies, and management, an analysis of key financial factors, a review for compliance with all laws and banking regulations, and an overall determination of the institution's solvency.

The Comptroller of the Currency, who is responsible for the chartering, supervision, and regulation of all national banks, examines those banks and provides the Fed with a copy of the report of each examination.

To fulfill its role as the primary supervisor of all bank holding companies, the Federal Reserve conducts on-site inspections of both the parent companies and their nonbank subsidiaries. These inspections include a review of nonbank assets and funding activities, an evaluation of policies and procedures as implemented by management, and a review for compliance with all relevant statutes.

Whenever the Fed determines that a bank or bank holding company is in unsatisfactory condition, it requires the organization to take corrective action. The organization's board of directors is responsible for carrying out the mandate of the Fed. If the situation deteriorates further, the Fed may act (either independently or in concert with other federal and state regulators) to bring about the acquisition of the institution by another bank holding company or state-chartered member bank. The Fed also may provide immediate liquidity assistance to a troubled institution through the discount window.

Federal Reserve Bank Services

The Federal Reserve also functions as a bank for banks and a bank for government (exhibit A.1). The accompanying chart illustrates these functions. Since its inception, the Federal Reserve System has played an important part in the nation's payment mechanism, through which billions of dollars are transferred every day. The Fed has established procedures for meeting the need for supplies of coin and currency, for expediting the collection and settlement of checks, and for wire transfers of funds throughout the country.

Nationwide check usage amounts to approximately 100 million items per day. Some 60 percent of these checks are processed through the 48 check-clearing centers established by the Fed, including the Regional Check Processing Centers (RCPCs).

The 12 Federal Reserve banks are directly involved in two types of Electronic Funds Transfer Services (EFTS), through the network of automated clearing houses (ACHs) and through wire transfers of funds. FedWire, which connects Federal Reserve facilities, depository institutions, the Department of the Treasury, and various government agencies, typically is used to transfer all large dollar payments. The ACH network provides a nationwide clearing and settlement mechanism that provides the processing for electronically originated debits and credits.

As the federal government's fiscal agent, the Federal Reserve banks and branches maintain the U.S. Treasury's "checking account" and issue

EXHIBIT A.1
BOUNDARIES OF FEDERAL RESERVE DISTRICTS AND THEIR BRANCH TERRITORIES

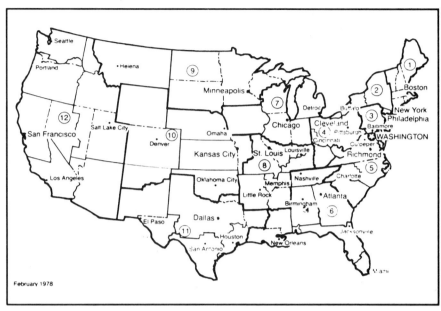

February 1978

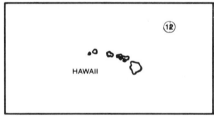

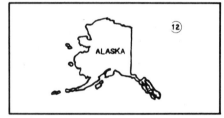

Legend:

——— Boundaries of Federal Reserve districts

——— Boundaries of Federal Reserve branch territories

★ Board of Governors of the Federal Reserve System

@ Federal Reserve bank cities

• Federal Reserve branch cities

Source: *Federal Reserve Bulletin.*

and redeem government securities. They also provide fiscal-agency services in connection with the financial activities of federal and federally sponsored agencies.

SUMMARY

A comprehensive overview of the Federal Reserve System is found in "The Federal Reserve System: Purposes and Functions," published by the Fed Board of Governors. This document periodically is updated to reflect regulatory and procedural changes, including the technological advances that the Fed has made in order to improve the efficiency of the payments mechanism in the United States. Virtually all of the material contained in this appendix has been excerpted from the abovementioned publication.

NOTES

1. Board of Governors of the Federal Reserve System, *73rd Annual Report*, Washington, D.C., 1986, p. 233.

2. *Ibid.*, p. 247.

3. *Ibid.*, p. 244.

4. *Ibid.*, p. 245.

APPENDIX B

A
GUIDE TO
FEDERAL
RESERVE
REGULATIONS

Excerpted from the booklet published by the Board of Governors of the Federal Reserve System, revised February 1985.

The Board of Governors of the Federal Reserve System and the Federal Reserve banks administer more than two dozen regulations affecting a wide variety of financial activities.

In broad terms, these regulations deal with the functions of the central bank and its relationships with financial institutions, the activities of commercial banks and bank holding companies, and consumer credit transactions. They are the Federal Reserve System's means of carrying out congressional policies embodied in various banking laws and assigned to the System.

A Guide to Federal Reserve Regulations provides a general understanding of the goals and scope of the regulations. This booklet is neither a substitute for the regulations, a comprehensive summary, nor a substitute for interpretations of the regulations. For answers to specific questions, the regulations themselves should be consulted. To obtain individual copies of the regulations, or for information about a subscription to the Federal Reserve Regulatory Service, please contact Publications Service, Board of Governors, Washington, D.C. 20551. Pamphlets explaining consumer credit regulations and margin regulations in more detail are also available.

REGULATION A

Regulation A governs borrowing by depository institutions at the Federal Reserve discount window.

The Federal Reserve discount window is open to any depository institution that maintains transaction accounts or nonpersonal time deposits. The regulation provides for lending under two basic programs. First, *adjustment credit* is advanced for brief periods to help borrowers meet short-term needs for funds when their usual sources, including such special industry lenders as the Federal Home Loan Bank Board, are not reasonably available. Second, *extended credit* is designed to assist depository institutions meet longer-term needs for funds. This category includes seasonal credit to smaller depository institutions lacking access to market funds; assistance to an individual depository institution that experiences special difficulties arising from exceptional circumstances; and assistance to address liquidity strains affecting a broad range of depository institutions. *Emergency credit* may also be advanced to entities other than depository institutions where failure to obtain credit would adversely affect the economy.

REGULATION B

Regulation B prohibits creditors from discriminating against credit applicants, establishes guidelines for gathering and evaluating credit information, and requires written notification when credit is denied.

The regulation prohibits creditors from discriminating against applicants on the basis of age, race, color, religion, national origin, sex, marital status, or receipt of income from public assistance programs. As a general rule, creditors may not ask (on applications) the race, color, religion, national origin, or sex of applicants. In addition, if the application is for individual, unsecured credit, the creditor may not ask the applicant's marital status. Exceptions apply in the case of residential mortgage applications. Creditors also may not discriminate against applicants who exercise their rights under the federal consumer credit laws.

Model credit application forms are provided in the regulation to facilitate compliance. By properly using these forms, creditors can be assured of being in compliance with the application requirements of the regulation. Creditors may use credit-scoring systems that allocate points or weights to key applicant characteristics. Creditors also may rely on their own judgment of an applicant's creditworthiness.

The regulation also requires creditors to give applicants a written notification of rejection of an application, a statement of the applicant's rights under the Equal Credit Opportunity Act, and a statement either of the reasons for the rejection or of the applicant's right to request the reasons. Creditors who furnish credit information, when reporting information on married borrowers, must report information in the names of each spouse.

The regulation establishes a special residential mortgage credit monitoring system for regulatory agencies by requiring that lenders ask residential mortgage applicants their race, national origin, sex, marital status, and age.

REGULATION C

Regulation C requires depository institutions making federally related mortgage loans to make annual public disclosure of the locations of certain residential loans.

The regulation carries out the Home Mortgage Disclosure Act of 1975, providing citizens and public officials with enough information to determine whether depository institutions are meeting the housing credit needs of their local communities.

The regulation applies to commercial banks, savings banks, savings and loan associations, building and loan associations, homestead associations, and credit unions that make federally related mortgage loans, with the exception of institutions with assets of $10 million or less and institutions that do not have an office in a metropolitan statistical area or a primary metropolitan statistical area. Institutions covered by the regulation must disclose annually, in central locations within their communities and at certain of their own offices, the number and total dollar amount of residential mortgage loans originated or purchased during the most recent calendar year, itemized by census tract in which the property is located.

The Board may exempt from Regulation C any institutions complying with substantially similar state or municipal laws or regulations which have adequate provision for enforcement.

REGULATION D

Regulation D imposes uniform reserve requirements on all depository institutions with transaction accounts or nonpersonal time deposits; defines such deposits and requires reports of deposits to the Federal Reserve; and sets phase-in schedules for reserve requirements.

Regulation D sets uniform reserve requirements on all depository institutions—including commercial banks, savings banks, savings and loan associations, credit unions, and industrial banks—that have transaction accounts or nonpersonal time deposits.

Transaction accounts are defined to include checking accounts, NOW accounts, share draft accounts, savings accounts that allow automatic transfers or third party payments by automated teller machines, and accounts that permit more than a limited number of telephone or preauthorized payments or transfers each month. The reserve requirement on transaction accounts is 3 percent of the first $29.8 million of net transactions balances and 12 percent of the rest.

Time deposits with original maturities of 1½ years or more presently are subject to a zero percent reserve requirement. Nontransferable time deposits (including personal savings deposits) with maturities of less than 1½ years do not have to be backed by reserves when they are owned by natural persons. Time deposits with a maturity of less than 1½ years owned by other than natural persons or that are transferable are subject to a 3 percent reserve requirement.

Time deposits are deposits or certificates with original maturities of at least 7 days, and savings accounts (including money market deposit accounts, regular share accounts at credit unions, and regular accounts at thrifts) that allow the institution to require at least 7 days' notice by the depositor before a withdrawal is made.

In order to relieve very small depository institutions from the burden of reserve requirements, each depository institution is subject to a zero percent reserve requirement on the first $2.4 million of its reservable liabilities.

Reserves are maintained in the form of vault cash or a noninterest-bearing balance held with a Federal Reserve bank on a direct or indirect basis.

Reserves for nonmember depository institutions are being phased in over an 8-year period that began in late 1980.

REGULATION E

Regulation E establishes the rights, liabilities, and responsibilities of parties in electronic funds transfers (EFT) and protects consumers using EFT Systems.

Regulation E prescribes rules for the solicitation and issuance of EFT cards; governs consumers' liability for unauthorized electronic funds transfers (resulting, for example, from lost or stolen cards); requires institutions to disclose certain terms and conditions of EFT services; provides for documentation of electronic transfers (on periodic statements, for example); sets up a resolution procedure for errors on EFT accounts; and covers notice of crediting and stoppage of preauthorized payments to and from a customer's account.

REGULATION F

Regulation F requires certain state-chartered member banks to register and file financial statements with the Board of Governors.

The regulation applies to state-chartered member banks that have 500 or more stockholders and at least $1 million in assets, or whose securities are registered on a national securities exchange. Generally, it does not apply to banks whose shares are owned by holding companies since these usually have fewer than 500 stockholders.

In general, these state-chartered member banks must file registration statements, periodic financial statements, proxy statements, statements of election contests, and various other disclosures of interest to investors. Officers, directors, and principal stockholders also must file reports on their holdings in the bank.

The regulation also prohibits tender offers for the stock of a bank subject to the regulation unless certain information is filed with the Board at the same time.

Regulations issued by the Board of Governors in this area are substantially similar to those issued by the Securities and Exchange Commission. Information filed under the provisions of Regulation F is available to the public at the offices of the Board of Governors in Washington, D.C. and at the Federal Reserve bank in the district where the registrant is located.

REGULATION G

Regulation G is one of four regulations concerning credit extended to finance securities transactions (see also Regulations T, U, and X). Regulation G governs credit secured by margin securities extended or arranged by parties other than banks, brokers, and dealers.

This regulation applies to lenders, other than broker-dealers and banks, who are required to register with the Board of Governors. Registration is required within 30 days after the end of the quarter during which credit (secured, directly or indirectly by margin stock) is extended in an amount of $200,000 or more or which exceeds $500,000 in total. Once a lender is required to be registered, the regulation applies to all loans which are secured, directly or indirectly by margin stock; if the loan is also for the purpose of purchasing or carrying margin stock, the margin requirements of the regulation apply. An exception to this general rule applies to lenders who extend credit via an eligible employee stock option plan which will be used to purchase margin stock of the employer.

Margin stock includes any equity security listed on or having unlisted trading privileges on a national stock exchange, any debt security convertible into such a security, most mutual funds, and any security included on the Board's list of OTC margin stocks (published three times annually and available at the Board or from any Federal Reserve bank).

REGULATION H

Regulation H defines the membership requirements for state-chartered banks, describes membership privileges and conditions imposed on these banks, explains financial reporting requirements, and sets out procedures for requesting approval to establish branches and for requesting voluntary withdrawal from membership.

The regulation sets forth the procedures for state-chartered banks to become members of the Federal Reserve System, as well as the privileges and requirements of membership.

State-chartered member banks are prohibited from engaging in practices that are unsafe or unsound or that result in violation of law, rule, or regulation. The regulation imposes specific restrictions on the conduct of some banking practices, including issuance of letters of credit, acceptances, and lending on the security of improved real estate or mobile homes located in flood hazard areas.

The regulation also requires state-chartered member banks, acting as securities transfer agents, to register with the Board and imposes requirements on registered state-member bank transfer agents or clearing agencies.

REGULATION I

Regulation I requires each bank joining the Federal Reserve System to subscribe to the stock of its district Reserve bank in an amount equal to 6 percent of the member bank's capital and surplus. Half the total must be paid on approval. The remainder is subject to call by the Board of Governors.

A 6 percent dividend is paid on paid-in portions of Reserve bank stock. The stock is not transferable and cannot be used as collateral.

Whenever a member bank increases or decreases its permanent capitalization, it must adjust its ownership of Reserve bank stock to maintain the same ratio of stock to capital. Payment for additional shares of Reserve bank stock, cancellation of shares, as well as semi-annual dividend payments, are made through the member bank's reserve account.

A member bank's ownership of Federal Reserve stock is subject to cancellation on discontinuance of operations, insolvency, or voluntary liquidation, conversion to nonmember status through merger or acquisition, or voluntary or involuntary termination of membership.

REGULATION J

Regulation J establishes procedures, duties, and responsibilities among Federal Reserve banks and (1) the senders and payors of checks and other cash items and noncash items, and (2) the originators and recipients of transfers of funds.

Regulation J provides a legal framework for depository institutions to collect checks and other cash items, and to settle balances through the Federal Reserve System. It specifies terms and conditions under which Reserve banks will receive items for collection from depository institutions and present items to depository institutions, and establishes rules under which depository institutions return unpaid items. The regulation also specifies terms and conditions under which Reserve banks will receive and deliver transfers of funds from and to depository institutions.

The regulation is supplemented by operating circulars issued by the Reserve banks and detailing more specific terms and conditions under which they will handle checks and other cash items, noncash items, and transfers of funds.

REGULATION K

Regulation K governs the international banking operations of banking organizations and of foreign banks in the United States.

Corporations organized to engage in international banking or other financial operations are chartered by the Board of Governors under section 25(a) of the Federal Reserve Act. This section of the act was introduced as an amendment in 1919 by Senator Walter E. Edge of New Jersey. Thus, these corporations are known as "Edge corporations."

The regulation permits Edge corporations to engage in a broad range of international banking and financial activities, subject to supervision, while limiting transactions within the U.S. to those clearly international in character. It also imposes reserve requirements, as specified in Regulation D, on certain deposits of these corporations and specifies prudent limits on their operations.

The regulation further authorizes, and sets forth the rules governing, Edge corporation and bank holding company investment in *de novo* or existing export trading companies.

As to foreign bank operations, the regulation reflects limitations on interstate banking and specific exemptions from nonbanking prohibitions.

With respect to loans by domestic banking organizations to foreign borrowers, the regulation provides for the establishment of special reserves against certain international assets which have been impaired and provides rules for accounting for fees on international loans.

REGULATION L

Regulation L seeks to avoid restraints on competition among depository organizations by restricting the interlocking relationships that a management official may have with depository organizations.

The regulation prohibits a management official of a state member bank or bank holding company from serving simultaneously as a management official of another depository organization if both organizations are not affiliated, or are very large, or are located in the same local area.

The regulation provides a 10-year grandfather period for certain interlocks and provides exceptions for certain interlocks. Some of these exceptions include depository organizations in low income or economically depressed areas, organizations owned by women or minority groups, newly chartered organizations, and organizations facing disruptive management loss or conditions endangering safety and soundness.

REGULATION M

Regulation M implements the consumer leasing provisions of the Truth in Lending Act.

Regulation M applies to leases of personal property for more than 4 months for personal, family, or household use. It requires leasing companies to disclose in writing the cost of a lease, including security deposit, monthly payments, license, registration, taxes, and maintenance fees, and, in the case of an open end lease, whether a "balloon payment" may be applied. It also requires written disclosure of the terms of a lease, including insurance, guarantees, responsibility for servicing the property, standards for wear and tear, and any option to buy.

REGULATION N

Regulation N is internal to the Federal Reserve System. It governs relationships and transactions among Reserve banks and foreign banks, bankers, and governments and describes the role of the Board of Governors in these relationships and transactions.

The regulation gives to the Board the responsibility for approving in advance negotiations or agreements by Reserve banks with any foreign banks, bankers, or governments. Reserve banks must keep the Board fully advised of all foreign relationships, transactions, and agreements.

Under direction of the Federal Open Market Committee, a Reserve bank maintaining accounts with a foreign bank may undertake negotiations, agreements, or contracts to facilitate open-market transactions. Reserve banks must report to the Board at least quarterly on accounts they maintain with foreign banks.

REGULATION O

Regulation O prohibits member banks from extending credit to their own executive officers and insured banks that maintain correspondent account relationships with other banks from extending credit to one another's executive officers on preferential terms.

Regulation O also limits the amount of credit that may be extended by a member bank to its executive officers. Regulation O implements the reporting requirements of the Financial Institutions Regulatory and Interest Rate Control Act of 1978, as amended by the Garn-St Germain Depository Institutions Act of 1982.

Each executive officer and principal shareholder of an insured bank is to report annually, to the bank's board of directors, the amount of his or her own indebtedness, and that of "related interests," to each of the insured bank's correspondent banks outstanding 10 days before the report is filed. The range of interest rates on such loans and other terms and conditions of the loans must also be reported. A "related interest" is a company controlled by political or campaign committees controlled by or benefiting bank officials and shareholders.

Each insured bank is required to include with its quarterly report of condition the aggregate extensions of credit by the bank to its executive officers and principal shareholders, together with the number of these individuals whose extensions of credit from the bank are 5 percent or more of the bank's equity capital or $500,000, whichever is less.

The regulation also requires each insured bank to disclose publicly, upon request, the names of its executive officers and principal shareholders who had extensions of credit outstanding to them or their related interests from their own or correspondent bank(s) of 5 percent or more of the reporting bank's equity capital or $500,000, whichever is less.

REGULATION P

Regulation P sets minimum standards for security devices and procedures state-chartered member banks must establish to discourage robberies, burglaries, and larcenies and to assist in identifying and apprehending persons who commit such acts.

A member bank must appoint a security officer to develop and administer a security program at least equal to the requirements of the regulation. The program must be in writing and approved by the bank's directors.

Each state-chartered member bank must annually file with its district Reserve bank a signed statement certifying its compliance with the regulation.

REGULATION Q

Regulation Q prescribes the maximum rates of interest that may be paid by member banks on time and savings deposits.

Under the Depository Institutions Deregulation and Monetary Control Act of 1980, limitations on maximum rates of interest that may be paid on time and savings deposits were to be phased out gradually and eliminated by 1986. In the interim, rules governing such deposits were prescribed by the Depository Institutions Deregulation Committee (DIDC). The secretary of the Treasury, chairman of the Federal Reserve Board, chairman of the board of directors of the Federal Deposit Insurance Corporation, chairman of the Federal Home Loan Bank Board, and chairman of the National Credit Union Administration Board were voting members of the committee; the Comptroller of the Currency was a nonvoting member.

The rules adopted by DIDC are incorporated by the Board into Regulation Q. In addition, Regulation Q includes rules governing the advertising of interest on deposits by member banks.

REGULATION R

Regulation R aims at avoiding interlocking relationships between securities dealers and member banks, and thus any potential conflict of interest, collusion, or undue influence on member bank investment policies or investment advice to customers.

The regulation restates the prohibition in the Glass-Steagall Act that prohibits individuals involved in various phases of securities activities (including issuance, flotation, underwriting, public sale, or distribution) from serving as a director, officer, or employee of a member bank.

The regulation provides an exemption for individuals in government securities transactions. These securities generally include, for example, those of the United States, the International Bank for Reconstruction and Development, the Tennessee Valley Authority, and the general obligations of states and municipalities.

REGULATION S

Regulation S establishes the rates and conditions for reimbursement to financial institutions for providing records to a government authority.

Regulation S implements that section of the Right to Financial Privacy Act of 1978 requiring government authorities to pay a reasonable fee to financial institutions for providing financial records of individuals and small partnerships to federal agencies. Costs for searching for, reproducing, or transporting books, papers, records, or other data requested are covered, with exceptions for such information as records furnished in connection with government loan programs or Internal Revenue summons.

REGULATION T

Regulation T governs credit extensions by securities brokers and dealers, including all members of national securities exchanges.

The regulation applies to broker-dealers and all national securities exchange members. In general, such entities may not extend credit to their customers unless the loan is secured by "margin securities" nor may they arrange for credit to be extended by others on terms better than they themselves are permitted to extend.

The term "margin securities," includes (1) any equity security listed on or having unlisted trading privileges on a national securities exchange; (2) most mutual funds; (3) OTC margin bonds, meeting criteria specified by the Board; (4) any OTC stock designated by the Securities and Exchange Commission as qualified for trading in the national market system; and (5) any security included on the Board's list of OTC margin stocks (published four times annually and available at the Board or from any Federal Reserve bank).

Generally, a broker-dealer may not extend credit on margin securities used as collateral in excess of the percentage of current market value permitted by the Board. For certain classes of securities, the Board allows a lending broker-dealer to use its judgment in determining how much collateral value can be assigned to any class of securities provided that the amount does not exceed 100 percent of the current market value of the particular security. This is called "good faith" value.

The regulation also prescribes rules governing cash transactions among brokers, dealers, their customers, and other brokers and dealers. It also limits the sources from which borrowing brokers and dealers may secure funds in the ordinary course of their business.

The regulation permits any registered self-regulatory organization or registered broker-dealer to establish more stringent rules than those required by the regulation.

REGULATION U

Regulation U governs extension of credit by banks for purchasing and carrying margin securities.

The regulation applies to banks which extend credit which is secured, directly or indirectly, by margin stock. Any time a loan is made in which a margin stock serves as collateral, the bank must have the customer execute a purpose statement regardless of the use of the loan. The margin requirements imposed by the regulation apply if the loan is both margin-stock secured and is for the purpose of purchasing or carrying margin securities. Certain exceptions exist for specified special purpose loans to broker-dealers, for loans to qualified employee stock option plans, for loans to plan lenders, or for emergencies.

Margin stock includes any equity security listed on or having unlisted trading privileges on a national securities exchange, any debt security convertible into such a security, most mutual funds, and any security included on the Board's list of OTC margin stocks.

REGULATION V

Regulation V facilitates and expedites the financing of contractors, subcontractors, and others involved in national defense work.

The Defense Production Act of 1950 and Executive Order 10480, as amended, authorize several federal departments and agencies to guarantee loans by private financing institutions to contractors, subcontractors, and others involved in national defense work. Regulation V spells out the authority granted to Reserve banks, as fiscal agents of the United States, to assist federal departments and agencies in making and administering these loan guarantees and sets maximum rates of interest, guarantee fees, and commitment fees.

REGULATION W

Regulation W was revoked in 1952.

Regulation W prescribed minimum down payments, maximum maturities, and other terms applicable to extensions of consumer credit. Such action was authorized by executive order during World War II, and by congressional legislation in 1947–48 and again during the Korean conflict. With the repeal of authorizing legislation in 1952, Regulation W was revoked.

REGULATION X

Regulation X extends the provisions of Regulations G, T, and U (governing extensions of credit for purchasing or carrying securities in the United States) to certain borrowers and to certain types of credit extensions not specifically covered by those regulations.

The regulation applies to United States persons and foreign persons controlled by or acting on behalf of or in conjunction with United States persons who obtain credit outside the United States to purchase or carry

United States securities, or within the United States to purchase or carry any securities. The following borrowers are exempt from the regulation and the controlling statute: (1) any borrower who obtains purpose credit within the United States unless the borrower willfully causes the credit to be extended in contravention of Regulations G, T, or U, and (2) any borrower whose permanent residence is outside the United States who has obtained or has outstanding during any calendar year no more than $100,000 in purpose credit obtained outside the United States.

In general, whenever the regulation applies, the borrower is responsible for ensuring that the credit conforms to one of the three margin regulations. The determination as to which one applies is dependent upon the nature of the lender and is specified in the regulation.

REGULATION Y

Regulation Y relates to the bank and nonbank expansion of bank holding companies and to the divestiture of impermissible nonbank interests.

Under the Bank Holding Company Act of 1956, as amended, a bank holding company is a company which directly or indirectly owns or controls a bank. The regulation contains presumptions and procedures the Board uses to determine whether a company controls a bank. The regulation also explains the procedures for obtaining Board approval to become a bank holding company and procedures to be followed by bank holding companies acquiring voting shares in banks or nonbank companies. The Board has specified in the regulation those nonbank activities that are closely related to banking and therefore permissible for bank holding companies.

REGULATION Z

Regulation Z prescribes uniform methods of computing the cost of credit, disclosure of credit terms, and procedures for resolving billing errors on certain credit accounts.

The credit provisions of the regulation apply to all persons who extend consumer credit more than 25 times a year or, in the case of real estate, more than 5 times a year. Consumer credit is generally defined as credit offered or extended to individuals for personal, family, or household purposes, where the credit is repayable in more than four installments or for which a finance charge is imposed.

The major provisions of the regulation require lenders to

- provide borrowers with meaningful, written information on essential credit terms, including the cost of credit expressed as a finance charge and an annual percentage rate
- respond to consumer complaints of billing errors on certain credit accounts within a specific period

- identify credit transactions on periodic statements of open end credit accounts
- provide certain rights regarding credit cards
- inform customers of the right to rescind certain residential mortgage transactions within a specified period
- comply with special requirements when advertising credit

REGULATION AA

Regulation AA establishes consumer complaint procedures.

Under the regulation, any consumer complaint about an alleged unfair or deceptive act or practice by a state member bank, or an alleged violation of law or regulation, will be investigated. Complaints should be submitted, preferably in writing, to the director of the Division of Consumer and Community Affairs at the Board of Governors of the Federal Reserve System, Washington, D.C. 20551, or to the Reserve bank for the district in which the institution is located.

The complaint should describe the practice or action objected to and should give the names and addresses of the bank concerned and the person complaining.

The Board will attempt to give a substantive reply within 15 business days, or, if that is not possible, will acknowledge the complaint within 15 business days and set a reasonable time for a substantive reply.

The Board will also receive complaints regarding institutions other than state member banks, and refer them to the appropriate federal agencies.

A person filing a complaint does not have to be a customer of the institution in question, and the acts or practices complained of do not have to be subject to federal regulation. Consumers may complain about acts or practices that may, in fact, be expressly authorized, or not prohibited, by a current federal or state law or regulation.

REGULATION BB

Regulation BB implements the Community Reinvestment Act (CRA) and is designed to encourage banks to help meet the credit needs of their communities.

Under Regulation BB, each bank office must make available a statement for public inspection indicating, on a map, the communities served by that office and the type of credit the bank is prepared to extend within the communities served. The regulation requires each bank to maintain a file of public comments relating to its CRA statement. The Federal Reserve Board, in examining a bank, must assess its record in meeting the credit needs of the entire community, including low and moderate income neighborhoods, and must take account of the record in considering certain bank applications.

SOURCES OF CURRENT INFORMATION

American Banker (daily except Sat., Sun., Holidays)
525 West 42nd Street
New York, New York 10036

Bank Administration (monthly)
Bank Administration Institute
60 Gould Center
Rolling Meadows, Illinois 60008

Bank Marketing (monthly)
Bank Marketing Association
309 West Washington Street
Chicago, Illinois 60606

Bankers Magazine (bi-monthly)
Warren, Gorham and Lamont
210 South Street
Boston, Massachusetts 02111

Bankers Weekly (weekly)
American Bankers Association
1120 Connecticut Avenue, N.W.
Washington, D.C. 20036

Banking (monthly)
(Journal of the American Bankers Association)
Simmons-Boardman Publishing Corporation
350 Broadway
New York, New York 10013

Federal Reserve Bulletin (monthly)
Division of Administrative Services
Board of Governors of the Federal Reserve System
Washington, D.C. 20551

Issues in Bank Regulation (quarterly)
Bank Administration Institute
60 Gould Center
Rolling Meadows, Illinois 60008

See also regional Federal Reserve publications.

These items represent only a few of the many resources available for banking information and study. For further information, contact the ABA Library at (202) 663-5221, or write to:

Library Assistance
American Bankers Association
1120 Connecticut Avenue, N.W.
Washington, D.C. 20036

GLOSSARY

ABA transit number. A unique identifying number assigned by the American Bankers Association under the National Numerical System. It has two parts, separated by a hyphen. The first part identifies the city, state, or territory in which the bank is located; the second part identifies the bank itself. The transit number appears in the upper right-hand corner of checks as the numerator (upper portion) of a fraction.

Acceptance. A time draft (bill of exchange) on the face of which the drawee has written the word *accepted*, the date it is payable, and his or her signature. After having accepted the draft, the drawee is called the acceptor. See also *banker's acceptance* and *certified check*.

Access. The right of entry to a safe deposit box so that authorized parties can examine, add to, or reduce the contents.

Account analysis. The process of determining the profit or loss to a bank in handling an account for a given period. It shows the activity involved, the cost of that activity as determined by multiplying unit costs by transaction volume, and the estimated earnings on average investable balances maintained during the period after all expenses have been listed.

Account reconciliation (reconcilement). The process of bringing a bank statement into proof; a service provided by banks to assist customers in reconciling by listing paid and/or outstanding items against an account.

Accounts receivable. Amounts due to a bank or business for merchandise sold on credit or for services rendered. Accounts receivable are short-term assets.

Accrual accounting. The method of accounting that records all income when it is earned and all expenses when they are incurred.

Activity charge. A service charge imposed on checking accounts of customers who do not maintain balances sufficient to compensate the bank for the expenses incurred in handling the account.

Adjustable rate loan. See *variable rate loan*.

Administrator. A party appointed by a court to settle an estate when (1) the decedent has left no valid will; (2) no executor is named in the will; or (3) the named executor cannot or will not serve. The legend *c.t.a.* with the word *administrator* means that the terms of the will dictate the settling of the estate.

Advice. A written acknowledgment by a bank of a transaction affecting an account; for example, debit or credit advices.

Advised line of credit. An expression of willingness by a bank as to the maximum amount of money it may lend to a customer, confirmed in writing to the customer. See *line of credit*.

Advising bank. A bank that has received notification from another financial institution of the opening of a *letter of credit*. The advising bank then contacts the beneficiary, reaffirming the terms and conditions of the letter of credit.

Affidavit. A voluntary statement of facts signed before a notary public, court officer, or other authority.

Agency. The relationship between agent and principal. The agent acts on behalf of the principal while the latter retains legal title to property or other assets.

Agent. A party who acts on behalf of another by the latter's authority.

Altered check. A check on which a material change, such as in the dollar amount, has been made. Banks are expected to detect alterations and are responsible for paying checks only as originally drawn.

American Bankers Association (ABA). An organization of commercial banks founded in 1875 to keep members aware of developments affecting the industry, to develop educated and competent bank personnel, and to seek improvements in bank management and service.

American Institute of Banking (AIB). A section of the American Bankers Association founded in 1900 to provide bank-oriented education for bank employees. AIB's activities are carried on through chapters and study groups throughout the country. In addition to its regular classes, the Institute conducts correspondence courses. Membership and enrollment are open to employees and officers of ABA member institutions.

Amortization. The gradual reduction of a loan or other obligation by making periodic payments of principal and interest.

Annual percentage rate (APR). The cost of credit on a yearly basis. Expressed as a percentage, the APR results from an equation that considers three specifically defined factors: the amount financed, the finance charge, and the term of the loan. The APR is usually expressed in terms of the effective annual simple interest rate.

Appraisal. A professional evaluation of the market value of some assets by an independent expert.

Asset. Anything owned that has commercial or exchange value. Assets may consist of specific property or of claims against others, in contrast to obligations due to others (liabilities).

Attorney-in-fact. A party who has been authorized by a bank's depositor to issue instructions to that bank regarding the account. The form by which the depositor conveys this authority is called a *power of attorney*. The rights of an attorney-in-fact last until the depositor dies or revokes them.

Audit. A formal or official examination and verification of accounts.

Auditor. In banking, an individual, usually appointed by the bank's directors and reporting directly to them, who is responsible for examining any and all phases of the bank's operations.

Authorized signature. The signature of those parties who have the legal right to issue instructions regarding an account.

Automated clearing house (ACH). A computerized facility that performs the clearing of paperless (electronic) entries between member financial institutions.

Automated teller machines (ATMs). Electronic facilities, located inside or apart from a financial services institution, for handling many customer transactions automatically.

Automatic transfer service (ATS). A service by which a bank moves funds from one type of account to another for its customer on a preauthorized basis.

Availability schedule. A list indicating the number of days that must elapse before deposited checks can be considered converted into usable funds.

Available balance. The portion of a customer's account balance on which the bank has placed no restrictions, making it available for immediate withdrawal.

Average daily float. *See float.*

Balance. The amount of funds in a customer's account. This term may refer to the *book (ledger) balance*, which simply shows the balance after debits and credits have been posted; the *collected balance*, which is the book balance less float; or the *available balance*.

Balance sheet. A detailed listing of assets, liabilities, and capital accounts (net worth), showing the financial condition of a bank or company as of a given date. A balance sheet illustrates the basic accounting equation: assets = liabilities + net worth. In banking, the balance sheet is usually referred to as the *statement of condition*.

Balloon payment. The last payment on a loan; it is substantially larger than the previous payments.

Bank check. A check, also known as a cashier's, treasurer's, or official check, drawn by a bank on itself. Since the drawer and drawee are one and the same, acceptance is considered automatic and such instruments have been legally held to be promises to pay.

Bank directors. The individuals elected by the bank's stockholders to constitute the board of directors and who form the active, governing body of the bank as a corporation.

Bank draft. A check drawn by a bank on its account with another bank.

Bank holding company (BHC). A corporation that owns, controls, or otherwise has the power to vote at least 25 percent of the voting stock in one or more banks. All BHCs come under the jurisdiction of the Federal Reserve.

Bank statement. A report, rendered by a bank to a customer, showing the account balance at the start of a period, the transactions affecting the account, and the closing balance.

Banker's acceptance. A time draft drawn on a bank and accepted by that bank. *See also acceptance.*

Banker's blanket bond. A broad-coverage insurance policy that provides protection against such hazards as embezzlement, burglary, fraud, robbery, and forgery.

Barter. The direct physical exchange of merchandise, not accompanied by an exchange of money.

Basis point. The movement of interest rates or yields, expressed in hundredths of one percent.

Batch. A group of deposits, checks, or records or documents that has been assembled for proof and processing.

Bearer. The party who is in possession of a check, security, or title document. A check made payable to "Cash" is a bearer instrument.

Beneficiary. The party who is to receive the proceeds of a trust, insurance policy, letter of credit, or other transaction.

Bequest. A gift of personal property provided for in a will.

Bilateral contract. An agreement made between two persons or two groups.

Bill. Money; paper currency.

Bill of exchange. *See draft.*

Bill of lading. A document issued by a transporter of goods (carrier) covering a shipment of merchandise. It may be issued in negotiable or nonnegotiable form and is a contract to ship the merchandise, a receipt for it, and a document of legal title.

Blank endorsement. The signature of a person or business on an instrument (check or note) making it payable to a holder in due course and containing no restrictions.

Blocked currency. Any currency that by law cannot be converted into the currency of another country.

Board of Governors. The seven-member group, appointed by the president and confirmed by the Senate for 14-year terms, that directs the operations of the Federal Reserve System.

Bond. An instrument that evidences long-term debt. The issuer (a corporation, unit of government, or other legal entity) promises to repay the stated principal at a specified date. Bonds may be *registered* (identifying the holder) or *bearer* (not identifying the holder).

Bond of indemnity. A written instrument issued to protect a party against loss.

Book balance. *See balance.*

Bookkeeping department. The bank unit that maintains and updates all records of depositors' accounts. It is also called the demand deposit accounting (DDA) unit.

Branch bank. A bank that maintains a head office and one or more branch locations. The ability to open branches is subject to state law.

Bulk cash. Rolled or bagged coin and/or banded currency.

Cable transfer. The movement of funds to or from a foreign country through cable instructions.

Call loan. *See demand loan.*

Call report. A sworn statement of a bank's financial condition as of a certain date, submitted in response to a demand from a supervisory agency or authority.

Capital. An accounting term describing the excess of assets over liabilities. Capital accounts include money raised through the sale of stock, retained earnings, and borrowings in the form of notes or debentures.

Capital ratio. A measure of profitability, determined by dividing stockholders' equity by total assets.

Capital stock. Usually synonymous with common stock; the total amount of shares of ownership in a corporation. The total amount of a corporation's common and preferred stock is authorized by its charter or certificate of incorporation.

Cash a check. To give money in exchange for a check drawn on another financial institution.

Cash accounting. The accounting system that posts debits and credits only when money is actually received or paid.

Cash dispenser. Equipment capable of automatically delivering amounts of cash to a customer, usually upon insertion of a bank card.

Cash item. Any item that a bank is willing to accept for immediate but provisional credit to a customer's account, thereby immediately increasing the book balance.

Cash letter. An interbank transmittal form, resembling a deposit slip, used to accompany cash items sent from one bank to another.

Cash management. A family of bank services for corporate customers that is designed to speed collection of receivables, control payments, reconcile accounts, provide information, and efficiently manage funds.

Cash surrender value. The amount that an insurer will pay to the insured upon surrender of a policy.

Cashier's check. *See bank check.*

Certificate of deposit (CD). A formal receipt issued by a bank for a specified amount of money left with the bank. CDs commonly bear interest, in which case they are payable at a specified future date or after a specified minimum notice of intent to withdraw. Some CDs are noninterest-bearing, in which case they may be payable on demand or at a future date. CDs may be issued in negotiable or nonnegotiable form. They are payable only upon surrender with proper endorsement, and are carried on the bank's general ledger rather than on individual customer account ledgers.

Certificate of origin. A document issued to certify the country of origin of goods or merchandise.

Certificate of quality. A document issued by an appraiser and attesting that goods being shipped conform to the buyer's specifications.

Certified check. A depositor's check across the face of which an authorized party in the drawee bank has stamped the word *certified* and added a signature. Through certification of a check, the drawee guarantees that sufficient funds have been set aside from the depositor's account to pay the item. A certified check is a bank's promise to pay.

Charge off. A loan, obligation, or cardholder account which the bank no longer expects to be repaid and is written off as a bad-debt expense.

Charter, bank. A document issued by a federal (for national banks) or state (for all other banks) supervisory authority, giving the bank the right to conduct its business under stated terms and conditions.

Chattel mortgage. A lien giving another party an interest in certain property.

Check. A demand draft drawn on a bank or other financial institution offering checking accounts.

Check digit. A suffix numeral used by bank computers, using a programmed formula to test the validity of a bank number or account number.

Check routing symbol. The denominator (lower portion) of a fraction appearing in the upper right-hand corner of checks drawn on all Federal Reserve member banks. The ABA transit number is the upper portion of this fraction. The check routing symbol identifies the Federal Reserve district in which the drawee is located, the Fed facility through which the check can be collected, and the availability assigned to the check under the Fed schedule.

Check truncation. Any one of several systems to reduce the physical load of processing of paper checks. In one approach the information on a check is converted into electronic impulses. Truncation may also refer to the bank service under which actual paid checks are not returned to the drawer with statements.

CHIPS (Clearing House Interbank Payment System). A private telecommunications service operated through the New York Clearing House for settlement among participating banks.

Clearing. The process or method by which checks and/or other point-of-sale transactions are moved, physically or electronically, from the point of origin to a bank or other financial institution that maintains the customer's account number.

Clearing house association. A voluntary association of banks who establish a clearing house (meeting place) for the exchanging and settling of checks.

Clearing item. A check or other item in the process of collection from another financial institution, usually one in the same community or geographic area.

Club account. An account offered by a bank to encourage customers to make periodic small deposits to be used for such future expenditures as Christmas or Hanukkah, vacations, or other purposes, usually within a year. These are informal accounts.

Coin. Metallic money, in contrast to paper money (currency).

Collateral. Specific property pledged by a borrower to secure a loan. If the borrower defaults, the lender has the right to sell the collateral to liquidate the loan.

Collateral note. A promissory note that pledges certain property as security for a loan.

Collected balance. Cash in an account, plus deposited checks that have been presented to a drawee for payment and for which payment has actually been received.

Collection item. Any item received by a bank for a customer's account and for which the bank does not or cannot give immediate, provisional credit. Also called a *noncash item*. Collection items receive deferred credit, often require special handling, usually are subject to special fees, and do not create float.

Co-maker. An individual who signs a note to guarantee a loan made to another party and is jointly liable with the maker for repayment.

Commercial bank. By law, an institution that accepts demand deposits and makes commercial loans. In practice, a full-service financial institution that offers deposit, payment, and credit services to all types of customers, in addition to other financial services.

Commercial invoice. A document listing goods sold and/or shipped and indicating the price and terms of the sale.

Commercial letter of credit. An instrument issued by a bank, substituting the credit of that bank for the credit of a buyer of goods. It authorizes the seller to draw drafts on the bank and guarantees payment of those drafts if all the stated conditions and terms have been met.

Commercial loan. Credit extended by a bank to a business, most frequently on a short-term and unsecured basis.

Commercial paper. Short-term, unsecured promissory notes issued by major corporations of unquestioned credit standing for borrowing purposes.

Common stock. Certificates evidencing ownership of a corporation and generally giving the stockholder voting rights. Common stockholders have rights inferior to those who hold the corporation's bonds, preferred stock, and other debts.

Compensating balance. The balance that a customer must keep on deposit with a bank in order to ensure a credit line, to gain unlimited checking privileges, and to offset the bank's expenses in providing various services.

Competitive Equality Banking Act. Legislation passed by Congress in 1987 and containing provisions regarding availability to bank customers of deposited checks, the operations of nonbank banks, and the authority of banks to offer certain services. Title IV of this act is called the Expedited Funds Availability Act.

Comptroller of the Currency. An official of the U.S. government, appointed by the president and confirmed by the Senate, who is responsible for the chartering, examining, supervising, and liquidating of all national banks.

Concentration account. A deposit account into which funds from other bank accounts are transferred.

Conservator. A court-appointed official responsible for the care and protection of the interests of an estate. Conservatorship is also referred to as *guardianship*.

Construction loan. A short-term loan to a builder or developer to finance the costs of construction. The lender generally requires repayment from the proceeds of the borrower's permanent mortgage loan. The lender may make periodic payments to the borrower as the construction work progresses.

Consular invoice. A form of certification, by a consul or other government official, covering a shipment of goods. It is used to ensure that the shipment does not violate any laws or trade restrictions, and also provides the government with statistical information on imports.

Consumer credit. The general term for loans extended to individuals or small businesses, usually on an unsecured basis and providing for monthly repayment. Bank card outstandings are also included in the total consumer credit figure. Also referred to as installment credit, personal loans, or personal finance.

Contract. An agreement, enforceable at law, between or among two or more persons, consisting of one or more mutual promises.

Contributory trust. An employee trust fund, such as a pension or profit-sharing plan, into which both employer and employees make payments.

Corporate resolution. A document presented to a bank by a corporation. It defines the authority given to the officers and specifies who may sign checks, borrow on behalf of the corporation, and otherwise issue instructions to the bank and conduct the corporation's business. The powers listed in the resolution are granted by the corporation's directors.

Corporation. A business organization treated as a legal entity and owned by a group of stockholders. The stockholders (shareholders) elect the directors who will manage the affairs of the corporation.

Correspondent bank. A bank that maintains an account relationship and/or engages in an exchange of services with another bank.

Cost accounting. An accounting system that relates all direct and indirect costs and expenses to specific functions performed.

Counterfeit money. Spurious (bogus) coins and currency that have been made to appear genuine. The act of creating counterfeit money is a felony, making the perpetrators subject to long prison terms and heavy fines. The U.S. Secret Service, a bureau of the Treasury Department, is responsible for tracking counterfeiters.

Country collections. A term describing all noncash items sent to drawees outside the geographic area in which the sending bank is located.

Coupon. One of a series of promissory notes of consecutive maturities, attached to a bond or other debt certificate and intended to be detached and presented on their respective due dates for payment of interest.

Covenant. A promise contained in a formal instrument and obliging a party to perform certain acts or to refrain from performing certain acts.

Credit. An advance of cash, merchandise, or other commodity in exchange for a promise or other agreement to pay at a future date, with interest if so agreed.

Credit balance. The net amount of funds in an account indicating an excess of total credits over total debits.

Credit card. A plastic card (or its equivalent) to be used from time to time by the cardholder to obtain money, goods, or services, possibly under a line of credit established by the card issuer. The cardholder is billed for any outstanding balance. *See also debit card.*

Credit department. The unit within a bank in which all information regarding borrowers is obtained, analyzed, and kept on file. The department's work may also include answering inquiries from outside sources. A bank's credit files contain the history of each account relationship and include all correspondence, memoranda, financial statements, and other material that must be retained.

Credit risk. The possibility that a debtor may not be able to repay. *See also market risk.*

Credit union. A voluntary cooperative association of individuals having some common bond (for example, place of employment), organized to accept deposits, extend loans, and provide other financial services.

Creditor. Any party to whom money is owed by another.

Cross-selling. Efforts to induce the user of one or more services to buy additional services from the same supplier.

Currency. Paper money, as opposed to coin.

Custody. A banking service that provides safekeeping for a customer's property under written agreement and also calls for the bank to buy, sell, receive, and deliver securities and collect and pay out income *only* when ordered to do so by the principal.

Cycle statement system. A system of dividing bank depositors' accounts into groups whose statements are then mailed at staggered intervals (cycles) during the month, thereby distributing the work load more evenly throughout the period.

Daily transaction tape. In fully automated demand deposit accounting, the disk or magnetic tape record of each day's debits and credits to all accounts, usually in account-number sequence. The daily transaction tape is also referred to as the *entry run.*

Debenture. An unsecured note of a corporation or bank.

Debit. A charge against a customer's deposit or bank card account. Debit entries increase the balance of an asset or expense account and decrease the balance of a liability or equity account.

Debit balance. The lack of funds in an account, indicating an excess of total debits over total credits.

Debit card. A plastic card enabling the cardholder to purchase goods or services, the cost of which is immediately charged to his or her bank account. Debit cards are used to activate point-of-sale terminals in supermarkets, gas stations, and stores. Together with credit cards, they are commonly referred to simply as bank cards.

Decedent. A term used in connection with wills, estates, and inheritances to describe a person who has died.

Deed. A written instrument, executed and delivered according to law, used to transfer title to property.

Deferred account. An account maintained with the Federal Reserve by a bank and credited with the proceeds of check collections.

Deferred credit. Credit given to a bank depositor for items that are not or cannot be given immediate, provisional credit.

Delivery. The transfer of possession of an item from one party to another.

Demand deposit accounting. A term referring to the processing, tracking, and posting of transactions affecting the demand deposits of a bank and the accounting for those deposits.

Demand deposits. Funds that may be withdrawn at any time, without prior notice to the bank. Checking accounts are the most common form of demand deposits.

Demand draft. A written order to pay at sight, upon presentation. A check is a demand draft, drawn on a bank or other financial institution.

Demand loan. A loan with no fixed maturity, payable whenever the bank calls for it. A *demand note* evidences this type of loan.

Deposit. Any placement of cash, checks, or other drafts with a bank for credit to an account. All deposits are liabilities of a bank, since they must be repaid in some form at some future date.

Deposit function. The banking process by which funds are accepted for credit to an account. In the case of checks, the function includes conversion of the items into available, usable funds.

Deposit slip. A listing of the items given to a bank for credit to an account. A copy of the deposit slip may serve as a receipt for the customer.

Depository transfer check. A preprinted, no-signature instrument used only to move funds from one bank account to another.

Deputy. An individual authorized to act for another in performing certain transactions, specifically in the case of safe deposit boxes. The deputy in a safe deposit relationship has the right of access to the box.

Direct deposit. The process by which a payor delivers data by electronic means directly to the payee's financial institution for credit to his or her account. The most common example is the federal government program for direct depositing of Social Security payments. Direct deposit systems substitute bookkeeping entries, received electronically, for paper checks.

Direct presenting. A demand for acceptance or payment, made by the holder of a negotiable instrument upon the maker of a note or the drawer of a check.

Direct sending. The method of check collection that forwards checks directly to the drawee bank for settlement.

Direct verification. The auditing procedure by which a bank confirms account balance, loan, or other information through direct contact with customers.

Directors. The individuals, elected by stockholders, who comprise the board of directors and therefore constitute the active, governing body of a corporation.

Discount. Interest withheld when a note, draft, or bill is purchased, or collected in advance at the time a loan is made.

Discount rate. The rate of interest charged by the Federal Reserve on loans it makes to financial institutions.

Discount register. A bank's book of original entry, in which a daily record is kept of loans made and paid. Interest collected and other transactions affecting loans are entered in this register.

Dishonor. A drawee's refusal to accept or pay a check, draft, or other instrument, or refusal by the maker of a note to pay it when presented.

Disintermediation. The flow of funds from one type of account into another, or from accounts into investments, for the purpose of obtaining higher yields.

Dividend disbursing agent. The service under which a bank acts on behalf of a corporation and issues periodic dividend payments (as instructed) to the corporation's stockholders.

Documentary draft. A written order to pay, accompanied by securities or other papers to be delivered against payment or acceptance.

Dormant account. A customer relationship that has shown no activity for a period of time.

Double-entry bookkeeping. An accounting system based on the premise that for every debit there must be an equal, corresponding credit; all transactions thus are posted twice.

Draft. A signed, written order by which one party (the drawer) instructs another (the drawee) to make payment to a third (the payee). In international banking, a draft is often called a bill of exchange.

Drawee. The party to whom the drawer issues instructions to make payment. In the case of checks, the drawee is a bank or other financial institution.

Drawer. The party who issues a set of written instructions to a drawee, calling for a payment of funds.

Drive-in window (drive-through window). A convenience offered to the public, with a teller's window facing the outside of a bank building so that customers can transact their business without leaving their cars.

Dual banking system. All commercial banks in the United States must be chartered either by the state in which they are domiciled (state banks) or by the federal government through the office of the Comptroller of the Currency (national banks). The side-by-side existence of the two types of banks creates a *dual* system.

Dual control. A bank procedure requiring that two members of the staff be involved in a transaction.

Earnings credit. An allowance to a customer, offsetting part or all of the service charges on an account and calculated on the basis of the average balance in the account during a period and the earnings credit rate in effect at the time.

Earnings per share. The most common method of expressing a company's profit. It is obtained by dividing the profits by the number of outstanding shares of common stock.

Edge Act. Federal legislation passed in 1919 that allows banks to establish offices outside their own states purely for the purpose of assisting in foreign trade transactions.

Electronic Funds Transfer Systems (EFTS). The use of automated technology to move funds in substitution for the use of paper checks.

Employee Retirement Income Security Act (ERISA). Legislation passed in 1974 that established federal minimum standards for employee benefit plans and an insurance program guaranteeing workers' pension benefits.

Employee trusts. Pension and profit-sharing trust funds established by employers for the benefit of employees.

Endorsement. Legal transfer of one's rights to an instrument.

Entry run. *See daily transaction tape.*

Equal Credit Opportunity Act. Federal legislation requiring all creditors to make credit equally available without any form of discrimination.

Equity. Ownership interest, represented by stockholders' investment and retained earnings; the excess of a firm's assets over its liabilities.

Escheat. The legal principle by which a state government is entitled to receive funds that have remained in dormant accounts for a period of time and whose owners have not been located.

Escrow. The holding of funds, documents, securities, or other property by an impartial third party for the other two participants in a business transaction. When the transaction is completed, the escrow agent releases the entrusted property.

Escrow agent. The third party in an escrow transaction, who acts as agent for the other two parties, carries out their instructions, and assumes the responsibilities of paperwork and funds disbursement.

Estate. The sum total, as determined by a complete inventory, of all the assets of a decedent.

Eurodollars. Deposits that are denominated in dollars but held in foreign branches or banks.

Executor. A party named in a decedent's valid will to settle an estate and qualified by a court to act in this capacity.

Expedited Funds Availability Act. A portion (title IV) of the Competitive Equality Banking Act of 1987 directed at limiting the amount of time checks can be placed on *hold*.

Factor. A financial firm that purchases at a discount the accounts receivable of other firms and assumes the risks and responsibilities of collection.

FDIC assessment. The annual premium, equal to one-twelfth of one percent of average deposits, paid by FDIC members for their insurance coverage.

Federal Deposit Insurance Corporation (FDIC). The agency of the federal government, established in 1933 to provide insurance protection, up to statutory limits, for depositors at FDIC member banks. All national banks and all Fed member banks must belong to FDIC; mutual savings banks may also join if they wish.

Federal funds. Member banks' excess reserves at the Fed, loaned on a daily basis to other banks. Fed funds are also used to settle transactions, with no float, among member banks involving transfers of funds.

Federal Home Loan Bank (FHLB). The supervisory agency and source of credit for federally chartered savings and loan associations.

Federal Reserve banks. The 12 district institutions that deal with member banks and the government. The district banks maintain branches and check processing centers as necessary.

Federal Reserve notes. The paper money issued by any one of the 12 Federal Reserve banks and officially designated by the federal government as legal tender. Each such note is an interest-free promise to pay on demand.

Federal Reserve System. The organization created by the Federal Reserve Act in 1913, consisting of the 12 district banks and their branches plus the member banks, who are the legal owners. The Fed Board of Governors, headquartered in Washington, exercises overall control over the nationwide operations of the System.

Federal Savings and Loan Insurance Corporation (FSLIC). The counterpart agency of FDIC, created by the federal government to provide insurance coverage on deposits at thrift institutions.

Fiduciary. An individual, bank, or other party to whom specific property is turned over under the terms of a contractual agreement.

Fiscal policy. The activities of Congress and the federal government concerning the budget and taxation.

Float. The dollar total of deposited cash items that have been given immediate, provisional credit but are in the process of collection from drawee banks; also known as uncollected funds.

Floor plan financing. Loans made to finance the purchase of inventory by dealers.

Foreign exchange. Trading or exchanging of the currencies of other countries in relation to one another or to U.S. currency.

Forged check. A demand draft, drawn on a bank, on which the drawer's signature is not genuine.

Forgery. The legal term for counterfeiting a check or other document with the intent to defraud.

Fraud. Intentional misrepresentation of a material fact by one party so that another party, acting on it, will part with property or surrender a right.

Free Banking Laws. The name given to a group of statutes passed by various states during the nineteenth century that made it possible for banks to open and operate with minimum controls and requirements.

Garn-St Germain Act. Federal legislation passed in 1982 that authorized the opening of new types of interest-free accounts and gave federal regulators additional powers to assist troubled banks and financial institutions.

General ledger. The consolidated, summary books of account in a bank, showing all changes in the bank's financial condition and bringing together all branch and departmental totals.

Genuine signature. The actual, valid signature of a drawer or maker, without forgery.

Glass-Steagall Act. Banking legislation passed in 1933; also known as the 1933 Banking Act.

Global risk analysis. An examination of all the elements and sources of risk that enter into international lending.

Guardian. A bank, individual, or other party named by a court to manage the property and/ or person of a minor or incompetent.

Guardianship. The court directive under which a guardian is named.

Guidance line of credit. An expression of the amount of money that a bank may be willing to lend to a customer. A guidance line of credit is not made known to the customer and is for the bank's internal use only.

Hedging. Taking action to neutralize risk. Hedging entails controlling the risk of one transaction by engaging in an offsetting transaction.

Hold. A restriction on payment of all or any part of the balance in an account.

Holder in due course. As defined in the Uniform Commercial Code, a party who accepts an instrument in good faith and for value, without notice that it has been dishonored, that it is overdue, or that there is any claim against it.

Holding company. A firm which owns stock in other corporations and usually exercises control over them.

House check. A demand draft deposited or otherwise negotiated at the bank on which it is drawn. Also called an *on-us check*.

Income statement. A record of the income and expenses of a bank or business covering a period of time. It is also called a *profit and loss statement*.

Indenture. A formal agreement executed by an issuer of bonds.

Individual retirement accounts (IRAs). Trust funds established by individuals for retirement purposes, as authorized by Congress.

Informal account. A bank account opened without detailed legal documentation.

Installment loan. A loan made to an individual or business and repaid in fixed, periodic payments.

Institutional trust. A trust fund consisting of assets of a university or other institution, turned over to a bank to be invested and managed.

Instrument. A document in which some contractual relationship is expressed or some right conveyed.

Insufficient funds. A banking term indicating that the maker's balance does not contain sufficient funds to cover a check or checks; commonly abbreviated NSF.

Insurance certificate. A document, issued by an insurer, providing a degree of protection for merchandise during transit.

Insured bank. A bank which is a member of FDIC.

Interbank loan. An extension of credit by one bank to another.

Interest. Money paid for the use of money.

Intestate. The legal term for a decedent who did not leave a valid will.

Investment. The exchange of money, either for a promise to pay at a later date (as with bonds) or for an ownership share in a business (as with stocks).

Investment portfolio. The sum total of the various securities owned by a bank, business, individual, or entity of government.

Invoice. A commercial bill for goods sold or services rendered.

Irrevocable. The term used to describe a letter of credit that cannot be amended or canceled, except by full mutual agreement between the parties.

Issuing bank. A bank that issues a letter of credit based on the application of a customer.

Joint account. A bank relationship in the names of two or more parties. Joint accounts may carry rights of survivorship or may be established on a tenants-in-common basis without such rights.

Joint tenancy. The holding of property by two or more parties on an equal basis, conveying rights of survivorship.

Journal. An accounting record of original entry in which transactions are listed and described in chronological order.

Judgment. A sum due for payment or collection as the result of a court order.

Keogh account. A retirement account for self-employed individuals. Contributions to the account are tax deductible.

Kiting. Attempting to draw against nonexistent funds for fraudulent purposes. A depositor issues a check, overdrawing an account at one bank, and deposits into that account a check drawn on another bank but also drawn against insufficient funds.

Ledger. An accounting record of final entry into which various transactions are posted after journal posting has taken place.

Ledger balance. *See balance.*

Legal reserves. The portion of banks' demand and time deposits that must be kept in the form of cash or acceptable equivalents for depositors' protection. Fed member banks maintain these reserves with the Fed in their district; others either use the Fed directly or use a correspondent bank that is a Fed member.

Legal tender. Government-backed currency that is acceptable in payment of all private and public debts.

Letter of credit. A bank instrument substituting the credit of the issuing bank for the credit of another party, such as an importer of merchandise.

Liability. Anything owed by a bank, individual, or business. A bank's largest liability is the sum total of its deposits.

Lien. A legal claim or attachment, filed against property as security for payment of an obligation.

Line of credit. An expression of the maximum amount of credit a bank is willing to lend to a borrower. *Confirmed* lines of credit are made known to the customer; *guidance* lines of credit are for the bank's internal use only.

Liquidity. The quality that makes an asset quickly and easily convertible into cash; also, the ability of a bank, business, or individual to meet current debts.

Liquidity needs. The amount that a bank calculates is necessary to cover estimated withdrawals or payments of funds and to meet the legitimate credit demands of customers.

Living trust. A trust fund that becomes effective during the lifetime of the trustor (settlor).

Loan. A business contract between a borrower and lender, covering an extension of credit.

Loan participation. The sharing of a loan to a single borrower by more than one lender.

Lobby depository. A receptacle located within the lobby of a bank that permits customers to deposit funds without the assistance of a teller.

Local items. Deposited checks drawn on other banks within the same geographic area or city.

Lock box. A banking service that assumes responsibility for receiving, examining, and processing incoming checks for a customer.

Loss reserve. Funds set aside to cover possible losses on loans.

Magnetic ink character recognition (MICR). The American Bankers Association program that provides for encoding of checks and documents with characters in magnetic ink so that they can be electronically "read" and processed.

Mail deposit. A deposit received through the mail, as opposed to an over-the-counter transaction.

Maker. The party who executes a draft or note.

Managing agent. The service by which a bank or other party assumes an active role in the management of another's property.

Margin. The excess of the value of collateral over the amount loaned against it. Also, the difference between the purchase price of a security and the amount actually paid for it at the time of purchase.

Market risk. The possibility of decline in the current value of a security; the loss that the holder of an investment may have to assume at the time of sale.

Master file. The updated record of the closing balance in each account at a bank. It is produced by merging the previous day's master tape with the current day's transaction tape (entry run).

Maturity. The date on which a note, draft, bond, or acceptance becomes due.

Maturity tickler. The reminder file maintained by a bank according to due dates to ensure that notes will be presented as they become due.

McFadden Act. Federal legislation enacted in 1927 that guarantees the rights of individual states to control the branching of national banks within their borders.

Member bank. A bank that belongs to the Federal Reserve System.

Merge. To combine into one sequenced file form two or more similarly sequenced files without changing the order of the items.

Merger. The combination of two or more formerly independent firms under a single ownership.

Microfilm. The photographic process that reduces checks and other documents for record-keeping and storage purposes.

Missort. A check or other instrument routed in error.

Monetary Control Act. The 1980 legislation that provided for the gradual phase-out of interest-rate ceilings, made all financial institutions subject to reserve requirements, and gave expanded powers to thrift institutions.

Monetary policy. The general term for the actions taken by the Federal Reserve to control the flow of money and credit.

Money. Legal tender; coin and currency declared by a government to be the accepted medium of exchange.

Money market deposit account. An account that provides banks and thrift institutions with a competitive instrument so that they can compete with money market funds.

Money market fund. A mutual fund that pools investors' contributions and invests them in various money market instruments.

Money market instruments. Short-term obligations; that is, obligations having a maturity of one year or less. These include U.S. Treasury bills, banker's acceptances, and commercial paper.

Money supply. The total amount of funds available for spending in the nation at any point in time.

Mortgage loan. Real estate credit, usually extended on a long-term basis with the property as security.

Municipal. A bond issued by any nonfederal government, government agency, or government authority.

Mutual savings banks. Thrift institutions that have no stockholders and are owned by the depositors.

National bank. A commercial bank operating under a federal charter and supervised and examined by the Comptroller of the Currency. The word *national* must appear in some form in the bank's corporate title. All national banks must belong to the Federal Reserve System and FDIC.

National numerical system. *See transit number.*

Negative verification. The auditing system by which a letter regarding balances, loans, or other data is sent to a customer; a reply is called for *only* if there is a discrepancy between the balance or other facts reported by the bank and the customer's own records.

Negotiable instrument. An unconditional written order or promise to pay a certain sum in money. The instrument must be easily transferable from one party to another. Various laws set forth the qualifications of negotiable instruments and the rights and liabilities of their parties.

Negotiable order for withdrawal (NOW) account. A type of account that permits the depositor to earn interest while at the same time having checkwriting privileges.

Net worth. The excess of assets over liabilities; the shareholders' equity in a bank or business.

Night depository. A convenience facility provided for merchants who wish to deposit their receipts after regular banking hours. A small vault, located on the inside of a bank but accessible outside the premises, is used.

Noncash item. Any instrument that a bank declines to accept on a cash basis; a collection item. Credit is not posted to the customer's account until final settlement takes place.

Nonpar bank. An institution that is not a Fed member and deducts an exchange charge from the face amount of checks drawn on it.

Nonperforming loan. A loan, made by a bank to a customer, that produces no income and becomes a nonearning asset. Loans in this category usually are related to or precede foreclosure or charge-off action.

Note. A written promise to pay.

Officer. Any executive of a bank or business to whom authority has been delegated, usually by the board of directors and/or senior management.

Official check. *See bank check.*

Offset. The bank's legal right to seize any funds that a debtor or guarantor may have on deposit, to cover a loan in default.

On-us check. A check deposited or negotiated for cash at the bank on which it is drawn. Also called a *house* check.

Open-market operations. Sales and purchases of government securities on the open market by the Federal Reserve Open Market Committee in order to influence the size of the money supply and the availability of credit. The Fed uses open market operations as its major tool for implementing monetary policy.

Opening bank. *See issuing bank.*

Order. Identification of the party to whom payment of funds should be made, as in "Pay to the Order of."

Overdraft. A negative (minus) balance in an account, resulting from the paying of checks for an amount greater than the depositor's balance.

Overdraft banking. A service offered to bank customers whereby checks drawn on insufficient funds are not returned to the presenter, but are paid from funds under a line of credit.

Par value. The nominal worth of a bond, note, or other instrument.

Participation. *See loan participation.*

Partnership. A business venture operated by two or more individuals in noncorporate form.

Partnership agreement. A contract or covenant between the partners of a business, wherein the rights, duties, and responsibilities of each are clearly defined.

Passbook. A record, supplied by a bank, showing customer transactions on an account.

Pay. To debit a check against a customer's account.

Payee. The beneficiary of an instrument; the party to whom payment is to be made.

Paying agent. The service by which a bank disburses dividends on a corporation's stock or the interest and principal on bonds and/or notes.

Paying teller. A bank representative responsible for the paying and cashing of checks presented.

Pension. A fixed sum paid to an individual or his or her family on a regular basis, usually by an employer following the individual's retirement from service.

Pension trust. A trust fund established by an employer (usually a corporation) to provide benefits for incapacitated or retired employees, with or without their contributions.

Personal identification number (PIN). A number or word, used by a cardholder or randomly assigned by the card issuer, to provide personal security in accessing a financial service terminal and prevent use of a bank card by unauthorized parties.

Platform. A term commonly used to describe that portion of a bank's lobby area where officers, new account representatives, and customer service personnel are located.

Point-of-sale (POS) system. An electronic system by which the purchaser of goods or services can use a plastic card in a terminal at the seller's place of business, thereby debiting the cardholder's account at a financial institution and crediting the seller's account.

Positive verification. The auditing system under which every customer contacted during a bank audit must reply to a letter of inquiry regarding balances, loans, and so forth.

Postdated check. An item bearing a future date. It is not valid until that date is reached.

Power of attorney. The legal document by which one party is authorized to act on another's behalf. *See attorney-in-fact.*

Preauthorized payments. A convenience service offered to customers, enabling them to request that funds be transferred from an account to a creditor's account on a regular, fixed basis.

Preferred stock. Securities that give the holder a right to share in a bank's or corporation's profits before common shareholders. If the institution is liquidated, preferred stockholders have a prior claim on its assets over common stockholders and certain other creditors. Preferred stock usually does not give the holder voting rights.

Presenting bank. A bank that forwards an item to another for payment.

Prime rate. A benchmark or guideline interest rate, offered by a bank to its most creditworthy customers, reflecting their deposit balances and financial strength.

Principal. (1) The sum of money stated in a contract, an account, or a financial instrument as distinguished from the sum of money actually to be paid. For example, the amount of a loan or debt exclusive of interest. (2) A person who is primarily liable on an obligation. (3) A person who appoints another party to act for him or her as agent. (4) The property of an estate, other than the income from that property. (5) The individual with primary ownership or management control of a business.

Probate. The judicial determination concerning the validity of a will and all questions that may pertain to that will.

Profit. The excess of revenues over the costs incurred in earning those revenues.

Profit-and-loss statement. *See income statement.*

Profit-sharing trust. A trust fund into which an employer places a portion of annual profits for the benefit of the employees.

Program. A sequence of instructions to a computer, written in a form that the computer can interpret and telling the system where to obtain input, how to process it, and where to show or place the results.

Promissory note. A written promise committing the maker to pay a certain sum in money to the payee, with or without interest, on demand or at a fixed or determinable future date.

Proof. Any process that tests the accuracy of a function or operation; also known as *balancing*.

Proof department. The central unit in a bank that sorts and distributes checks and other work and arrives at control figures for all transactions.

Proof machine. Equipment that simultaneously sorts items, records the dollar amount of each item, provides totals for each sorted group, and balances the total to the original input amount.

Proprietor. A person who has an exclusive right or interest in a business venture.

Proprietorship. A business venture operated by a single owner.

Protest. A legal document, usually notarized, that provides evidence that an instrument was presented and dishonored.

Prove. The process of verifying the accuracy of calculations performed by an individual or department.

Public funds accounts. Accounts established for any government, agency of government, or political subdivision.

Purpose statement. A signed affidavit from a borrower whose loan is secured by certain types of stock market collateral. Under Federal Reserve Regulation U, the borrower must state the use(s) to which the proceeds of the loan will be put.

Qualified endorsement. An endorsement on a check or other instrument containing the words *without recourse* or similar language intended to limit the endorser's liability.

Qualified plan or trust. An employer's trust fund or plan that qualifies under the Internal Revenue Code of 1954 for the exclusive benefit of employees or their beneficiaries. A qualified plan entitles the payments made by the employer to the deductions and benefits set forth in that code.

Quick deposit box. *See lobby depository.*

Raised check. An item on which the dollar amount has been fraudulently increased.

Receiving teller. A bank representative who accepts and verifies deposits and issues receipts for them, but has no paying or cashing duties.

Redlining. Systematic exclusion of certain geographic areas—usually high-risk, low-income neighborhoods—from mortgage investment.

Regional check processing centers (RCPCs). Special facilities established by the Fed in its 12 districts to expedite the handling, presenting, and collecting of transit checks.

Registrar. A bank or trust company appointed by a corporation to ensure that the number of shares of outstanding stock does not exceed the authorized limit. A registrar is agent both for the corporation and the latter's stockholders, since it protects the interests of both.

Repurchase agreements (Repos). Contracts between a seller and a buyer, usually involving federal government obligations. The seller agrees to buy back the securities at an agreed-upon price after a stated period of time. Repos often are executed on an overnight basis.

Reserves. Portions of a bank's funds set aside to meet legal requirements and/or for known or potential expenses or losses.

Resolution. An official document, executed under seal by a corporation, certifying that specified officers can open a bank account for the corporation and conduct business with the bank on its behalf.

Restrictive endorsement. An endorsement that limits the future actions of the next holder. The most common example includes the words "For Deposit Only."

Return items. Checks, drafts, or notes that have been dishonored by the drawee or maker and are sent back to the presenter.

Return on assets (ROA). A financial measurement that indicates how efficiently a bank's assets are being employed. It is usually determined by dividing net profits by average total assets.

Return on equity (ROE). A financial measurement that indicates how efficiently the bank's equity capital has been invested. It is usually calculated by dividing net profit by net worth.

Revenue bonds. Obligations, usually municipal, secured by the income from the operations of specific enterprises, such as bridges or toll roads. These bonds are not backed by the "full faith and credit" of the issuer.

Revocable. A term usually associated with letters of credit. It allows the letter of credit to be canceled or amended by either party without the approval of the other.

Revolving credit. A line of credit arrangement that permits the borrower to withdraw funds or charge purchases up to a specified dollar limit. Also referred to as *open-end credit*.

Right of survivorship. The right of one individual to take full possession of a specific asset upon the death of the co-owner.

Routing symbol. *See check routing symbol.*

Safekeeping. The banking service by which the bank issues a receipt for, maintains records of, and provides vault facilities for a customer's property.

Safety. The ideal perception by customers that the bank is in a position to honor all anticipated demands for withdrawals of funds and that the bank has taken all appropriate measures to provide full protection for all property entrusted to it.

Savings account. An interest-bearing relationship used by a customer to accumulate funds. Savings accounts have no fixed maturity date.

Savings and loan association (S&L). A federally chartered or state chartered thrift institution that accepts various types of deposits and uses them primarily for mortgage loans. By making deposits, the members of a cooperative S&L are actually buying stock in it.

Savings bank. A thrift institution specializing in savings accounts but also offering other forms of deposit relationships, including checking accounts. *See also mutual savings bank.* Many savings banks have become federally chartered, rather than state chartered.

Savings certificate. A written instrument, evidencing the depositing of a stated sum of money, usually for a specific time frame at a specified rate of interest. The certificate must be surrendered to the issuing bank to obtain funds.

Secured loan. A borrower's obligation which includes the pledging of some form of collateral to protect the lender.

Security officer. A bank representative who has been given responsibility for various phases of internal controls, such as protective devices.

Service charge. A fee levied by a bank for services rendered.

Settlor. A person who creates a trust (such as a living trust) to become operative during his/her lifetime. Also called *grantor, trustor,* or *donor.*

Share draft. A check-like instrument used by customers of credit unions as a payment medium and drawn against the issuer's deposit balance.

Sight draft. A written order to pay upon presentation or delivery.

Sight letter of credit. An instrument, issued by a bank, by which the bank's credit is substituted for that of an individual or corporation. In merchandise shipments, a sight letter of credit permits payment of the funds immediately upon presentation of the documents evidencing the shipments.

Signature. A sign or mark made by the drawer or maker of a negotiable instrument. A signature may include thumbprints and may be printed, typed, or stamped.

Software. A set of programs and procedures that direct the operation of a data processing system.

Sorter-reader. Electronic equipment having the ability to "read," sort, and process MICR-encoded checks and other documents.

Special endorsement. An endorsement that names the party to whom an instrument is being transferred.

Specie. "Hard" currency; gold and/or silver, as opposed to paper money.

Split deposit. A transaction in which a customer wishes to have part of a check credited to an account and the remainder paid out in cash.

Spot audit. A procedure by which certain bank accounts, areas, or procedures are randomly selected for testing.

Spread. (1) The difference between the return on assets and the cost of liabilities; the profit margin. (2) The difference between the buying rate and selling rate of a currency or marketable security (stock, bond).

Stale-dated check. An instrument bearing a date 6 months or more in the past, prior to its presentation. The Uniform Commercial Code states that banks are not required to honor such checks.

State bank. A commercial bank chartered by the state in which it is headquartered.

Statement of condition. *See balance sheet.*

Statement savings. A savings account in which a periodic statement replaces the passbook.

Stop payment. A depositor's instructions to the drawee, directing it to dishonor a specific item.

Subsidiary ledger. A component of the general ledger identifying individual banking activities, such as types of accounts, loans, and so forth.

Super NOW account. A relationship that is interest-bearing and is similar to a money market deposit account, *but* (1) subjects the funds to reserve requirements, (2) is not available to corporations, and (3) has no limit on monthly transaction volume.

Surplus. That portion of a bank's capital accounts derived from retained earnings over a period of time and from stockholders' contributions.

Survivorship. The right of a surviving party, subject to legal considerations, to the property of a decedent.

Sweep account. A relationship in which all the funds in an account, over and above a specified figure, are automatically transferred into an investment pool.

Tenants in common. The holding of property by two or more persons in such a way that each has an undivided interest that, at the death of one, passes to the heirs or devisees and not to the survivor(s).

Terminal. An electronic device, often connected to a computer, that can supply information and accept instructions to initiate transactions.

Testamentary trust. A trust fund created under the terms of a will.

Testate. The legal term for one who has died, leaving a valid will; the opposite of intestate.

Testator. A decedent who has made and left a valid will.

Thrift institution. The broad term used to describe savings banks and savings and loan associations, whose primary function is accepting deposits and granting mortgage loans.

Time deposit. An account which carries a specific maturity date, with limitations on withdrawals before that date.

Time draft. A written order directing payment at a fixed or determinable future date.

Time letter of credit. A letter of credit containing a specific maturity date for payment.

Time loan. An extension of credit with a specific repayment date.

Title. Legal evidence of ownership of property.

Trade acceptance. A time draft drawn on the buyer of goods by the seller and accepted by the buyer before maturity.

Trade name. A fictitious name used for business purposes. The laws of many states require that trade names be legally registered.

Transaction account. Under the terms of the Monetary Control Act of 1980, an account with a financial institution that allows for transfers of funds to third parties.

Transit check. Any item that a bank chooses to classify as not payable locally; an out-of-town check.

Transit number. *See ABA transit number.*

Traveler's check. A negotiable instrument sold by a bank or other issuer in various denominations for the convenience of individuals who do not wish to carry cash. These checks are readily convertible into cash upon proper identification, usually by a signature in the presence of the cashing party.

Traveler's letter of credit. An instrument issued by a bank for the convenience of an individual who is going abroad. It allows the traveler to draw drafts against it and present them at a foreign branch of the issuing bank or at an office of the issuer's foreign correspondent, thereby obtaining local currency.

Treasurer's check. *See bank check.*

Truncation. A banking system that reduces the need to send or physically handle checks for customers' accounts.

Trust. An agreement or contract established by agreement or declaration, in a will, or by order of a court, under which one party (the trustee) holds legal title to property belonging to another, with a specific benefit in mind.

Trust company. A financial institution chartered specifically to offer trust services. It may also be authorized, under its charter, to provide banking services.

Trust receipt. A written agreement creating a special type of secured loan and often extended to an importer of goods. The borrower is allowed to take possession of merchandise to which the bank holds legal title.

Trustee. The party holding legal title to property under the terms of a trust.

Trustor. *See settlor.*

Truth in Lending laws. Federal and/or state legislation requiring that a lender provide each borrower with full information as to the terms and conditions of a loan.

Uncollected funds. *See float.*

Undivided profits. An account in a bank's general ledger that is part of capital; it represents funds that have not been paid out as dividends or transferred to the surplus account.

Uniform Commercial Code. The body of laws, adopted in whole or in part by all states, pertaining to various types of financial transactions.

Uniform Gifts to Minors Act. Legislation that provides tax relief for individuals who make irrevocable gifts of money or property to underage beneficiaries.

Unit bank. An institution that maintains no branch offices.

Unit teller. A bank representative who handles both paying and receiving functions.

Unsecured loan. Credit extended without collateral.

Updating. Modifying a master file with current information.

Usury. Excessive, illegal, or punitive interest charges.

Variable rate loan. A loan that allows the lender to make periodic adjustments in the interest rate, according to fluctuating market conditions. Also referred to as an *adjustable rate loan.*

Verification. The auditing process in banking by which bank records are confirmed through direct contact with customers.

Waiver. The voluntary relinquishing of a right or privilege.

Ward. A person who by reason of age, mental incompetence, or other incapacity is under the protection of a court, either directly or through another party.

Warehouse receipt. A document evidencing the storage of specific property in a bonded facility. The receipt may be issued in negotiable or nonnegotiable form and serves as a title document.

Wildcat banking. The system that established offices of banks at remote locations for the redemption of notes.

Will. A formal, written, witnessed instrument by which a person gives instructions for the disposition of his or her estate.

Wire transfer. A transaction by which funds are electronically moved from one bank to another and/or from account to account, upon a customer's instructions, through bookkeeping entries.

Without rights of survivorship. An account in which the joint tenancy ends upon the death of one of the parties.

Working capital. The excess of a business venture's current assets over its current liabilities; the liquid funds available to a business for its daily needs.

Writ of attachment. A legal document, frequently served on a bank, making the assets of a debtor subject to the terms of a court order.

Yield. (1) In *investments*, the rate of return, expressed as a percentage of the investment. (2) In *loans*, the total amount earned by a lender, expressed on an annual percentage basis.

Zero proof. A banking procedure by which a control figure is first entered into a machine or system, and all postings are successively subtracted from that figure to arrive at a zero balance, thus indicating that all entries have been correctly posted.

INDEX